THE STORY OF RHODESIAN SPORT
Volume One : 1889-1935

THE STORY OF RHODESIAN SPORT

VOLUME ONE

1889-1935

by

J. de L. Thompson

Reproduction of the 1935 edition of *A History of Sport in Southern Rhodesia, 1889-1935*, to a reduced format and incorporating a new Foreword and Author's Preface.

BOOKS OF RHODESIA

BULAWAYO

1976

BOOKS OF RHODESIA PUBLISHING CO. (PVT.) LTD.

P.O. Box 1994, Bulawayo.

Publishers of Rhodesiana Reprints
and New Rhodesian Literary Works

First published 1935

Reprinted 1976

© J. de L. Thompson 1935

© Preface to the reprint edition: J. de L. Thompson 1976

ISBN 0 86920 150 6

PRINTED IN RHODESIA BY MARDON PRINTERS (PVT.) LTD., BULAWAYO

PREFACE TO THE REPRINT EDITION

IN the forty-odd years since this book first came out the Rhodesian sporting scene has undergone a major transformation. Most of the changes have been very much for the better; a few, perhaps, may be regretted. What immediately strikes one when turning the pages of this history is the basic difference in attitudes between the two eras. Then, sportsmen were amateurs in the old-fashioned (though not necessarily better) sense of the word; they played games because it was fun to do so. Now the approach, if not the technical status, tends to be a lot more professional and competitive. Which of course has its merits: standards are a lot higher, facilities are much better and the general public—the spectator—has benefited greatly from the improvements.

Probably the most important contributory factor to the progress of Rhodesian sport has been the development of air travel. I can recall, for instance, one Currie Cup cricket tour around South Africa by a Rhodesian team in 1930. It was scheduled to play four matches—against Griquas at Kimberley, against the Orange Free State at Bloemfontein, against Border at King William's Town, and against Eastern Province at Port Elizabeth. The players travelled by train and the tour lasted three weeks—a long time for a man to be away from his work. Moreover, it was costly from a financial point of view, and the jolting of the train and cramped living conditions *en route* were poor preparation for any game.

Today, teams can fly to Cape Town and back in half a day. This means that they are able to travel more and in greater comfort, and so players in all sports benefit from constant contact with their counterparts beyond our borders.

Another notable improvement has been the grassing of playing fields. The hard, bare and often very dusty grounds of yester-year diminished not only the pleasure of the sportsmen but, most importantly, of the spectators as well, especially on windy days when clouds of dust enveloped players and public alike. When I see the modern cricketer or rugby player skidding along the turf I cannot help remembering what would have happened to him on the harsh gravel fields of my day: the cost to him in terms of torn clothes, torn skin and painful gravel rash was considerable.

With less freedom of movement—there were fewer cars and motorcycles on what then passed for roads—the young men of earlier days hadn't so many diversions and were rather restricted to the popular sports then in vogue. The population, too, was smaller. The end result was that a lot of men took part and sometimes excelled in several different activities. Today, with so great a variety of sports and the demanding fixture lists—a direct consequence of swifter travel facilities—there seem to be far fewer all-rounders and each game has to compete for the available talent. In this connection it is interesting to note that, on some of the major sports fields, there are fewer, or at least no more, teams competing today than there were forty years ago.

The entry of the African into the world of Rhodesian sport is another relatively new feature. During the period covered by this volume Africans tended to be somewhat unsophisticated, and their sporting activities were confined largely to meetings held on high days and holidays and organised by the mining companies and such like. But in recent years the African has come very much to the fore, excelling especially in athletics, soccer and cycling. At the moment most other sports are beyond his economic means, but this state of affairs is of course changing, and the leading exponents are offered jobs where their sporting prowess is encouraged.

Finally, we now have specialist coaches, engaged on a professional basis, often subsidised by the sporting associations with funds donated by various sponsors. Professional coaches have had an enormously beneficial effect on the quality and character of Rhodesian sport, and these sponsors merit high tribute for their generous and valuable contribution.

Praise is also due, today, to the Press and broadcasting media for the support they give to sport, particularly in pre-event publicity. The Press, especially, comes in for more brickbats than bouquets, yet the big crowds which bring in much-needed revenue would not be in evidence without the 'free advertising' in the newspapers and on radio and television.

This book was written and published in 1935 and is here reprinted as the first of a series of three volumes which, when complete, will carry the story of Rhodesian sport through to 1976. The fact that two books—almost twice as many pages, more than twice as many printed words—are needed to cover less than half the period since the Pioneers played their famous rugby game on the Shashi river, is a measure of our sporting progress during the past few years.

J. de L. T

Bulawayo,
July 1976.

FOREWORD TO THE REPRINT EDITION

by the Prime Minister of Rhodesia
The Hon. I. D. Smith, I.D., M.P.

THE reappearance of this work will bring pleasure to all Rhodesians. Virtually every facet of sport in our country, from the earliest days, has been dealt with by the author. But here we have something more than a record of men and women who were household names even before the turn of the century. There are fascinating glimpses of an earlier way of life, and of the firm foundations which were laid for our outstanding achievements in the sporting sphere.

To have these glimpses readily available for reference is something that will be welcomed by all. I believe Rhodesian sportsmen will join with me in acknowledging our gratitude and appreciation to the author and publishers for once more placing at our disposal this outstanding history of Rhodesian sport.

I was very pleased to learn that this book—an 'old friend' from my school days—is to be joined by two additional volumes. These supplementary works will fill a gap which is necessary to bring up to date the sporting history of Rhodesia.

In the last decade we have increasingly witnessed the tragic embroilment of sport in politics. However, this has not prevented Rhodesians from carrying our name into many international sporting fields. Their great achievements have brought resounding credit to both them and our country.

In this volume, Colonel Thompson illustrates repeatedly that neither isolation nor difficulties could deter our early sports enthusiasts. Just as our country's early representatives overcame all obstacles—for 'the sake of the game'—so their successors of all races continue to overcome the almost insuperable problems which are placed in their way.

Let us pay our gratitude and respect to Rhodesia's sporting ambassadors, who carry our flag and our image with such credit, wherever they may go.

Salisbury,
August 1976.

PUBLISHER'S NOTE

This, the first volume of a three-volume history of Rhodesian sport covering the years 1889-1976, is a facsimile reproduction of Col J. de L. Thompson's book, *A History of Sport in Southern Rhodesia, 1889-1935*, first published in a small edition by the Rhodesian Printing and Publishing Company Limited in 1935. We are grateful to that Company for their courtesy in permitting us to reproduce the original work. The reprint edition, re-titled and in slightly reduced format, carries a Foreword by the Prime Minister of Rhodesia, the Hon. I. D. Smith, I.D., M.P., an Author's Preface, and a new dust jacket design.

CECIL JOHN RHODES.

A HISTORY OF SPORT

IN

SOUTHERN
RHODESIA

(Illustrated)

1889 - 1935

By

J. de L. THOMPSON

THE RHODESIAN PRINTING AND
PUBLISHING COMPANY LIMITED
BULAWAYO
1935

To
J. B. B.

CONTENTS

FOREWORD

I N asking me to write a foreword for his book, "A History of Sport in Southern Rhodesia," the author, Mr. J. de L. Thompson, remarked that I am one among those Rhodesians who have successfully combined work with play. That may be so but, in sending this book on its way, with my good wishes, I feel I must comment upon the significant fact that in this sporting record there appear the names of almost all the men who have given personal service for the Colony. As Rhodesians we should be proud to think that sport can hold such an important position in our lives and yet be in no way detrimental to our work.

It is more than forty years since organised sport first took root in Southern Rhodesia and any later effort than the author's to recall its beginnings and trace its progress might have been made too late. The pioneers of sport had not always the forethought to preserve a record of their doings and the happy company of those who were among the first to transfer the national games of their home countries to the unturned soil of a new Colony is rapidly diminishing as the years take their toll.

Human memory is not always reliable and this record has been compiled just in time to recapture precious memories of the past before they vanish forever.

I first came to the Colony in 1897 and since that time have watched with interest the development of the facilities which we have here for recreation. I have always held the view that physical fitness, particularly in a new country where our first task is to tame the wilderness, is not only desirable but essential. For a country as young as ours the growth of sport has been truly remarkable and for this we owe much to that real sportsman, the late Sir William Milton, who in his earlier years was an outstanding figure on cricket and rugby fields.

The author has taken upon himself a considerable task but, having represented Rhodesia at rugby against the famous All Blacks in 1928 and in cricket against the M.C.C. in 1930, he has special qualifications for writing on the subject of sport in Rhodesia. It gives me very real pleasure in wishing his book every success.

INTRODUCTION

OUTHERN Rhodesia may well be proud of her achievements in the realm of sport. With a small population scattered over a vast area the country's sportsmen encounter many difficulties but the great obstacle of distance has been overcome by the fine sporting spirit that pervades the Colony and by the generous assistance of the Rhodesia Railways, which have had a succession of General Managers who have all shown a splendid consideration of the great handicap which travelling expenses must necessarily be to young sportsmen. The Railway Company's contribution to sport in Rhodesia has been of inestimable benefit. Not only have members of the staff been among Rhodesia's best performers on the various fields, but the administration itself has gone out of its way to give all games every encouragement by means of generous concessions on all its lines to sporting teams.

No such assistance was available, however, for those who, in the eighteen-nineties, pioneered sport in this Colony. The pity of it is that these men left so few written records and cameras were bulky things in those days, not to be carried in the 30-lb. pack, including blankets, allowed to the pioneer. There is, therefore, very little information available to-day of how contests were lost and won in the good old days for most of the old sportsmen have long since joined the great majority.

So, with the absence of written records, much of this book has been built up on the reminiscences of a few of the old hands. The uncertainty in recalling incidents of thirty or forty years ago with clarity and in accurate chronological sequence must be apparent. Old faces fade, names are forgotten and years merge into periods so that, despite every endeavour towards a true record of the games played in this country, omissions or faulty statements may occur. Perhaps, however, the defects will be overlooked if the allusions to names and incidents here and there strike a happy chord in the memories of those who lived through Rhodesia's early days.

Some of the photographs reproduced are, unfortunately, not very clear, but many of them were taken from very old prints and others of more recent years were the best obtainable. There is much that could be added to make this History complete and the writer would be glad to hear from anyone who would assist towards a revised edition.

The principal towns of Southern Rhodesia are Bulawayo, Salisbury, Gwelo and Umtali, and it is with these centres that Rhodesian sporting records are chiefly concerned. The various games, when first organised, existed in a few clubs, with occasional inter-town matches, and it was not until quite recently that controlling bodies were formed. Even of some of these, however, the white ants have had the records. The huge area over which the games are spread, the difficulty and expense of travelling, went a long way towards hindering the progress of King Sport in his new domain, but small, enthusiastic bands of devotees, eager for some form of recreation, set the various sports going and it is the development and growth of these that I am endeavouring to trace here.

When I tabulated all the sports I should have to deal with, there were no fewer than nineteen different kinds. The Colony is certainly up-to-date in the world of sport and this was equally true forty years ago. The only difference lies in that the youth of to-day is exceptionally well provided for in every branch of sport whereas the pioneer had to face many restrictions before he could obtain the recreation he desired.

It is a fact that sport makes for sound constitutions and those in authority were not slow to recognise the value of this when enlisting men for the Pioneer columns. Consequently the lists of the early settlers contain many names familiar to South African sportsmen. The call of adventure brought these men to the young Colony, and it was in response to this same summons that, though beset by numerous obstacles and sometimes faced with possible dangers, they played their games. Small wonder, then, that sport, as played in the dashing style of those adventurers, reached the heights it did. One hopes that this heritage will remain without blemish to keep true the words of Mr. J. H. Tandy, a member of Mr. I. D. Difford's touring team in 1913, who said, referring to Rhodesia, " The sporting spirit is to be found everywhere. It is in the air."

The greatest of all Rhodesians, Cecil John Rhodes, gave sport a high place in his curriculum of life. He made it one of the major qualifications for the world-prized scholarships he endowed and left as a maxim for his Rhodes scholars, " *Mens sana in corpore sano.*" The Rhodes Cup for horse racing and the Rhodes Challenge Cups for tennis are among the donations, many of them monetary, which he made to assist the development of sport in the Colony. Financial assistance has also been given by the Beit Trust.

One of Rhodesia's chief advantages is that its climate permits of games being played all the year round. Taken roughly, the summer months are October to March, inclusive, and the great summer game, Cricket, is played during that half of the year. This period is also the rainy season so that the summer sports, even though they are played during the hottest months, are made pleasanter by intermittent rains. The winter climate, from April to September, is exceptionally pleasant with a succession of clear, sunny days, cold enough for the invigorating exercise of the winter games such as football and hockey. Apart from cricket, swimming, football and hockey, which naturally fall into definite seasons, all sports can be played throughout the year.

Easter, as a general rule, is the high season for tennis, golf and bowls and most of the national tournaments are held then. The Rhodes and Founders holidays, being the second Monday and Tuesday in July, are often taken advantage of by clubs arranging sporting fixtures.

A handicap to sportsmen that is being gradually overcome with the laying down of turf fields has been the fact that Rhodesia's games have had to be played on hard grounds. Cricket, for instance, is a totally different game when played on a hard bumpy ground instead of on turf and fielding becomes a test in expecting the unexpected. However, more difficult conditions develop more efficient teams and cricket at present maintains a very high standard. Soccer in Rhodesia is faster because of the higher bouncing of the ball but less ball control is in evidence than on a turf field. Hockey is similarly affected by the terrific pace at which the ball travels.

There are, however, several turf fields now in existence, one in Bulawayo, two in Salisbury and one in Umtali, and in time it is possible that all sport will be played on turf. The laying down of these turf fields marks the beginning of a new era for Rhodesian sportsmen.

The award of "colours" for Rhodesian representatives is vested in a Colours Control Board. This council is comprised of the Presidents of all the governing bodies of sport. When any branch wishes to recommend its representatives to have colours the interested body applies to the Control Board and if the application is granted those players are registered

A

and may then wear the Rhodesian colours—dark green and white. A green blazer is worn, with silver buttons embossed with the Rhodesian lion which is repeated, embroidered in white, on the left breast pocket. Each branch of sport has its own initials embroidered on the pocket, together with the date on which the wearer appeared for Rhodesia.

The following are the various governing bodies:—

Rhodesia Cricket Union (R.C.U.).
Rhodesia Rugby Football Union (R.R.F.U.).
Rhodesia Amateur Athletic and Cycling Union (R.A.A. and C.U.).
Rhodesia Bowling Association (R.B.A.).
Rhodesia Hockey Association (R.H.A.).
Rhodesia Amateur Swimming Association (R.A.S.A.).
Southern Rhodesia National Rifle Association (S.R.N.R.A.).
Southern Rhodesia Football Association (S.R.F.A.).
Rhodesia National Amateur Boxing Association (R.N.A.B.A.).
Rhodesia Lawn Tennis Association (R.L.T.A.).

With the exception of lawn tennis and, in 1935, bowls, all these bodies are affiliated with the corresponding controlling bodies in South Africa with whom close relations are maintained. It is through affiliation of this kind that Rhodesia has been included in the itinerary of so many overseas teams that have visited the Union and has occasionally been the venue for inter-provincial tournaments.

Rhodesia being a self-governing Colony, its status in sport is not provincial, and in most departments the Colony is acknowledged to have a national status. This is particularly the case in athletics and the Colony is entitled to independent representation at Olympic and Empire Games meetings. Rhodesia's geographical position, however, and the close link that exists between all sportsmen in the sub-continent, makes it advantageous for all organised sport to be affiliated with the bodies controlling it in South Africa. Northern Rhodesian sport is similarly linked with South African or Southern Rhodesian and in course of time there will be a much closer relationship in sport between the two Rhodesias than there is at present.

THE HON. G. M. HUGGINS,
The Prime Minister of Southern Rhodesia, who has always taken
a keen interest in all branches of sport in the Colony.

ACKNOWLEDGMENTS.

The writer tenders his sincere thanks to all those sportsmen in the Colony and outside it, as far away as New Zealand, who have given valuable assistance in the compilation of this record and also to: The Government of Southern Rhodesia for financial assistance and encouragement; the Rhodesian Printing & Publishing Company, Limited, for access to files and use of blocks, and to Mr. G. D. Smith, Sports Editor of "The Bulawayo Chronicle"; "The Sunday News," Bulawayo, and Messrs. Hortors, Limited ("British South Africa Annual) for permission to reproduce certain articles; Mr. I. D. Difford for permission to quote from the "History of South African Rugby"; the Rho-Anglo Ad-Service for gift of blocks; the Rhodesia Cricket Union, the Southern Rhodesia Football Association, the Southern Rhodesia National Rifle Association, the Rhodesia Rugby Football Union, the Rhodesia Lawn Tennis Association, the Bulawayo and District Cricket Association, the Matabeleland Rugby Football Board, the Matopo Yacht Club, the Rhodesia Amateur Swimming Association, the Matabeleland Amateur Boxing Association, the Rhodesia Bowling Association, the Mashonaland Cricket Association, the Royal Salisbury Golf Club, the Bulawayo Golf Club, the Rhodesia Hockey Association, for donations towards the cost of publication; the Rhodesia Advertising Contractors, Ltd., for loan of block.

SALISBURY v. QUEEN'S CLUB, 1895.

Back Row: R. A. Sidgreaves, G. A. Tucker, H. H. D. Christian, H. J. Mordaunt, O. H. Ogilvie, J. Purcell, H. E. Galt, D. Dollar, C. S. Gill, Baragwanath, H. B. Farquhar (Scorer).

Middle Row: Backhouse, H. M. Taberer, G. Cripps, E. C. Sharp, Money, A. B. Bramwell, C. Southey.

Front Row: G. Hill, P. E. Craven, A. Hill, H. B. Douslin, ———, Fergusson, Macdonald, Macfarlane.

S. J. Goldsmith

CRICKET.

WITH such a large percentage of Englishmen among Rhodesia's first inhabitants, it was only natural that cricket became popular very early. The first record of the game appears in the cyclostyle newspaper of Victoria, which, on February 27, 1893, published details of a cricket meeting. Subsequently a series of matches was played at Victoria.

At Umtali, also, the game provided delightful recreation for the pioneers, and in December, 1893, the local newspaper records the scores of a Country v. Town match. Douglas Dollar and Cooper Hodgson helped the Country to win by six runs.

In Bulawayo the game flourished in the Queen's, Bulawayo Athletic, and Matabeleland Mounted Police clubs, which came into being in 1894.

In '94 Salisbury endeavoured to stage a quadrangular tournament to which Victoria, Umtali, and Bulawayo were invited. The Bulawayo players made all arrangements for the trip, which was to be accomplished by mule-coach at a cost of roughly £200, but unfortunately the tournament fell through.

The Gwelo Cricket Club started in 1894, and a little later clubs at Gatooma and Hartley were instituted.

Since the early days when Zeederberg's coaches were the only link in the 300 miles between Bulawayo and Salisbury, great rivalry has existed in the two centres. In December, 1895, a Salisbury team visited Bulawayo for the first real trial of cricket strength. Three matches were played, against Queen's, B.A.C. and Bulawayo, in the order named. H. M. Taberer captained the visitors and he proved an able and popular skipper. The first game provided Salisbury with an easy victory, but B.A.C., for whom A. G. Hay played two useful innings, defeated the visitors after a keen game. Bulawayo then beat Salisbury by an innings and 83 runs.

In September, 1897, a carnival was held at Salisbury, to which a Bulawayo eleven journeyed by coach. The journey was broken at Gwelo and two matches were played. Bulawayo won both, thanks principally to L. G. Robinson and R. A. Blanckenberg. The ground was a little rough, having

Back Row:
H. Sanderson,
L. C. Wigg,
E. T. Kenny,
G. Candler,
A. E. Holloway,
W. Collins,
J. E. Nicholls,
C. Bailey.

Middle Row:
E. Coxwell,
J. A. Edmunds,
J. H. Kennedy,
A. B. Rankine,
G. Bowen,
W. Strachan,
R. le S. Fisher.

Bottom Row:
H. A. Harper,
A. H. Newnham,
E. C. Sharpe,
G. W. Fermanner,
R. Benn,
C. E. Wells,
P. E. Craven.

A GATHERING OF VETERANS AND PIONEERS, 12th SEPTEMBER, 1900, SALISBURY.

been recently ploughed and, owing to its sandy nature, white-wash would not " take," so white tape had to be used for the creases!

The team then proceeded to Salisbury. Two hours after debarking from the coach, Bulawayo had to play Salisbury, and the latter won easily. W. S. Taberer was in great bowling and batting form, while "Joey" Milton (afterwards Sir William, the Administrator) who had previously rattled up 36 and 40 against the first English team to visit South Africa and knocked little Johnny Briggs' bowling about, also gave a good display. Robinson was top scorer for Bulawayo.

The 7th Hussars were just off the veld from fighting or looking for Mashonas, and they were Bulawayo's next opponents. In this match R. A. Blanckenberg registered the only century of the tournament and helped Bulawayo into a winning position, but Capt. R. M. Poore saved the day for the soldiers.

Then the two towns met for the cup presented by Mr I. H. Hirschler, and Bulawayo won, A. E. Fitzgerald, the Bulawayo captain, batting well.

In 1899 a visit by Lord Hawke's team was arranged, and two matches were played in Bulawayo, one against a local XVIII and the other against a Rhodesia XV. The visitors won both comfortably.

Mr. J. D. Logan was an interested spectator of these matches and, in commemoration of Lord Hawke's visit, promised a cup for inter-town competition, deputing Lord Hawke to select the trophy on his return to England. The Hirschler Cup was not a floating trophy, and when Bulawayo won it in 1897 it became the local First League cup.

The Salisbury contingent for Rhodesia v. Lord Hawke's team had a most eventful ten days' journey. The coach had to be pulled out of a morass at Charter by a span of thirty oxen, and they were then held up by the Hunyani River in flood. H. M. Taberer established communication with the further bank by throwing over a cricket ball with line attached. A skip was then constructed and the team conveyed across the river and taken to Bulawayo by another coach, arriving shortly before the hour of play.

In 1910, H. D. G. Leveson-Gower brought up a side composed of some of his M.C.C. team, then touring South Africa, and several prominent South African cricketers. There was difficulty in raising the guarantee of about £600 for the visit,

RHODESIA v. LEVESON-GOWER'S TEAM, 1910.

Standing: B. F. Wright, J. Hopley, G. Hopley, C. E. Duff, G. R. Payne, C. Pfaff, H. S. Keigwin, T. E. Bourdillon, P. Lewis, P. W. Sherwell, H. S. Kaye, G. Anderson, H. O. Coker.

Sitting: M. C. Bird, R. O. Schwarz, F. L. Fane, Sir Raleigh Grey, W. S. Taberer, Judge Watermeyer, H. D. G. Leveson-Gower, G. H. Simpson-Hayward, L. G. Robinson, J. W. Zulch.

In front: F. G. Brooks, P. Henwood, A. E. Cook.

so the much-abused B.S.A. Company assumed responsibility and were considerable losers. The visitors beat Rhodesia in Bulawayo fairly easily, Simpson-Hayward with his underhands amusing the spectators, but not the batsmen. For Rhodesia L. G. Robinson, W. S. Taberer and H. S. Keigwin all batted well, while G. M. Stephenson's 5 for 104 was the result of excellent bowling. P. Henwood constantly beat the batsmen but could not hit the stumps. Among the visitors' big scores was a rapid 45 by P. W. Sherwell. The latter is now a popular resident of Bulawayo, and is a great mentor on the Cricket Union. In 1907 he captained what was a very successful South African team in England, and led the Springboks on their Australian tour of 1910-11. Mr. Sherwell at one time held the South African tennis singles title. During the Rhodesia-M.C.C. match the B.S.A. Police Band rendered musical selections! The M.C.C. then defeated a Midlands XVIII, for whom A. J. Bradley and R. L. Juul batted well and A. Bailey bowled with great effect. In the return match in Salisbury against Rhodesia the latter had the better of a drawn game. In the first innings G. Anderson took 7 of the M.C.C. wickets for 78 runs and C. E. Duff 4 for 11 in the second. L. G. Robinson in both innings batted splendidly, and Keigwin gave a fine display for 111. Fred Brooks batted well and did some wonderful work in the outfield.

Three years later I. D. Difford's team, captained by E. A. Halliwell, visited the country, but was not superior to the leading towns, and suffered defeat in Salisbury, while it could only draw with Bulawayo. This was the first side to make a general tour of Rhodesia, and the visit did a great deal of good.

After the war, in 1922, the results of a similar tour by the Green Point Club showed that cricket in Rhodesia was at a high standard. In March, 1923, a strong Transvaal team was bowled out for 99 in Bulawayo, V. L. Robinson (a son of L. G.) doing most of the damage. After a drawn game with Rhodesia, in which P. Rabinson bowled well, the Transvaalers overwhelmed Rhodesia in a return match. Rabinson was again outstanding with some great bowling. Late in 1923 the Rhodes University College toured Rhodesia and played fourteen matches. In 1925 they played thirteen matches in the Colony and in 1928 nine games. The amount of good derived from these visits is inestimable. Most teams visiting

M.C.C. v. RHODESIA, 1930.

Top Row: D. Morris (12th man), N. I. Boast, W. A. Napier, D. S. Tomlinson, W. Farrimond, W. Voce, H. de V. Moll, C. J. R. Hayward, M.C.C. Baggage Man.

Middle Row: T. P. Syminton, R. J. Crisp, A. Hyde, W. R. Hammond   M. Leyland, M. Allom, M. Turnbull, I. A. R. Peebles.

Front Row: J. de L. Thompson, M. W. Tate, J. C. White, A. G. Hay (Pres., R.C.U.), A. G. E. Speight (Capt. Rhodesia), A. P. F. Chapman (Capt. M.C.C.), W. A. Sewell (M.C.C. Manager), R. E. S. Wyatt, H. J. O'Reilly.

Rhodesia have time only to play in Bulawayo and/or Salisbury. The R.U.C. team, however, went to every cricketing town in Rhodesia, with tremendously beneficial results. On each visit R.U.C. was captained by a Rhodesian, the respective skippers being I. Campbell-Rodger, A. G. E. Speight and H. B. Dugmore. The best incident was related by the 1928 team, and occurred at Umtali. A Rhodes batsman who was suffering from a leg-strain drove a ball which disappeared in some grass inside the boundary. The fielder, after some searching, discovered the Wisden down an ant-bear hole. He summoned aid but no arm was long enough to get the ball. Meanwhile the batsmen ran eight runs, at which stage the lame one refused to go on! Eventually another ball was requisitioned to allow the game to continue.

In 1924 Lionel Tennyson's " Jolly Souls " team played Rhodesia and won easily. S. A. Cowper bowled well and there were several good knocks by R. H. Catterall, F. H. Morgan, W. Wood, E. C. Arnold, Dr. A. Campbell and H. Campbell-Rodger. The Transvaal, a province that has done much for Rhodesian cricket, came up again in 1928, led by A. S. Frames. By this time the pre-war cricketers who had returned and kept the game going were being superseded by those who are still playing to-day, and in 1928 Rhodesian teams were composed of very young men. In the match in Bulawayo Rhodesia's best bowler was F. Dollar, and the best innings was that of C. J. R. Hayward. G. E. Fletcher, W. Wood, H. Campbell-Rodger and E. C. Arnold also batted splendidly, and the visitors gained a very narrow victory. In the capital, however, they won by a big margin after being lucky to force a draw against Mashonaland.

The biggest event of recent years was the visit in 1930 of the M.C.C. side to Rhodesia. The Colony did remarkably well against A. P. F. Chapman's team, and two memorable knocks were those of C. J. R. Hayward and T. P. Symington. N. I. Boast batted well, too, and " kept " splendidly. Of the bowlers H. J. O'Reilly, D. S. Tomlinson, and R. J. Crisp performed with credit. H. de V. Moll took no wickets but bowled really well.

The first Rhodesian team to cross the border of the Colony took part in the Currie Cup tournament of 1905. Only one match was played which Transvaal won comfortably.

D. S. TOMLINSON.

A. J. BELL.

DUNCAN DOLLAR.

C. H. BLANCKENBERG.

In 1930, after a 25 years' absence, Rhodesia re-entered the Currie Cup tournament and followed this none too happy venture by an entry in 1931-32 that was more successful than even the most sanguine had expected.

Several Rhodesians have earned recognition in the front ranks of South African cricket. In 1905, against the Transvaal team, five of whom were ultimately chosen for the 1906 overseas tour, G. Anderson's bowling figures were: 28 overs, 2 maidens, 91 runs, 7 wickets. Anderson is reckoned the finest left-arm bowler this country has ever had. In 1910 T. E. Bourdillon impressed Leveson-Gower's team with his all-round ability, and before the 1912 Springbok overseas team was selected he was invited South for trials. R. H. Catterall, the Transvaal Springbok, spent a season in Bulawayo playing for Raylton, before proceeding overseas with the 1924 South African team. In 1935 Rhodesians have at last found their way into the Springbok team. A. J. Bell, who had already played for South Africa in England and Australia but who has been resident in Bulawayo long enough to be termed a Rhodesian, has been re-selected. D. S. Tomlinson, Rhodesian-born and taught, is the first essentially Rhodesian cricketer to gain a Springbok cap. Incidentally, another member of the team, R. J. Crisp, learned and played all his cricket in this country up to a few seasons ago.

Cricket in Rhodesia is ably administered. Each of the four provinces—Manicaland, Mashonaland, Matabeleland and Midlands—has its own Board affiliated to, and with delegates on, the Rhodesia Cricket Union. Northern Rhodesia is similarly affiliated and represented. The present President of the Union is Mr. A. G. Hay, who has held office for many years, and the game owes much to his services. An ex-President and benefactor of the game is Mr. P. J. Phillips. Mr. C. H. Blanckenberg, a splendid batsman-wicketkeeper in his day, was honorary secretary of the Union for many years, and has given valuable assistance in the compilation of this record.

CRICKET IN MASHONALAND.

In 1891 Salisbury's first cricket pitch lay partly across the present Manica Road in the shadow of the historic Kopje. On this Ranche Ground, as it was called, many a fine game was seen with that much-revered Rhodesian, Archdeacon Upcher at cover-point, Tim Finnicane behind the wickets,

Fatty Beaven, a left-arm bowler, Canon Balfour, who umpired, and such men as Percy Craven, Haasie Newmeyer, G. Candler, Colonel Rhodes, Judge Vintcent, H. M. Taberer (of Oxford, Essex, Natal, Rhodesia and Transvaal), H. J. Borrow, J. Spreckley, Skipper Hoste, Eyre, Geo. St. Hill, Ernest Graham, Sid Arnott, Morris, Newnham, Cooper Hodgson, Bly Hopley, Crouchley, Jock Drysdale, Grimmer, Jeff Clinton and Jack Carruthers.

Salisbury was divided into two parts by a deep and wide ditch, or donga, the two divisions of the town being known as " Kopje " and " Causeway." The latter was the administrative or Government side, and Kopje the commercial section and, as there was a natural cleavage, so, too, was there a rivalry in all matters, including sport. The Kopje Club left the Ranche Ground after a time and used the centre of the racecourse, with the grandstand for a pavilion. The surface of the ground was as hard as iron and not too smooth, and a good deal of pluck was required to stop hard drives. The Causeway Club's field was what is still known as Cecil Square, which is now laid out as a small park.

For many years the Causeway or Salisbury Club had matters all its own way. Among its stars were Colin Duff (also a fine rugby player), D. W. Hook, Ken Fairbairn, E. C. Sharpe, who is well remembered as one of Salisbury's famous comedians, W. S. Taberer, who made a good 51 for a King Williamstown XXII. against Lord Hawke's 1895-96 team, Frames, J. P. Kennedy and later, Fred Brooks; whilst Kopje, which later became the Alexandra Club, had a good slow left-arm bowler in Liversley, two useful bats in Copeland and Moorcroft, and Fitzgerald, Lonsdale, Harry Harper, who did so much spade-work for the Club, C. E. Slocock and A. D. Fradgeley. In 1899 Mr. E. Vigne presented a handsome trophy for inter-club competition. During the first fifteen years of its existence the Salisbury Club won it on thirteen occasions. The Kopje's first success came when the Blanckenbergs (R. A. and C. H.) played, in 1901. Kopje won one match by one run, Fradgeley making 50 not out, and C. H. Blanckenberg 99 not out. Umtali also competed for the Vigne Cup, and at Umtali Reg. and Charlie Blanckenberg went in first for Salisbury and knocked up 250 runs before being separated, each scoring a century. A third brother, W. R., was also prominent in Rhodesian cricket after coming from the Diocesan College with a fine reputation. Only a few years ago, playing for the Bar and Side Bar against the Police, a match arranged by Sir Murray Bisset, who took a keen interest in Rhodesian cricket, " W. R." took 6 wickets for 2 runs, which is a good index to his earlier form. He was also a fine bat.

Early Umtali stalwarts were L. Winslow, one time of the champion King Williamstown team, Andrew Puzey, who played against Major Wharton's team for Transvaal, D. Dollar, a splendid bowler, Tulloch, Palmer, J. L. Crawford, and A. J. Tomlinson, of the B.S.A. Police (now Colonel) and father of the 1935 Springbok. An Umtali side captained by Dr. Craven scored a great victory over Alexandra, skippered by Dr. O'Keefe, a big share of the win going to J. S. Holland, who took 8 for 28 and scored 104. Cricket was in a healthy condition in Umtali, and other notables were the brothers Tom and Jim Gilbert, Gubb, a medium-paced bowler, Carey, a useful left-hander, Frank Myburgh and his brother Ryk, the Magistrate, A. L. Baker, Jordan of the Police, Frank Howe-Ely, a first-class bowler, and Reg. Lark. Tom Gilbert was regarded as the safest catch in Umtali. On one occasion he was fielding at slip where he dropped a catch, an unheard-of offence as far as Tom was concerned. He changed positions, where he dropped another, and when he went into the covers he dropped a third, and his side lost the match. Tom had his leg pulled about that for many a day, but he was never again seen to drop a catch.

Among the records of these earlier days in Salisbury is an account of Salisbury's dismissal of the Police for 16 runs. They suffered one of the heaviest defeats known in the Capital for, besides their being beaten by an innings, only one Salisbury batsman was dismissed before the innings was declared. The highest score recorded was Salisbury's 450 for 5 wickets against Kopje, and in this game C. E. Duff made a record score of 250 not out. The largest number of wickets in a single innings was captured by W. R. Blanckenberg who, for All-Comers against Home-Born, took 10 for 17 runs.

Just before the Great War cricket was very strong in Salisbury, the Salisbury Club fielding two senior teams of equal strength against Alexandra and the Police. Players who achieved success were L. C. Vernon, G. R. Payne, W. A. and L. Brooks, H. O. Coker, F. Kendle, of Eastern Province, and R. H. Wood.

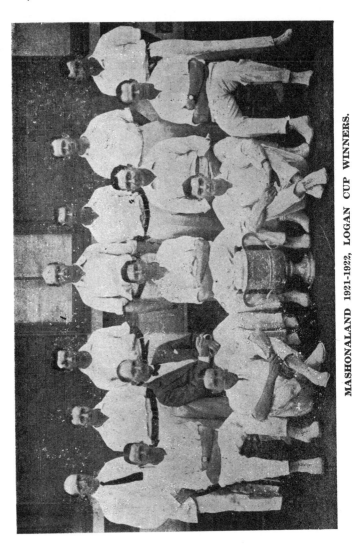

MASHONALAND 1921-1922, LOGAN CUP WINNERS.

Standing:
R. Allen (Secty.),
R. A. Gower,
C. W. Charter,
J. von Bonde,
R. J. Herholdt,
F. J. Townsend,
E. E. Wright,

Middle Row:
G. Gemmell,
W. E. Thomas
(President),
D. G. Elliott
(Captain),
S. A. Cowper,
H. T. Bell.

Bottom Row:
T. Fisher,
C L. Roberts.

Soon after the war cricket was in full swing again, and new clubs were Raylton, Old Hararians and Territorials. So many new players were enrolled that three leagues were organised. It is impossible to mention all who have been instrumental in the building up of Mashonaland cricket, but of the later players mention should be made of V. L. Robinson, a worthy successor to his famous father, Leo. Robinson, Don Elliott, a tip-top wicket-keeper, Austin Cowper, C. L. Roberts, the Hydes, Pat O'Reilly, A. L. Fielding, Eric Thomas, R. Tomlinson, D. Tomlinson, D. P. C. Gumpertz, E. H. Beck, E. G. Smith, who has worked hard for cricket in this country, John Hopley, C. Pfaff, R. J. Herholdt, G. Gemmell, and R. A. Gower. In Umtali there are Major F. R. Lark, a fine all-rounder, B. Howard, H. H. Smetham, K. Rowell and L. D. Elworthy, who in a Lawley Cup match against Beira in 1932 took all 10 ten wickets for 41 runs. Salisbury, Umtali and Beira, where E. Jarvis is a great enthusiast, compete annually for the Lawley Cup.

Beira is like an oasis for cricketers where the hospitality only misses being overwhelming by being completely spontaneous and genuine. Recently a Salisbury team went there and returned with " The Ashes," which consisted of " Johnny Walker " corks and caps. These were reverently burned at the Drill Hall in Salisbury with appropriate honours, and now repose in a glass jar for annual competition.

There are playing fields ample for the requirements of the game in Salisbury, for which thanks are due to the Municipality for granting long leases of portions of the town land to clubs at very low rentals. Grass is now being grown on most of the grounds, and a bright future for cricket in the Capital can be confidently expected.

CRICKET IN MATABELELAND.

The year 1894 marks the beginning of cricket in Bulawayo when Queen's, B.A.C., 7th Hussars and the Matabeleland Mounted Police were great rivals. The Hussars had their camp near the Old Nick Mine, to which visiting teams went by bicycle or mule-cart. After matches there was royal entertainment in the Officers' Mess, where prints from illustrated papers depicting Prince Teck leading charges against the Matabele in the Matopos were displayed on the walls and were the subject of much good-natured derision. Very

A. G. HAY.   L. G. ROBINSON.

Queen's Pavilion wrecked by hail storm, 1900.

popular were the Colonials v. Home-born matches, and a great festival fixture was the Licensed Victuallers' match, in which old Harry Lloyd and Ted Slater figured prominently. Bulawayo had some fine players in Major Poore, of the Hussars, who played for Natal and South Africa in 1893, and some years later captained Hampshire, G. Cripps, vice-captain of the first South African side that went Home, H. J. Mordaunt, a Cambridge " Blue," C. W. Cosnett, known as "Gobo the Wily," Leo. G. Robinson, once of Natal, M. G. Linnell, H. Hallward of Lancing XI, G. D. Katanakis, who later played for Hampshire, C. H. Blanckenberg, J. C. Coghlan, ex-Griqua Currie Cup player, Dr. E. Head, H. G. ("Sonny") Board, J. Bissett, Magnus Spence, L. P. Ashburnham, a Western Province Currie Cup man and brilliant field, R. H. Jones, H. A. de Beer, C. S. Gill, S. H. Walker, C. J. Robinson, who at one time opened the batting for Somerset, A. L. Jones, and " Bunks " Copeland. Queen's and B.A.C. were in a flourishing condition and it may interest present members to learn that in December, 1898, B.A.C. had a cash balance of £1,300 and a membership of 250.

In 1898 a Second League was organised to meet the influx of players, and it was at this period that St. George's School, destined to play an important part in all Bulawayo athletics, was founded. The visit of Lord Hawke's team in 1899 gave cricket a fillip, and among new players were Tommy Routledge, the Springbok, R. A. Sidgreaves, A. C. L. Webb, C. T. Stuart, a Currie Cup player, that keen B.A.C. supporter, Donald Welsh, who was a walking " Wisden's," Captain Foley (Cambridge and Middlesex) whose off-play was so attractive, and G. M. Campbell.

In 1900, during the rainy season, a terrific storm struck Bulawayo. The Queen's pavilion roof was lifted right off and the building looked as if it had been bombarded by heavy artillery.

In 1902 Raylton and King's clubs entered the leagues. A. E. Speight and G. S. Stapleton were additions to local cricket, and also W. P. T. Hancock, a medium-paced right-hand bowler with a wonderful length, and the great G. Anderson. J. Willing was a most unorthodox but useful cricketer. No batsman could let the ball come nearer to his stumps and yet stop it at the last moment. He had a wonderful eye. In McCormack, Bulawayo possessed an outstanding wicket-

QUEENS CLUB, 1901.

Top Row: Sgt. Alder, W. P. T. Hancock, W. Haddon, H. O. Coker, C. Parkin, W. P. Puree, A. J. Tomlinson, C. Campbell, A. Gruno, Mrs. Bush.

Middle Row: W. G. Swanson, H. E. O. Green, G. W. Wood, C. S. Gill, Knowles, C. G. Smitherson, C. W. Cosnett, Bush.

Bottom Row: A. P. Heeley, C. J. Robinson, Major Masterson, H. A. Cooper, Judge C. Ward, A. G. Hay, Harry Lloyd. M. G. Linnell, E. F. Henderson.

Teddy Bush.

keeper. Bulawayo has always been fortunate in filling this position. Mackendrick, Blakeney and Jack Huntley were well above the average and there were Linnell and two of the Blanckenbergs who could fill the gap, and later came N. Henwood and J. Walker, of Raylton. Perhaps the most unobtrusive and best we ever had was Williamson of Queen's. More recently there have been E. C. Arnold, R. H. J. Dickinson, E. G. Burton and F. Morgan of B.A.C.

Later a team from Messrs. Haddon and Sly entered the Second League and there were regular friendlies among Messrs. Smart and Copley's team, Past and Present Police, The Bulawayo Chronicle, S.R. Volunteers, S.R. Constabulary, Uitlanders and Teetotallers. In 1905 the Matopo Athletic Club was born, piloted by that dear old sportsman, Teddy Hull, and many pleasant games were played amid the hills. Jock Pender, E. Selfe, C. R. Gunner and E. C. Weaver were all Matopos stalwarts. New players at this time were F. B. and W. A. Brooks, brothers of the redoubtable Fred; W. A. was a vigorous bat and Frank a polished bat with a great variety of strokes. Then there were W. Bell, H. A. Cloete, M. Tait and A. Tait, W. W. Dawson, D. G. Davies and S. S. Shipman. R. Henwood came to Bulawayo in 1906, and there were more new names such as C. Burrows, R. Lanning and J. D. Mackenzie (later Judge).

In 1906, in a First League match, A. H. Tummell, who had a variety of unorthodox strokes that were the despair of all bowlers, created a record by knocking up 226. The previous best had been Linnell's 176 not out. In 1923 W. Wood approached this record with 204 not out.

In 1907 B.A.C. were beaten by Gwelo, who thus won the First League Cup. In this year St. John's School came into being. Later this became the Milton School, the *alma mater* of so many splendid Rhodesian sportsmen. By 1907, too, Plumtree School were figuring prominently in the scheme of things, and this school has also produced many fine cricketers. In the 1908-1909 season, St. George's School came up into the First League to join issue with Queen's, B.A.C. and Gwelo. The schoolboys were remarkably good fielders and Basil Howard, Pat and Sonny Walsh, were all good bats, and the last a useful fast bowler. No less worthy of record was a slim youth, a good bat and bowler and a brilliant slip-field, known to-day as "Doc" Campbell—no longer slim, but as keen as ever. The Doc, one of the most popular sportsmen in Bulawayo, played for the Cape Town and Edinburgh Universities, obtained Scottish trials and subsequently played for and captained Rhodesia.

In 1911 Leo. Robinson captained the first team to Livingstone. One of the Bulawayo side celebrated his 21st birthday there and, making acquaintance with that old-timer, Van der Hum, retained on the journey home sorrowful recollections of the encounter. Another tale told of the North, in later days, is about a Wankie umpire's unorthodoxy, and the reply it provoked is vouched for by members of the Bulawayo team which played cricket in Wankie in a temperature of 110 degrees. The game was about to begin and the visitors' opening batsman had just reached the crease. He looked up towards the umpire and asked for guard.

"What will you have?" said the umpire as the other's bat hovered between middle and leg.

"Beer!" was the laconic reply.

King's, promoted to the Senior League in 1910, were a well-balanced batting and keen fielding side, with D. G. Elliott, Guy Davis, Jack Lea, Ben Rabinson, P. Harvey, D. Brown, F. Wood, P. Rabinson, and H. D. Guest. B.A.C. at that time acquired T. E. Bourdillon who, until a few years ago, was an outstanding performer with bat and ball in Rhodesian cricket. A. W. Seccull, of South African fame, also joined B.A.C. and, though past his prime, his advice and guidance in local cricket were much appreciated. C. H. Milton, son of that well-known sportsman, Sir William, E. Montgomery, H. B. Dawson and E. J. Leslie also played for them. The last-named was a fine wicket-keeper. G. P. L. ("Pondo") Matthews, a fine all-rounder, was a great acquisition to Queen's, and also Syd. Ashley, the rugger Springbok, a wily slow left-arm bowler. A. K. Castor, a beautiful bat, and H. D. Keigwin, a medium-paced left-hand bowler and forcing bat, were two fine performers.

In 1913 E. A. Green, playing for Chemists against King's, bowled remarkably, taking 9 wickets for 34 runs, and H. O. ("Chappie") Frielinghaus, for Queen's, took 9 Raylton wickets for 29 runs. Tom Gilbert, E. M. Wells, R. J. Herholdt, C. Myles and G. C. Hopley, an outstanding batsman, formed the backbone of the Raylton side which was promoted, after some years in the Second League.

The Great War period marked a suspension of all senior sport in the Colony. Games were kept going only by schools and women players until the gradual revival of serious competition, which began in 1919. Cricket attained to a high standard when organised afresh in 1919, and among a fine collection of players were E. F. Harris, an unorthodox but prolific run-getter and a great slip-catch, A. N. Cranswick, who captained Queen's, G. C. Hopley, W. H. Melville, good bat and brilliant cover-point, rivalled in this position in the field only by P. Peiser and J. W. Rackham; R. L. Juul, a solid batsman who later did good work on the administrative side, C. P. Harvey, wily as ever; the veteran C. H. Blanckenberg, as good as any of them; Tom Bourdillon and his brother Victor, a useful all-rounder; D. G. ("Tommy") Lewis, a googly bowler; T. A. Hubbard, a fine bowler who would have been outstanding if he had played regularly; F. Wood and J. W. Miller, two splendid all-rounders; good bowlers in H. Evans and R. T. Murray; two sparkling batsmen in S. Hepker and H. Clarke; Major A. M. Miller of flying fame; C. Wynne, V. L. Robinson, a splendid bat and bowler who has also done much off the field for the game; P. Rabinson, a clever bowler and as fine a type of sportsman as one could wish to meet; T. P. Gilbert, who collected many wickets and runs, and G. W. Ledeboer, a stylish left-hand bat when he got going and a useful right-arm fast bowler. " George " is a really big-hearted sportsman, and his perseverance and success as a coach have earned him a lasting reputation in Bulawayo. In fact, nearly all the prominent local cricketers have at some time profited by his teaching.

St. George's School had now lapsed into the Second League, and the senior sides were B.A.C., Queen's, Raylton and King's. Matches were keenly contested, with B.A.C. and Raylton battling for premier honours. In 1921 a Bulawayo record for a first-wicket partnership and also for the rate of scoring was set up by A. N. Cranswick and W. Melville, who knocked up 249 in 100 minutes for Queen's against King's. Newcomers to local cricket who maintained this high standard were A. C. Curle, a powerful hitter, G. E.

Fletcher, a dour bat who afterwards captained and made many runs for Matabeleland; O. P. S. W. Green, of the same calibre as Curle; F. H. Morgan, a keen all-rounder; E. C. Arnold and W. Wood, a splendid bat, bowler and fielder.

In 1924 R. H. Catterall came to reside in Bulawayo, and his Raylton side carried all before it. The famous Springbok discovered and made J. A. Adamson, who for many years now has been easily the best left-arm bowler in Rhodesia. In 1927, in a league match, Adamson made 101 and took 10 wickets for 83 runs.

R. H. Catterall.

The year 1925 saw the birth of the Ramblers XI, composed of young cricketers under 21 years of age. The idea was to stick to this age-limit, but it was found impracticable, and to-day there are several of the original side still playing. The Ramblers, during their ten seasons, have won the senior competition six times, and have been runners-up on three occasions. Prominent ex-Ramblers are J. W. Rackham, a brilliant fielder, W. Wood, T. F. B. Gilbert, E. C. Arnold, W. H. Strachan, a fine left-arm bowler and useful bat, and H. de V. Moll, a most accurate bowler. While the Ramblers were making their debut their great rivals were Raylton. The latter were strengthened by Dr. A. Campbell, O. L. Olver,. a fine forcing batsman, E. Sim, a medium-paced bowler, F. Mathieson, a useful wicket-. keeper and batsman, R. D. Gloak and R. P. Easterbrook. Other notables among the Bulawayo clubs in recent years have been T. P. Syminton, a left-hand bat with numerous scoring strokes, E. A. Maughan, V. N. Hepker, who afterwards played for Transvaal against Rhodesia, K. P. Neall, a stylish left-hand bat, W. A. Napier, a very useful all-rounder, I. Campbell-Rodger, a fine forcing bat and fast bowler, E. Zacks, another in the list of Bulawayo's wicket-keeper batsmen, G. Gemmell (Cantab.) one of the finest sportsmen in Rhodesia, and a really polished batsman; A. H. Minter, a good all-rounder; F. Dakyn Hockin, a good fast bowler unfortunately crocked at football; J. A. A. Thompson, medium right-hand " stock " bowler, and C. R. Ridgway, who had made useful scores for Staffordshire. Mr. Ridgway has been chairman of the Matabeleland Cricket Association for many years and its representative on the Cricket Union. He has captained Matabeleland and Rhodesia and has generally done great work for the game.

Cricket in Matabeleland to-day is in a healthy condition. Some outstanding performers are J. C. Tones, a prolific run-getter, J. H. Charsley, a splendid all-rounder, M. Napier, the Province's best slip catch, good bat and change bowler, A. S. Ward, ex-Griqua Currie Cup player, Gordon Cunningham, who took up cricket only three seasons ago and made 50 in his first Logan Cup appearance; S. R. Lanning, promising left-hand bat and splendid field; A. S. Hancock, an unlucky bowler with a wonderful length; Chappell, keen as mustard; A. Genner, Queen's stock bowler; Jock Henderson, and that big-hearted sportsman, K. O. (" Porky ") Goldhawk.

Other useful men are W. E. G. Wilson, an opening bat, M. W. Clarke, J. H. Fuller, F. Payne, L. Walkden, captain of B.A.C., F. C. Robinson, with a deceptive break either way, J. M. Fox and G. H. Burne.

Hitters always delight the crowd, and among the " go-getters " are D. R. Paterson, B. L. Calderwood, J. W. Willing and C. A. W. Bartels, who seems to enjoy a duck as much as a century. But cricket is like several games in one, and fielding by itself can be a sheer delight. The batsman and bowler are forgotten when the fielder streaks for the ball and a smart pick-up with a good throw-in never fails to earn deserved applause. In Bulawayo one takes no chances when Bob Reid is in the covers. T. M. Davies, B. W. ("Brom") Bland, the popular Queen's captain, and F. S. Haslett, in the out-field, are all quick off the mark and safe as houses.

RHODESIA v.
TRANSVAAL, 1928.

Back Row:
E. Munnik (Umpire),
E. C. Arnold, G. E. Fletcher, J. W. Rackham
(12th man), C. J. R. Hayward, H. Campbell-Rodger, W. P. T. Hancock (Umpire).

Front Row: R. N. Tomlinson, J. de L. Thompson,
A. Hyde, C. R. Ridgway
(capt.), W. Wood, F. Dollar, D. S. Tomlinson.

The Matabeleland Cricket Association has a staunch supporter in Sir Richard Goode, an Old Fettesian, while others are Major R. Gordon, D.S.O., O.B.E., H. Johnston, Colonel Fenwick, and "Daddy" Hubbard, beloved by all cricketers for his keenness and his artistry in the preparation of pitches.

THE CURRIE CUP ENTRIES.

In March, 1905, a Rhodesian team went to Johannesburg and played the Transvaal. This was before the Fourteen Streams and Zeerust railway lines were constructed and the team, travelling by coach from Mafeking to Potchefstroom, came upon heavy weather. For 26 hours they braved the perils of land and flood, of which the survivors even to-day speak with awe. But this extremely uncomfortable and hazardous journey had, it is said, its compensating features. These included the unfailing good humour and whimsical wit of Tummell who was perched precariously on the outside of the swaying, water-logged coach; the ridiculous grief of the man, Scotch by absorption if not by birth, who having lost his luggage treasured a cork-screw, and the comic plight of the non-cricketing passenger who, having vehemently refused to remain on the coach while it dashed foolhardily through a swollen ford, braved the flood with desperate breast-stroke in pursuit of the vanishing coach and its cheery occupants, his only refuge from the terrors of the desolate veld. There are even more humorous but less recordable tales told at sundown.

The team arrived in Johannesburg shortly before the hour of play in anything but a fit condition for cricket and Transvaal won fairly easily. Only F. G. Brooks, who played a fine innings of 61, and G. Anderson with 7 wickets for 91 runs, did justice to themselves. After the match a friendly was played against a Wanderers XI., which included most of the Transvaal team, and Rhodesia won comfortably, thus showing that the previous game was not a true index of the real form of the team.

The Rhodesian team was: L. G. Robinson (capt.), C. T. Stuart, F. G. Brooks, M. G. Linnell, A. H. Tummell, W. S. Taberer, C. E. Duff, W. R. Blanckenberg, W. P. T. Hancock, C. P. Richardson, J. V. McCormack and G. Anderson.

CURRIE CUP, 1930.

Standing: W. H. Strachan (Scorer), C. J. R. Hayward, T. P. Syminton, J. de L. Thompson, R. N. Tomlinson, F. Dollar, W. Wood, C. R. Ridgway (Manager).

Middle Row: D. Fowler, R. H. J. Dickinson, F. H. Morgan, Dr. A. Campbell (capt.), A. Hyde, E. Sim, H. J. O'Reilly.

J. W. Willing, C. L. Roberts.

THE SECOND CURRIE CUP ENTRY.

After an interval of twenty-five years Rhodesia in 1930 ventured South once again to participate in the Currie Cup series.

The team left Bulawayo on January 7 and returned on the 30th. The twenty-three days were occupied by twelve days' cricket, two days of rest, and nine days' travel in which the players covered 2,655 miles by train, which must be a record in itself for a Currie Cup tournament. This excess of train travelling was not conducive to good cricket, but apart from that Rhodesia was well beaten in each of the four three-day fixtures.

The touring team was: Dr. A. Campbell (captain), F. H. Morgan (vice-captain), R. H. J. Dickinson, C. J. R. Hayward, T. P. Syminton, W. Wood, J. W. Willing, J. de L. Thompson, A. Hyde, R. N. Tomlinson, H. J. O'Reilly, E. Sim, D. Fowler, C. L. Roberts and F. Dollar. The Manager was Mr. C. R. Ridgway.

Rhodesia was first beaten by the Griquas. Rhodesia started the match well by getting the first three wickets for three runs, but thereafter Balaskas and Co. piled up a record Currie Cup score of 602, which the Griquas subsequently surpassed when playing the Western Province. But the Rhodesians dropped many catches. O'Reilly bowled magnificently. The tourists' batting in the face of that big score was excellent and Hyde and Syminton gave fine displays. In Rhodesia's second innings Sim and O'Reilly made a great stand that added 94 for the last wicket and also averted the innings defeat.

On the Ramblers' ground the Free Staters had the Rhodesians at their worst, considering the conditions were so like those in the Colony. Hayward was the only batsman, with Wood and Sim quite good among the bowlers. Wood was the "stock" trundler on the tour and bowled with great heart.

Then at Kingwilliamstown, where the change to sea-level, though benefiting health, did the cricket no good, the Rhodesians were hopeless in the heavier atmosphere. Syminton alone showed any form and in fact he was the most consistent run-getter of the tour. "Pat" O'Reilly again bowled well.

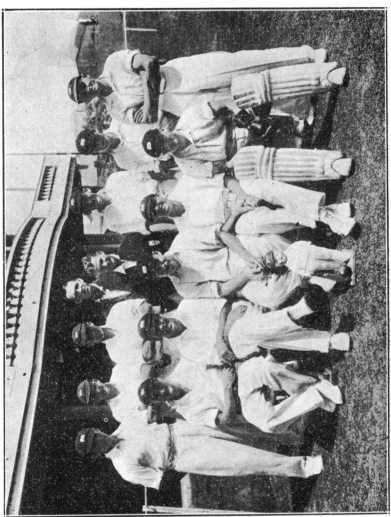

CURRIE CUP, 1931-32.

Standing: G. C. Grant, C. J. R. Hayward, D. S. Tomlinson, J. de L. Thompson, V. Hyde, M. H. Quinn, J. A. Adamson, H. de V. Moll.

Sitting: A. Hyde, A. H. Pattison, H. Campbell-Rodger (capt.), V. L. Robinson, R. Forbes.

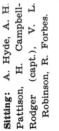

The fourth match, at Port Elizabeth, found the Rhodesians more acclimatised and several of the side batted well, particularly Hayward, Hyde, Syminton and Wood. Dickinson, who " kept " splendidly on the tour, came to light with the bat in this game. Sim, who up to this match had been unlucky in his bowling, met with a change of fortune and returned fine figures.

For the last game of the tournament Transvaal came up to Bulawayo where they won easily. A. Hyde played two good innings and Wood and Crisp bowled well.

THE THIRD CURRIE CUP ENTRY.

It was with feelings of mingled trepidation and confidence that Rhodesia proceeded to Johannesburg at the end of 1931. The Colony had fared so badly in the previous tournament that it was felt the other Provinces could hardly consider the Rhodesians as much of an opposition. On the other hand, most of the lessons learnt in 1930 had been assimilated, and fairly creditable performances against the visiting Transvaalers and the M.C.C. showed that Rhodesia would never again be the " wooden spoonists." The 1931 team, as it turned out, was more successful than even the most sanguine had expected. In Johannesburg an old friend, Mr. J. R. Con Mackey, became its able and energetic manager, while H. M. Taberer, that fine old sportsman, now unfortunately dead, " fathered " the team. Mention must be made of Isaac, a Cape Malay, who accompanied the team as baggage-man and who performed so many and varied duties as to become almost indispensable. Those who travelled to Johannesburg were: H. Campbell-Rodger (captain), A. H. Pattison, C. J. R. Hayward, G. C. Grant, H. de V. Moll, J. A. Adamson, R. Forbes, M. H. Quinn, J. de L. Thompson, V. L. Robinson (vice-captain), A. Hyde, V. Hyde and D. S. Tomlinson.

After the previous tour the Rhodesians had a lot to avenge and their first victim was the Orange Free State. Pattison scored a century and the skipper batted attractively while Henry Moll hit up a hectic 45. Quinn, as in every match, bowled well, and so did Tomlinson. This big victory over the Orange Free State alarmed the Transvaal and they considerably strengthened their original team to play

Rhodesia by the inclusion of E. P. Nupen and Cochrane.
Nupen was in great form, but Rhodesia was saved from total
disgrace by fine knocks by Campbell-Rodger, who notched a
great century, and Hayward. The only poor umpiring
encountered on the tour was in this match, and there were
several doubtful decisions on each side. Quinn again bowled
well, but the others' averages suffered before some fine batting
by Bob Catterall, Susskind and Anderson.

The Rhodesians felt far from happy at the prospect of
playing next day on turf, but on a wicket slightly damped
by the overnight dew, Quinn, helped by Tomlinson, rattled
out the opposition. In the second innings Border also failed
and Adamson took wickets cheaply. Robinson was the only
bat on the turf, with Grant playing two useful knocks, but
Rhodesia managed to win through.

Rhodesia's narrowest win was against the Griquas.
Adamson and Quinn caused their first innings collapse, but
then the Rhodesians failed miserably also. Only Hayward
and Thompson could cope with McNally, whose leg-theory
was disastrous for Rhodesia. In their second innings the
Kimberley men piled up a useful aggregate and the Northerners were set a big job. Grant and Pattison made the first
stand and the position looked good. A minor collapse made
all expressions glum but a stand by Robinson and Thompson
brightened the outlook until they were both run out, just
as they had fairly got the measure of the bowling. The last
men, Quinn and Adamson, were in with several runs required
and during alternate moments of cheering and of tense
silence this pair got the runs somehow and the Rhodesians
won by one wicket. Whew! Those last minutes were a
nerve-racking period!

The Eastern Province gave the tourists little trouble.
All the Rhodesian bowlers were in form and the opposition
were given no chances in the field. Tomlinson batted well
for a century while Campbell-Rodger registered his second
three-figure score, and the Rhodesians ran up a huge total.

Unfortunately there were no extra points for an outright
victory compared with a win on the first innings, otherwise
Rhodesia would have won the Currie Cup.

The first three positions in the log were as follows:—

	P.	W.	L.	1st inns. W.	L.	D.	Pts.
Western Province	5	1	0	3	0	1	9
Rhodesia	5	4	1	0	0	0	8
Transvaal	5	3	0	1	1	0	8

Rhodesia emerged from the tournament with the under-mentioned honours:—(1) Runners up; (2) Scorers of the highest innings total of the tournament (437) against Eastern Province; (3) The only team to win four outright victories; (4) The only team against which no centuries were scored; (5) the team that recorded the highest number (4) of centuries in the tournament.

After the tournament several Rhodesians gained distinction in South African cricket. The captain, H. Campbell-Rodger, was selected as captain of the best eleven chosen from the tourney. In that side too were included A. H. Pattison, C. J. R. Hayward and D. Tomlinson. In The Rest XI J. de L. Thompson was chosen as the wicket-keeper. On their performances when the Western Province cricket festival was held over Christmas, 1933, H. Campbell-Rodger captained The Rest of South Africa team chosen from Rhodesia, Griqualand West, Orange Free State, Border and Eastern Province, and for this team were also chosen D. Tomlinson, C. J. R. Hayward and J. de L. Thompson.

FIRST CURRIE CUP ENTRY·

TRANSVAAL v. RHODESIA.

Played at Johannesburg, March 15th and 16th, 1905.   Transvaal
won by an innings and 170 runs.

TRANSVAAL.

L. J. Tancred, lbw, b Anderson	8
J. H. Sinclair, c Brooks, b Duff	57
M. Hathorn, b Anderson	43
R. O. Schwarz, c Robinson, b Anderson	7
J. J. Slatem, c Anderson, b Robinson	154
E. G. McDonald, b Duff	0
E. A. Halliwell, b Anderson	7
D. M. Sinclair, lbw, b Anderson	0
C. E. Floquet, b Anderson	26
W. Hazelhurst, c Stuart, b Anderson	2
R. W. Norden, not out	13
Extras (b. 15, l.-b. 8)	23
Total	340

RHODESIA.

Robinson, c Tancred, b Hazelhurst	18	—c Hathorn, b Norden	13
Stuart, c and b J. Sinclair	5	—b Schwarz	12
Brooks, c D. Sinclair, b Norden ...	61	—b Norden	1
Linnell, lbw, b Schwarz	15	—b Norden	6
Tummell, c Schwarz, b Norden ...	2	—b Norden	0
Taberer, b Norden	0	—b Norden	9
Duff, b Norden	3	—hit wicket, b Norden	0
Blanckenberg, b Schwarz	0	—b Norden	1
Hancock, b Schwarz	0	—not out	5
Richardson, lbw, b Schwarz	0	—c Schwarz, b Norden	0
Anderson, not out	0	—st Halliwell, b Schwarz	2
Extras (b 7, lb 1, w 3)	11	—Extras (b 1, lb 3, nb 2)	6
Total	115	Total	55

12th man: J. V. McCormack.

RHODESIA BOWLING.

	O.	M.	R.	W.		O.	M.	R.	W.
Anderson ...	28	2	91	7	Tummell ... ...-	2	0	13	0
Duff	30	5	104	2	Linnell	3	0	24	0
Blanckenberg .	4	1	27	0	Richardson ...	4	0	26	0
Taberer	8	1	31	0	Robinson ...	0.2	0	1	1

TRANSVAAL BOWLING.

	O.	M.	R.	W.	O.	M.	R.	W.
Sinclair	9	0	32	1				
Schwarz	13	3	29	4	2.5	1	9	2
Hazelhurst	5	2	15	1	10	3	28	0
Floquet	5	2	7	0				
Norden 11.1		3	21	4 ·	12	8	12	8

SECOND CURRIE CUP ENTRY.

GRIQUALAND WEST v. RHODESIA.

Played at Kimberley, 9th, 10th and 11th January, 1930. Griqualand West won by 9 wickets.

GRIQUALAND WEST.

J. Glover, c Dickinson, b O'Reilly	0	—not out 15
K. Viljoen, lbw, b O'Reilly	0	—not out 26
W. V. Ling, b O'Reilly	0	
F. Nicholson, lbw, b Sim	50	—lbw, b O'Reilly 2
C. D. McKay, b Sim	85	
X. Balaskas, b O'Reilly	206	
R. Henderson, c Thompson, b O'Reilly	62	
J. McNally, b Hyde	61	
L. Lowe, lbw, b O'Reilly	22	
D. Daly, b Wood	70	
H. Promnitz, not out	22	
Extras (b 8, lb 11, nb 5)	24	—Extras 0
Total	602	Total (for 1 wkt.) 43

RHODESIA.

Thompson, c Balaskas, b Henderson	34	—c Glover, b Lowe ... 2
A. Hyde, lbw, b Promnitz	80	—b Viljoen 6
Hayward, lbw, b Balaskas	29	—c Glover, b Promnitz 34
Tomlinson, c Nicholson, b Daly ...	35	—c McNally, b Balaskas 17
Syminton, c McKay, b McNally ...	23	—c Viljoen, b Balaskas 84
Morgan, b Balaskas	10	—c McKay, b Ling ... 1
Sim, run out	14	—st Nicholson, b Balaskas 61
O'Reilly, b Daly	5	—not out 37
Wood, c McNally, b Viljoen	49	—lbw, b Promnitz 9
Dickinson, b Daly	10	—b McNally 0
Campbell, not out	27	—c Promnitz, b McNally 37
Extras (b 5, lb 12, nb 1)	18	—Extras (b 11, lb 8) ... 19
Total	334	Total 307

RHODESIA BOWLING.

	O.	M.	R.	W.	O.	M.	R.	W.
O'Reilly	43	3	166	6	7	0	27	1
Tomlinson	16	2	54	0	6	1	12	0
Sim	25	3	123	2	1	0	4	0
Morgan	24	3	110	0				
Wood	25.3	4	61	1				
Dr. Campbell	7	0	35	0				
Hayward	3	0	11	0				
Hyde	5	0	18	1				

GRIQUALAND WEST BOWLING.

	O.	M.	R.	W.	O.	M.	R.	W.
Daly	31	9	69	3	14	3	32	0
Viljoen	12.4	3	22	1	8	1	36	1
Lowe	5	1	9	0	12	3	31	1
Balaskas	19	3	57	2	12.4	0	64	3
McNally	28	7	78	1	10	1	47	2
Promnitz	17	2	48	1	11	1	47	2
Henderson	12	0	33	1	3	0	19	0
Ling	—	—	—	—	2	0	12	1

ORANGE FREE STATE v. RHODESIA.

Played at Bloemfontein, January 13th, 14th and 15th, 1930. Orange
Free State won by 184 runs.

ORANGE FREE STATE.

A. G. Reid, lbw, b O'Reilly	2	—b Dollar	5
A. Kaplan, b Dollar	0	—lbw, b Morgan	45
M. Francis, b Sim	55	—lbw, b Sim	38
J. C. Newton, lbw, b Wood	13	—c Hyde, b Sim	67
E. Conlon, c Wood, b O'Reilly ...	3	—st Fowler, b Sim ...	15
C. W. Travers, c Fowler, b O'Reilly	4	—c Thompson, b Wood	38
S. Barry, run out	51	—b Wood	16
P. Withers, b Dollar	62	—c and b Wood	38
B. Hill, lbw, b Dollar	8	—lbw, b Wood	33
F. S. Campling, not out	5	—not out	4
A. Conlon, b Wood	10	—lbw, b Wood	2
Extras (b 6, lb 4, nb 2)	12	—Extras (b 21, lb 2, nb 1)	24
Total	225	Total	325

RHODESIA.

Thompson, b Withers	25	—b Hill	28
Hyde, c Barry, b Conlon	2	—b Hill	14
Hayward, run out	56	—b Francis	86
Roberts, b Reid	12	—c Francis, b Campling	1
Syminton, c Newton, b Reid	21	—b Campling	23
Wood, lbw, b Campling	3	—c A. Conlon, b Hill ...	6
Sim, b Reid	0	—c Francis, b Campling	0
Morgan, lbw, b Campling	12	—b Francis	31
Fowler, b Reid	2	—b Hill	0
O'Reilly, not out	12	—b Campling	9
Dollar, b Campling	0	—not out	1
Extras (b 4, lb 4, w 1, nb 2.)	11	—Extras (b 4, lb 6, w 1)	11
Total	156	Total	210

RHODESIA BOWLING.

	O.	M.	R.	W.	O.	M.	R.	W.
O'Reilly	18	2	58	3	16	0	60	0
Dollar	13	3	40	3	13	1	41	1
Wood	14	2	32	2	24.5	6	67	5
Morgan	8	0	44	0	15	0	71	1
Sim	9	3	29	1	14	2	48	3
Syminton	2	1	10	0				
Hyde	—	—	—	—	4	1	14	0

ORANGE FREE STATE BOWLING.

	O.	M.	R.	W.	O.	M.	R.	W.
Conlon	14	4	25	1	9	2	23	0
Hill	7	0	21	0	15	3	33	4
Reid	19	5	45	4	12	0	47	0
Campling	11.1	3	21	3	13	2	75	4
Travers	7	2	12	0	3	1	8	0
Withers	3	1	9	1				
Francis	3	0	12	0	5.3	0	13	2

BORDER v. RHODESIA.

At Kingwilliamstown, January 17th, 18th and 20th, 1930. Border won by 162 runs.

BORDER.

C. Fraser-Grant, b Dollar	0	— b O'Reilly	1
S. Farrer, c Hayward, b Dollar ...	3	— c Thompson, b Wood	8
S. Hubbard, c Dickinson, b O'Reilly	1	— c Campbell, b O'Reilly	12
L. Miles, b Willing	24	— c Dollar, b Hyde	66
C. Warner, c Hayward, b Willing	39	— b Wood	24
F. Goldschmidt, b Wood	50	— b O'Reilly	0
A. Beveridge, c Dickinson, b Willing	2	— b Wood	22
J. Whitehead, c Thompson, b O'Reilly	8	— b O'Reilly	3
D. Phillips, run out	5	— b O'Reilly	39
K. Muzzell, c Syminton, b Wood ...	8	— b Dollar	2
M. Warner, not out	2	— not out	0
Extras (b 2, lb 2, nb 9)	13	— Extras (b 2, lb 1, nb 9)	12
Total	155	Total	189

RHODESIA.

Thompson, lbw, b Whitehead	9	— lbw, b Muzzell	4
Willing, b M. Warner	21	— c Hubbard, b Muzzell	2
Hayward, b Whitehead	0	— c and b Beveridge ...	5
Hyde, lbw, b Whitehead	0	— b Whitehead	11
Syminton, c and b Phillips	34	— b Whitehead	18
Wood, b Phillips	21	— c and b Muzzell	10
Campbell, b Phillips	1	— c Goldschmidt, b Whitehead	1
Sim, c Miles, b Phillips	14	— b Muzzell	0
O'Reilly, b Phillips	9	— c Grant, b Whitehead	2
Dickinson, lbw, b Phillips	9	— not out	0
Dollar, not out	0	— c Hubbard, b Muzzell	0
Extras (b 1, nb 3)	4	— Extras (b 6, nb 1) ...	7
Total	122	Total	60

RHODESIA BOWLING.

	O.	M.	R.	W.	O.	M.	R.	W.
O'Reilly	15.2	7	28	3	19.5	5	44	5
Dollar	15	4	32	2	16	3	50	1
Wood	7	1	12	1	20	6	52	3
Willing	16	0	50	3	5	0	20	0
Hyde	—	—	—		2	0	11	1
Sim	4	1	10	0				
Campbell	4	2	10	0				

BORDER BOWLING.

	O.	M.	R.	W.	O.	M.	R.	W.
Phillips	22	16	16	6	13	6	18	0
Whitehead	16	3	38	3	6	2	13	4
M. Warner	4	1	10	1				
Muzzell	12	2	29	0	15	8	14	5
Beveridge	5	1	9	0	5	2	8	1
Miles	2	0	7	0				
Hubbard	4	0	9	0				

EASTERN PROVINCE v. RHODESIA.

At Port Elizabeth, January 23rd, 24th and 25th, 1930. Eastern Province won by 166 runs.

EASTERN PROVINCE.

Batsman	1st	2nd	
Mardon, b Sim	45	—c Wood, b Campbell .	75
Van den Berg, b O'Reilly	0	—run out	43
S. White, lbw, b Wood	30	—lbw, b Sim	0
H. B. Cameron, b Sim	67	—st Dickinson, b Sim	23
H. E. Pagden, c Dollar, b O'Reilly	80	—not out	91
E. Q. Davies, b Willing	0		
B. C. Philpot, b Wood	19		
E. L. Burgess, b Sim	0	—b Sim	4
D. M. Brown, c Dollar, b Sim	21	—b Dollar	29
T. C. Whitlock, lbw, b Wood	13	—b Sim	3
W. Boltman, not out	0		
Extras (b 5, lb 10, nb 5)	20	—Extras (b 12, lb 6, w 1, nb 2)	21
Total	295	Total (for 7 wkts declared)	289

RHODESIA.

Batsman	1st	2nd	
Hyde, c White, b Boltman	0	—b Davies	51
Willing, b Davies	3	—lbw, b Whitlock	11
Hayward, c Cameron, b Whitlock	73	—st Cameron, b Davies	3
Wood, lbw, b Burgess	25	—c Pagden, b Whitlock	45
Syminton, c Mardon, b Davies	0	—c Cameron, b Mardon	44
Dickinson, lbw, b Whitlock	26	—c Davies, b Philpot .	18
Morgan, b Boltman	2	—b Mardon	36
Sim, b Boltman	5	—b Philpot	26
O'Reilly, b Boltman	2	—c Boltman, b Davies .	1
Campbell, not out	5	—not out	10
Dollar, b Boltman	2	—b Davies	4
Extras (b 9, lb 6)	15	—Extras (b 2, lb 7, w 1, nb 1)	11
Total	158	Total	260

RHODESIA BOWLING.

	O.	M.	R.	W.	O.	M.	R.	W.
O'Reilly	15	2	40	2	14	1	73	0
Wood	15	1	58	3	9	0	39	0
Sim	19.2	5	50	4	25	5	76	4
Morgan	10	0	34	0	4	0	19	0
Willing	9	1	47	1	5	1	26	0
Dollar	6	1	46	0	8	3	12	1
Campbell	—	—	—	—	6	0	23	1

EASTERN PROVINCE BOWLING.

	O.	M.	R.	W.	O.	M.	R.	W.
Davies	15	4	19	2	14	3	36	4
Whitlock	7	4	5	2	15	2	50	2
Boltman	21.1	5	53	5	26.5	8	66	0
Philpot	14	3	33	0	18	5	40	2
Burgess	8	0	25	1	7	1	20	0
Brown	3	2	5	0	2	0	4	0
White	1	0	3	0	3	0	14	0
Mardon	—	—	—	—	11	5	19	2

TRANSVAAL v. RHODESIA.

At Bulawayo on March 29th, 30th ant 31st, 1930. Transvaal won by an innings and 11 runs.

TRANSVAAL.

S. H. Curnow, b Crisp	... ...	44
L. G. Duffus, c Dickinson, b Crisp	... ...	7
V. N. Hepker, lbw, b Crisp	... ...	0
H. W. Taylor, c Wood, b Tomlinson	... ...	139
W. H. Foley, c Napier, b Sim	... ...	153
G. Parker, b Wood	... ...	35
C. E. Cawse, b Tomlinson	... ...	8
J. Cochrane, b Wood	... ...	1
K. E. Bull, b Wood	... ...	2
F. Elworthy, c Hayward, b Wood	... ...	0
S. Brissenden, not out	... ...	1
Extras (b. 11, l.-b. 10, w. 3, n.b. 3)	... ...	27
Total	... ...	417

RHODESIA.

V. L. Robinson, b Brissenden	... ...	3	—lbw, b Parker	22
D. S. Tomlinson, b Cawse	... ...	28	—c Duffus, b Bull	11
W. A. Napier, b Cochrane	... ...	4	—c Foley, b Brissenden	38
A. Hyde, b Brissenden	... ...	60	—c Duffus, b Cochrane	55
Hayward, c Taylor, b Cawse	... ...	0	—c and b Bull	32
W. Lee, c Duffus, b Cochrane	... ...	30	—c and b Cawse	5
Syminton, c Duffus, b Cochrane	...	1	—not out	20
Wood, lbw, b Elworthy	... ...	13	—c Curnow, b Cawse ...	0
Crisp, b Brissenden	... ...	3	—b Cawse	4
Dickinson, not out	... ...	18	—c Cawse, b Bull	12
Sim, c Bull, b Brissenden	... ...	12	—c Cawse, b Cochrane	1
Extras (b 13, lb 8, w 1)	... ...	22	—Extras (b 4, lb 7, w 1)	12
Total	... ...	194	Total	212

RHODESIA BOWLING.

	O.	M.	R.	W.			O.	M.	R.	W.
Napier	12	2	47	0		Wood	7.5	0	38	4
Robinson	7	2	15	0		Tomlinson ...	21	1	111	2
Crisp	20	2	88	3		Hyde	3	0	17	0
Sim	17	1	60	1		Lee	2	0	14	0

TRANSVAAL BOWLING.

	O.	M.	R.	W.	O.	M.	R.	W.
Brissenden	17.5	2	34	4	18	6	31	1
Bull	10	3	16	0	18	6	44	3
Cochrane	11	3	34	3	20	8	39	2
Cawse	21	5	51	2	16	3	47	3
Elworthy	16	5	37	1	10	3	20	0
Parker	—	—	—	—	8	3	19	1

THIRD CURRIE CUP ENTRY.

In Johannesburg.

ORANGE FREE STATE v. RHODESIA.

On the Pirates' ground, December 21st and 22nd, 1931. Rhodesia
won by 209 runs.

RHODESIA.

Pattison, c de Villiers, b Machin	128	—b de Villiers 48
Robinson, c Machin, b de Villiers	7	—lbw, b Sparks 42
Hyde, lbw, b de Villiers	6	—c Travers, b Sparks . 0
Hayward, b de Villiers	2	—b de Villiers 4
Grant, c Ashman, b de Villiers	4	—c Newton, b Machin ... 17
Campbell-Rodger, b de Villiers ...	22	—c Machin, b de Villiers 58
Tomlinson, lbw, b de Villiers	27	—lbw, b de Villiers ... 17
Moll, b Machin	45	—b de Villiers 0
Adamson, b Machin	6	—b de Villiers 5
Forbes, lbw, b Sparks	1	—not out 6
Quinn, not out	4	—st Ashman, b Dick ... 13
Extras (b 13, lb 7, w 1, nb 4)	25	—Extras (b 18, lb 1, w 1) 20
Total	277	Total 230

ORANGE FREE STATE.

C. J. Kaplan, c Campbell-Rodger, b Quinn	10	—b Tomlinson 32
J. C. Newton, b Quinn	4	—c Grant, b Moll 6
E. Warner, lbw, b Quinn	0	—b Quinn 16
R. Dick, c Grant, b Moll	10	—c Pattison, b Tomlinson 28
H. Stevenson, lbw, b Quinn	1	—lbw, b Tomlinson ... 27
S. Quin, b Quinn	0	—b Adamson 3
C. W. Travers, not out	39	—b Campbell-Rodger ... 3
A. B. Machin, c Tomlinson, b Adamson	5	—b Tomlinson 10
L. de Villiers, lbw, b Tomlinson ...	23	—c Moll, b Tomlinson . 9
H. Sparks, b Adamson	3	—c Moll, b Adamson ... 11
G. R. Ashman, c Hyde, b Adamson	2	—not out 0
Extras (b 23, lb 4)	27	—Extras (b 27, lb 2) ... 29
Total	124	Total 174

ORANGE FREE STATE BOWLING.

	O.	M.	R.	W.	O.	M.	R.	W.
Machin	18.2	4	50	3	11	1	35	1
Sparks	15	3	25	1	9	1	30	2
de Villiers	23	9	56	6	22	6	52	6
Dick	12	0	40	0	14.2	5	31	1
Travers	5	1	27	0	6	0	19	0
Quin	5	1	17	0	4	0	30	0
Stevenson	4	0	15	0	3	0	13	0
Newton	4	1	22	0				

RHODESIA BOWLING.

	O.	M.	R.	W.	O.	M.	R.	W.
Quinn	9	3	23	5	12	4	23	1
Moll	9	4	19	1	11	3	16	1
Adamson	12.1	2	34	3	9.2	0	34	2
Campbell-Rodger .	2	0	.4	.0	7	0	17	1
Tomlinson	4	0	17	1	14	0	55	5

TRANSVAAL v. RHODESIA.

On the Old Edwardians' ground, December 23rd and 24th, 1931.
Transvaal won by 9 wickets.

RHODESIA.

Thompson, lbw, b Nupen	21	c Baines, b Nupen ... 23
Pattison, c Baines, b Cochrane ...	1	b Keightly-Smith ... 14
Grant, c Anderson, b Catterall ...	40	b Nupen 11
V. Hyde, b Nupen	0	b Cochrane 0
Campbell-Rodger, b Nupen	108	lbw, b Nupen 49
Hayward, lbw, b Nupen	86	not out 35
Tomlinson, c Foley, b Nupen	2	c Venn, b Cochrane ... 5
A. Hyde, b Nupen	0	c van Weizel, b Nupen 39
Moll, not out	4	b Cochrane 0
Adamson, c Foley, b Nupen	0	c Cochrane, b Nupen 4
Quinn, c Anderson, b Catterall ...	7	b Nupen 4
Extras	3	Extras 4
Total	272	Total 188

TRANSVAAL.

Venn, c Grant, b Moll	8	
Anderson, lbw, b Quinn	63	not out 20
Susskind, lbw, b Quinn	64	not out 60
Catterall, c Thompson, b Quinn ...	91	lbw, b Quinn 4
Van Weizel, st Thompson, b Tomlinson	13	
Baines, b Adamson	37	
Foley, b Grant	6	
Keightly-Smith, c Moll, b Grant ...	4	
Grieveson, not out	21	
Nupen, c Pattison, b Adamson ...	31	
Cochrane, c and b Quinn	13	
Extras	25	Extra 1
Total	376	Total (for 1 wkt) . 85

TRANSVAAL BOWLING.

	O.	M.	R.	W.	O.	M.	R.	W.
Cochrane	24	4	82	1	16	3	60	3
Catterall	17.1	2	68	2	7	1	26	0
Nupen	26	6	77	7	15	5	25	6
Baines	4	0	21	0	8	0	33	0
Keightly-Smith ...	3	0	21	0	9	1	40	1

RHODESIA BOWLING.

	O.	M.	R.	W.	O.	M.	R.	W.
Quinn	19.4	5	60	4	6	2	20	1
Moll	25	5	79	1	5	1	7	0
Tomlinson	22	0	109	1				
Adamson	19	0	56	2	2.1	0	24	0
Campbell-Rodger .	4	0	19	0	2	0	15	0
V. Hyde	3	0	23	0	3	1	10	0
Grant	4	1	5	2	2	0	8	0

BORDER v. RHODESIA.

On the Pirates' ground (turf) on December 26th and 28th, 1931.
Rhodesia won by 6 wickets.

BORDER.

Phillips, lbw, b Quinn	0	—c Thompson, b Adamson 26
Chubb, b Tomlinson	8	—b Tomlinson 7
C. White, lbw, b Quinn	6	—b Campbell-Rodger ... 1
Wilkins, b Quinn	2	—c Campbell-Rodger, b Quinn 31
Perry, b Adamson	0	—c Pattison, b Campbell-Rodger 12
O. Flemmer, c Thompson, b Quinn	22	—lbw, b Adamson 1
Whitehead, run out	1	—lbw, b Adamson 2
Closenberg, st Thompson, b Tomlinson	9	—c Campbell-Rodger, b Tomlinson 3
Kidson, b Quinn ... ..., ...	27	—b Moll 0
Dam, c Grant, b Tomlinson	2	—b Adamson 11
Muzzell, not out	8	—not out 12
Extras	23	—Extras 15
Total	108	Total 121

RHODESIA.

Thompson, lbw, b Kidson	18	—lbw, b Muzzell 1
Robinson, st Flemmer, b Wilkins	59	—run out 32
Grant, c White, b Closenberg ...	17	—c and b Muzzell 33
Hayward, c and b Wilkins	1	—b Muzzell 1
Pattison, b Muzzell	19	—not out 5
Campbell-Rodger, lbw, b Wilkins	5	—not out 3
A. Hyde, b Closenberg	12	
Tomlinson, b Closenberg	7	
Moll, lbw, b Kidson	1	
Adamson, not out	2	
Quinn, b Kidson	1	
Extras	9	—Extras 5
Total	151	Total (for 4 wkts.) 80

RHODESIA BOWLING.

	O.	M.	R.	W.	O.	M.	R.	W.
Quinn	15.1	3	25	5	13	4	23	1
Moll	2	1	1	0	13	1	26	1
Grant	2	0	6	0				
Tomlinson	15	3	35	3	7	0	29	2
Adamson	6	2	17	1	8	4	19	4
Hyde	2	1	1	0				
Campbell-Rodger	—	—	—	—	5	1	9	2

BORDER BOWLING.

	O.	M.	R.	W.	O.	M.	R.	W.
Muzzell	13	1	24	1	9.1	0	35	3
Kidson	10.4	2	23	3	6	2	9	0
Closenberg	16	1	34	3	5	0	12	0
Chubb	5	0	19	0	2	0	10	0
Dam	5	1	12	0	3	1	5	0
Wilkins	7	0	28	3				
Whitehead	5	4	2	0	3	0	4	0

GRIQUALAND WEST v. RHODESIA.

On the Wanderers Ground, December 29th and 30th, 1931. Rhodesia
won by 1 wicket.

GRIQUALAND WEST.

C. D. McKay, b Quinn	0	—c Thompson, b Grant .	13
F. Nicholson, c Thompson, b Quinn	4	—b Campbell-Rodger	10
Helfrich, lbw, b Adamson	36	—c Grant, b Tomlinson	27
Boggan, c Thompson, b Adamson	8	—c Campbell-Rodger, b	
		Quinn	19
Dunn, c Grant, b Tomlinson	22	—c Thompson, b Quinn	17
J. McNally, b Quinn	18	—b Adamson	9
L. Lowe, c Hayward, b Adamson	13	—run out	1
Bock, c Hayward, b Adamson	1	—c Grant, b Campbell-	
		Rodger	78
J. Glover, lbw, b Adamson	9	—lbw, b Tomlinson	48
Viljoen, st Thompson, b Adamson	7	—not out	0
H. Promnitz, not out	1	—b Campbell-Rodger	35
Extras (b 3, lb 4)	7	—Extras (b 23, lb 5)	28
Total	126	Total	285

RHODESIA.

Thompson, lbw, b McNally	28	—run out	47
Robinson, b Viljoen	6	—run out	25
Grant, c McNally, b Viljoen	0	—c McNally, b Viljoen	68
Hayward, not out	45	—run out	0
Pattison, c Helfrich, b McNally	2	—c McNally, b Bock	65
Campbell-Rodger, b McNally	0	—c Viljoen, b McNally	35
Hyde, c McKay, b McNally	2	—c Bock, b Viljoen	16
Tomlinson, lbw, b McNally	5	—b Promnitz	6
Moll, b McNally	0	—c McNally, b Bock	2
Adamson, b McNally	2	—not out	24
Quinn, run out	0	—not out	5
Extras (b 14, lb 3)	17	—Extras (b 7, lb 7)	14
Total	107	Total (for 9 wkts)	307

RHODESIA BOWLING.

	O.	M.	R.	W.	O.	M.	R.	W.
Quinn	10	1	31	3	17	1	46	2
Moll	2	0	9	0	2	0	16	0
Campbell-Rodger	4	1	6	0	12.3	2	41	3
Adamson	16.4	2	38	5	23	4	74	1
Tomlinson	10	0	35	2	14	2	49	2
A. Hyde	—	—	—	—	3	0	9	0
Grant	—	—	—	—	6	0	22	1

GRIQUALAND WEST BOWLING.

	O.	M.	R.	W.	O.	M.	R.	W.
Viljoen	11	2	25	2	19	0	68	2
Dunn	3	0	8	0				
McNally	16	2	35	7	29.5	4	96	1
Promnitz	6.2	1	12	0	26	5	60	1
Bock	3	0	10	0	12	1	42	2
Glover	—	—	—	—	2	0	16	0
Lowe	—	—	—	—	4	1	11	0

EASTERN PROVINCE v. RHODESIA.

On the Wanderers Ground, January 1st and 2nd, 1932.   Rhodesia
won by an innings and 81 runs.

EASTERN PROVINCE.

Gardiner, b Adamson	30 — c Pattison, b Quinn .	0
Freakes, c Pattison, b Quinn	0 — c A. Hyde, b Adamson	41
White. b Adamson	9 — c Hayward, b Campbell-Rodger	4
Mardon, b Campbell-Rodger	7 — b Tomlinson	38
Cawood, lbw, b Tomlinson	19 — c and b V. Hyde	11
Finlayson, run out	5 — lbw, b V. Hyde	32
Turner, c Hayward, b Tomlinson	19 — b Adamson	1
Whitlock, c Thompson, b C.-Rodger	32 — c V. Hyde, b Tomlinson	0
Marais, lbw, b Campbell-Rodger ...	45 — run out	1
Stein, not out	29 — not out	1
Boltman, st Thompson, b Tomlinson	10 — b Tomlinson	1
Extras	17 — Extras	4
Total 222	Total 134	

RHODESIA.

A. Hyde, b Stein	22
Tomlinson, run out	109
Pattison, c Mardon, b Whitlock	9
Hayward, lbw, b Stein	65
Grant, b Boltman	25
Campbell-Rodger, b Freakes	105
Thompson, lbw, b Freakes	29
Robinson, c White. b Turner	34
V. Hyde, not out	17
Adamson, run out	5
Quinn, c Freakes. b Boltman	0
Extras	17
Total	437

RHODESIA BOWLING.

	O.	M.	R.	W.	O.	M.	R.	W.
Quinn	10	0	32	1	4	0	10	1
Grant	11	1	34	0				
Campbell-Rodger .	13	3	47	3	5	1	25	1
Adamson	16	2	56	2	4	0	20	1
Tomlinson	8.4	0	36	1	10.1	3	19	4
V. Hyde	—	—	—	—	13	1	56	2

EASTERN PROVINCE BOWLING.

	O.	M.	R.	W.		O.	M.	R.	W.
Mardon	11	2	52	0	Freakes ...	17	2	56	2
Stein	33	5	111	2	Cawood ...	7	0	29	0
Whitlock ...	17	3	56	1	White	3	0	12	0
Boltman ...	14.4	1	74	2	Turner	5	0	30	1

THE STORY OF THE LOGAN CUP.

The Logan Cup, chosen by Lord Hawke, arrived in Rhodesia in 1899. The trophy, a massive silver cup on an ebony stand, is two feet six inches high. On it is engraved the Rhodesian coat of arms and the following inscription: " Presented by the Hon. J. D. Logan, M.L.C., to the Rhodesia Cricket Association in commemoration of the first visit of an English team of Lord Hawke's, March, 1899." The trophy cost one hundred guineas.

The cup lay in Bulawayo for four years until the intertown competition was resuscitated and the first Logan Cup match was played in 1904.

Salisbury came down early that year and were beaten after leading by 199 on the first innings. W. S. Taberer took seven wickets for 12 runs in Bulawayo's first knock, and F. G. Brooks played a splendid innings of 99 for Salisbury. The veteran, C. W. Cosnett, took 88 off the Salisbury bowling in the second innings and followed this up by bowling them out, and did much to win the match for his side. In the final Gwelo were easily beaten when Bulawayo ran up what is still the record score, a total of 478, of which M. G. Linnell scored 117 and A. H. Tummell 96 not out. The competition lapsed for another four years and then Bulawayo and Salisbury played the only two drawn games of the whole series. In the first C. H. Blanckenberg scored 98 and L. G. Robinson 93. In 1909, G. Anderson and H. S. Keigwin played a large part in Mashonaland's victory. In the following year Midlands made their second entry but lost to Matabeleland who also, thanks to Leo Robinson's fine captaincy, beat Mashonaland. For the latter Anderson again proved his bowling ability. There were three schoolboys in the winning team, each of whom performed creditably— A. Bennett, W. Walsh and the present Dr. A. Campbell. In 1911-12 Linnell's highest score record went by the board when T. E. Bourdillon scored 147. C. H. Blanckenberg notched 88 not out and young Ben Rabinson compiled a splendid 81. Mashonaland failed badly, H. O. ("Chappie") Frielinghaus being almost unplayable. The next year Mashonaland turned the tables on their rivals to win by eight wickets. C. Pfaff hit up a brilliant and chanceless century for the winners while Matabeleland could not cope with the bowling of Frank Howe-

THE LOGAN CUP.

Mule Coach.

Ely. In the last season before the war Mashonaland defeated Midlands, A. Campbell appearing for the latter and Dawes scoring 80. The winners piled up 313 against a weak attack. In the final in Bulawayo the homesters scored 415, Linnell notching his second century of the series just ten years after his first. Tom Bourdillon batted well and also bowled with success. R. J. Herholdt, a left-arm " find," was also too much for Mashonaland.

After the war Midlands produced a fine bowler in E. Sim, a medium paced spin merchant, but Matabeleland with C. P. Harvey, a googly bowler, were the stronger team. Harvey then did well against Mashonaland when T. A. Hubbard also took wickets and R. L. Juul came to light with two good knocks. For the losers W. E. Thomas and S. A. Cowper batted well. The next season C. W. Charter's bowling was mainly responsible for Mashonaland's victory. G. Gemmell batted well and after 17 years the name of C. H. Blanckenberg still appeared in the Matabeleland side. W. H. Shaw, of St. George's School, was in the same team and secured useful wickets. In 1922-23 Midlands and Matabeleland tried twice to come to a decision, but on each occasion rain spoilt the match and the competition was abandoned. V. L. Robinson appeared for the first time for Matabeleland and batted splendidly.

R. H. ("Bob") Catterall, the Springbok cricketer, captained Matabeleland against Midlands in 1923-24, when F. H. Morgan scored 128 against the province he had played for the previous season. W. H. Shaw is now seen taking Matabeleland wickets. The Matabeleland team for the final contained three school-boys, H. Campbell-Rodger (Plumtree), J. de L. Thompson (Milton), who have both captained the Province XI since, and C. C. W. Ingham (Plumtree). G. E. Fletcher batted well and J. A. Adamson got a fine bag of wickets. The Mashonaland captain, G. Gemmell, scored a sparkling century. Mashonaland and Midlands then met for the first time in 1924 and the latter won with the veteran G. Anderson helping them. P. Rabinson, ex-Matabeleland, appeared for Midlands and then in the next season for Mashonaland. Dr. A. Campbell (Matabeleland and Midlands) played in this match for Mashonaland. G. Anderson also got his third provincial cap here. D. S. Tomlinson, of Salisbury High School, played for Mashonaland. From

1925-26 Manicaland have made regular appearances in semi-finals but never reached the finals. In this season J. de L. Thompson took six wickets for 40 runs, performing the hat-trick.

In the following season G. E. Fletcher joined the centurions with 114 against Midlands. In the final in Bulawayo the brothers Tomlinson won the cup for Mashonaland. Ray scored 114 and took eight wickets, while Dennis scored 66 and 62 and captured eight wickets also. W. Wood, for Matabeleland, took 5 for 51, including the hat-trick in this performance, while Dr. A. Campbell established a new Logan Cup record with a score of 155. Another record was created in 1927-28 by H. F. Edmonds, of Manicaland, who opened against Mashonaland and scored 52 not out.

In 1927-28 Midlands beat Matabeleland, thanks mainly to fine bowling by F. Dollar who has been Midlands' standby for many years. At Salisbury, however, Midlands were well beaten, W. Wood assisting Mashonaland. In 1928-29 V. L. Robinson helped Matabeleland to victory with a fine 147, despite a great effort by the Mashonaland captain, A. G. E. ("Jock") Speight. This player's death in an aeroplane accident robbed the Colony of a fine cricketer. In 1930 C. J. R. Hayward scored 100 for Matabeleland against Midlands, who made only 60, R. J. Crisp getting 8 for 21. Against Mashonaland in Salisbury J. de L. Thompson made a new Logan Cup record by going in first and carrying his bat. He scored 108 not out.

In 1931-32 V. L. Robinson made two fine scores for Mashonaland, but the latter lost to Matabeleland for whom G. E. Fletcher scored a great 97. In the semi-final between Midlands and Matabeleland the game was started in Gwelo on a Saturday afternoon when rain stopped all further prospects of play for the week-end. On Sunday morning the teams motored forty miles to Que Que where Matabeleland just gained a first innings decision before rain again flooded the ground.

In 1933, against Midlands, R. J. Oliver obtained the present highest individual score record with 159. Midlands' reply to Matabeleland's 465 was to the tune of 326 runs in which total there were no byes—that province's record innings total. Their captain, R. H. J. Dickinson (ex Matabeleland), made a fine 64. L. Hanson also batted well.

In 1933 Mashonaland won easily, thanks to the captaincy and batting of V. L. Robinson and good knocks by A. Hyde and N. I. Boast, despite great bowling by Adamson.

In 1934 Matabeleland won after a great recovery by M. Napier and A. J. Bell, the Springbok, while in 1935, after Matabeleland had beaten Midlands in a low scoring match, they were thoroughly trounced by Mashonaland for whom Vic Robinson again batted excellently and D. P. C. Gumpertz knocked up a useful 94. Mashonaland had previously beaten Manicaland whose score of 33 is the lowest of the series.

A. L. Fielding.

M. Napier.

THE LOGAN CUP COMPETITION.

1903-04—Semi-Final:	Matabeleland beat Mashonaland.
Final	Matabeleland beat Midlands.
1907-08—Final	Mashonaland drew with Matabeleland.
1908-09—Final	Matabeleland drew with Mashonaland.
1909-10—Final	Mashonaland beat Matabeleland.
1910-11—Semi-Final:	Matabeleland beat Midlands.
Final	Matabeleland beat Mashonaland.
1911-12—Final	Matabeleland beat Mashonaland.
1912-13—Final	Mashonaland beat Matabeleland.
1913-14—Semi-Final:	Mashonaland beat Midlands.
Final	Matabeleland beat Mashonaland.
1920-21—Semi-Final:	Matabeleland beat Midlands.
Final	Matabeleland beat Mashonaland.
1921-22—Final	Mashonaland beat Matabeleland.
1922-23—Semi-Final:	Matabeleland v. Midlands.
	Midlands v. Matabeleland.
	Competition abandoned.
1923-24—Semi-Final:	Matabeleland beat Midlands.
Final	Matabeleland beat Mashonaland.
1924-25—Semi-Final:	Midlands beat Mashonaland.
Final	Midlands scratched to Matabeleland.
1925-26—Semi-Final:	Matabeleland beat Midlands.
	Mashonaland beat Manicaland.
Final	Matabeleland beat Mashonaland.
1926-27—Semi-Final:	Matabeleland beat Midlands.
	Mashonaland beat Manicaland.
Final	Mashonaland beat Matabeleland.
1927-28—Semi-Final:	Midlands beat Matabeleland.
	Mashonaland beat Manicaland.
Final	Mashonaland beat Midlands.
1928-29—Semi-Final:	Matabeleland beat Midlands.
	Mashonaland beat Manicaland.
Final	Matabeleland beat Mashonaland.
1929-30—Semi-Final:	Matabeleland beat Midlands.
	Mashonaland beat Manicaland.
Final	Mashonaland beat Matabeleland.
1930-31—Semi-Final:	Matabeleland beat Midlands.
	Mashonaland beat Manicaland.
Final	Matabeleland beat Mashonaland.
1931-32—Semi-Final:	Matabeleland beat Midlands.
	Mashonaland beat Manicaland.
Final	Matabeleland beat Mashonaland.
1932-33—Semi-Final:	Matabeleland beat Midlands.
	Mashonaland beat Manicaland.
Final	Mashonaland beat Matabeleland.
1933-34—Semi-Final:	Matabeleland beat Midlands.
	Mashonaland beat Manicaland.
Final	Matabeleland beat Mashonaland.
1934-35—Semi-Final:	Matabeleland beat Midlands.
	Mashonaland beat Manicaland.
Final	Mashonaland beat Matabeleland.

THE LOGAN CUP.

1903-04

SEMI-FINAL—BULAWAYO v. SALISBURY, at Bulawayo.

BULAWAYO (won by 54 runs).

L. G. Robinson (capt.), C. W. Cosnett, M. G. Linnell, H. S. Keigwin, L. P. Ashburnham, K. B. Fairbairn, J. Bissett, M. Spence, A. H. Tummell, E. C. Sharpe, J. V. McCormack

1st innings, 49 (Taberer 7 for 12, W. R. Blanckenberg 3 for 29).

2nd innings, 309 (Cosnett 88, Linnell 62, Brooks 4 for 62, W. R. Blanckenberg 4 for 70).

SALISBURY.

W. S. Taberer (capt.), F. G. Brooks, R. T. Bower, W. R. Blanckenberg, G. Grimmer, G. R. Johnson, F. J. Blanckenberg, W. L. Winnett, G. Parson, Grant, B. Wright.

1st innings, 248 (Brooks 99, Grimmer 52, W. R. Blanckenberg 49, Cosnett 4 for 49, Spence 3 for 43).

2nd innings, 55 (Cosnett 5 for 16, Robinson 4 for 28).

FINAL—GWELO v. BULAWAYO, at Bulawayo.

BULAWAYO (won by an innings and 252 runs).

C. W. Cosnett, M. G. Linnell, H. S. Keigwin, K. B. Fairbairn, L. P. Ashburnham, E. C. Sharpe, A. H. Tummell, M. Spence, C. Devitt J. Huntly, G. Anderson.

1st innings, 478 (Linnell 127, Fairbairn 63, Tummell 96 not out). No bowling analysis recorded.

GWELO.

G. Watkinson, L. C. Masterson, E. S. Clegg, B. Norris, C. T. Stuart (capt.), J. H. Bellasis, A. J. R. Peel, J. Watkinson, G. W. Puzey, H. J. Sparks, A. N. Stenning.

1st innings, 120 (Stuart 79, Anderson took 4 wickets and Cosnett 3).

2nd innings, 106 (Anderson 6 wickets). No bowling analysis recorded.

1907-08.

FINAL—BULAWAYO v. SALISBURY, at Salisbury.

Result: A Draw.

BULAWAYO.

C. H. Blanckenberg, L. G. Robinson (capt.), M. C. Linnell, N. Henwood, L. P. Ashburnham, W. P. T. Hancock, A. H. Tummell, N. Nightingale, G. M. Stephenson, G. P. L. Matthews, G. M. Tait.

1st innings, 106 (Cole took 6 wickets and Anderson 4).

2nd innings, 298 for 6 wickets declared (Blanckenberg 98, Robinson 93).

SALISBURY.

C. E. Slocock, W. S. Taberer (capt.), H. S. Keigwin, W. R. Blanckenberg, F. Kendle, G. Anderson, C. von Levetzow, H. O. Coker, Robins, W. C. Palgrave, W. A. Ludgater.

1st innings, 211 (Slocock 53, Robinson 4 wickets).

2nd innings, 128 for 3 wickets (Slocock 45, Kendle 42 not out). No bowling analysis recorded.

1908-09

FINAL—MATABELELAND v MASHONALAND, at Bulawayo.

Result: A Draw.

MATABELELAND.

L. G. Robinson (capt.), W. P. T. Hancock, F. B. Brooks, C. H. Blanckenberg, N. Henwood, P. Henwood, L. P. Ashburnham, G. P. L. Matthews, P. Walsh, G. M. Stephenson, L. Bester.

1st innings, 109 (Duff 4 for 27, Taberer 4 for 34).

2nd innings, 88 (Anderson 6 for 42).

MASHONALAND.

H. S. Keigwin, S.M . Wood, C. E. Slocock, W. S. Taberer (capt.), G. Anderson, E. H. Jalland, W. R. Blanckenberg, C. E. Duff, W. Kendle, H. O. Coker, F. Howe-Ely.

1st innings, 76 (Henwood 6 for 32).

2nd innings, 29 for 3 wickets.

1909-10

FINAL—MATABELELAND v. MASHONALAND, at Salisbury.

MASHONALAND (won by 8 wickets).

H. S. Keigwin, J. V. Kerr, G. Anderson, C. E .Slocock, W. S. Taberer (capt.), C. Pfaff, W. R. Blanckenberg, L. Brooks, R. R. McGee, W. L. Brereton, L. C. Vernon.

1st innings, 179 (Keigwin 81, P. Henwood 3 for 57, Stephenson 3 for 36).

2nd innings, 128 for 2 wickets (Taberer 52).

MATABELELAND.

L. G. Robinson (capt.), C. H. Blanckenberg, B. Howard, N. N. Henwood, E. C. Weaver, H. O. Frieiinghaus, D. G. Elliott, P. Henwood, L. Henwood, J. Lea, G. M. Stephenson.

1st innings, 163 (Frielinghaus 48, Anderson 4 for 37, Brereton 4 for 60).

2nd innings, 143 (Anderson 4 for 39).

1910-11

SEMI-FINAL—MATABELELAND v. MIDLANDS, at Bulawayo.

MATABELELAND (won by an innings and 14 runs).

C. H. Blanckenberg (capt.), D. G. Elliott, L. G. Robinson, F. B. Brooks, W. Walsh, H. O. Frielinghaus, M. G. Linnell, G. P. L. Matthews, P. Henwood, S. Ashley, L. Goldsmidt.

1st innings, 165 (Blanckenberg 41, Jones 6 for 45).

MIDLANDS.

T. P. Jones, C. C. Ritchie, R. L. Juul, C. T. Stuart, Fowler, T. Greenfield, J. J. de C. Walsh, Wright, Morsehead, W. F. C. Palgrave, Collier.

1st innings, 63 (Ashley 6 for 22, Brooks 3 for 26).

2nd innings, 88 (Frielinghaus 4 for 36, Henwood 3 for 3).

FINAL—MATABELELAND v MASHONALAND, at Salisbury.

MATABELELAND (won by 35 runs).

D. G. Elliott, A. C. Morgan, L. G. Robinson (capt.), C. H. Blanckenberg, M. G. Linnell, W. Walsh, H. O. Frielinghaus, A. Dawson, G. P. L. Matthews, A. Campbell, A. Bennett.

1st innings, 192 (Morgan 50, Anderson 3 for 51, Hopley 4 for 29).

2nd innings, 114 (Walsh 47, Duff 4 for 37, Anderson 5 for 20).

MASHONALAND.

E. H. Beck, E. G. Smith, F. G. Brooks, G. Anderson, C. Pfaff, F. J. V. Hopley, M. Graham, W. S. Taberer, C. E. Duff, J. B. Fradgley, W. L. Brereton.

1st innings, 151 (Robinson 4 for 13).

2nd innings, 120 (Anderson 45, Bennett 5 for 41, Frielinghaus 3 for 20).

1911-12
FINAL—MATABELELAND v MASHONALAND, at Bulawayo.

MATABELELAND (won by an innings and 156 runs).

M. G. Linnell, T. E. Bourdillon, D. G. Elliott, L. G. Robinson (capt.), W. Walsh, B. Rabinson, C. H. Blanckenberg, H. O. Frielinghaus. R. W. Travis, A. C. Morgan, A. Bennett.

1st innings, 429 (Bourdillon 147, Rabinson 81, Blanckenberg 88 not out, Molyneux 4 for 111).

MASHONALAND.

E. G. Smith, E. H. Beck, H. W. McCowan, J. H. E. Koch, C. Pfaff, C. H. Richardson, K. Mackenzie, G. Innes, L. J. Molyneux, F. H. Ely, G. Matthews.

1st innings, 140 (Beck 51, Frielinghaus 3 for 35, Morgan 3 for 28, Elliott 4 for 23).

2nd innings, 133 (Rabinson 3 for 26).

1912-13
FINAL—MATABELELAND v. MASHONALAND, at Salisbury.

MASHONALAND (won by 8 wickets).

A. C. Jennings, C. H. Richardson, E. H. Jalland, J. H. E. Koch, L. C. Vernon, E. G. Smith, C. Pfaff, G. P. L. Matthews, F. H. Ely, G. Anderson, W. S. Taberer.

1st innings, 254 (Jennings 48, Pfaff 115, Matthews 44 not out, Bourdillon 4 for 25, Robinson 3 for 75, Bennett 3 for 55).

2nd innings, 46 for 2 wickets.

MATABELELAND.

T. E. Bourdillon, T. P. Gilbert. A. Dawson, G. C. Hopley, A. Walsh, Fox, A. C. Morgan, L. G. Robinson, H. Baird, A. Bennett, E. Wells.

1st innings, 167 (Hopley 51, Ely 5 for 24).

2nd innings, 131 (Ely 4 for 28).

1913-14

FINAL—MATABELELAND v. MASHONALAND, at Bulawayo.

MATABELELAND (won by an innings and 209 runs).

T. E. Bourdillon, A. K. Castor, T. P. Gilbert, M. G. Linnell, C. H. Blanckenberg, L. G. Robinson, A. van Rooyen, G. C. Hopley, H. O. Frielinghaus, H. Herholdt, E. J. Leslie.

1st innings, 415 (Bourdillon 76, Linnell 128, Robinson 52, Hopley 56 not out, Matthews 4 for 78).

MASHONALAND.

J. C. Elsworth, A. R. W. Davis, A. W. Whiley, E. H. Beck, Dr. Hill, Bester, G. A. Carroll, S. M. Edwards, G. P. L. Matthews, W. C. Robertson, W. S. Taberer.

1st innings, 112 (Herholdt 5 for 21).

2nd innings, 94 (Bourdillon 6 for 28, Herholdt 4 for 27).

1920-21

FINAL—MATABELELAND v. MASHONALAND, at Salisbury.

MATABELELAND (won by 3 wickets).

R. L. Juul, C. P .Harvey, V. E. Bourdillon, E. G. Smith, D. G. Lewis, A. N. Cranswick (capt.), S. Hepker, C. Wynne, W. Melville, F. Wood, T. A. Hubbard.

1st innings, 198 (Juul 40, Smith 76, Gemmell 4 for 28, Charter 3 for 53).

2nd innings, 222 for 7 wickets (Juul 44, Melville 46 not out).

MASHONALAND.

H. S. Keigwin, W. S. Taberer, H. T. Bell, W. E. Thomas, G. Gemmell, D. G. Elliott, R. A. Gower, S. A. Cowper, R. J. Herholdt, E. E. Wright, C. W. Charter.

1st innings, 259 (Thomas 67, Harvey 3 for 70).

2nd innings, 159 (Cowper 56, Hubbard 4 for 51, Harvey 3 for 44).

1921-22

FINAL—MATABELELAND v. MASHONALAND, at Bulawayo.

MASHONALAND (won by 1 wicket).

G. Gemmell, F. Townsend, H. T. Bell, E. E. Wright, R. A. Gower, J. von Bonde, C. L. Roberts, S. A. Cowper, D. G. Elliott. C. W. Charter, R. J. Herholdt.

1st innings, 228 (Gemmell 85, Miller 3 for 35, Bourdillon 3 for 47).

2nd innings, 182 for 9 wickets (Cowper 52, Shaw 3 for 24).

MATABELELAND.

V. E. Bourdillon, T. E. Bourdillon, P. Peiser, E. H. Beck, C. H. Blanckenberg, J. W. Miller, F. Wood, A. M. Miller, W. L. H. Melville, T. A. Hubbard, W. H. Shaw.

1st innings, 266 (Blanckenberg 46, J. W. Miller 60, Charter 5 for 56, Cowper 3 for 103).

2nd innings, 143 (Wood 43 not out, Charter 5 for 30).

1922-23.

Competition abandoned.

1923-24

FINAL—MATABELELAND v. MASHONALAND, at Salisbury.

MATABELELAND (won by 10 wicket).

T. E. Bourdillon (capt.), G. E. Fletcher, H. Campbell-Rodger, O. P. S. W. Green, F. H. Morgan, J. de L. Thompson, W. Wood, R. A. Gower, C. Wynne, W. Ingham, J. A. Adamson .

1st innings, 285 (Fletcher 77, Campbell-Rodger 56, Wood 53, Cowper 4 for 82, Campbell 3 for 60)

2nd innings, 27 for 0 wickets.

MASHONALAND.

G. Gemmell (capt.), W. E. Thomas, F. B. Brooks, A. L. Wynne, A. Campbell, S. A. Cowper, E. M. Saunders, C. L. Roberts, R. J. Herholdt, C. W. Charter, A. M. Kuys.

1st innings, 176 (Gemmell 102, Adamson 6 for 55).

2nd innings, 134 (Cowper 46, Adamson 4 for 29, Bourdillon 3 for 22, Green 3 for 27).

1924-25

Midlands, who beat Mashonaland by 5 wickets, scratched, and Matabeleland won the Cup by default.

1925-26

FINAL—MATABELELAND v. MASHONALAND, at Salisbury.

MATABELELAND (won by 6 wickets).

T. F. B. Gilbert, V. N. Hepker, E. F. Harris, W. Wood, J. de L. Thompson, F. H. Morgan (capt.), O. Olver, Dr. A. Campbell, J. A. Adamson, F. Mathieson, E. Sim.

1st innings, 148 (Morgan 41, Rabinson 6 for 49, Herholdt 3 for 31).

2nd innings, 128 for 4 wickets (Wood 43).

MASHONALAND.

D. G. Elliott, G. Gemmell, A. G. E. Speight, C. L. Roberts, E. Saunders, R. N. Tomlinson, A. Hyde, P. Rabinson, T. J. Lilford, R. J. Herholdt, D. S. Tomlinson.

1st innings, 137 (Thompson 6 for 40, hat-trick).

2nd innings, 135 (Wood 4 for 50, Campbell 3 for 17).

1926-27

FINAL—MATABELELAND v. MASHONALAND, at Bulawayo.

MASHONALAND (won on first innings by 76 runs).

J. G. Simpson, D. S. Tomlinson, E. M. Saunders (capt.), A. G. E. Speight, A. Hyde, W. Melville, R. N. Tomlinson, D. G. Elliott, L. Sinclair, A. C. Lilford, A. L. Wynne.

1st innings, 230 (D. S. Tomlinson 66, Melville 54, Bourdillon 3 for 31).

2nd innings, 356 (D. S. Tomlinson 62, R. N. Tomlinson 114, Wood 5 for 51, hat-trick).

MATABELELAND.

T. E. Bourdillon, G. E. Fletcher, T. F. B. Gilbert, A. C. Curle, W. Wood, E. C. Arnold, F. H. Morgan, K. P. Neall (capt.), Dr. A. Campbell, W. Ingham, J. A. Adamson.

1st innings, 154 (Gilbert 52, D. Tomlinson 6 for 42, R. Tomlinson 3 for 52).

2nd innings, 367 for 9 wickets (Campbell 155, Curle 53, R. Tomlinson 5 for 123).

1927-28

FINAL—MASHONALAND v. MIDLANDS, at Salisbury.

MASHONALAND (won by an innings and 10 runs).

F. W. L. Cadwallader, V. Hyde, Q. A. Austin, C. L. Roberts, W. Wood, R. N. Tomlinson, O. P. S. W. Green, A. Hyde, B. Ulyett, D. G. Elliott, A. L. Wynne.

1st innings, 250 (Austin 86, Elliott 46 not out, Dollar 3 for 69, McCabe 3 for 57, Shaw 3 for 57).

MIDLANDS.

E. H. Beck, A. J. Bradley, H. A. Bradley, L. Harris, R. Fowler, J. C. McCabe, F. Dollar, A. M. Kuys, J .Holland, D. D. Homan, W. H. Shaw.

1st innings, 66 (Tomlinson 5 for 29, V Hyde 5 for 15).

2nd innings, 174 (Wynne 4 for 58, Wood 5 for 25)

1928-29

FINAL—MATABELELAND v. MASHONALAND, at Salisbury.

MATABELELAND (won on 1st innings by 30 runs).

J. de L. Thompson, G. E. Fletcher, V. L. Robinson, C. J. R. Hayward, H. Campbell-Rodger, T. P. Symington, W. Wood, Dr. A. Campbell, F. H. Morgan, P. Peiser, R. H. J. Dickinson.

1st innings, 271 (Robinson 147, Crisp 4 for 47).

2nd innings, 168 1or 3 wickets (Thompson 73, Robinson 40).

MASHONALAND.

O. P. S. W. Green (capt.), D. S. Tomlinson, Q. A. Austin, C. L. Roberts, A. Hyde, J. G. Simpson, E. M. Saunders, A. G. E. Speight, R. J. Crisp, H. J. O'Reilly, G. French.

1st innings, 241 (Speight 50 not out).

1929-30

FINAL—MATABELELAND v. MASHONALAND, at Bulawayo.

MASHONALAND (won on 1st innings by 53 runs).

A. J. Bradley, K. Paterson, H. Campbell-Rodger, C. L. Roberts, A. Hyde, D. Tomlinson, R. N. Tomlinson, S. Sawyer (capt.), H. J. O'Reilly, A. L. Fielding, A. Wynne.

1st innings, 204 (Hyde 42, D. Tomlinson 54, I. Campbell-Rodger 4 for 52, Adamson 3 for 75).

MATABELELAND .

J. de L. Thompson, R. J. Oliver, C. J. R. Hayward, R. Stewart, T. P. Symington, I. Campbell-Rodger, W. Wood, Dr. A. Campbell (capt.), R. H. J. Dickinson, J. A. Adamson, P. Rabinson.

1st innings, 151 (Campbell 42 not out, O'Reilly 4 for 30).

2nd innings, 140 for 5 wickets (Thompson 48, Hayward 44 not out, O'Reilly 3 for 13).

1930-31

FINAL—MATABELELAND v. MASHONALAND, at Salisbury.

MATABELELAND (won on 1st innings by 27 runs).

J. de L. Thompson, G. E. Fletcher (capt.), T. F. B. Gilbert, C. J. R. Hayward, J. C. Tones, T. P. Syminton, J. H. Charsley. J. W. Willing, H. de V. Moll, A. S. Hancock, J. A. Adamson.

1st innings, 276 (Thompson 108 not out, Morris 4 for 30, Tomlinson 3 for 69).

2nd innings, 134 for 3 wickets (Gilbert 52 not out, Hayward 48).

MASHONALAND.

D. S. Tomlinson, V. L. Robinson, A. Hyde, A. G. E. Speight. A. L. Fielding, C. Brown, V. Hyde, A. Holden, J. Reid-Rowland. D. Morris, H. J. O'Reilly.

1st innings, 249 (Speight 65, Tomlinson 56, Hancock 3 for 21).

2nd innings, 212 (A. Hyde 52, Moll 6 for 34, Adamson 3 for 1).

1931-32

FINAL—MATABELELAND v. MASHONALAND, at Bulawayo.

MATABELELAND (won by 7 wickets).

J. W. Willing, G. E. Fletcher, M. Napier, J. C. Tones, A. S. Ward, H. Campbell-Rodger, J. H. Charsley, J. de L. Thompson. J. A. Adamson, P. Rabinson, M. H. Quinn.

1st innings, 267 (Fletcher 97, Charsley 51 not out, Stein 4 for 47, Tomlinson 4 for 104).

2nd innings, 156 for 3 wickets (Ward 43 not out).

MASHONALAND.

D. S. Tomlinson, Q. A. Austin, V. L. Robinson (capt.), A. Hyde, C. B. Taberer, R. Slocock, C. L. Roberts, A. L. Fielding, Easterbrook, A. Stein, B. B. Napier.

1st innings, 185 (Robinson 62, Fielding 40, Adamson 7 for 61).

2nd innings, 233 (Robinson 59, Hyde 56, Ward 4 for 49).

1932-33

FINAL—MATABELELAND v. MASHONALAND, at Salisbury.

MASHONALAND (won by an innings and 8 runs)

V. L. Robinson (capt.), V. Hyde, S. Irvine, A. Hyde, N. I. Boast, D. S. Tomlinson, R. N. Tomlinson, C. Dale, J. D. Burne. A. L. Fielding, H. J. O'Reilly.

1st innings, 270 (Robinson 62, A. Hyde 61, Boast 81, Adamson 7 for 74).

MATABELELAND.

G. E. Fletcher (capt.), B. W. Bland, C. J. R. Hayward, M. Napier, J. C. Tones, J. de L. Thompson, J. H. Charsley, A. S. Ward, J. A. Adamson, L. Myles, A. S. Hancock.

1st innings, 126 (O'Reilly 3 for 29).

2nd innings, 136 (Irvine 4 for 24).

1933-34

FINAL—MATABELELAND v. MASHONALAND, at Bulawayo.

MATABELELAND (won on 1st innings by 108 runs).

J. de L. Thompson (capt.), R. J. Oliver, T. F. B. Gilbert, C. J. R. Hayward, J. H. Charsley, A. S. Ward, M. Napier, G. A. Cunningham, A. J. Bell, J. A. Adamson, M. H. Quinn.

1st innings, 199 (Napier 76, Bell 34, Oliver 33, Hyde 5 for 42, Tomlinson 3 for 65).

2nd innings, 70 for 4 wickets.

MASHONALAND.

C. L. Roberts (capt.), V. L. Robinson, D. Morris, M. Holman, D. Tomlinson, C. R. Allin, V. Hyde, A. L. Fielding, C. A. Lilford, J. Reid Rowland, R. Forbes.

1st innings, 91 (Charsley 3 for 18, Adamson 3 for 19).

1934-35

FINAL—MASHONALAND v. MATABELELAND, at Salisbury.

MASHONALAND (won on 1st innings by 221 runs).

V. L. Robinson, C. B. Taberer, M. Napier, R. Cornell, D. Morris, D. P. C. Gumpertz, Moir, M. W. Grant (capt.), J. P. Pattinson, C. A. Lilford, Den.

1st innings, 317 (Gumpertz 94, Robinson, 63, Cornell 55, Charsley 5 for 73).

MATABELELAND.

J. H. Fuller, F. D. W. Payne, J. C. Tones, C. J. R. Hayward (capt.), L. Walkden, J. H. Charsley, S. R. Lanning, H. Evans, G. A. Cunningham, W. H. Shaw, D. Johnstone.

1st innings, 96 (Morris 3 for none).

2nd innings, 44 for 1 wicket.

THE 1895 TOURNAMENT IN BULAWAYO.

SALISBURY v. QUEENS CLUB.

Queens—
53 (G. A. Tucker 5 for 4 runs, H. M. Taberer 3 for 9 runs).
150 (A. B. Bramwell 36, H. J. Mordaunt 30, C. S. Gill 5 for 22).
Salisbury—
185 (E. C. Sharpe 58, G. Hill 39, Mordaunt 3 for 68, Ferguson 3 for 24).
20 for 1 wicket.

Salisbury won by nine wickets.

SALISBURY v. B.A.C.

B.A.C.—
197 (D. Ingram 42, G. Cripps 37, A. G. Hay 26, Gill 3 for 63).
122 (Hay 26, Taberer 5 for 15, H. H. D. Christian 3 for 35).
Salisbury—
136 (Taberer 79, A. Hill 4 for 24).
141 (Taberer 49, Goldsmith 5 for 44, Cripps 3 for 35).

B.A.C. won by 42 runs.

SALISBURY v. BULAWAYO.

Bulawayo—
241 (Cripps 98, Mordaunt 42, Money 40, Gill 4 for 72, Taberer 3 for 46, G. Hill 3 for 15).
Salisbury—
34 (Goldsmith 6 for 9 runs).
124 (Taberer 31, Mordaunt 6 for 53).

Bulawayo won by an innings and 83 runs.

THE 1897 TOURNAMENT IN SALISBURY.

BULAWAYO v. SALISBURY.

Bulawayo—
143 (A. E. Fitzgerald 45, G. T. B. Hepburn 44, W. S. Taberer 6 for 46)
181 (L. G. Robinson 70, Fitzgerald 36, W. S. Taberer 6 for 40).
Salisbury—
331 (W. S. Taberer 65, W. H. Milton 60, H. M. Taberer 54).

Salisbury won by an innings and 7 runs.

BULAWAYO v. 7th HUSSARS.

Bulawayo—
142 (Fitzgerald 53, W. Jackson 50).
294 for 3 wickets declared (R. A. Blanckenberg 118, Robinson 83, Fitzgerald 34 not out).
7th Hussars—
126 (Robinson 5 for 42).
146 for 2 wickets (Capt. R. M. Poore 75 not out).
Match drawn.

BULAWAYO v. SALISBURY.

Bulawayo—
271 (Fitzgerald 80 not out, Robinson 58, Hepburn 34, Gleeson 4 for 52).
Salisbury—
81 (Robinson 4 for 28, M. G. Linnell 4 for 31).
181 (W. S. Taberer 55, Robinson 6 for 54).

Bulawayo won by an innings and 9 runs.

ENGLAND v. RHODESIA XV.

Played at Bulawayo, March 4th, 6th and 7th, 1899.

England won by an innings and 65 runs.

ENGLAND.

F. Mitchell, b Taberer	5
P. F. Warner, c Board, b Routledge	80
Tyldesley, c Mackendrick, b Taberer	71
Cuttell, c Hallward, b Taberer	16
Haigh, c Sharpe, b Bissett	27
Trott, b Bissett	1
F. W. Milligan, b Taberer	5
C. E. M. Wilson, b Taberer	32
H. R. B. Davenport, c Hallward, b Bissett	2
Board, c Jones, b Bissett	17
A. G. Archer, not out	1
Extras (b 18)	18
Total	275

RHODESIA XV.

R. B. Beatson, c and b Trott	8	—c Mitchell, b Trott ...	0
G. D. Katinakis, b Haigh	0	—b Trott	0
E. C. Sharpe, c Board, b Trott ...	4	—b Milligan	2
L. G. Robinson, lbw, b Trott	*	—run out	7
R. A. Blanckenberg, b Haigh	4	—b Trott	13
H. M. Taberer, b Haigh	0	—b Milligan	2
H. Hallward, c and b Trott	52	—b Milligan	8
G. Finch, b Haigh	0	—c Wilson, b Cuttell ...	0
H. G. Board, c Trott, b Haigh	0	—b Milligan	0
M. H. Routledge, b Trott	3	—b Haig	15
C. E. Duff, b Haigh	1	—b Haig	27
A. L. Jones, b Haigh	0	—run out	4
R. H. Jones, b Haigh	2	—lbw, b Haigh	1
J. Bissett, b Haigh	21	—b Haigh	2
R. Mackendrick, not out	0	—not out	4
Extras	19	—Extras (b. 2, lb. 2) ...	4
Total	121	Total	89

RHODESIA XV. BOWLING.

	O.	M.	R.	W.		O.	M.	R.	W.
Bisset	40	9	85	4	Katinakis ...	2	0	12	0
Taberer	38	15	62	5	Robinson	12	6	37	0
Duff	25	9	45	0	Routledge ...	9	3	14	1
Finch	3	0	2	0					

ENGLAND BOWLING.

	O.	M.	R.	W.	O.	M.	R.	W.
Haigh	24	9	36	3	10.1	7	8	4
Trott	24.2	13	35	5	22	10	31	3
Cuttell	4	1	9	0	6	2	23	1
Wilson	4	2	9	0				
Milligan	4	0	13	0	18	10	23	4
B. Davenport	3	3	0	0				

LEVESON-GOWER'S XI v. RHODESIA.

At Bulawayo, March 22nd, 23rd and 24th, 1910. Leveson-Gower's XI. won by an innings and 120 runs.

RHODESIA.

L. G. Robinson, c Schwarz, b Zulch	20	—c Schwarz, b Cook ...	20
T. E. Bourdillon, b Simpson-Hayward	4	—b Cook	10
C. H. Blanckenberg, b Schwartz ...	0	—b Cook	7
W. S. Taberer, b Cook	45	—c S.-Hayward, b Bird	42
F. G. Brooks, lbw, b Simpson-Hayward	0	—run out	15
L. P. Ashburnham, b Zulch	11	—st Sherwell, b Zulch...	4
N. Henwood, c Lewis, b Cook	4	—run out	0
H. S. Keigwin, b Schwarz	35	—b Zulch	16
H. O. Frielinghaus, c Zulch, b Cook	3	—c and b S.-Hayward...	21
P. C. Henwood, st Sherwell, b Schwarz	15	—not out	6
G. M. Stephenson, not out	19	—c and b Zulch	3
Extras	8	—Extras	8
Total	164	Total	152

LEVESON-GOWER'S XI.

F. L. Fane, lbw, b Stephenson	8
J. W. Zulch, c Frielinghaus, b Stephenson	168
H. S. Kaye, b P. Henwood	6
M. C. Bird, c sub., b Stephenson	17
A. E. Cook, c Blanckenberg, b Bourdillon	101
P. S. T. Lewis, b Bourdillon	0
R. O. Schwarz, b Stephenson	63
P. W. Sherwell, not out	43
F. J. V. Hopley, c sub., b Stephenson	10
Extras	20
Total (for 8 wkts., declared)	436

G. H. Simpson-Hayward and H. D. G. Leveson-Gower did not bat.

LEVESON-GOWER'S XI BOWLING.

	O.	M.	R.	W.	O.	M.	R.	W.
Schwarz	11.2	0	46	3	16.3	4	47	0
Simpson-Hayward	...	10	3	24	2	4	0	16	1
Bird	6	0	28	0	8	4	11	1
Cook	9	0	35	3	12	3	42	3
Zulch	7	3	23	2	12	3	28	3
Kaye	—	—	—	—	1	1	0	0

RHODESIA BOWLING.

	O.	M.	R.	W.		O.	M.	R.	W.
Taberer	16	2	73	0	Frielinghaus	3	1	12	0
Stephenson ...	28	8	104	5	Bourdillon ...	11	1	51	2
P. Henwood ...	25	2	99	1	Robinson ...	6	1	23	0
Brooks	9	0	54	0					

LEVESON-GOWER'S XII. beat a MIDLANDS XVIII. by 3 wickets.

Midlands XVIII.

    104 (A. J. Bradley 31, Schwarz 7 for 25, Simpson-Hayward 6
       for 17, Cook 3 for 19).

    99 (R. L. Juul 26).

Leveson-Gower's XII.

    144 (Zulch 44, A. Bailey 8 for 81).

    60 for 7 wkts. (Collier 4 for 20, Bailey 3 for 36).

LEVESON-GOWER'S XI. v. RHODESIA.

At Salisbury, March 31st, and April 1st and 2nd, 1910. Result a
draw.

LEVESON-GOWER'S XI.

Fane, b Coker	103	
Zulch, b Duff	9—c and b Duff	0
Cook, c Keigwin, b Anderson	72—b Duff	6
Bird, b Anderson	3—b Duff	0
Schwarz, c Taberer, b Coker	48	
Simpson-Hayward, c and b Anderson	19	
G. Hopley, c Keigwin, b Anderson	55—not out	0
Sherwell, c Robinson, b Anderson...	10	
Kaye, not out	6—c Henwood, b Duff ...	5
Lewis, b Anderson	1—not out	11
Leveson-Gower, c Duff, b Anderson	0	
Extras	23—Extras	0
Total	379 Total (for 4 wkts.)	22

RHODESIA.

L. G. Robinson, b Simpson-Hayyard	95—c and b Hopley	57
H. S. Keigwin, lbw, b Simpson-Hayward	34—b Schwarz	111
F. G. Brooks, b Simpson-Hayward...	10—c Cook, b S.-Hayward	51
T. E. Bourdillon, b Leveson-Gower...	10—st Sherwell, b Schwarz	15
G. Anderson, b Schwarz	1	
W. S. Taberer, b Simpson-Hayward	25—not out	14
C. Pfaff, b Simpson-Hayward	0	
C. E. Duff, not out	11—b Hopley	7
Payne, b Schwarz	9	
H. O. Coker, b Schwarz	0	
P. C. Henwood, b Simpson-Hayward	0—not out	5
Extras	12—Extras	14
Total	207 Total (for 5 wkts., declared)	304

RHODESIA BOWLING.

	O.	M.	R.	W.	O.	M.	R.	W.
Duff			95	1			11	4
Anderson			78	7			11	0
Henwood			20	0				
Taberer			35	0				
Coker			78	2				
Bourdillon			28	0				
Payne			6	0				
Robinson			16	0				

LEVESON-GOWER'S XI. BOWLING.

	O.	M.	R.	W.		O.	M.	R.	W
Hopley			16	0				63	2
Bird			29	0				50	0
Cook			19	0				16	0
Zulch			12	0				19	0
Schwarz			57	3				62	2
Simpson-Hayward ...			38	6				67	1
Leveson-Gower			24	1				13	0

THE TRANSVAAL (Mr. I. D. Difford's) TEAM'S VISIT, 1913.

v. MATABELELAND AT BULAWAYO.

Matabeleland—
267 (B. Rabinson 54, M. G. Linnell 54, T. E. Bourdillon 48, L. G.
Robinson (Capt.) 46; J. H. Tandy 5 for 31).

Transvaal—
197 (W. J. Bird 50; H. D. Keigwin 4 for 60, H. O. Frielinghaus
3 for 72).

Matabeleland—
139 for 6 wickets declared (Tandy 4 for 34).

Transvaal—
85 for 4 wickets.

Match drawn.

---

v. MIDLANDS AT GWELO.

Transvaal—
252 (T. T. Cradock 64, W. V. Ling 41; F. Candler 5 for 75).

Midlands XV.—
68 (Ling 6 for 25, A. S. Frames 4 for 18).
53 (W. S. Amos 28 not out; C. Platt 4 for 7, J. Howden 4 for 2,
L. E. Tapscott 3 for 8).

Transvaal won by an innings and 131 runs.

---

v. SALISBURY AT SALISBURY.

Transvaal—
58 (Extras 20; G. Anderson 6 for 16, F. Howe-Ely 3 for 17).

Salisbury—
164 (A. Redick 4 for 32).

Transvaal—
184 (J. Howden 67 not out; G. Anderson 6 for 54, C. E. Duff
3 for 35).

Salisbury—
79 for 2 wickets (E. H. Beck 36).

Salisbury won by 8 wickets.
    v. Salisbury—match drawn.
    v. Gatooma—Transvaal won by an innings and 80 runs.
    v. Umtali—Transvaal won by an innings and 58 runs.
    v. Beira—Transvaal won by an innings and 74 runs.

Summary: Played 7, won 4, lost 1, drew 2.

THE GREEN POINT TOUR, FEBRUARY, 1922.

v. Midlands at Gwelo.

Midlands—
123 (G. Sewell 41; F. Smith 5 for 41).

Green Point—
183 (W. Colson 55; E. Sim 6 for 81).

Result, a draw.

v. Mashonaland at Salisbury.

Mashonaland—
191 (S. A. Cowper 48; S. V. Brown 5 for 58, Smith 3 for 3).

Green Point—
158 (L. Fox 61; Cowper 4 for 64).

Mashonaland—
119 (G. Gemmell 62 not out; G. Mercer 5 for 22, Brown 3 for 47).

Green Point—
95 (E. Wright 4 for 12, Cowper 4 for 46).

Mashonaland won by 57 runs.

v. Mashonaland at Salisbury.

Mashonaland—
111 (Smith 6 for 44).

Green Point—
319 for 9 wickets declared (Colson 169 not out, Fox 45; Cowper
5 for 89).

Mashonaland—
189 (F. W. Townsend 85; Smith 6 for 57).

Green Point won by an innings and 19 runs.

v. Que Que at Que Que.

Green Point—
93.

Que Que—
108.

Green Point—
280 for 9 wickets declared (Colson 135).

Que Que—
133.

Green Point won by 132 runs.

v. Matabeleland at Bulawayo.

Green Point—
312 (Colson 119; J. W. Miller 5 for 74).

Matabeleland—
175 (J. W. Miller 57; W. Stephen 5 for 31, Smith 3 for 66).

Matabeleland—
195 for 7 wickets (P. Peiser 75 not out, F. Wood 43 not out).

Result, a draw.

v. Matabeleland at Bulawayo.

Matabeleland—
367 (T. E. Bourdillon 100, Peiser 68, A. M. Miller 59, G. C. Hopley
52; Stephen 3 for 58, Brown 3 for 90).

Green Point—
129 (J. W. Miller 6 for 38, T. E. Bourdillon 3 for 21).

Green Point—
243 for 5 wickets (S. Stuart 57 not out, Colson 55).

Result, a draw.

Summary: Played 6, won 2, lost 1, drew 3.

THE TRANSVAAL TEAM, MARCH, 1923.

v. Midlands at Gwelo.

Midlands—
110 (Skottowe 4 for 14, Meintjies 3 for 24).

Transvaal—
208 (Frank 64, Kerr 49; Chalmers 3 for 38, L. D. Elworthy 3 for 46, Sewell 3 for 46).

Midlands—
128 (Skottowe 5 for 25, Jardine 4 for 45).

Transvaal—
31 for 1 wicket.

Transvaal won by 9 wickets.

v. Matabeleland at Bulawayo.

Transvaal—
99 (A. Kennedy 46 not out; V. L. Robinson 3 wickets for 4 runs).

Matabeleland—
136 (G. C. Hopley 46; Skottowe 4 for 26, D. Meintjies 3 for 41).

Transvaal—
103 for no wickets (R. H. Catterall 69).

Result, a draw.

v. Mashonaland at Salisbury.

Transvaal—
230 (Catterall 95; C. E. Duff 3 for 42).

Mashonaland—
140 (F. G. Brooks 49; Kennedy 5 for 39, Meintjies 3 for 39).

Transvaal—
68 for 2 wickets.

Result, a draw.

R. J. Oliver.

J. C. Tones.

C

TRANSVAAL v. RHODESIA.

In Salisbury, 15th March, 1923.

Result, a draw.

RHODESIA.

G. Gemmell, b Skottowe	10
T. E. Bourdillon, b Meintjies	4
V. L. Robinson, b Skottowe	3
F. B. Brooks, st. Whyttock, b Murray	28
A. J. Bradley, c and b Kennedy	13
F. W. Townsend, not out	22
P. Rabinson, b Murray	6
S. A. Cowper, b Murray	0
F. H. Morgan, b Murray	3
D. G. Elliott, c and b Murray	23
J. Bain, b Kennedy	6
Extras	—
Total	118

TRANSVAAL.

C. N. Frank, c Elliott, b Rabinson	0
R. H. Catterall, c Cowper, b Rabinson	1
D. J. Mentjies, l.b.w. b Rabinson	31
A. S. Frames, hit wkt. b Morgan	13
Whyttock, c Robinson, b Rabinson	5
N. Lindsay, c Bourdillon, b Morgan	6
E. C. Murray, b Morgan	0
A. Kennedy, not out	23
Foster, c Bradley, b Cowper	3
McCubbin, not out	5
Extras	7
Total (for 8 wickets)	94

Skottowe did not bat.

BOWLING.

Transvaal.	O.	M.	R.	W.	Rhodesia.	O.	M.	R.	W.
Meintjes	14	5	28	1	Rabinson	12	4	23	4
Skottowe	10	1	32	2	Bourdillon	3	0	15	0
Kennedy	11.5	1	36	2	Cowper	8	0	24	1
Murray	8	2	22	5	Morgan	8	1	25	3

TRANSVAAL v. RHODESIA.

At Bulawayo on March 17th, 18th and 19th, 1923.
Transvaal won by an innings and 133 runs.

TRANSVAAL.

R. H. Catterall, lbw, b Rabinson	6
E. C. Murray, b Rabinson	0
C. N. Frank, l.b.w. b Cowper	63
A. S. Frames, c Bradley, b Gemmell	13
J. F. Kerr, b Cowper	4
D. J. Meintjies, l.b.w. b Rabinson	31
N. Lindsay, not out	160
Whyttock, c F. Wood, b Rabinson	23
Kennedy, c Bourdillon, b Rabinson	4
McCubbin, c Bourdillon, b Rabinson	97
Extras	43

Total (for 9 wickets declared) 444

Skottowe did not bat.

RHODESIA.

G. Gemmell, c and b Lindsay	34	—c Kerr, b Meintjies ...	0
T. E. Bourdillon, b Meintjies	24	—c Whyttock, b Meintjies	0
A. J. Bradley, b Meintjies	19	—b Kerr	8
E. Lang, c Kerr, b Meintjies	29	—b Meintjies	12
V. L. Robinson, c Whyttock, b Meintjies	10	—b Meintjies	14
A. C. Curle, b Murray	34	—b Meintjies	8
G. C. Hopley, c and b Kennedy	17	—b Meintjies	22
P. Rabinson, b Murray	7	—b Meintjies	4
S. A. Cowper, c Catterall, b Kennedy	18	—b Meintjies	10
F. Wood, b Kennedy	4	—not out	21
F. H. Morgan, not out	1	—run out	3
Extras	7	Extras	5

Total	204	Total	107

RHODESIA BOWLING.

	O.	M.	R.	W.		O.	M.	R.	W.
Rabinson	36.3	9	89	6	Bourdillon ...	13	5	26	0
Cowper	43	6	141	2	Wood	2	0	14	0
Robinson	10	3	24	0	Curle	1	0	14	0
Gemmell	23	5	51	1	Morgan	12	2	42	0

TRANSVAAL BOWLING.

	O.	M.	R.	W.		O.	M.	R.	W.
Meintjies	24	5	64	4		20	5	63	8
Frames	5	0	20	0		7	2	24	0
Murray	13	3	29	2		5	3	4	0
Kennedy	13.1	1	42	3		3	1	6	0
Lindsay	7	2	29	1					
Catterall	1	0	13	0					
Foster						1	0	1	0
Kerr						3	2	3	1
McCubbin						2.4	1	1	0

RHODES UNIVERSITY COLLEGE TOUR, 1923.

1. Plumtree School and Town 123 (E. Weir 5 for 25).
   R.U.C. 209 (A. G. E. Speight 59, L. Johnson 52).
   R.U.C. won by 86 runs.

2. Plumtree School 175 (Yates 44).
   R.U.C. 188 (H. McPherson 69, K. MacRobert 48).
   R.U.C. won by 13 runs.

3. Combined Bulawayo Schools 94 (J. de L. Thompson 55 not out;
     K. MacRobert 6 for 25).
   R.U.C. 124 for 6 wickets.   R.U.C. won by 4 wickets.

4. R.U.C. 152 (I. Campbell-Rodger 55; F. H. Morgan 5 for 42).
   Raylton (Bulawayo) 275 for 3 wickets declared (R. H. Catterall
     156).
   R.U.C. 185 for 4 wickets (A. Woods 66, Weir 57).
   Raylton won on the first innings by 123 runs.

5. Queens 155 (E. Watkinson 5 for 17; Brown 50).
   R.U.C. 315 for 3 wickets declared (Woods 140, I. Campbell-
     Rodger 87, A. H. Pattison 54 not out).
   R.U.C. won by 7 wickets.

6. R.U.C. 123 (Weir 51; P. Rabinson 4 for 25, A. Brewer 4 for 32).
   Kings and B.A.C. combined 293 (MacRobert 5 for 63; P. Rabinson
     53, E. Grewers 53).
   Kings and B.A.C. combined won by 170 runs.

7. R.U.C. 214 (Woods 86 not out; C. E. Duff 4 for 53, J. J. Bain
     4 for 68).
   Salisbury Club 71 (Weir 6 for 12).   Salisbury Club 98.
   R.U.C. won by an innings and 45 runs.

8. Alexandra 203 (G. Gemmell 65, D. G. Elliott 42; Woods 4
     for 55).
   R.U.C. 61.   R.U.C. 83 for 5 wickets.
   Alexandra won on the first innings by 142 runs.

9. Raylton (Salisbury) 111 (Woods 4 for 18).
   R.U.C. 256 (Woods 59, Pattison 41; E. M. Saunders 5 for 62).
   R.U.C. won by 145 runs.

10. Midlands 187 (H. T. Bell 56; Weir 4 for 39).
    R.U.C. 250 (Pattison 86, Woods 43).
    Midlands 117 (MacRobert 4 for 53).
    R.U.C. 56 for 6 wickets.   R.U.C. won by 4 wickets.

11. R.U.C. 115 (McPherson 52 not out).
    Umvuma 109 (Woods 5 for 35).
    R.U.C. won by 6 runs.

12. Bulawayo 45 (MacRobert 6 for 9).
    R.U.C. 174 (Woods 73; J. A. Adamson 7 for 64).
    Bulawayo 185 for 6 wickets (O. P. S. W. Green 81, G. W. Lede-
      boer 50).
    R.U.C. won on the first innings by 129 runs.

13. Broken Hill 44 (Woods 4 for 7, I. Campbell-Rodger 3 for 16).
    R.U.C. 206 for 6 wickets declared (R. Rein 70 not out, C.
      Cummings 51).
    R.U.C. won by 162 runs.

14. Broken Hill 71 (Woods 4 for 10).
    R.U.C. 222 for 6 wickets (I. Campbell-Rodger 66, Watkinson
      47 not out, Woods 40).
    Broken Hill 83 (Cummings 3 for 3).
    R.U.C. won by an innings and 68 runs.

Summary: Played 14, won 11, lost 3.

SOLLY JOEL'S ENGLAND XI. v. RHODESIA.

At Bulawayo on December 5th, 6th and 8th, 1924.

England won by 8 wickets.

RHODESIA.

G. Gemmell, b Geary	1	c Bowley, b Geary ...	0
A. J. Bradley, c Bowley, b Geary ...	4	lbw, b Marriott	19
H. Campbell-Rodger, b Geary	2	c and b Kennedy	22
R. H. Catterall, b Jameson	38	lbw, b Geary	10
T. E. Bourdillon, b Kennedy	2	b Geary	9
F. H. Morgan, lbw, b Marriott	25	b Geary	50
W. Wood, not out	19	st. Bartley, b Bowley .	28
Dr. A. Campbell, lbw, b Jameson ...	3	c Bowley, b Geary ...	22
S. A. Cowper, b Jameson	0	not out	18
E. C. Arnold, c Bartley, b Geary ...	13	b Marriott	15
R. D. Gloak, b Kennedy	3	st Bartley, b Bowley	8
Extras (b. 6, lb. 5)	11	Extras (b. 6, lb. 5) ...	11
Total	121	Total	212

ENGLAND.

P. Holmes, c Bradley, b Cowper ...	32		
F. W. Nicholas, c Gloak, b Bourdillon	2	lbw, b Catterall	2
E. H. Bowley, c Catterall, b Morgan	131		
A. C. Russell, lbw, b Cowper	1		
L. H. Tennyson, c Gemmell, b Cowper	8	not out	16
A. Kennedy, c and b Morgan	5		
A. H. H. Gilligan, b Cowper	1	b Catterall	19
G. Geary, c and b Morgan	2		
T. O. Jameson, not out	90	not out	1
F. W. S. Bartley, c. Catterall, b Wood	5		
C. S. Marriott, b Gloak	4		
Extras (b. 5, lb. 8)	13	Extras (b. 2, lb. 1, w. 1)	4
Total	294	Total (for 2 wkts.)	42

ENGLAND BOWLING.

	O.	M.	R.	W.	O.	M.	R.	W.
Geary	22	7	38	4	33	5	70	5
Kennedy	15.3	7	40	2	18	5	51	1
Marriott	10	2	19	1	18	5	39	2
Jameson	6	4	13	3	6	1	20	0
Bowley					7	0	21	2

RHODESIA BOWLING.

	O.	M.	R.	W.	O.	M.	R.	W.
Catterall	7	0	23	0	4	0	24	2
Bourdillon	12	2	36	1	3.1	1	14	0
Cowper	25	4	65	4				
Gloak	16.1	2	45	1				
Morgan	26	2	85	3				
Wood	12	1	27	1				

RHODES UNIVERSITY COLLEGE TOUR, 1925.

1. Combined Bulawayo Schools 148 (V. Hepker 52; MacRobert
   4 for 63, A. H. Pattison 3 for 12).
   R.U.C. 181 for 6 wickets declared (Pattison 79, A. G. E. Speight
   52).
   Combined Schools 76 for 6 wickets (MacRobert 4 for 14; H.
   Campbell-Rodger 49).
   R.U.C. won on the first innings by 33 runs.

2. Gwelo 126 (Morgan 55, Hurrell 49, Pattison 5 for 28).
   R.U.C. 140.
   Gwelo 92 (MacRobert 4 for 25).
   R.U.C. 84 for 7 wickets (F. Dollar 4 for 22).
   R.U.C. won by 3 wickets.

3. R.U.C. 183 (Robertson 45, Rein 44, H. Bennett 41).
   Selukwe 111 (H. Bennett 6 for 51; MacRobert 4 for 48).
   R.U.C. won by 72 runs.

4. R.U.C. 332 for 9 wickets declared (O. Flemmer 57 not out, Rein
   88, Workman 48).
   Que Que 148 (Pattison 8 for 47).
   R.U.C. won by 184 runs.

5. R.U.C. 161 (Speight 98; Roberts 4 for 29, Goldberg 3 for 18).
   Umtali 81 (Bennett 4 for 36).
   R.U.C. 215 for 4 wickets declared (Pattison 104 not out).
   Umtali 116.
   R.U.C. won by 179 runs.

6. R.U.C. 290 for 7 wickets declared (Speight 132, Flemmer 70).
   Mr. E. M. Saunders' XI 85 (MacRobert 6 for 31; H. St. Croix 45).
   Mr. E. M. Saunders' XI 105 for 7 wickets (Bennett 4 for 20).
   R.U.C. won by 205 runs on the first innings.

7. R.U.C. 247 for 7 wickets declared (Speight 62, Pattison 62).
   Mr. D. Elliott's XI 155 (MacRobert 4 for 56).
   R.U.C. won by 92 runs.

8. Mr. W. E. Thomas's XI 219 for 9 wickets declared.
   R.U.C. 137 for 6 wickets (Flemmer 56).
   Match drawn.

9. R.U.C. 189.
   Norton 144 (Pattison 7 for 41).
   R.U.C. won by 45 runs.

10. R.U.C. 225 (Robertson 58, Pattison 44; A. McCullam 6 for 56).
    Gatooma 108 (Speight 3 for 17; Ingham 46).
    Gatooma 126.
    R.U.C. 10 for no wickets.
    R.U.C. won by 10 wickets.

11. R.U.C. 231 for 4 wickets declared (Pattison 104, Speight 40).
    Broken Hill 119 (Pattison 4 for 42).
    R.U.C. won by 112 runs.

12. R.U.C. 217 for 2 wickets declared (Flemmer 97, Speight 54 not
    out).
    Broken Hill 141 for 6 wickets (MacRobert 4 for 61).
    Match drawn.

13. R.U.C. 194 (Farrar 61; W. Wood 5 for 73, J. de. L. Thompson
    4 for 16).
    Raylton (Bulawayo) 109 (Speight 3 for 14).
    R.U.C. won by 85 runs.

Summary: Played 13, won 11, drew 2.

THE TRANSVAAL TEAM, MARCH, 1928.

v. Matabeleland at Bulawayo.

Matabeleland—

281 (E. C. Arnold 40; Conyngham 3 for 26, Mitchell 3 for 75).

Transvaal—

200 (Frames 56; H. Campbell-Rodger 5 for 55).

Matabeleland—

156 for 6 wickets declared (W. Wood 51 not out; Brissenden 3 for 15, Mitchell 3 for 38).

Transvaal—

190 for 2 wickets (Langebrink 102 not out, Christy 67).
Result, a draw.

v. Mashonaland at Salisbury.

Mashonaland—

175 (Walsh 4 for 41, Conyngham 3 for 36).

Transvaal—

159 (Christy 61; R. Tomlinson 5 for 19, Q. Austin 3 for 9).

Mashonaland—

249 (Crisp 57 not out; Conyngham 5 for 51, Mitchell 3 for 61).

Transvaal—

88 for 9 wickets (Reid Rowland 3 for 20).
Result, a draw.

v. Livingstone at Livingstone.

Livingstone—

153 (E. J. Whindus 64; Mitchell 5 for 41, Campbell 4 for 39).

Transvaal—

246 (Mitchell 51; A. Grill 3 for 29).

Livingstone—

149 for 5 wickets declared (S. F. Turner 55, G. C. Latham 53 not out).

Transvaal—

49 for no wickets.

Transvaal won on first innings by 93 runs.

TRANSVAAL v. RHODESIA.

At Bulawayo, March 31st and April 1st and 2nd, 1928.
Transvaal won by 3 wickets.

RHODESIA.

J. de L. Thompson, b Frames	6	—b Conyngham	22
G. E. Fletcher, c Kennedy, b Walsh	31	—lbw, b Brissenden ...	51
C. J. R. Hayward, c Campbell, b Walsh	72	—run out	11
R. N. Tomlinson, c Walsh, b Mitchell	25	—c Conyngham, b Brissenden	0
H. Campbell-Rodger, lbw, b Christy	47	—b Conyngham	1
W. Wood, lbw, b Kennedy	18	—not out	60
E. C. Arnold, c Chappell, b Walsh	57	—b Brissenden	28
A. Hyde, c Chappell, b Walsh	8	—b Brissenden	0
D. S. Tomlinson, c Mitchell, b Brissenden	12	—b Christy	1
C. R. Ridgway, b Brissenden	0	—c Frames, b Christy	5
F. Dollar, not out	10	—lbw, b Christy	0
Extras (b 8, lb 9)	17	Extras (b 4, lb 1) ...	5
Total	303	Total	184

TRANSVAAL.

A. C. Langebrink, b Dollar	0	—c C.-Rodger, b Hyde	68
A. B. Kennedy, c Hayward, b Dollar	32	—c C.-Rodger, b Dollar	13
J. A. Christy, c Hayward, b Hyde	40	—c Dollar, b C.-Rodger	103
B. Mitchell, b Dollar	54	—not out	45
A. S. Frames, c and b Hyde	6	—h Wood	8
C. S. Chappell, st Arnold, b Hyde ...	0	—lbw, b D. Tomlinson	0
A. J. Jardine, lbw, b Wood	0	—not out	10
D. P. Conyngham, c Arnold, b Wood	8	—lbw, b Wood	5
F. Walsh, c Fletcher, b Dollar	2		
H. Campbell, c Arnold, b D. Tomlinson	28	—c Thompson, b Hyde	8
S. Brissenden, not out	14		
Extras (b 18, lb 3)	21	Extras (b 11, lb 12)	23
Total	205	Total (for 7 wkts.)	283

TRANSVAAL BOWLING.

	O.	M.	R.	W.	O.	M.	R.	W.
Frames	8	0	27	1	7	0	32	0
Brissenden	17	2	75	2	14	2	38	4
Conyngham	9	3	25	0	13	1	58	2
Walsh	18.2	3	62	4	4	1	4	0
Mitchell	10	0	48	1	4	1	10	0
Campbell	5	1	13	0	4	0	16	0
Christy	4	0	11	1	6.4	1	13	3
Kennedy	11	2	25	1	5	2	8	0

RHODESIA BOWLING.

	O.	M.	R.	W.	O.	M.	R.	W.
Fletcher	4	1	23	0				
Dollar	18	1	46	4	8	3	20	1
Wood	8	3	19	2	20	3	49	2
D. Tomlinson	11.3	2	45	1	19	0	58	1
Hyde	8	1	34	3	15	3	49	2
Campbell-Rodger .	7	2	17	0	12	1	38	1
R. Tomlinson	—	—	—	—	14	1	46	0

TRANSVAAL v. RHODESIA.

At Salisbury, April 7th, 8th and 9th, 1928.

Transvaal won by an innings and 159 runs.

TRANSVAAL.

Langebrink, c R. Tomlinson, b Saunders	2
Farquharson, b R. Tomlinson ... ...'..	40
Christy, c Saunders, b D. Tomlinson	175
Mitchell, run out	20
Frames, c Arnold, b D. Tomlinson	16
Kennedy, c Arnold, b Campbell-Rodger	8
Campbell, c Green, b D. Tomlinson	17
Conyngham, hit wkt, b Saunders	63
Duffus, not out	47
F. Walsh, b Campbell-Rodger	2
Brissenden, b D. Tomlinson	0
Extras	33
Total	423

RHODESIA.

D. Tomlinson, c Duffus, b Campbell	7	—c Walsh, b Conyngham	14
R. J. Oliver, c Duffus, b Brissenden	11	—c Mitchell, b Campbell	2
Q. A. Austin, b Mitchell	25	—b Campbell	0
E. M. Saunders, c and b Campbell	2	—injured, did not bat.	
A. G. E. Speight, b Mitchell	18	—c and b Mitchell	12
W. Wood, lbw, b Mitchell	0	—b Campbell	0
E. C. Arnold, b Walsh	13	—b Brissenden	8
O. P. S. W. Green, b Brissenden ...	23	—c and b Conyngham .	5
H. Campbell-Rodger, run out	20	—b Brissenden	26
R. N. Tomlinson, not out	10	—no out	44
A. Hyde (indisposed, did not bat).		c Kennedy, b Mitchell ...	1
Extras	6	Extras	17
Total ... ...'.. ...	135	Total	129

RHODESIA BOWLING.

	O.	M.	R.	W.		O.	M.	R.	W.
					Campbell-				
Saunders	21	7	62	2	Rodger	19	3	58	2
R. Tomlinson .	32	8	86	1	Austin	17	1	29	0
D. Tomlinson .	31.3	7	105	4	A. Hyde	5	2	8	0
Wood	15	7	28	0	Green	2	1	14	0

TRANSVAAL BOWLING.

	O.	M.	R.	W.	O.	M.	R.	W.
Frames	3	0	10	0				
Brissenden	15	3	31	2	16	2	43	2
Campbell	13	3	28	2	14	4	38	3
Conyngham	6	0	28	0	4	0	10	2
Mitchell	5	0	13	3	4	0	21	2
F. Walsh	7	2	19	1				

RHODES UNIVERSITY COLLEGE TOUR 1928.

1. Matabeleland 335 for 4 wkts. dec. (J. de L. Thompson 103, H. Campbell-Rodger 73, T. E. Bourdillon 55, C. J. R. Hayward 53 not out, T. P. Symington 42).
   R.U.C. 192 (H. B. Dugmore 70, V. L. Robinson 4 for 59, J. de L. Thompson 3 for 9).
   R.U.C. 100 for 4 wickets.

   Matabeleland won the first innings by 143 runs.

2. R.U.C. 277 for 5 wkts. dec. (B. Gillett 67 not out, Dugmore 59, A. Brown 49, F. Dollar 3 for 65).
   South Midlands 87 (G. Pote 6 for 27, Dugmore 4 for 34).
   South Midlands 128 (H. Stranger 47 not out, J. Perry 4 for 43).

   R.U.C. won by an innings and 62 runs.

3. A Salisbury XI. 139 (Robertson 40, Dugmore 5 for 43).
   R.U.C. 259 for 9 wkts. dec. (J. Perry 71 not out).
   A Salisbury XI. 144 for 7 wickets dec. (S. Sawyer 69).

   R.U.C. won on the first innings by 120 runs.

4. Mashonaland 429 (V. Hyde 109, A. Saunders 77, A. L. Wynne 76, A. Hyde 52, Dugmore 6 for 163).
   R.U.C. 382 (Dugmore 101, Gillett 70, D. Purdon 44, E. Schaefer 43).

   Match drawn.

5. R.U.C. 219 for 9 wkts. dec. (Dugmore 100, Small 5 for 51).
   Umtali 102 (Dugmore 4 for 46, Perry 3 for 4).
   Umtali 65 for 3 wickets.

   R.U.C. won on the first innings by 117 runs.

6. Umtali 233 (K. W. Rowell 82, C. Brymer 59, C. Taberer 5 for 54).
   R.U.C. 157 (Purdon 43, L. D. Elworthy 5 for 54).

   Umtali won on the first innings by 76 runs.

7. Que Que 127 (Dugmore 4 for 37).
   R.U.C. 281 for 6 wkts. dec. (Dugmore 66, V. Schaefer 62. Brown 59).
   Que Que 163 (H. Bradley 49, Purdon 3 for 15).
   R.U.C. 33 for 0 wkts.

   R.U.C. won by 10 wickets.

8. A Bulawayo XI. 230 (V. L. Robinson 90, R. H. J. Dickinson 46, Dugmore 4 for 69).
   R.U.C. 244 (L. Gillespie 87, V. Schaefer 59, P. Rabinson 5 for 89).

   A Bulawayo XI. won on the first innings by 6 runs.

9. Livingstone 33 (Dugmore 5 for 17, Taberer 4 for 16).
   R.U.C. 62 (A. Morton 6 for 34).
   Livingstone, 89 for 4 wickets (S. F. Turner 45).

   R.U.C. won on the first innings by 29 runs.

   Summary: Played 9; Won 5; Lost 3; Drew 1.

M.C.C. v. RHODESIA.

Played on the Queen's Ground, Bulawayo, December 6th, 8th and 9th, 1930.

Result: A Draw.

M.C.C.

J. C. White, lbw, b Tomlinson ...	22	—b Crisp	9
R. E. S. Wyatt, c Boast, b O'Reilly	78	—c Boast, b Tomlinson	16
W. R. Hammond, st Boast, b Tomlinson	7	—retired	49
M. Leyland, run out	1	—c O'Reilly, b Crisp ...	169
M. J. Turnbull, lbw, b Crisp	8	—st Boast, b Tomlinson	16
A. P. F. Chapman, c Napier, b O'Reilly	48		
W. Farrimond, c Tomlinson, b O'Reilly	7	—lbw, b Crisp	10
I. A. R. Peebles, c Moll, b Tomlinson	28	—run out	1
M. W. Tate, c Speight, b Tomlinson	28	—b Hyde	19
W. Voce, hit wicket, b Tomlinson	28	—not out	25
M. J. C. Allom, not out	5		
Extras (b 6, lb 8, w 2, nb 2) ...	18	—Extras	8
Total	278	Total (for 8 wickets)	322

RHODESIA.

J. de L. Thompson, lbw, b White	13
D. S. Tomlinson, lbw, b Tate	0
C. J. R. Hayward, c Chapman, b Allom	95
A. Hyde, b Peebles	2
T. P. Syminton, b Leyland	60
A. G. E. Speight, b Peebles	2
W. A. Napier, c and b Peebles	19
N. I. Boast, not out	33
H. J. O'Reilly, b Peebles	9
R. J. Crisp, b Peebles	0
H. de V. Moll, c Turnbull, b Peebles	5
Extras (b 5, lb 5)	10
Total	248

RHODESIA BOWLING.

	O.	M.	R.	W.	O.	M.	R.	W.
Moll	19	3	48	0	17	4	61	0
Crisp	14	1	39	1	18.2	3	64	3
O'Reilly	10	0	49	3	8	2	27	0
Tomlinson	22.5	3	106	5	13	1	85	2
Napier	4	2	9	0	8	1	46	0
Hyde	2	0	9	0	4	0	13	1
Hayward	—	—	—	—	3	0	18	0

M.C.C. BOWLING.

	O.	M.	R.	W.		O.	M.	R.	W.
Tate	14	3	30	1	White	11	3	23	1
Allom	18	4	47	1	Hammond ...	3	0	11	0
Voce	17	4	38	0	Leyland	9	1	32	1
Peebles	24.3	5	57	6					

THE BULAWAYO FIRST LEAGUE CUP.

1896-97: B.A.C.	1913-14: Raylton.
1897-98: Queens.	1919-20: Raylton.
1898-99: Civil Service.	1920-23: B.A.C.
1900-04: B.A.C.	1923-25: Raylton.
1904-05: United Banks.	1925-26: Ramblers.
1905-06: B.A.C.	1926-27: Raylton.
1906-07: Gwelo.	1927-28: Ramblers.
1907-10: Queens.	1928-29: Raylton.
1910-11: B.A.C.	1929-31: Queens.
1911-13: Queens.	1931-35: Ramblers.

THE VIGNE CUP (Salisbury).

1899-1901: Salisbury.	1924-25: Alexandra.
1901-02: Kopje.	1927-29: Salisbury.
1902-07: Salisbury	1929-31: Raylton.
1908-14: Alexandra.	1931-33: Salisbury.
1920-21: Umtali & Alexandra.	1933-34: Raylton.
1921-22: Alexandra.	1934-35: Salisbury.

THE J. F. JONES CUP (Umtali).

The trophy was lost between 1906 and 1930.

1903-05: Civil Service.	1932-33: Forresters.
1905-06: Railway.	1933-34: Crusaders.
1929-31: Railway.	1934-35: Ramblers.

THE LAWLEY CUP.

1924-26: Salisbury.	1929-30: Beira.
1926-27: Umtali.	1930-34: Salisbury.
1927-29: Salisbury.	1934-35: Umtali.

SOCCER

ASSOCIATION football was first played in Rhodesia by members of the Pioneer Column soon after their arrival at Fort Salisbury at the end of 1890. Conspicuous among the early players were Charlie Hall, Cooper Hodgson, Bill Strachan, Bly Hopley, Willie Grimmer, Joe Clinton, Spreckley, who represented Johannesburg in 1889, and P. C. ("Sally") Nunn, who was killed with Allan Wilson in 1893. The first clubs were Police, Kopje, and Causeway, the two latter eventually changing their names to Alexandra and Salisbury respectively. In 1898 Mr. H. J. Deary presented a cup for competition on the league system. This trophy is the present senior championship cup and its donor became president of the first committee formed to control soccer. Vice-president of this Salisbury Association League which in 1904 became the Mashonaland Football Association, was Mr. R. B. Mitchell, who in his early years was a keen player and in later years an able performer with the whistle. He laid the foundations and then did most of the building up of the game in Mashonaland and his son Russell is the well-known Mashonaland and Rhodesia rugby scrum half. W. Smith is another of the old hands who did not forsake the game when he stopped playing and last season was president of the Mashonaland Football Association.

Prominent early stalwarts in the capital were R. L. Phillips, a recent Mayor of Salisbury, who kept goal for Alexandra for several seasons, George Candler, W. A. Ludgater, B. R. Greenhalgh, G. Hinds, D. M. Lewis, a Welsh international (whose two sons, "Tommy," a fine full-back, and Jack, a tip-top forward, incidentally became noted rugby players in Rhodesia), F. G. Brooks, a terror in front of the goal, Jenkinson of Western Province, splendid goalies in C. J. W. Andrews and Fred Kettle of the Police, G. B. Jennings of the famous Sussex County XI, Tim Percy, H. D. Smith, G. B. Reilly and A. F. Williams. Major Drury of the Police gave soccer every assistance. He would scan a list of men for transfer from Salisbury and rule out anyone whom he thought would be useful in the football fields, much to the chagrin of the Regimental Sergeant Major! With such players as those mentioned, and others too numerous to set down here, it would have been difficult to find an abler and

MANICALAND, 1902.

Standing:

A. C. Addecott, J. B. Gilbert, F. Hitch, A. Shaw, F. A. Yates, S. E. Good, C. K. Spencer, G. Cramp, T. P. Gilbert.

Sitting:

D. M. Lewis, F. R. Myburgh, T. R. Cox (capt.), F. C. Wibberley, H. Allen.

more enthusiastic selection of Association footballers in any young Colony such as Rhodesia was 25 years ago.

Salisbury's nearest rival was Umtali, 170 miles distant, and though the only means of transport was by mule coach there were frequent inter-town matches. Soccer was very strong in Umtali until 1911, when the railway headquarters were moved to Bulawayo. As instancing Umtali's strength, in 1898 when the Deary Cup competition was held in Salisbury, Umtali's twelfth man, Jim Gilbert, was picked for Mashonaland. That Umtali side included Harry Allen, vice-president of the Southern Rhodesia Football Association and probably the finest forward ever seen in Rhodesia. In 1899 he played for Derby County against Sheffield United in the English Cup Final at the Crystal Palace. He played inside to Johnny Goodall, who had left Preston North End to play for Derby County. Then there was Reg. Elkin of Middlesex and his brother Syd, a fine full-back, both brothers of Bert Elkin of South African golf fame who, incidentally, played for Tottenham Hotspur. Others were Watty Ross, who to everyone's wonder always played with his boots only half laced; that well-known all-rounder, Tom Gilbert, whose son has done well at cricket and rugger; Jimmy Hendry, W. Bennett, J. H. Davidson and Chas. Eickhoff, captain of this redoubtable team, who played against the 'Spurs over forty years ago and just before coming to this country took part in a London Cup Tie. A fine sportsman, Mr. Eickhoff has done a tremendous amount for all games in Manicaland. Other Umtali giants were T. R. Cox, S. E. Good, A. C. Addecott, C. K. Spencer, P. Gubb, F. C. Wibberley and F. R. Myburgh.

Soccer also had a good start in Bulawayo. In 1895 the B.S.A. Police had a team mostly composed of Public School boys just out from Home, many well-known schools being represented by such players as Scott, Marks, Baker, Constable, C. H. Blanckenberg, Hoskens and others. In August, 1896, an interesting match took place when Plumer's Relief Force at Usher No. 2 invited out a team from town. On a Saturday afternoon the visitors started off gaily in a mule trolley but this had to be abandoned just beyond Hillside owing to the poor condition of the mules. Undeterred, the party walked the rest of the way and arrived at the camp in the early hours of Sunday morning. The soldiers had gone to a great deal of trouble for the entertainment of their guests but when they arrived, weary and footsore, the dinner and

smoking concert were long over. However, a spread of ham, jam-tarts and whisky was brought out and though there was no bread and little water, the repast was fully appreciated. On Sunday afternoon the Bulawayo team won a great game by one goal to nil. Among the winners were T. Lockie, "Scotty" Ewing, Platt, Hyde, C. Granger, Roy, Thompson (goalie), Jowett, and Bill Marley and in Plumer's team were Bram Watson, M. G. Linnell, "Fatty" Russell, A. J. Webb, Lieut. Dent, Perkins and Hoskens.

Later some splendid games were played between the town and the 7th Hussars who were camped just beyond the suburbs.

In 1897 and 1898 association football was firmly established in Bulawayo since when it has enjoyed a large following and a well-deserved popularity. As in Salisbury and Umtali, Bulawayo was rich in talent with players from home counties, crack English clubs, and South African teams, a sprinkling of professionals, and teams from the various regiments stationed here from the year of the first rebellion, 1893, until after the Boer War. The B.S.A.P. had Magnus Spence, a member of the Western Province team that won the first Currie Cup tournament in 1892. He played for the Province again in 1895 when he was awarded the gold medal for the best player in the tournament. Others in the Police team were Howitt, Wilkinson, Stewart, Katinakis (also a fine cricketer), prince of centre-halves in Knight, the speedy Sergeant H. Agar who played with Jim Atter on the right wing for Middlesex, Davy Bruce, Currie, and Cameron, a professional from a north of England club who went down with the s.s. "Titanic." Queens had an imposing array, too, with Harrison (Westminster and Casuals), capped for England as full-back, Halsey, a centre-half noted for his excellent head work, J. Collyer, now Postmaster-General, two fine players in Charles and Bob Granger, a good half-back in C. H. Blanckenberg, Leo. Robinson, Dr. E. Head, G. M. Tait, a clever centre-forward in the Rev. O'Leary who played in that position for Western Province in 1896, Watson, and a first-class player in D. E. Williams who, at the early age of nineteen was picked in the first Matabeleland team in 1903. In the B.A.C. side were two fine men in the brothers T. and A. Roy, M. G. Linnell, who is one of the best all-rounders Rhodesia has known, Reg. Payne, A. Ruxton, the brilliant Hallward at centre-half with his white boots, Routledge, an ex-Crusader (England), in goal, E. W. Clarkson of Surrey,

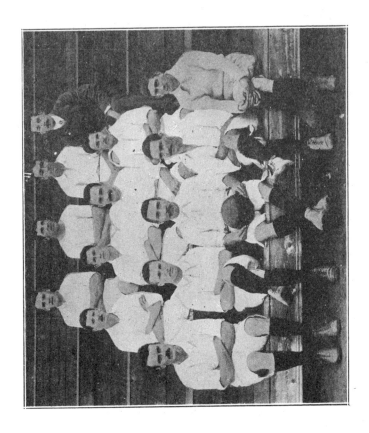

BULAWAYO, 1906.
Winners Metcalfe Inter-
Town Cup.

Top Row:
S. Smith, J. Hodgkinson, A.
Loggie, H. Carr.

Middle Row:
Goldie, G. P. L. Matthews,
A. T. Tait, Williams.

Front Row:
Wilkinson, P. Henwood, G.
M. Tait, T. H. Cooke, Mit-
chell.

Loosley and T. H. Cooke, one of the best wings ever seen here. Then in the Rhodesia Scottish team there were Mac-Arthur, a tip-top full back, Dunbar on the wing, McKenzie and Burnett.

Towards the end of the Boer War the King's Own Scottish Borderers beat all the local teams. Their football kit was not registered and did not conform to any rules but the old grey-back shirt, blue, or any other colour trousers, and ammunition boots did the trick. They had several well-known Scottish professionals. In 1903 - King's Club joined in, then Callies and later Raylton and soccer was strengthened by such men as J. H. Robison, who was chosen to go down as full-back against the visiting English side of 1910. Unfortunately, on the eve of his departure he was accidentally killed. Before coming to Rhodesia he had played against an earlier English team, was captain of Eastern Province and then Orange Free State and captain of the South African team that toured the Argentine. Other notables were H. Evans the goalie, Syd Cartwright, Syd Smith, Alec Tait, Francis Diack of Western Province, and Jimmy Rogers. Joe Agutter was also prominent in Bulawayo soccer circles.

St. George's School was for many years a great soccer nursery in Rhodesia and among their best products are Pat Walsh who played for Rhodesia while still at school, Dr. Aidan Campbell, A. Carroll, W. E. Popkiss, V. G. Isaac, H. R. Smith and Stanley Howard.

On one occasion the school won the Charity Shield and the story goes that the authorities demanded a £50 deposit before it could be taken away. The school indignantly refused the terms but, waiting until the trophy was locked up and the coast all clear, the boys effected a burglary and carried the shield to their school where it was allowed to remain until the following season.

Organised sport in the Midlands suffers from many handicaps, chiefly the fact that the players, mostly farmers and miners, are scattered over a large area with their several clubs so many miles apart that while the playing of inter-club matches is accomplished only by an excessive amount of travelling, it will be readily appreciated how difficult it is to choose, and then get into the field, a representative Midlands team.

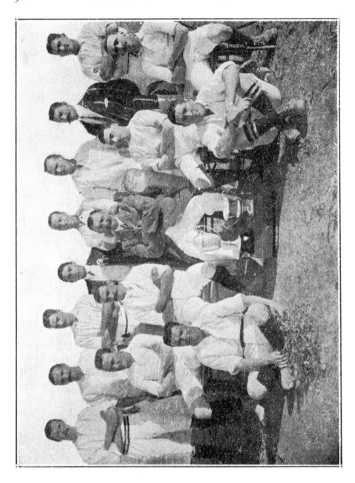

SEBAKWE & DISTRICT
FOOTBALL CLUB, 1912.
Midlands League.
Holborn Cup.

Standing:
Sgt. Paley, A. W. Marshall,
T. Greenfield, E. Furniston,
T. Liddle, W. Ross, H. Matt-
hews, E. Brown.

Sitting:
G. Austin, T. Wellings
(capt.), H. Shimmin (President), T. Crow, A. Rimmer,

In front:
B. Kyle, T. Curtis.

If enthusiasm may be measured in miles, there is no lack of the sporting spirit in Rhodesia. Challenges are flung from one end of the country to the other and journeys involving hundreds of miles are undertaken for a single match. When one considers the state of the roads and the vagaries of the weather it is small wonder that some of the stories told might stagger the credulity of even Mr. Ripley. In the earlier days, travel was by mule or ox transport but to-day, where there is no convenient railway, the motor car is universally used, particularly in the Midlands. Even this means of transport is not without its hazards, especially during the rainy seasons when a sudden tropical downpour converts the roadway into a muddy channel inches or even a foot deep, and dry river beds are suddenly transformed into raging torrents. Many are the teams that, caught between two swollen rivers, have had to camp the night waiting for the waters to subside. This may sometimes be fun, but the humour becomes rather grim when the roar of the rushing waters is accompanied by the roar of the lion and other uncanny night noises of the veld. That the Midlands should take the prominent part it does in Rhodesian sport is always a matter for wonder and appreciation.

From the earliest days of the occupation of the now prosperous farming and mining district, wherever it was possible to raise sufficient men to form a team, one found the round ball being kicked about. The first teams were from the Que Que, Selukwe and Falcon Mines and Gwelo and there was such keen rivalry between these sides that in 1912, Mr. Holborn of Gwelo donated the present league cup. The first winners were the Sebakwe and District Football Club, now the Que Que and District Football Club.

In 1913 the Midlands Football Association was formed with Mr. R. Barnes, of Gwelo, its first president and Mr. H. Daws, one of its keenest supporters. Among the best Midlands players were Walker, C. Fraser, Cecil Spearpoint, A. Goldie and H. S. Taylor, who were all picked for Matabeleland against Mashonaland, A. Woodvine, E. A. Rainsford, Geitzman, Waterhouse, F. K. Taylor, Brown, Salt, G. M. Hughes, A. MacIntosh, P. Duckenfield and H. Bradley. In recent years, the Midlands control board has been well served by Mr. M. Jacobson, honorary life member, Mr. G. B. Ledger, who was secretary for many years, and Messrs. J. L. Jackelow, A. E. White and M. Cohen.

J. N. Wilkinson.

In 1908 Rhodesia made her debut in the Currie Cup competition and though the team met with little success, several of the players distinguished themselves, notably Paddy Walsh at outside left, T. H. Cooke, A. G. Williams and W. J. Percy.

Rhodesia was not dismayed and in 1911 sent a second team to try conclusions with the provinces in the south. Arriving in Maritzburg on a Saturday, the team played seven matches before it left on the Monday week. Despite this strenuous programme and the unfamiliarity of the turf fields, the Rhodesians gave a good account of themselves. Green, J. N. Wilkinson, Pfaff, H. Allen and G. P. L. Matthews were the best of the Rhodesians.

In 1922 soccer in the Colony was at a high standard and in this season the Rhodesians made their third and most successful Currie Cup entry. The team played dashing football in each game except against Natal when Rhodesia, at the end of a path of glory, tripped and fell heavily. Natal's only win was over Rhodesia. However, Rhodesia finished third on the log and the soccer reputation of the Colony was greatly enhanced. Among those who drew special praise from the southern critics were J. S. McNeillie in goal, G. G. McKenzie, H. Linde and E. M. Goveia.

After the excellent form of the previous year, the 1923 entry was distinctly disappointing. On their own hard and fast grounds the Rhodesians had developed kick and rush tactics owing to the high bounce of the ball and its speed over the hard surface. On the Durban turf, however, this policy did not pay and in an endeavour to change, Rhodesia's lack of combination and ball control was very noticeable. E. W. Burke, T. P. Morgan and H. Levy were outstanding for Rhodesia, together with G. E. Fletcher and G. G. McKenzie who in 1924 were invited south for trials prior to the selection of the Springbok team to tour Great Britain.

The De Beer's Club, Kimberley, was the first side to visit this Colony. The tour was a great success. The visitors lost only one match and that was in a great game against Bulawayo when E. F. Harris scored the only goal before breaking his collar-bone. Tommy Cairns (S.A. International) was in the Bulawayo team with A. H. Minter, L. Bester, C. Wells and L. Ayres prominent.

Then the Great War intervened and all sport came to a standstill. There was a great revival, however, after the

**MARIST BROTHERS v.
MIDLANDS.**

Gwelo, 1920.

Top Row:

J. Green, A. Broderick, S. J. Pitts, J. Crole, R. Ferguson, R. Kilfoil, R. Meintjes, J. Prentice, A. E. Lowe, R. J. Thominet, Cullen, C. Spearpoint, J. Lea, B. Phillips, T. Baker, A. Bailey, A. McIntosh, T. P. Gilbert.

Bottom:

C. M. Starck, A. Surtees, G. Plaskett, M. Klopper, J. Ritchie, F. Mathieson, J. Mathieson, W. H. Rickards, H. Munro Samuel.

Front:

R. McCue, S. S. Fulton.

War and the Rhodesia Football Asssociation lost no time in restoring the game to its previous high standard. The Marist Brothers' Old Boys, Johannesburg, accepted an invitation in 1920 and their team included several Transvaal representative players and three Springboks in Alf Lowe, the Springbok captain, Joe Green and R. McCue. The local sides, particularly Midlands, did very well against this powerful combination.

In 1921 another good team came up and a great improvement in the local play was noticeable. The visitors, Transvaal, lost to Búlawayo, drew with Salisbury and just managed to beat the strong Umvuma team óf which the brothers Mathieson, H. G. Bateman, the cricket enthusiast, W. H. Rickards, and S. S. Fulton were the stars.

Since 1923 the conditions of the Currie Cup.competition have been changed and the excessive travelling and expense consequent upon this change made it practically impossible for Rhodesia to compete. The Rhodesia Football Association, however, were determined not to neglect the welfare of the game and a series of tours by teams outside the Colony became an essential part of the local authorities' policy, a policy that has met with gratifying success.

A flying visit in 1925 to Bulawayo from the South African Railways (Johannesburg) Club in which they beat two strong local teams, was followed in 1926 by a second Transvaal visit. The Southerners had little difficulty in beating the teams they met but the tour was of great benefit to Rhodesian soccer. The following local players were outstanding: J. B. Day, R. H. Jordan, A. Marnie, C. L. Roberts, who has captained Mashonaland at cricket, and J. A. Q. Scrutton, in the capital; J. A. Winter, W. G. Wilson, the brothers J. and W. Wood, W. Robinson and R. Rayne, in Bulawayo, and S. E. Stowe, T. P. Morgan, R. A. Killick and F. Dollar, the well-known cricketer, in the Midlands.

Soccer was greatly encouraged by the visit of a Natal team in 1927 and a Griqualand West team in 1928. Each of these sides lost to Bulawayo and Salisbury and met with strong opposition in other centres so that those who had been anxious for the welfare of the game in the Colony had their fears completely allayed.

The year 1929 was a proud one, for the Colony was honoured by a visit from the English Football Association's

SOUTHERN RHODESIA
v. ENGLAND,
Salisbury, June 27th, 1929.

Left to Right, Top:
N. Innes, S. H. Perkins, C. E. Ramsay, A. Robinson (Referee), O. L. Olver, C. N. MacKenzie.

Sitting:
W. Wood, A. Evans T. P. Morgan (capt.). F. T. Mc-Adam, A. L. Dewar, R. H. Jordan.

team captained by Jimmy Seed. The first representative Rhodesian team to play on Rhodesian soil opposed this formidable side in Salisbury and in Bulawayo. They were well beaten but in the Bulawayo game Rhodesia succeeded in scoring one goal, no mean feat, as was the opinion of the Football Association, for they awarded their gold medal to the scorer, T. P. Morgan.

In the first game in Salisbury, England won 4—0. Rhodesia's chief weakness was in the half-back line. In the first half Wood tested their goalkeeper with a good shot and shortly after Rhodesia made three successive raids in which Evans and McAdam were prominent. They led at the interval 1—0. Rhodesia opened the second half with a pretty bit of work which Morgan finished off with a good shot that was just saved at the expense of a corner. Play was very fast, practically all in the Rhodesian half, and Ramsay saved well time after time. The Englishmen, however, were not to be denied as they were a vastly superior combination. Perkins and Wood were good.

The second game, in Bulawayo, was won by the tourists, 6—1. There was again no link between the half-backs and the forwards and the two lines did not work in together. In the first half, Ramsay effected some brilliant saves. The Rhodesian score came from a good solo effort by Morgan who beat two men. Shortly afterwards Dewar hit the goal post with the keeper well beaten. It was a great shot worthy of a better reward. The Englishmen led 2—1 at the interval. On the resumption McAdam put in some good work, but Blake, after a fine effort, shot over. The last quarter of an hour was uninteresting. England was too good and appeared to ease off while the Rhodesians seemed fatigued. Such splendid soccer as displayed by the Englishmen had never before been seen in Rhodesia and many lessons of value were learnt.

In 1933 a Southern Transvaal team came to Rhodesia and was beaten both in Bulawayo and Salisbury.

Another visit was from the famous Motherwell Club (Scotland) in 1934, who played Matabeleland in Bulawayo and Mashonaland in Salisbury. Matabeleland played very well indeed, particularly H. Arnott, H. L. St. Croix, J. A. French, J. T. Bell and A. L. Robinson. The latter gave such a fine exhibition in goal that he was chosen for a South African XI in the third "test" against Motherwell when he played another splendid game.

MOTHERWELL A.F.C. (Scotland) v. MATABELELAND. Played at Bulawayo, Thursday, 7th June, 1934.
Result: Motherwell 3, Matabeleland 0.

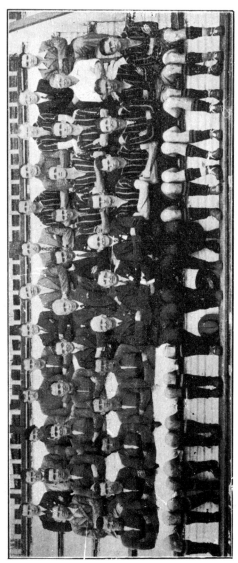

Back row (left to right): J. McKenzie (M), J. Crapnell (M), "Pud." Allen (M), A. McClory (M), B. Ellis (M), J. McMenemy (M), A. S. Hemming (Act. Hon. S.A. Manager), C. Whiteson (Hon. Sec., S.R.F.A.), H. St. Croix (Mat.), A. L. Robinson (Mat.),

Centre Row (left to right): W. McFadyen (M), H. Wales (M), J. Blair (M), W. Telfer (M), E. Weston (Mem. S.A. Selection Committee), A. Muirhead (Director, Motherwell A.F.C.), V. Williams (Hon. Treas., B. & D.F.A.), M. du Plessis (Mat.), R. Dunn (Mat.), W. Walker (Motherwell Trainer), W. Stewart (M).

Front Row (left to right): D. Ogilvie (M), J. Johnstone (M), M. Crawley (M), G. Stevenson (M), R. Ferrier (Capt. Motherwell), J. Hunter (Manager, Motherwell), D. Macintyre, M.P. (Pres., S.R.F.A.), F. Mathieson (Hon. Sec., B. & D.F.A.), A. Genner (Mat.), H. Arnott (Capt. Matabeleland, S. B. Adams (Referee), J. A. French (Mat.), A. G. Rastall (Mat.), J. Bell (Mat.), W. Wood (Mat.) H. Collins (Mat.). (M) Motherwell; (Mat.) Matabeleland.

In 1935 Southern Rhodesia extended a warm welcome to the Combined Services team, a team representing the three branches of the fighting forces of the Imperial Government, namely, the Navy, the Army and the Air Force. The first match was against Mashonaland in Salisbury where the visitors gave a masterly display of clever football to win by 9 goals to nil. The local side held their own in the early stages of the game, the first goal being scored after 30 minutes' play. After that, however, the game became a one-sided affair and the visitors treated the spectators to an exhibition of splendid ball control, passing, positional play and clever dummying.

Saric, the goalkeeper, was the hero of the Mashonaland side and brought off many fine saves from pile-driving shots. Gledhill stood out as the best defender but all the local players worked hard against a much superior combination. Fraser, Wilson and Cornish were nippy and often their dangerous crosses deserved a better fate.

In Bulawayo, Combined Services beat Matabeleland by 5 goals to 1. The losers fought gallantly and once they had settled down they gave a good, if erratic, account of themselves. Their main weakness lay at half-back and centre-forward. Louth was brilliant in goal and Botterill at full-back was sound throughout. The Matabeleland goal was scored by Hyde when the ball rebounded to him after hitting the crossbar from a hot shot by Logie.

There have been few Rhodesian teams chosen since the war, but even so there has been an abundance of good material and the following are some of the prominent players who only missed representative colours through lack of opportunity.

After the war inter-town and inter-provincial games were resumed in 1920. In that year J. Winter kept goal for Matabeleland while other outstanding players were G. W. Ledeboer, who was a tower of strength as full-back, F. Wood, A. H. Minter, E. F. Harris, a deadly shot at centre-forward, C. Dunckley, a tricky forward, R. A. Gower and A. Marnie. For Umvuma, who won through to the final of the Metcalfe Cup, were E. A. Rainsford, a fine exponent, and F. Mathieson.

In 1921, Jimmy Miller came to the fore. A brilliant centre-half, he was chosen as captain of the 1923 Currie Cup team, but was unable to get away. Andrew Ross, the tennis

COMBINED SERVICES v. MATABELELAND.

Back Row: C. Whiteson (Hon. Sec., S.R.F.A.), W. A. Blezard (Linesman), Lt. W. V. H. Robins, L/Cpl. M. Lally, Aircraftsman I. J. E. Scruton, Marine D. E. A. Renouf, G. D. Ward (Referee), Leading Telegraphist H. Hayles, Stoker W. C. Peart, V. W. Williams (Hon. Treas. B. & D.F.A.), Pte. R. Williams, Pte. L. H. Bird, A. W. Clelland (Hon. Sec. B. & D.F.A.), Leading Aircraftsman J. F. Hamlet, Aircraftsman I. T. G. Hurrell, W. J. Webb (Trainer), C. R. Turkington (Linesman).
Middle Row: W. Methven (Groundsman), T. Woods (Pres., Referees' Assn.), Flying Officer J. M. Warfield, Capt. H. Allen (Vice-Pres., S.R.F.A.), Commander F. C. Baker, R.N., D. Macintyre, M.P. (Pres., S.R.F.A.), Major A. Webb, D.C.M., E. N. Watts (Hon. Sec., S.A.F.A.), R. Dunn (Capt.), Rigger H. L. Coates (Capt.), Marine R. C. James.
Front Row: C. A. Goodyear, B. H. Louth, H. Collins, C. S. Lineham, A. Hyde, L/Cpl. S. Eastham, R. H. Hoare, Officers Steward, R. Pearce, M. S. Bambrough, Pte. S. Rochester, C. Botterill, J. McPherson, F. Logie.

star, was a grand outside right. Many will remember G. A. Tebbitt, a fine outside left, H. A. Fear at centre-half, and H. S. Cross who figured prominently for Mashonaland.

In the 1924 season when many of the older players dropped out of football, among the new men were F. D. Hockin, Matabeleland's right wing, C. Allen at full-back, Johnny Wood, another member of the well-known sporting family, the nippy J. G. Simpson and George Gemmell whose exhibitions at centre-forward were a treat to watch.

In 1925 H. Arnott was playing grand football and so also was J. Iverson. In the Midlands ranks were R. A. Killick, who subsequently took up the whistle with success, G. B. Ledger, Bert Shimmin, a fine player, and S. E. Stowe. In 1926, J. Winter was still Matabeleland's goalkeeper but new men were H. Collins who still represents this province at outside right, H. Hill, J. A. Q. Scrutton, who was a brilliant player, and A. Hyde who has played for Mashonaland, Midlands and Matabeleland. R. P. Easterbrook represented Matabeleland from 1927 to 1933. He had a powerful shot. H. T. Bell, the Midlands cricketer, was another good player, and also C. Whiteson, a full-back with a terrific " boot."

M. S. Bambrough first appeared in 1930 for Mashonaland and since then for Matabeleland. He played this year against the Combined Services team. T. N. Lindeque was a versatile player with an accurate goal shot.

In 1932, B. H. Louth, Matabeleland's present goalkeeper, came into prominence and so did R. Dunn, A. G. Rastall, a splendid forward, L. A. Hardy, Mashonaland's fine goal-keeper, A. Gledhill, J. Saric, F. J. Nevett, and J. Bell who played for Matabeleland for many seasons.

Apart from football against sides outside the Colony, the game subsists principally on well-organised leagues and inter-town and inter-provincial matches. In 1903, Sir Charles Metcalfe donated a cup for inter-town games and in 1908 the inter-provincial trophy was presented by the late Brigadier-General W. Bodle, C.M.G. Great keenness is displayed in these annual games which are played alternately in Salisbury and Bulawayo, except that the semi-final for the Metcalfe Cup is played each year in Gwelo and Umtali. Mr. John Austen, M.B.E., of Que Que, a great sporting benefactor, presented a handsome cup for club competition with a proviso

MASHONALAND, 1904.

Standing: Cole, S. Elkin, R. L. Phillips, G. Watt, Whatley.
Middle Row: A. G. Williams, D. Bruce, R. Elkin, F. G. Brooks, (Capt.), Laurence, H. Allen, J. Hendry.
Bottom Row: Sims, W. Smith, Cooke.

that the semi-final and final be played in Que Que. This proviso has now been lifted and the finals are played in the big
towns in rotation. Each season the best club side in each province, determined by preliminary rounds, proceeds to the
venue of the semi-finals and final and as the winner is, in
effect, the champion club in the Colony, the Austen Cup is
considered the "blue riband" of Rhodesian soccer. Younger
soccer players are exceptionally well provided for, but as most
of the schools do not play soccer the lack of nurseries is
keenly felt.

In 1916 the English Football Association presented the
South African Football Association with a trophy for competi-
tion among the juniors, and with the inauguration of the
South African Under 16 Schools Tournament, Southern
Rhodesia sent a team to Natal in 1927, and to East London
in 1928. These teams were under the charge of Mr. D. J.
Avery and Mr. C. Whiteson respectively. In 1929 (Mr. R.
S. Brown in charge) and 1930 (Mr. C. Whiteson in charge)
the Rhodesian boys were sent to Johannesburg and Bloemfontein respectively and in 1932 the tournament was held in
Rhodesia, the matches being played in Bulawayo. The
occasion was a memorable one. Teams from the Transvaal,
Natal, Orange Free State and Rhodesia competed. Large
crowds witnessed the games and were astonished to see the
splendid football played by the boys. Although the Rhodesians did not meet with a great deal of success in the
tournaments, the lessons learnt were very valuable. The
educational value of the visits to the South was considerable.
Many of the boys had not been out of Rhodesia before and
in the various centres they did a lot of sight-seeing, including
visits to factories, mines, whaling-stations, etc.

Owing to the depression, a Rhodesian team has not been
able to compete since, and the tours have had to be abandoned
for the time being, but they will be resumed at the first
opportunity.

The increasing importance of Southern Rhodesia in the
Junior Football world was recognised by the South African
Football Association as early as 1925, when that body allocated
the Upington Cup for competition in Southern Rhodesia.
This trophy was presented by Mr. B. Upington, K.C., to
the South African Football Association for annual competition by junior clubs of affiliated Divisional Associations, and

S.R.F.A. COUNCIL, 1933.

J. McMeekan (S.), M. Cohen (G), H. Higgo (Q.), J. Gillespie (B.), A. J.
Horne (G.), F. H. Morgan (B.), R. L. Abbott (Q.), S. B. Adams (B.),
P. J. le Cordeur (B.).

J. G. Simpson (S.), G. Young (S.), D. Macintyre, M.P. (Chairman), C.
Whiteson (Hon. Sec.), W. Harrison (G.)

G—Gwelo.   Q—Que Que.   S—Salisbury.   B—Bulawayo.

CHAS. EICKHOFF.

G. F. HUNT,
a pioneer and the Raylton Club's
groundsman for many years.

the cup is allocated in rotation to Natal, Transvaal, Western Province, etc. In 1925 the trophy was won by St. George's School, and in 1932 when Rhodesia's turn came round again, Bulawayo Juniors annexed it.

The Southern Rhodesia Football Association began to officiate in 1905, as the Rhodesia Football Association which name was changed to the present title in 1930 when Northern Rhodesia became affiliated to the S.A.F.A. The early records of the Association have been lost but no books are needed to recall the valuable services given to the game by that great enthusiast, F. O. John, E. Dechow, secretary and treasurer for so many years, Ben Wilson, actively associated with all forms of sport from the earliest years, N. Cook, the Rev. Father D. Brand, Edgar Jenkins, D. MacGillivray, D. Macintyre, M.P., president of the S.R.F.A. and C. Whiteson, a useful full-back, who has really worked hard for soccer off the field of play.

At one time there were four provincial associations, but in 1920 the Manicaland Board, which was revived in 1935, became defunct and the remaining associations govern Mashonaland, Midlands and Bulawayo district. The latter controls the Callies, Raylton Rovers, Raylton Rangers, United Services, Queens, Old Georgians and Raylton Clubs, which represent about twenty teams, senior and junior. An important body is the Bulawayo and District Referees' Association. Some of the first referees were Advocate J. D. MacKenzie (afterwards Judge), G. F. Stapleton, L. Makin, a keen cricketer, M. G. Linnell and E. L. Loosley. In 1909 the Referees' Association was formed and the magnitude of its work may be realised from the fact that it now controls well over 200 games in a season. Among those who have given valuable service as referees are W. Thomson, first chairman, G. C. Salmon, first secretary, J. Ellman Brown, W. W. Feigenbaum, S. Burns, Sid Dennett, H. H. Montgomery, S. S. Grossberg, G. Y. Shearer, J. Dobson, A. E. Clegg, T. P. Gilbert, W. A. Blezard, A. Robinson, who was president of the S.R.F.A. for three years, T. Woods, now president of the Referees' Association, F. W. Harrison, R. A. Killick, who has played for Midlands, S. B. Adams, F. Mathieson and J. M. McDonald, the present chairman.

The clubs affiliated to the Mashonaland Association are Raylton, Police, Salisbury, Alexandra, Territorials and Postals and during the football season a large number of

GWELO, F.C., 1923.

Winners of all the Trophies in the Midlands that year: Holborn Cup (League), Globe & Phoenix Shield (Knock-out), Wilkins Cup (Knock-out), Shiff & Jacobson Cup (Knock-out).

Back Row:

J. Avery, J. Holgate, A. McIntosh, J. Hogg, F. Dollar, C. Ross.

Middle Row:

Griffiths, Roberts, T. Morgan, M. Jacobson (President), Bell, Liebenberg, E. Garland.

Front Row:

L. Phillips, D. Bourne.

teams are placed in the field. The principal trophies for competition are the H. J. Deary Cup, the Salisbury Challenge, the
Tim Percy and the Charity Cups. Among the workers for
the game in the capital are B. Thomas, J. G. Simpson, a
good all-rounder, J. R. Robertson, G. Gemmell, a Mashonaland captain and popular sportsman who had been capped
three times for England after playing for Cambridge, R. T.
Anderson, E. W. Popkiss, and J. McMeekan, the present
chairman of the Association.

H. H. CORNISH
(Mashonaland).

R. REID
(Matabeleland)

THE FIRST CURRIE CUP TEAM TO LEAVE RHODESIA, 1908.

Standing (left to right): J. Rodger, Pat Walsh, Kerr, R. B. Mitchell (Referee), F. W. Kettle, W. A. Ludgater, G. M. Tait, W. Sargent, P. Henwood.

Sitting (left to right): A. V. Williams, D. Bruce, P. J. de Stadler (Manager), S. Cartwright (capt.), W. Ross, S. Smith, W. J. Percy.

In front (left to right): A. G. Williams, T. H. Cooke.

THE CURRIE CUP TOURNAMENTS.

(1908) JOHANNESBURG.

Rhodesia: S. Cartwright (captain), F. W. Kettle, G. M. Tait, P. C. Henwood, A. V. Williams, P. Walsh, J. H. Rodger, W. Ross, S. Smith, Kerr, T. H. Cooke, D. Bruce, W. A. Ludgater, W. H. Sargent, A. G. Williams, W. J. Percy, A. Ruxton. Referee: R. B. Mitchell. Manager: P. J. de Stadler.

Opponents:	Results:		
Transvaal	Lost	5 —	1
(Percy.)			
Western Province	Lost	4 —	0
Griqualand West	Drew	1 —	1
(Bruce.)			
Natal	Lost	4 —	1
Orange River Colony	Lost	4 —	2
(Percy, an opponent.)			
Frontier	Won	3 —	0
(Cooke, A. G. Williams (2).)			
Eastern Province	Drew	1 —	1
(A. G. Williams.)			

1911 (MARITZBURG).

Rhodesia: H. Allen (captain), G. Eckard, S. Smith, G. B. Jennings, C. Pfaff, C. J. W. Andrews, Pearson, H. D. Smith, F. G. Diack, G. P. L. Matthews, B. Matthews, J. Rodger, J. N. Wilkinson, F. J. Wilkinson, R. C. D. Napier, Green, E. W. Clarkson. Manager: Jock Hutchinson.

Opponents:	Results:		
Orange Free State	Lost	4 —	0
Natal	Lost	4 —	1
(Green.)			
Frontier	Won	3 —	0
(Green, Allen (2).)			
Western Province	Lost	2 —	1
(G. P. L. Matthews.)			
Eastern Province	Lost	3 —	1
(B. Matthews.)			
Griqualand West	Won	1 —	0
(Allen.)			
Transvaal	Lost	4 —	0

RHODESIAN 1922
CURRIE CUP
TEAM.

Top Row:
F. O. John, G. Robertson, W. Wilson, R. H. A. Rayne, J. B. Day, R. H. Jordan, E. W. Popkiss.

Second Row:
W. W. Feigenbaum, E. Golding, A. Packer, J. S. McNeillie, H. Levy, W. Abrahams, H. Linde, E. Dechow.

Third Row:
C. L. Roberts, E. Goveia, G. E. Fletcher, T. P. Gilbert, G. Eckard, C. F. Spearpoint, V. John.

Front Row:
G. G. McKenzie, R. H. Metcalfe, F. H. Morgan, R. D. Gloak.

Inset:
T. P. Morgan.

1922 (JOHANNEBURG).

Rhodesia: G. E. Fletcher (captain), J. S. McNeillie, H. L. Levy, R. D. Gloak, W. B. Abrahams, C. F. Spearpoint, W. G. Wilson, A. H. Packer, G. Eckard, R. H. Jordan, E. Golding, J. B. Day, G. G. McKenzie, E. M. Goveia, H. H. Linde, G. Robertson, R. H. Metcalfe, F. H. Morgan, T. P. Morgan, R. H. Rayne, V. John, C. L. Roberts, S. Lambourne, J. Mathieson. Referees: E. W. Popkiss and A. Feigenbaum. Managers: T. P. Gilbert and E. Dechow.

Opponents:	Results:	
Eastern Province ... ... (McKenzie, Linde.)	Won	2 — 1
Frontier ... ... (Packer, Goveia.)	Won	2 — 1
Western Province ... ... (F. H. Morgan, McKenzie.)	Lost	3 — 2
Transvaal ... ... (Goveia.)	Drew	1 — 1
Natal	Lost	1 — 0

1923 (DURBAN).

Rhodesia: T. P. Morgan (captain), E. W. Burke, H. L. Levy, R. D. Gloak, W. Amos, H. T. Bell, W. G. Wilson, G. E. Fletcher, R. H. Catterall, D. J. Avery, H. Ambler, R. H. Jordan, G. G. Mckenzie, H. H. Linde, D. Killen, F. H. Morgan, R. H. Rayne, J. Hazelhurst, C. H. Ashort. Managers: T. P. Gilbert and Porter.

Opponents:	Results:	
Natal ... ... (Rayne.)	Lost	5 — 1
Western Province	Lost	2 — 0
Frontier ... ... (McKenzie.)	Won	1 — 0
Transvaal ... ... (T. P. Morgan.)	Lost	4 — 1
Eastern Province	Lost	2 — 0

DE BEERS (Kimberley) v. BULAWAYO.

21st June, 1913.

Top Row:

T. Watson, L. M. Campbell, A. H. Harley, J. T. Thompson, H. Herbert, G. McCartney, J. Hutchinson (hon. sec. R.F.A.), L. Bester, V. Isaac, P. J. le Cordeur, H. D. Smith, T. Gilbert.

Middle Row:

H. Knight, S. G. Watkins, A. Mauchline, J. Innes (capt.), D. Demster, Jack Lea (Referee), P. Hargreaves (Manager), F. Diack, J. Rodger, A. McMasters, W. Thompson, S. J. Smythe.

Front Row:

R. W. Moore, J. A. Moore, C. Robertson, H. Hargreaves, W. Laxson, Lt.-Col. Baxendale (Pres. M.F.A.), L. Ayres, G. Hopley, E. F. Harris, H. Allen (capt.), T. Cairns, Ben Wilson (Hon. Sec. M.F.A.).

THE DE BEERS (KIMBERLEY) VISIT, 1913.

This was the first occasion in the history of Association Football in Rhodesia that a Soccer Team from outside Rhodesia visited this Territory. The results were:—

Versus Bulawayo at Bulawayo	Won	4 — 1
Versus Bulawayo at Bulawayo	Lost	0 — 1
Versus Salisbury at Salisbury	Won	3 — 0
Versus Salisbury at Salisbury	Drawn	1 — 1
Versus Midlands at Gwelo	Won	2 — 0
Versus Livingstone at Livingstone	Drawn	0 — 0

Bulawayo: H. D. Smith (captain), T. Cairns, L. Fox, E. F. Harris, W. Walsh, A. H. Minter, A. McMasters, A. Woods, P. J. le Cordeur, L. Bester, C. Wells, H. Allen, G. Hopley, L. Ayres, J. Rodger, F. G. Diack, V. G. Isaac.

Salisbury: Harnetty, Steer, Winward, Aston, O. Pearson, Gale, Bowley, Cater, Jennings, A. Carroll, Champion, Cullen.

Midlands: Mercer, Fraser, Irons, Daly, Huxtable, Waterhouse, Moore, Bester, Kirby, Taylor, Remmer. Referee T. P. Gilbert.

De Beers: T. Watson, L. M. Campbell, A. H. Harley, J. T. Thompson, H. Herbert, G. McCartney, H. Knight, S. G. Watkins, A. Manckline, J. Innes (captain), D. Dempster, W. Thompson, S. J. Smythe, R. W. Moore, J. A. Moore, C. Robertson, H. Hargreaves.

THE MARIST BROTHERS VISIT, 1920.

The results were:—

Versus Bulawayo at Bulawayo	Won	3 — 1
Versus Salisbury at Salisbury	Won	6 — 2
Versus Gatooma at Gatooma	Won	6 — 0
Versus Bulawayo at Bulawayo	Won	7 — 0
Versus Midlands at Gwelo	Won	2 — 0

Bulawayo: J. A. Winter, P. Smith, W. Wilson, F. Wood, G. Eckard, J. W. Miller, A. H. Minter, E. F. Harris, A. Wilson, C. Dunckley, Rev. H. Young, J. Rodger, R. H. Rayne.

Salisbury: H. L. Levy, K. R. Rowell, C. M. Dowling, H. S. Cross, Tysoe, Brown, Dancer, Brooks, Saville, Murray, Dunseith.

Midlands: J. Lea, E. A. Rainsford, F. Mathieson, R. J. Thominet, W. H. Rickards, A. Bailey, Cullen, T. Baker, S. S. Fulton, B. Phillips, J. Mathieson.

Marist Brothers: A. Surtees, A. Ferguson, M. Klopper, C. M. Starck, J. Green, J. Gibb, J. Crole, A. Broderick, J. Prentice, J. Ritchie (captain), A. E. Lowe, R. Kilfoil, R. Meintjes, G. Plaskett, R. McCue.

MARIST BROTHERS v.
BULAWAYO, 1920.

Top Row:

E. Dechow (Hon. Sec. M.F.A.), J. Crole, S. J. Pitts (Manager), L. L. French (Pres. S.A.F.A.), T. P. Gilbert, W. J. Atterbury (Pres. M.F.A.)

Second Row:

R. McCue, G. Plaskett, R. Meintjes, P. Smith, J. Winter, W. Wilson, T. Kennedy.

Third Row:

R. Kilfoil, C .M. Starck, M. Klopper, A. E. Lowe, J. Ritchie, F. Wood, G. Eckard, J. W. Miller (capt.), W. Feigenbaum.

Bottom Row:

A. Broderick, J. Green, R. Ferguson, A. Surtees, J. Prentice, H. Minter, E .F. Harris, A. Wilson, C. Dunckley, Rev. H. Young.

THE TRANSVAAL TOUR, 1921.

The results were:—

Versus Bulawayo at Bulawayo	Lost	1 — 2
Versus Salisbury at Salisbury	Drawn	3 — 3
Versus Salisbury at Salisbury	Won	2 — 1
Versus Umvuma at Umvuma	Won	1 — 0
Versus Midlands at Gwelo	Won	5 — 0
Versus Bulawayo at Bulawayo	Won	2 — 0

Bulawayo: J. S. McNeillie, C. Spearpoint, W. Wilson, G. Baker, J. W. Miller (captain), F. Wood, A. Ross, R. Rayne, D. Killen, C. Dunckley, G. Tebbitt.

Salisbury: H. L. Levy, C. M. Dowling, S. Porter, H. S. Cross, H. G. Brown, A. Packer, F. Crick, Leach, G. Gemmell, F. W. Murray, J. B. Day, R. H. Jordan, Ellis, Cockerton, Evans.

Midlands: J. Lea, G. Kuhn, E. A. Rainsford (captain), McMasters, F. Mathieson, W. H. Rickards, Viljoen, F. Fulton, Koch, J. Hogg, Bresler.

Umvuma: H. G. Bateman, J. Mathieson, E. A. Rainsford, W. H. Rickards, E. Golding, F. Mathieson, A. Bailey, S. S. Fulton (captain), G. Devitt, G. Hinds, G. Lucas.

Transvaal: R. McCue, M. A. Broderick, B. C. Nicoll, P. A. Street, D. A. Dewar, M. Klopper, R. W. Fawcett, F. H. Morgan, T. P. Morgan, R. F. Ferguson, C. C. Jackson (captain), A. H. Surtees, J. Collier, G. G. McKenzie.

VISIT OF SOUTH AFRICAN RAILWAYS JOHANNESBURG CLUB, 1925.

Results:—

Versus Railway Recreation Club, Bulawayo	Won	2 — 0
Versus Bulawayo	Won	2 — 1

J.S.A.R.: A. Watson, R. Abbott, D. J. Langford, H. Hamilton, A. E. Strecker (captain), A. Langford, H. J. Sutherland, E. Meggy, W. Ferguson, E. Clark, S. Brown, J. D. Crookes.

R.R.C.: J. A. Winter, R. D. Gloak (captain), W. Wilson, C. Pienke, O. Olver, J. Dewar, M. Iverson, R. H. Rayne, F. H. Morgan, R. P. Easterbrook, G. G. McKenzie.

Bulawayo: J. S. McNeillie, R. D. Gloak (captain), W. Wilson, J. Dewar, O. Olver, H. Arnott, M. Iverson, R. H. Rayne, R. P. Easterbrook, R. H. Metcalfe, G. G. McKenzie.

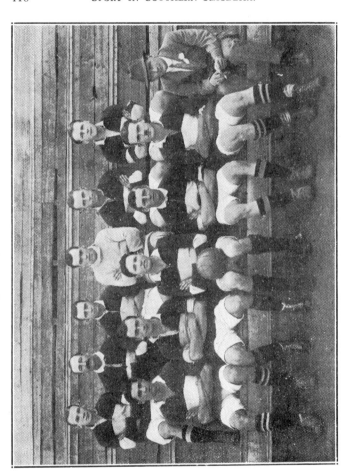

BULAWAYO
REPRESENTATIVE TEAM
AGAINST TRANSVAAL
TOURING TEAM,
Season 1921.

Top Row:

F. Wood, G. Tebbitt, A. Ross,
J. S. McNeillie, D. Killen,
W. Wilson.

Bottom Row:

G. Baker, C. Dunckley, J. W.
Miller (capt.), R. Rayne, C.
Spearpoint, N. Cook (Hon.
Sec., M.F.A.)

This team defeated the
Transvaal by 2—1 in
Bulawayo.

THE TRANSVAAL VISIT, 1926.

Results:—

Versus Bulawayo at Bulawayo	Won	5 — 1
Versus Midlands at Gwelo	Won	7 — 0
Versus Que Que at Que Que	Won	4 — 1
Versus Salisbury at Salisbury	Won	2 — 1
Versus Salisbury at Salisbury	Won	6 — 3
Versus Bulawayo at Bulawayo	Won	5 — 1
Versus Eiffel Flats at Gatooma	Won	4 — 1

Transvaal: L. Mandy, G. T. Leemhuis, T. D. Young, C. C. Jackson (captain), C. D. Macrae, H. A. Hurry, B. Stevenson (vicecaptain), W. V. E. Schuurman, R. Sharpe, J. Jackson, H. J. Sutherland, E. Jarvis, S. Levy, J. T. Morrison, J. Prentice, W. F. Gibb, Maton, Dunn, A. V. Middlewick, Ferreira.

Bulawayo: J. A. Winter, W. Robinson (captain), W. G. Wilson, J. Wood, O. Olver, H. Arnott, H. Collins, C. Adams, W. Wood, R. H. Metcalfe, G. G. McKenzie, N. Jenkins, R. H. Rayne, R. P. Easterbrook.

Midlands: T. P. Morgan (captain), R. A. Killick, C. Spearpoint, Barnes, Jackelow, D. J. Avery, B. Shimmin, S. E. Stowe, H. Stranger, R. C. D. Napier, F. Dollar.

Que Que: J. D. Wakefield, C. Spearpoint, T. Wallis, Skinner, McLeod, R. C. D. Napier, B. Shimmin.

Salisbury: H. Levy, A. R. Green, Brooke, Merrington, Ramsay, T. H. Jordan, J. B. Day, R. H. Jordan, A. Marnie, A. N. Evans, C. L. Roberts, J. A. Q. Scrutton, N. Innes, Moffat, Murray.

NATAL TOURING TEAM VISIT, 1927.

Results:—

Versus Bulawayo at Bulawayo	Won	3 — 1
Versus Bulawayo at Bulawayo	Lost	4 — 1
Versus Que Que at Que Que	Won	4 — 0
Versus Eiffel Flats at Eiffel Flats	Won	4 — 0
Versus Salisbury at Salisbury	Lost	1 — 0
Versus Mashonaland at Salisbury	Won	4 — 1
Versus Bulawayo at Bulawayo	Won	3 — 2

Que Que: Wilkinson (captain), J. D. Wakefield, W. Gow, Radford, Van Heerden, Hunt, Paul, J. Stewart, Ramsey, C. Campbell, C. Brown. Referee: Higgo.

Salisbury: H. L. Levy, W. G. Gale, G. F. Kuhn, R. H. Jordan, A. Marnie, A. R. Green, F. W. Murray, A. Hyde, W. Wood, A. N. Evans, G. C. Barker.

Mashonaland: L. A. Hardy, W. G. Gale, G. F. Kuhn, R. H. Jordan, J. A. Q. Scrutton, A. R. Green, F. W. Murray, A. Hyde, W. Wood, A. N. Evans, G. C. Barker. Referee: J. R. Robertson.

Eiffel Flats: J. A. Q. Scrutton (captain), Porter, McCabe, Jamieson, Garton, D. J. Avery, H. T. Bell, W. Poley, J. Kelly, R. Moffat, Lemmer.

Bulawayo: G. E. Fletcher (captain), J. S. McNeillie, C. Allen, O. L. Olver, B. Melville, J. Wood, R. Reid, H. Hill, F. H. Morgan, J. Dewar, F. G. Jackson, R. Rayne, H. Arnott, H. Collins, G. McKenzie. Referees: A. Robinson, T. Woods and F. Mathieson.

TRANSVAAL v. UMVUMA FOOTBALL CLUB, 1921.

Top Row: E. A. Rainsford, R. McCue, T. Stranger, A. Surtees, J. Mathieson, J. Collier, Broderick, J. Walsh.
Second Row: W. Mawdsley, W. Ferguson, Nicoll, H. G. Bateman, G. Devitt, W. H. Rickards, J. Hines, F. H. Morgan, J. C. Elworthy.
Sitting: W. Dewar, E. Golding, M. Klopper, S. S. Fulton, H. T. Brett, J. H. Williams (Transvaal Manager), C. Jackson (Transvaal Captain), F. Mathieson, T. P. Morgan, A. Bailey.
Sitting on ground: G. Lucas, G. G. McKenzie, B. Fawcett.

GRIQUALAND WEST VISIT, 1928.

Results:—

Versus Salisbury at Salisbury	Lost	3 — 1
Versus Mashonaland at Salisbury	Lost	4 — 1
Versus Gatooma & District at Eiffel Flats	Won	2 — 0
Versus Que Que at Que Que	Drawn	1 — 1
Versus Midlands at Gwelo	Won	4 — 0
Versus Bulawayo at Bulawayo	Lost	2 — 0

Bulawayo: A. Robinson, A. L. Ault, O. L. Olver, L. Scott, H. Arnott, A. L. Dewar, W. J. Poley, H. H. Hill, W. Wood, J. Dewar, W. Brown.

Salisbury: J. Saric, H. McGilton, A. R. Green, H. G. Denby, A. Marnie, T. G. Saric, C. Melville, L. Blake, A. Mylne, M. G. Evans, C. H. Ashort. Referee: G. B. Ledger.

Mashonaland: L. Ramsay, W. G. Dale, G. C. Barker, A. Mylne, N. Innes, T. G. Saric, McAdam, Burnett, M. G. Evans, A. N. Evans, F. S. Barker. Referee: Humphries.

Midlands: T. P. Morgan (captain), J. D. Wakefield, H. T. Elkington, S. E. Stowe, J. M. Attwell, A. E. G. Cooney, R. Thomas, J. Carpenter, R. Moffat, C. Rau, F. Patterson.

Que Que: J. Stewart (captain), J. D. Wakefield, O'Leary, Woram, Smith, Attwood, Van Heerden, Campbell, C. Rau, Douglas, J. Carpenter. Referee: A. H. A. Hutchinson.

THE ENGLISH VISIT, 1929.

Results:—

Versus Rhodesia at Salisbury	Won	4 — 0
Versus Rhodesia at Bulawayo	Won	6 — 1

Rhodesia: T. P. Morgan (captain), C. E. Ramsay, S. H. Perkins, O. L. Olver, A. L. Dewar, N. Innes, R. H. Jordan, F. T. McAdam, W. Wood, A. N. Evans, C. N. McKenzie, A. Mylne, S. Blake, J. L. Dewar. Referees: A. Robinson and F. Mathieson.

England: E. A. Hart, W. P. Thompson, L. Armitage, A. E. L. Keeping, A. Barrett, R. Osborne, A. Harrison, F. A. Shelley, B. A. Olney, H. Hibbs, J. Landells, H. A. Davies, W. Pease, A. Chandler, J. M. Seed (captain), R. J. Turnbull, W. J. Price, J. J. Williams.

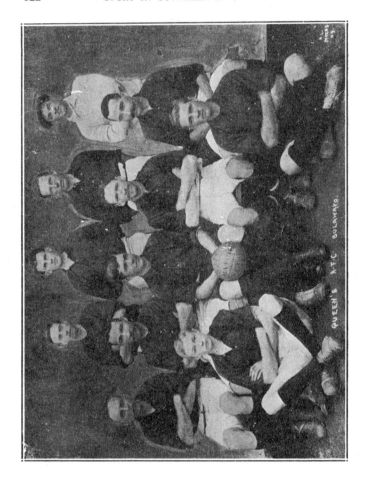

QUEEN'S SPORTS CLUB,
1909.

Top Row:
Jackson, Shipman, Stevenson,
M. O'Brien.

Middle Row:
S. Cartwright, G. M. Tait,
L. Bester, T. Wilson, A. T.
Tait.

Front Row:
C. Napier, E. Shipman.

THE SOUTHERN TRANSVAAL VISIT, 1933.

Results:

Versus Bulawayo at Bulawayo	Won	2 — 1
Versus Bulawayo at Bulawayo	Lost	2 — 5
Versus Gwelo at Gwelo	Won	6 — 0
Versus Que Que at Que Que	Won	2 — 1
Versus Mashonaland at Salisbury	Won	2 — 1
Versus Mashonaland at Salisbury	Lost	1 — 4

Bulawayo: B. Louth, H. L. St. Croix, R. Dunn, A. Genner (captain), H. Carroll, H. Arnott, R. J. Oliver, W. Wood, J. T. Bell, J. Bryson, J. A. French, R. P. Easterbrook, S. Rastall.

Mashonaland: A. L. Robinson, W. Nevett, C. Jamieson, A. Mylne, A. N. Evans, P. du Plessis, King, D. Fraser, C. Melville, A. R. Kerr, Mackenzie, L. Blake, E. J. Clarke.

Gwelo: Christie, H. T. Elkington, Malt, James, Baldwin, S. E. Stowe, S. Aronowitz, J. Cary, Robertson, J. Carpenter, A. Taylor.

Que Que: Smith, Seiler, H. Stewart, C. Campbell, C. Rau, Calder, M. Aronowitz, Faulds, D. Campbell, S. Aronowitz, White.

THE MOTHERWELL CLUB'S VISIT, 1934.

Results:—

Versus Matabeleland at Bulawayo	Won	3 — 0
Versus Mashonaland at Salisbury	Won	6 — 0

Motherwell: R. Ferrier (captain), W. McFadyen, A. McGlory, M. Crawley, J. Johnson, W. Telfer, B. Ellis, D. Ogilvie, W. Allen, G. Stevenson, J. Blair, J. McKenzie, J. McMenemy, H. Wales.

Matabeleland: A. L. Robinson, R .Dunn, H. L. St. Croix, H. Arnott (captain), A. Genner, R. du Plessis, J. A. French, A. G. Rastall, J. T. Bell, W. Wood, H. Collins. Referee: S. B. Adams.

Mashonaland: J. Saric, W. H. Nevett, C. I. Jamieson, T. G. Saric, J. Harvey (captain), C. R. Allin, E. J. Clarke, A. R. Kerr, H. Cornish, C. H. Ashort, A. N. Evans. Referee: J. R. Robertson.

THE COMBINED SERVICES TOUR, 1935.

Results:—

Versus Mashonaland at Salisbury	Won	9 — 0
Versus Matabeleland at Bulawayo	Won	5 — 1

Mashonaland: J. Saric, J. Carroll, A. Gledhill, O. Palmer, R. Hyde, P. du Plessis (captain), J. Wilson, D. Fraser, H. Cornish, A. N. Evans, J. McPhun.

Matabeleland: B. H. Louth, C. Botterill, R. Dunn (captain), C. A. Goodyear, M. S. Bambrough, J. Macpherson, F. Logie, C. S. Lineham, R. H. Hoare, A. Hyde, H. Collins.

Combined Services: T. G. Hurrell, M. Lally, W. C. Peart, S. Eastham, J. F. Hamlet, H. W. Hales, I. J. E. Scruton, R. Williams, T. Rochester, H. L. Coates (captain), R. Pearce, J. M. Warfield, L. H. Bird, D. E. A. Renouf. The three last named played in Bulawayo in place of Coates, Pearce and Hurrell.

Referee: A. E. Yeats and G. D. Ward.

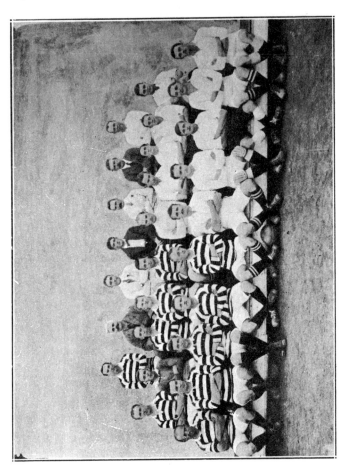

MATABELELAND FOOT-BALL ASSOCIATION.

(Bodle Cup.)

Matabeleland v. Mashonaland
Bulawayo, September, 1914.

Top Row:

E. H. Jenkinson, J. Ellman-Brown (Referee), A. R. W. Davis (Manager Mashonaland team), H. N. Gosse, Ben Wilson (Hon. Sec. M.F.A.), T. P. Gilbert (Referees' Assn.), P. J. le Cordeur.

Middle Row:

A. R. Cockerton, J. Mann, A. Carroll, H. Bowley, H. Cross, Jack Lea, R. McKillop, R. N. Reid, L. Ayres, C. Fraser (Que Que).

Bottom Row:

T. Tod Hunter, E. B. Goldsbury, L. Bester, S. G. Searle, O. R. Pearson (capt.), H. Fear (capt.), E. F. Harris, H. Grosch, H. S. Taylor (Que Que), H. Minter.

INTER-PROVINCIAL CAPTAINS.

Year.		Matabeleland.	Mashonaland.
1903	—	D. M. Lewis.	W. Ross.
1904	—	D. M. Lewis.	F. G. Brooks.
1905	—	S. Cartwright.	W. Smith.
1907	—	G. M. Tait.	H. Allen.
1908	—	G. M. Tait.	R. Kerr.
1909	—	J. H. Robison.	H. Allen.
1910	—	F. J. Wilkinson.	R. Kerr.
1912	—	H. Allen.	G. W. Ledeboer.
1913	—	H. A. Fear.	O. R. Pearson.
1920	—	G. Eckard.	H. G. Brown.
1921	—	J. W. Miller.	G. Gemmell.
1922	—	G. E. Fletcher.	S. Porter.
1924	—	T. P. Morgan.	E. B. Goldsworthy.
1926	—	D. J. Avery.	R. H. Jordan.
1927	—	G. E. Fletcher.	J. A. Q. Scrutton.
1928	—	T. P. Morgan.	N. Innes.
1929	—	J. Dewar.	S. H. Perkins.
1930	—	G. G. McKenzie.	D. M. Adams.
1931	—	A. L. Dewar.	V. Brown.
1932	—	M. S. Bambrough	A. N. Evans.
1933	—	H. Arnott.	A. N. Evans.
1934	—	H. Arnott.	C. R. Allin.
1935	—	R. Dunn.	A. N. Evans.

THE METCALFE CUP.

Year:	Winner:	Result:	Year:	Winner:	Result:
1903:	Bulawayo	1 — 0	1922:	Bulawayo	4 — 1
1904:	Bulawayo	3 — 1	1924:	Salisbury	2 — 0
1905:	Salisbury	5 — 2	1925:	Bulawayo	1 — 0
1906:	Drawn	1 — 1	1926:	Bulawayo	2 — 1
	Bulawayo	4 — 0	1927:	Salisbury	5 — 0
1907:	Bulawayo	5 — 1	1928:	Bulawayo	3 — 2
1908:	Bulawayo	2 — 0	1929:	Salisbury	5 — 2
1909:	Salisbury	3 — 0	1930:	Bulawayo	4 — 1
1910:	Drawn	1 — 1	1931:	Bulawayo	3 — 1
1912:	Salisbury	2 — 1	1932:	Salisbury	5 — 2
1914:	Drawn	2 — 2	1933:	Bulawayo	2 — 1
1920:	Salisbury	4 — 3	1934:	Bulawayo	3 — 1
1921:	Bulawayo	2 — 0	1935:	Salisbury	2 — 0

UMVUMA FOOTBALL
CLUB (Association).
Season 1920.

Trophies: Wilkins Cup, G. &
P. Shield, Holborn Cup.

Back Row:

G. Hinds, W. Mawdsley, J.
Mathieson, A. H. M. Hughes,
G. Devitt, A. Bailey (jnr.),
W. H. Rickards.

Front Row:

F. Mathieson, R. C. D.
Napier (Vice-Capt.), W. Wil-
son (President), E. A. Rains-
ford (Capt.), S. L. Fiander
(Hon. Sec.), S. Fulton, E.
Golding.

THE BODLE CUP.

Year:	Winner:	Result:	Year:	Winner:	Result:
1908:	Matabeleland ...	3 — 1	1927:	Mashonaland ...	6 — 2
1909:	Drawn	1 — 1	1928:	Drawn	3 — 3
1910:	Matabeleland ...	1 — 0	1929:	Matabeleland ...	1 — 0
1912:	Drawn	1 — 1	1930:	Matabeleland ...	2 — 0
1914:	Mashonaland ...	3 — 2	1931:	Matabeleland ...	5 — 2
1920:	Matabeleland ...	2 — 1	1932:	Matabeleland ...	3 — 1
1921:	Mashonaland ...	2 — 0	1933:	Mashonaland ...	3 — 1
1922:	Matabeleland ...	3 — 0	1934:	Mashonaland ...	5 — 3
1924:	Drawn	1 — 1	1935:	Matabeleland ...	2 — 0
1926:	Mashonaland ...	3 — 1			

THE AUSTEN CUP.

1924:	Bulawayo Callies.	1930:	Salisbury Alexandra.
1925:	Bulawayo Rovers.	1931:	Bulawayo Rovers.
1926:	Que Que.	1932:	Salisbury Alexandra.
1927:	Salisbury Alexandra.	1933:	Salisbury Alexandra.
1928:	Bulawayo Rovers.	1934:	Bulawayo Rovers.
1929:	Bulawayo Rovers.	1935:	Salisbury Postals.

THE BULAWAYO FIRST LEAGUE CUP.

Donated by the Local Association.

1898:	B.S.A.P.	1919:	Kings.
1899:	B.S.A.P.	1920:	Raylton.
1901:	Queens.	1921:	Queens.
1902:	B.S.A.P.	1922:	Rovers.
1903:	Queens.	1923:	Rovers.
1904:	Queens.	1924:	Rovers.
1905:	Raylton.	1925:	Rovers.
1906:	Raylton.	1926:	Rovers.
1907:	Queens.	1927:	Rovers.
1908:	Queens.	1928:	Rovers.
1909:	Callies.	1929:	Queens.
1910:	B.A.C.	1930:	Callies.
1911:	Raylton.	1931:	Rangers.
1912:	Raylton.	1932:	Rovers.
1913:	Raylton.	1933:	Rovers.
1914:	Raylton.	1934:	Rovers.

BULAWAYO & DISTRICT FOOTBALL ASSOCIATION

Winners Metcalfe Cup 3—1.
Winners Bodle Cup 5—2.
At Salisbury, 22 Aug., 1931.

Back Row:

J. N. Dick, S. Perkins, J. A. Winter, A. J. French, H. Macfarlane.

Middle Row:

J. Bell, B. Catella, S. G. Scott, R. P. Easterbrook, I. Sachs.

Bottom Row:

Ben Wilson (Manager), Les. Dewar (Capt.), D. Macintyre (President), M. S. Bambrough (Vice-Capt.), Major Trott (Trainer).

In the final of the Bodle Cup, 1931, after losing two players in the first few minutes of the game, and being two goals down at half-time, this team went on to win by 5 goals to 2.

THE CHARITY SHIELD.

This handsome trophy, costing about one hundred guineas, was purchased through the generosity of Bulawayo sportsmen. The Shield was handed to the football authorities with a condition that " gates " were to be donated to the Memorial Hospital. There were 24 seasons' play until the hospital became a Government institution and the " charity " competition thereupon became defunct.

1898:	B.S.A.P.	1910:	Callies and Queens.
1899:	B.S.A.P.	1911:	St. Georges School.
1900:	Queens.	1912:	Raylton.
1901:	Queens.	1913:	Raylton.
1902:	B.S.A.P.	1914:	Old Crocks.
1903:	B.A.C.	1919:	Raylton.
1904:	B.A.C.	1920:	Loco.
1905:	Raylton.	1921:	Queens.
1906:	B.A.C.	1922:	Rovers.
1907:	Queens.	1923:	Rovers.
1908:	Queens.	1924:	Rovers.
1909:	Callies.	1925:	Rovers.

THE CELTIC CHARITY CUP, Bulawayo.

This was presented by the Celtic Football Club, Glasgow through the good offices of the Rev. Fr. David Brand, S.J. Gate monies go into a fund to assist players injured at football.

1926:	Rangers.	1931:	Callies.
1927:	Rovers.	1932:	Queens.
1928:	Rovers.	1933:	Rovers.
1929:	Rangers.	1934:	Rovers.
1930:	Queens.		

THE SALISBURY FIRST LEAGUE CUP.

1898:	Police.	1919:	Alexandra.
1899:	Kopje.	1920:	Alexandra.
1900:	Umtali.	1921:	Alexandra.
1901:	Kopje.	1922:	Alexandra.
1902:	Umtali.	1923:	Callies.
1903:	Umtali and Salisbury.	1924:	Police.
1904:	Police.	1925:	Police.
1905:	Police.	1926:	Raylton.
1906:	Police.	1927:	Raylton.
1907:	Salisbury.	1928:	Alexandra.
1908:	Umtali.	1929:	Police.
1909:	Umtali.	1930:	Alexandra.
1910:	Alexandra.	1931:	Raylton.
1911:	Police.	1932:	Alexandra.
1912:	Police.	1933:	Postals.
1913:	Alexandra.	1934:	Terriers.

SALISBURY CHARITY CUP.

1930:	Alexandra.	1933:	Alexandra.
1931:	Raylton.	1934:	Raylton.
1932:	Terriers.		

BULAWAYO RAYLTON ROVERS.

Winners First League Championship and Celtic Charity Cup, 1933.

Back Row:

A. G. Rastall, S. Perkins, W. Clegg, H. van Blerk, W. Wood, G. R. Campbell, S. Dare.

Sitting:

E. R. Baldock, G. G. McKenzie, H. Arnott, H. Collins, F. H. Morgan.

Front Row:

W. Fulton, C. Goodyear.

TIM PERCY CHALLENGE CUP.

1932: Raylton.   1934: Alexandra.
1933: Alexandra.

SALISBURY KNOCK-OUT CUP.

1921: Raylton.	1928: Raylton.
1922: Raylton.	1929: Police.
1923: Police.	1930: Rovers.
1924: Avondale.	1931: Raylton.
1925: Police.	1932: Alexandra.
1926: Police.	1933: Alexandra.
1927: Police.	1934: Alexandra.

THE MacGILLIVRAY CUP.

The MacGillivray Cup was presented in 1932 by D. MacGillivray, Esq., and is played for on the knock-out principle, the proceeds from " gates " being set aside for the express purpose of fostering junior soccer.

| 1932: Queens. | 1934: Rovers. |
| 1933: Queens. | 1935: Callies. |

THE BEN WILSON CUP.
(For Second League Teams.)

1911: Raylton.	1927: Rovers.
1912: Raylton.	1928: Rovers.
1913: Raylton.	1929: Queens " A."
1920: King's	1930: Queens " A."
1921: King's.	1931: Lonely Mine.
1922: Raylton.	1932: Rovers.
1923: B.A.C.	1933: Postals.
1924: B.A.C.	1934: Queens " B."
1925: Rangers.	1935: Queens " B."
1926: St. George's School.	

THE OFFICERS' MESS CUP.
(For Second League Teams on the knock-out system.)

1922: Senior Cadets.	1929: B.S.A.P. and Queens " A."
1923: B.A.C.	1930: Queen's " A."
1924: Queens.	1931: Queens " A."
1925: Rovers.	1932: B.S.A.P.
1926: St. George's School.	1933: Postals.
1927: Queens.	1934: Bellevue.
1928: Rovers.	

RUGBY

T HE first game of football in Rhodesia was a rugby match which took place in the bed of the Shashi River. By some error the Pioneers got it into their heads that it was the Tuli River, and so called their camp Fort Tuli. The game was played on July 5, 1890. The date is fixed because it was on the next day that Troop "B" of the Pioneers started cutting the road to Mount Hampden, a day that is commemorated annually on the Rhodes and Founders holidays. The field selected for the game was a patch of heavy sand in the river bed. No one was hurt, for the game was very slow with the men toiling laboriously after each other through the sand—a very different tale from those told of the matches nowadays on the present hard grounds when every game has its toll of minor injuries.

When the column reached Fort Victoria two definite teams were formed, Police and Pioneers, both strong sides, and some good rugby resulted. Later in Salisbury, where Borrow and Spreckley encouraged the game further, more matches took place. The Pioneer Corps contained some very fine players and among their number were H. J. Borrow and J. Spreckley, of the Grahamstown Rovers, E. Burnett, Birkley, R. Adcock, A. Elliott, J. Grimmer and R. Coryndon, all of Kimberley, Darter, Halkett and L. Vintcent, of the Western Province, L. Cripps, Chase, C. B. Lovemore, of the Olympics, Port Elizabeth, W. H. Harbor, Puzey, of East London, and J. Mahon, of Dublin, the C.M.R., and the B.B.P. In the B.S.A. Company Police were H. M. Heyman, of the C.M.R., C. van der Byl, G. van der Byl and R. Morkel, of the Western Province, and I. FitzGerald and I. Brabant, of East London. Of the twenty-two named only seven are alive to-day. Captain H. J. Borrow and Sergeant W. H. Birkley were killed on the Shangani in 1893 and Ted Burnett in the '93 Rebellion.

Later rugby was played even more enthusiastically in Bulawayo where in 1894 the Colony's oldest Clubs, Queens and B.A.C., were formed. Right from the start there was a great number of good players in the town and the game had a fine send-off. For years Queens were overwhelmingly strong and their early stars included C. S. Gill, E. J. Lang,

QUEEN'S RUGBY TEAM, 1895.

Left to right:

Top Row:
W. BROWNLIE-WALKER,
M. B. JOBSON,
R. M. MACKENDRICK,
H. B. DOUSLIN,
J. N. NORMAND.

Middle Row:
C. SALMONSON,
W. A. PERRY,
M. J. FARQUHAR,
R. L. HULSE.

Bottom Row:
HIGGINBOTHAM,
J. A. SPRECKLEY,
W. E. BIDDULPH,
D. I. C. MONTGOMERIE,
J. HYDE,
P. H. ROSS.

T. B. Hepburn, the Springbok, whose son played for Matabeleland last year, Scott, of Blackheath, D. I. C. Montgomerie, W. A. Perry, whose two sons are prominent in local rugby, and W. G. Swanson. B.A.C. was much weaker than Queens but had some fine players in M. G. Linnell, the well-known cricketer, C. Brown, who afterwards played for South Africa, Clarkson Tredgold (now Sir Clarkson), an ex-Villagers forward who coached the S.A. College team when Colin Duff was captain, A. Hill, H. U. Moffat, later the Colony's Prime Minister, and Clinton. For a field B.A.C. used the old Ingubu Kraal as it was the only piece of level ground available. Later on, when this ground was required to be the site for the present railway station, Mr. Rhodes gave the club £500 towards levelling and improving the ground they now own. For the past twenty years Mr. George Johnson has been president of this, the oldest club in Rhodesia, and sportsmen in general owe much to his magnanimity. As the club's honorary secretary Mr. T. E. ("Tinker") Taylor has also been a hard worker for many years.

At the time when the new B.A.C. grounds were being prepared, the Matabeleland Mounted Police also had a strong team, with Magnus Spence, an old Bishops' three-quarter and one of the finest full-backs Western Province ever turned out, Giles, F. A. Hodson, W. S. Spain, W. Jackson, of Yorkshire, G. F. Scott, of Blackheath, D. M. MacBarnett and B. de V. Heatlie, brother of the famous Springbok captain. The first cup match was played on July 20, 1895, when Queen's beat M.M.P. by 9 points to 3.

There was not so much keenness in Salisbury as in Bulawayo, but with the formation of the Kopje and Causeway Clubs the game gradually commanded a larger following. These clubs were great rivals and their struggles were epic and sanguinary, especially on the Kopje ground, which was very hard and pebbly. Some of the early players of note were C. E. Duff, E. W. Graham, Hood, Peter de Stadler and G. N. Fleming, donor of the tennis trophies that bear his name.

The first record of rugger in the Midlands appears in June, 1899, when Gwelo paid a visit to Selukwe. The visitors were winning handsomely, despite the fact that the referee

CURRIE CUP, 1898.

Back Row: F. A. Hodson, H. B. Douslin, R. Mackendrick, E. S. W. Hutchinson, Giles, W. Jackson, B. E. Dugmore.

Middle Row: Mather, D. Davies, G. F. Scott, T. B. Hepburn (capt.), H. H. Forbes, B. de V. Heatlie, C. Brown.

Front Row: M. G. Linnell, L. Phillipson, C. Duff.

Missing: E. W. Graham, D. I. C. Montgomerie, D. W. Hook, W. S. Spain, G. N. Fleming, M. Spence.

was obviously against them, when suddenly the referee produced a pen-knife and, grabbing the ball, proceeded to cut it up, saying, "I'm damned if you fellows will win!" The game ended in pandemonium. Selukwe were captained by Ben Andrews, a Transvaal star, while other notables were J. Ferguson of Gwelo, J. M. Harris and H. R. Cumming.

Rugby was so keen in Bulawayo and Salisbury that in 1898 the two centres combined to send the first Rhodesian side to compete in Currie Cup rugger. The tournament was held at Cape Town and the cost of the tour was £800. The journey South by train lasted a week and the pace of the train may be judged by the fact that the team donned footer togs and, with a ball, ran round and ahead of the train for exercise. The journey was broken at Kimberley for a match against the Griquas, who won 13—8. The score was 8—0 in favour of the Griquas at half-time, but Duff and Hepburn combined to enable the latter to score a fine try. Ten minutes from time a pretty piece of passing right across the field saw Hepburn score behind the posts and when Scott converted the scores were level. Play became rough and fast. In the last few minutes the home team scored the winning points.

The first game at the Cape was against the Transvaal and Hepburn opened the scoring with an early try that Duff converted. The latter hit the upright with a place kick from half-way. Rhodesia led 5—0 at half time and then added three more points when Linnell, near the Transvaal line, dashed over on his own. Fine forward rushes characterised Rhodesia's play, but Larrard on the Transvaal scrum was always dangerous and eventually he scored and converted. Just before time a Transvaal forward went over to equalise and a great game ended in a draw. Against Eastern Province Rhodesia from the start carried the scrums with Duff doing great work at fly-half. Early on he initiated a fine move and Forbes scored. Later the Eastern forwards had the better of the game but their backs were unable to use it to advantage. Rhodesia had the better of the first half against Western Province, in which there was no score. In the second spell Krige scored the three tries by which the Province won. The Free State were beaten by 25 points to nil, Hepburn scoring three tries and Linnell two. Rhodesia finished third on the log and earned high praise for

1899 CURRIE CUP TEAM.

Standing: B. A. Helm, B. E. Dugmore, G. F. Scott, H. G. Morris, C. S. Gill (Manager), A. H. Newton, S. Arthur,
R. Mackendrick, F. Hopley.
Middle Row: H. B. Douslin, G. Fussel, C. E. Duff, T. B. Hepburn (Capt.), W. F. Alexander, T. S. Cloete, R.
Heard.
Front Row: A. L. Jones, P. C. Farquharson, M. G. Linnell, L. P. Ashburnham.

what has proved to be the Colony's most successful Currie Cup venture.

Rhodesian teams have crossed the boundary on four other occasions to play in the Cup series. Encouraged by the success of 1898, a side went to Kimberley the following season. The first match was remarkable. Rhodesia scored 9 points in the first ten minutes after which, through over-confidence, she lost her grip on the game and Eastern Province scored 11 points to win.

In the second match Duff kicked over four drop goals, Hepburn scored three tries which he converted and Border were beaten by 31 points to nil. The losers had a memorial card printed on which was represented a tombstone with the following inscription : " In memory of the Border Team who met their death August 24, 1899, at the hands of Roo-de-seer, aged 31 points." With due ceremony the card was presented to the winners. The incident serves to illustrate the friendliness that existed between all the competing teams. Rhodesia was unlucky against the Griquas. During the first half the Northerners had to play against a veritable hurricane. To show the severity of this, the canvas screening round the top of the iron palisading was ripped and blown away. After changing ends, the fortune of the weather was still with the Griquas as the wind dropped completely and the exhausted Rhodesians, especially the forwards, were unable to do themselves justice and the result was a draw. Owing to the growing friction between Briton and Boer only the four teams mentioned took part in this tournament.

The next entry, in 1906, was not a successful one. Rhodesia won only one match in seven and filled the bottom place on the log. Actually too many in the team were past their best and were unable to stand up to the rigours of the tour. Injuries took their toll and only four men, le Cordeur, van der Spuy, Blackwell and Keigwin, played in every match. Rhodesia's only victory was certainly a grand one. Griquas goaled first. Then Duff broke away and set off up-field accompanied by le Cordeur and Brooks. The latter took Duff's pass and transferred to le Cordeur who in turn reversed for Brooks to go over and score a grand try. Keigwin converted with a fine kick. The score was five all at half-time. Griquas scored with a drop-goal, but Rhodesia took the final lead when Brooks intercepted and beat his

CURRIE CUP TEAM, 1906.

Standing—
A. FORD.
H. T. ALMOND.
S. D. EVANS.
J. J. DOBSON.
H. COKER.
A. R. GILLETT.
J. McCORMACK.
E. R. S. TAYLOR.

Middle Row—
F. J. GATER.
P. J. le CORDEUR.
C. E. DUFF.
T. B. HEPBURN.
(Capt.)
H. A. CLOETE.
F. G. BROOKS.
H. S. KEIGWIN.

Front Row—
C. BLACKWELL.
W. van der SPUY.
H. C. THWAITES.
G. M. TAIT.
J. P. KENNEDY.

pursuers to the line for Keigwin to goal with another fine kick. In view of this victory the match with Western Province was looked forward to with interest but Rhodesia was badly beaten. Transvaal also inflicted a heavy defeat. Eastern Province and O.F.S. were much superior, too, but grim tackling kept the scoring low and for this McCormack at full-back deserves special mention. The games against Border and Natal were very even but Rhodesia played without any dash or spirit. After the tournament the Springbok team to tour Britain was chosen and Brooks just missed a place by failing in the then existing residential qualification of five years. However, he went to England on leave, where, playing for the South of England versus the North, he scored several tries. Then, picked for the Old Country, he scored the equalising try against the South Africans in a drawn match at the Crystal Palace. H. C. Milton, son of Sir William, was asked to play for England in this match but was unable to accept. Cecil Milton and Fred Brooks had played together for Bedford School, and later for Mashonaland in 1903 when Milton scored the winning try against Matabeleland on the Queens ground. Milton, a grand centre, was capped for England after playing in Rhodesia so that both he and his father were internationals.

Like that of 1906, the 1908 Currie Cup entry was not a successful one and Rhodesia won only one match in eight. There were some outstanding players: F. G. Brooks, Bradley, Devine, of the backs, with Coker, Ford, " Blinder " Evans, Hughes, Monk, and van der Spuy, of the forwards, but the general standard of the team's play was well below that of the other sides.

After the disastrous tour of 1908 Rhodesia in 1914 selected a strong side to play in the tournament at Durban, but it drew only one match in nine and lost eight. The Colony, however, did much better than would appear from her scalpless record and time and again the smallest slice of luck would have turned a match in her favour. But Fortune failed Rhodesia. There was an incredibly long list of players incapacitated through sickness or injury and the team had to call on G. Blackbeard, on holiday in Durban, to play in two matches. It was all very disappointing. Not once

1908 CURRIE CUP TEAM.

Two at Back: E. H. Clothier, G. E. Henderson.
Back Row: G. Hughes, A. Ford, S. D. Evans, H. D. Monk, H. A. Cloete, C. von P. Helm, K. M. Webb, J. C. Taylor, C. von Levetzow.
Middle Row: T. E. Wylde, V. Devine, A. J. Bradley, H. O. Coker, F. G. Brooks (Capt.), G. P. L. Matthews, W. T. B. Urquhart, L. A. N. Brooks, W. van der Spuy.
Front Row: P. E. Shone, C. Devitt, A. von Levetzow.

was the best fifteen fielded. However, there was some consolation in that several of the players distinguished themselves. Of the forwards, Hopley, Ferris, Morton and Bolus bore the brunt of the tournament while "Gappo" Thomas and "Togo" Moll showed to advantage in the games in which they played. L. Rabinson, youngest member of the side, played in every match and was called on to play fullback, centre, and half-back, all positions he filled with credit. Phil Rabinson was brilliant on attack and so at times was Ben. At half-back Wright and Eddie Green showed good form throughout.

In 1923 a Rhodesian team went South on tour. There was a great deal that mitigated against the possibility of the team doing itself justice. The protracted nature of the tour meant that many of the players were not available and Rhodesia fielded a side far from her best. A series of gruelling matches at short intervals, after tedious and restless train journeys; variations in the climatic conditions and the extremes of altitude between Johannesburg and the coast towns, and variations in the quality of grounds—turf, plough, gravel, etc. (it was necessary to have the team re-shod on three occasions)—were all factors that re-acted unfavourably. The tour, though strenuous and exhausting, was happy and helpful. Rhodesia's programme consisted of 7 representative matches in 18 days, played successively at Johannesburg, Potchefstroom, Kimberley, Bloemfontein, Maritzburg, Durban and Pretoria, and in all the team travelled 2,761 miles by train from Bulawayo and return.

Each of the seven games was lost, and only in one game, that against the Griquas, did Rhodesia look at all convincing. In the forward line Thomas proved himself a capable leader, while Salonika, Brown and Reynolds played some sterling games. Steele, Holland and Mitchell were effective halfbacks, with Gower and McIntyre the best of the outsides.

It is now twelve years since a Rhodesian team went South and it is a great pity such tours have not been more frequent. The Colony has, however, had a welcome number of teams from the South and overseas which have done much to stimulate the game here.

The first rugby side that visited the Colony was one picked from the New Zealand contingent during the Boer War. In 1900 this team came up and played Bulawayo.

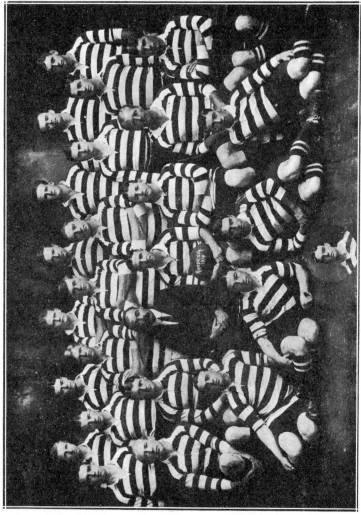

CURRIE CUP, 1914.

First Row—
R. A. GOWER.
A. F. B. CURRAN.
J. J. PHILIPS.
G. A. P. THOMAS.
P. H. BOLUS.
W. M. ATTWELL.
D. T. KOCK.

Second Row—
E. A. GREEN.
E. HARE.
E. W. EYLES.
W. H. BROOKS.
A. B. MORTON.
W. C. ROBERTSON.
J. C. ELSWORTH.

Third Row—
J. F. S. CURTIS.
H. T. MOLL.
T. B. HEPBURN
    (Manager).
S. ASHLEY (Capt.)
C. C. D. FERRIS
    (Vice-Capt.)
F. J. V. HOPLEY.
E. WRIGHT.

Fourth Row—
V. R. C. HOETS.
B. RABINSON.
P. RABINSON.
L. RABINSON

Inset—
E. H. BECK

The names of the visitors cannot be traced but Bulawayo was represented by G. M. Tait, E. J. Lang, B. A. Helm, T. B. Hepburn (capt.), A. C. L. Webb, L. P. Ashburnham, F. A. Hiscock, G. F. Scott, H. B. Douslin, P. Paley, P. Farquharson, B. E. Dugmore, W. A. Perry, J. M. Gibson and C. Swanson. Referee: R. Mackendrick. The New Zealanders, who won 10—3, gave their war-cry before and after the game. The local try was scored by Douslin after a fine run by Hepburn.

Four overseas teams have played here. The British team in 1910 was the first Home side ever to visit Rhodesia and one match was played in Bulawayo. Rhodesia drew first blood when, after less than five minutes' play, near the British line, Freddy Wunder (who afterwards, in an official capacity worked so hard in the interests of a game he loved) slipped through from an opening by Devitt and scored in a good position, le Cordeur converting. Then, in a brilliant movement that brought the crowd cheering to its feet, the ball travelled right along the three-quarter line to Horne who dived over in the corner. Just before half-time Devitt goaled from a penalty to make Rhodesia's score 11 points to Britain's 13. Thereafter the visitors were superior all round and they scored 11 more points before " no side." The Britishers played splendid rugger and the visit was a highly successful one.

The second overseas team was also a British one— Cove-Smith's side—which Rhodesia played in Salisbury. The Colony lost 3—16 but the defeat is one upon which Rhodesia can look with some pardonable pride, the more so that she drew first blood and at half-time held a three points lead, the result of a fine penalty by Coaton. The light Rhodesian forwards played up well and the tackling was excellent, especially that of Coaton. Coaton incidentally is the only Rhodesian who has played rugby for each of the four provinces, Matabeleland, Midlands, Mashonaland, Manicaland, and Rhodesia. The Rhodesian halves, Steele and Green, played well and Thomas was a tower of strength to his pack. It was in this match that the dummy was sold to the scrum!

The third overseas team came from New Zealand, in 1928, and the following account of the game is taken from *The Bulawayo Chronicle*:—

" The famous ' All Blacks ' attracted to Bulawayo the biggest crowd that has ever attended a rugby match in Rho-

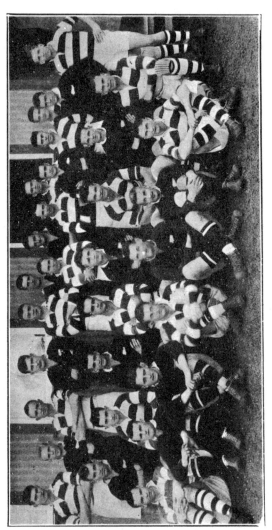

NEW ZEALAND v. RHODESIA, 1928.

Standing: D. Farquharson, W. Dalley, L. J. Hancock, G. T. Alley, H. P. Charles, I. Finlayson, V. Crowther, E. Snow, A. Gardiner, J. de L. Thompson, J. P. Swain, G. F. A. Aston, D. Lindsay, A. Robilliard, E. Meikle.

Middle row: J. Hore, W. A. Cunningham, G. Scrimshaw, G. J. Smith (capt.), M. Brownlie (capt.), L. Rae, F. W. Lucas, A. G. E. Speight.

Front row: A. McIntosh, A. C. Lilburne, C. Rushbrook, F. H. Yates, W. Hazlett, L. Johnson, J. W. Rackham.

desia. Three of the South African selectors were present, this being the first official visit of members of the S.A. Rugby Board to Rhodesia. The Rhodesians were completely non-plussed in the first half and their tackling was most ineffective, while the New Zealanders gave an exhilarating show of open football. The visitors led 31—0 at the interval. Rhodesia's inspiring rally in the second half made amends for their failure in the first half when their defence, with the exception of Thompson, the full-back, crumpled up under the pressure of the persistent thrusts launched from all angles of the field. In the second spell Rhodesia were admirably served by Crowther and Cunningham and effected some fine movements. For Rhodesia Thompson kicked a penalty goal and converted a try by McIntosh. The latter intercepted in the visitor's back-line, short-punted over the full-back and gathered again to score a good try. The scoring in the second half (13—8) was a good indication of the trend of the game. Rhodesia owed much to the sterling play of Thompson at full-back and Cunningham, the Irish international, who was sound at stand-off." The forwards, who won more scrums and line-outs than their opponents, played splendidly. Only in two other games were the All Blacks beaten in the line-out —in the Third Test and against Western Province. Smith was a good leader and was well supported by Farquharson, Aston and Rae. Hancock played a great loose game and time and again went across the field and tackled their three-quarters. Rhodesia nominated several players for the Spring-bok trials in this year but only J. W. Rackham went South, where he made a good impression.

The fourth overseas team was from Australia. The Wallabies played two matches against Rhodesia. The first was at Salisbury where the tourists won 24—5. They completely overwhelmed Rhodesia at the start, but as the game wore on the Rhodesians became more confident. Australia led 16—0 at half-time. In the second half the scoring was a fair index to the play and Rhodesia played splendidly. Her score was obtained by Cunningham and was the result of a very fine combined movement in which the wing and Crowther used the reverse pass. Robinson goaled. The best on the Rhodesian side were Robinson whose fielding was brilliant, Cunningham who ran well on the wing, Crowther at centre, Lardant whose defence round the scrum was splendid, and in the pack Louw and Cluff.

WALLABIES v. RHODESIA, AT BULAWAYO, 24th JUNE, 1933.

Top row: B. W. Love, M. A. Mackenzie, F. M. Royston, G. M. Cooke, M. Rest, M. Grace,

2nd row: G. V. Bland, H. P. Charles, O. L. Bridle, N. Morgan, R. B. Louden, R. L. Robinson, C. N. Campbell, S. H. Compton, J. B. Young, W. Cluff, G. Green.

3rd row: F. M. McPhillips, G. A. Cunningham, G. Sturtridge, E. Maytham, D. L. Cowper (capt.), P. K. Louw (capt.), M. F. Morton, A. P. Wheeler, W. H. Cerutti.

4th row: S. L. Wolffe, W. G. Bennett, M. Napier, P. Rabinson (referee), J. D. Crowther, M. C. White, J. J. Lardant.

At Bulawayo Rhodesia made a grand start and held the Australians for a full twenty minutes. Thereafter, however, the defence was nil and the visitors, scoring almost as they wished, won 33—0. The only time Rhodesia looked like getting over was when Cunningham dashed infield from the wing and punted up, but the bounce did not favour him. For the home side Lardant was outstanding, with Napier, Royston and Charles also prominent on occasions. The Wallabies played fine open football, unlike the orthodox rugby seen here, and much more spectacular.

Several teams from the Union have paid the Colony visits from time to time. In 1912 came the South African College team. The students won all their matches fairly easily, but the tour was of great educational value. It revealed that there were many fine players in the country and Ben and Phil Rabinson, F. J. V. Hopley, A. C. ("Sport") Hoare, and T. Louw were invited to Newlands for the South African trials. The Rabinsons were outstanding among the three-quarters and their omission from the Springbok team was a mystery to all who saw them play. In the first trial Phil scored two tries and Ben one. In the second Ben scored twice and Phil once, while in the final try-out each scored two tries!

In 1922 the second Southern side to play here was composed of a strong combination from the Western Province Country Clubs. They met several centres and finished the tour with a match against Rhodesia. The game was a very even one, but in the last few minutes the visitors got the advantage forward and registered the only score. Peiser pleased with his play; Scully played a great game at half and was well supported by Huddy; du Plessis was sound, and the pick of the forwards were Thomas, Carmichael and Salonika. This side gave Rhodesian post-war rugby a fine fillip.

Continuing with its progressive policy the Rhodesia Rugby Union in 1925 invited up the Transvaal University College whose combined forward play particularly was an object lesson.

Three seasons later, just before the New Zealand match, came the Witwatersrand University who treated us to some fine football.

RHODESIA v. W.P.
COUNTRY CLUBS,
1922.

Standing—
  J. BARRETT.
  I. H. SALONIKA.
  R. J. LUCAS.
  C. C. D. FERRIS.
  W. E. THOMAS
    (Capt.)
  K. CARSTENS.
  I. MacGILLIVRAY.
  R. A. GOWER.
  P. PEISER.

Sitting—
  E. J. BUSHELL.
  D. V. SCULLY.
  J. V. KERR.
  D. HUDDY.
  F. J. du PLESSIS.
  J. CARMICHAEL.

In 1930 Griqualand West, the first South African provincial side to come here, was beaten both in Salisbury and Bulawayo. As a result of their form against the Griquas, J. D. Crowther and G. A. Cunningham went to Newlands in 1931 for the trials prior to the selection of the Springbok team to tour Britain. Cunningham especially did well and in 1932 he was chosen for the Junior Springbok team that went to the Argentine where he earned a big reputation.

In 1934 the next Southern team, S.A.C.S., now known as the University of Cape Town, paid Rhodesia their second visit after 22 years and taught some valuable lessons, particularly demonstrating that the pace at which the game was being played here was much too slow.

In 1935, Mr. L. Rabinson, the well-known Rhodesian player, now a first-class referee on the Rand, brought up a Transvaal team which played several matches in the Colony. Their fine open rugby was a great attraction and the tour did an immense amount of good for the game here.

Although Rhodesian rugby was practically dormant during the Great War, many Rhodesians took a prominent part in matches organised by various regiments at Home and at the various fronts. A team, representative of the South Africans and Rhodesians at Inkerman Barracks, Woking, was frequently engaged in matches in London and country towns. Among other teams met was a representative New Zealand Army side. In the team the following Rhodesians played regularly, whilst in training at Woking, D. T. Koch, E. J. Hacking, C. van Blerk, M. A. Graham and J. C. Elsworth.

In 1918, the English R.F.U. invited the New Zealanders and South Africans to select representative Army teams to meet each other in a Mobbs Memorial Match at Northampton. (E. R. Mobbs was a prominent English player killed in the War.) The South African side was captained by "Billy" Millar (W. A. Millar, the 1912 Springbok captain), and the following Rhodesians played: M. A. Graham, C. van Blerk and J. C. Elsworth. The All Blacks won 14—9. This team later toured Wales where four matches were played.

J. C. Elsworth captained the Air Force team at Oxford and the following Rhodesians played in inter-area matches: Eric Eyles and Balfour Carnegie.

THE RHODESIAN RUGBY TOURING TEAM, 1923.

Standing—
P. PEISER.
H. LING.
R. W. BROWN.
J. LEWIS.
L. HANCOCK.
T. C. RICKETTS.
J. HARDMAN.
R. A. GOWER.

Middle Row—
E. J. BUSHELL.
E. WHITE.
R. DAVIES.
A. L. REYNOLDS.
F. H. HOLLAND.
C. H. STEELE.
V. MORKEL.
C. W. G. McINTYRE.
J. KIRSTEIN.
J. CARMICHAEL.

Front Row—
W. H. STEAD.
J. R. MITCHELL.
W. E. THOMAS
(Capt.)
T. M. FAIRLAMB
(Manager).
I. H. SALONIKA.
J. C. COATON.
S. LONGDEN.

In France the 2nd Rhodesian Platoon of the 2nd K.R.R. played the rest of the battalion just behind the front-line at Lillers, in December, 1915, and won an historic game by a small margin.   Ben Munro captained this team and amongst those remembered were the Greenfield Brothers, J. D. D. Dick, H. B. Dawson and MacMillan.

Again, on the eve of the second battle of Ypres, the First Rhodesian Platoon of the K.R.R. played the rest of the battalion in a shell-pocked field at Poperinghe.   The Rhodesian wing scored a disputed try in a shell hole from which he was extricated with much difficulty.   At half-time, however their opponents insisted on switching over to soccer, as the Rhodesians were too good for them.

On another occasion at Lillers, the 2nd Rhodesian Platoon, assisted by C. N. Lowe, the English international, met a French Army team which included four French international players.   This game resulted in a win for the Rhodesians by over 30 points to nil.

At the beginning of 1915, during the South-West African campaign, an inter-regimental competition was played at Walvis Bay.   This was won by the 1st Rhodesians, who never lost a match against such teams as the Imperial Light Horse, Rand Rifles and South African Irish, whose teams included several Springboks.   Among the Rhodesians were Tommy Thomas, full-back, D. du Toit, Ben Rabinson, Tom Bourdillon, "Curly" Wright, G. Blackbeard, Erikson, G. A. P. Thomas, C. Ferris, D. Philip, Major Methuen, J. J. Phillips and Reg. Hart, who also did some refereeing.

It should be added that the above episodes are not recorded from official documents but obtained from actual eye-witnesses and participants in these games.

Sir Donald Currie, the late head of the Castle Mail Packets Company, presented valuable floating trophies to the Cricket, Rugby and Association Football sections of South African sport and the annual tournaments are important national events.   Southern Rhodesia has sent five teams to compete in the South African Rugby Board's inter-provincial tournaments for the Currie Cup.   These Rhodesian teams all went South before the Great War, but since the War only one team has left the Colony on tour.   That was in 1923.

RAYLTON CLUB, 1928.

(Winners, McGregor Shield, Globe and Phoenix Shield, and First League Cup.)

Back row: J. G. Lewis, L. Rae, T. P. B. Gilbert, P. Siebert, J. Waddington, C. H. Frielick, D. Murray.

Middle row: D. M. Ross, G. A. Cunningham, J. A. P. Evans, N. M. Moolman, E. R. M. Manning, W. F. Bromehead, J. Birnie, T. H. Dyke, J. L. Veale.

Front row: F. St. J. Bromehead (Coach), J. W. Rackham, Capt. H. Allen (Chairman) J. de L. Thompson (Captain), R. W. Brown, J. B. Gilbert (Hon. Secretary), J. D. Crowther.

It is a great pity that more Rhodesian teams have not been sent outside the Colony's borders because such excursions can be of great benefit to the players and to the game and because from time to time Rhodesia has been in a position to field a really strong XV that would have done very well in the Union. The various teams that have visited the Colony since the War have done a great deal of good, but it is thought more benefit would be derived by sending Rhodesian sides away occasionally. It is with no thought of substitution that one is prompted to state that a tour down South lasting about three weeks is cheaper by far than having a side visit this Colony.

Rugby has its lean and its good years, and the teams that have come here have not always struck Rhodesia's best years. The Rhodesian teams picked against the visitors have been very carefully selected but as only fifteen men go to make up a team it is only natural that on each occasion there have been a few players who just failed to find a place in the best XV.

Having already dealt with the representative matches, it is now my intention to mention some of the more prominent of the post-war players who have not played for Rhodesia because of non-selection or because no Rhodesian team was picked in their day.

The Colony's rugby talent is revealed in the annual inter-provincial and inter-town matches. Each of the four provinces and each town, competes in its respective competition, which is on the knock-out principle, so that the finals provide not only excellent rugby but a sure index to the standard of the game in the country.

The first of the series after the war was in 1920, and from then to 1922, when a Rhodesian team met the combined Western Province Country Clubs, there were some fine footballers in Tommy Lewis, a safe full-back, J. L. Veale, a nippy half-back, A. N. Cranswick, who could fill most positions behind the pack, E. Grewers, scrum-half, H. Hefer and C. MacLaren, two fine forwards, useful three-quarters in S. A. Cowper and J. W. Leach, a dashing centre in V. Eriksen, B. J. Carnegie, a fearless wing, who is now Secretary to the Rhodesia Rugby Union, a great hooker in A. H. Knoesen, who later took to coaching, Bert Greenfield, a tip-

Lieut.-Col. A. C. L. Webb, V.D.,
President of the Rhodesia Rugby
Football Union.

Lieut.-Col. Sir Melville Heyman,
A Pioneer of Rhodesia and
Rhodesian Rugby.

A. C. Burgess.

J. M. Fox.

top forward, and another of his ilk from the Midlands in R. Biffen, more good forwards in H. N. Titterton, S. M. Stringfield and A. C. Wienand, who played in the Matabeleland pack when at Milton School.

Among the candidates for the Rhodesian team that met Cove-Smith's side in 1924 were A. M. Tillie, a splendid full-back; D. J. Avery, who played soccer for Rhodesia; the popular A. C. Amyot, a great rugger enthusiast; T. H. Dyke, a fine forward; three good three-quarters from Mashonaland in P. J. Power, 'L. Kirschner and H. Lovemore; R. L. Strobel, full-back; and two excellent forwards in H. Steyn and J. Betts.

There was no Rhodesian team in the seasons 1925, 1926 and 1927, but there flourished in that period many who made a name for themselves on the Colony's rugger fields. First there was A. C. Burgess, in the writer's opinion the best wing three-quarter Rhodesia has produced in the last decade. In 1926 J. M. Fox came to the fore and in 1935 this versatile full-back was still one of the Colony's leading players. He has a splendid record. D. Newman was another fine full-back, and in 1926 P. G. Morkel, the famous Springbok full-back, played for Mashonaland. His equally famous brother, " Boy " Morkel, spent several seasons in Bulawayo, where he gave his services as a referee and a selector.

Forwards of note in 1926 were C. P. Laurens, L. -H. Playford, F. Olver, the huge S. C. ("Bull") Geyle, and that splendid scrummager, Andy Hogg, of Shabani. Among the backs were E. J. Gordon and N. M. Hathaway, a useful pair of halves; B. B. Napier, who has done good work on the administrative side; L. Huddy, scrum-half; and two fine centres in D. Meikle and A. L. Fielding.

There was a host of players from 1927 to make more difficult the task of the selectors who were to pick a side to meet the All Blacks in 1928. T. M. Davies was a useful full-back; E. A. Barbour, E. H. Driver, A. J. Liebenberg and W. Myburgh, a quartette of good half-backs; J. Livingston, J. R. Franks, D. M. Ross and G. D. Smith, useful three-quarters, and splendid forwards in K. T. Widdicombe-Smith, K. O. Goldhawk, P. Siebert, C. F. Watterworth, J. H. van Niekerk, B. D. B. Thomas, H. Widdows and J. Ward.

MIDLANDS RUGBY TEAM, 1932.

Reading from left to right.

Back row:

C. PHILLIPS,
A. THWAITES,
E. T. LINES,
C. F. PARKER,
T. WATSON,
S. MORRIS.
P. DU PLESSIS.

Centre Row:

S. HATFIELD,
D. McFARLANE,
J. S. VAN RENSBURG,
L. R. TARR,
W. H. LEONARD
        (Captain),
C. R. VAN LENNEP,
P. J. EDMEADES,
        (Manager.)

Front Row:

D. M. KIRSTEIN,
A. F. HOLMES,
E. M. KENNY,
A. W. ROSE.

From 1929 to 1932 there was another long period without a Rhodesian XV, but during that time there was a wealth of talent in the various provinces. Prominent among the forwards was that fine leader, W. H. Leonard; A. Matthews, the Matabeleland captain; L. Mitchell, N. H. B. Longhurst, B. Joelson, W. C. Douglas, A. S. Fulton, C. H. Frielich, J. L. Gazet, J. A. du Plessis, A. Thwaites, A. F. Holmes, S. Morris, C. F. Parker, N. Wood and C. J. Birnie. Of the three-quarters, S. Hatfield, I. S. Evans, W. F. S. Belton, C. R. ("Pom") van Lennep, H. van der Linden, and J. B. Johnstone were the pick, while D. M. Kirstein, C. J. Fleming and F. Phillips were splendid half-backs from the Midlands.

In recent seasons there have been some excellent forwards in H. Fox, a first-class hooker, R. A. G. Stupart, D. L. Burke, R. E. Walker, V. H. Abrams, A. Garside, W. Bamberger, L. E. May, and I. P. Potgieter; a fine scrum-half in L. Gruber, and other useful backs in E. M. Kenny, A. W. Rose, B. W. Bland, L. J. Coley, full-back; P. J. van Blerk, scrum-half; B. van der Kooi, S. Lemmer, J. H. Charsley, L. Taylor, D. Baker and W. E. C. Atherstone.

As in most other things, there has always been keen rivalry between Bulawayo and Salisbury in regard to rugby. These centres first met in 1901, the Matabeleland fifteen travelling to the Capital by mule-coach, driven most of the way by that great old sportsman, Balfour Helm. In 1909, Advocate William Russell presented a cup for these inter-provincial contests. Up to 1912 the winner was decided on one match, but thereafter two matches were played annually until 1924, the aggregate of points deciding the winner. In 1925 one of the inter-province matches became inter-town, for which Lord Woolavington gave the "Black and White" Cup as a floating trophy. An exceptionally high standard of rugby is seen in these games each season.

An important competition is that for the shield presented by the Globe & Phoenix Gold Mining Company. This is open to all clubs in Rhodesia, a condition being that the semi-finals and final must be played in Que Que. Another valuable trophy was presented by G. V. van der Byl (who in his day was a splendid rugger player and represented Rhodesia) for inter-province school rugby football competition. The conditions have been altered to allow juniors, whether attending school or not, to play. "Juniors" must be under nineteen

MASHONALAND,
1901.

Standing—
    P. GUBB.
    B. de V. HEATLIE.
    W. HUGO.
    C. BENNETT.
    R. H. WOOD.
    D. W. HOOK.

Middle Row—
    G. VAN DER BYL.
    J. B. GILBERT.
    F. R. MYBURGH.
    A. E. FITZGERALD
        (Capt.)
    T. P. GILBERT.
    W. S. LANGER-
        MAN.

Front—
    H. N. WATTERS.
    R. MOORCROFT.
    W. S. TABERER.

years of age on the 1st of April of the year in which the competition is played. The shield was presented in 1914, after the first official match had been played in 1913. The van der Byl Shield is the most handsome trophy in the possession of the Rhodesia Rugby Union. At the top of the shield are two inscriptions: "Discrimine salus" and "Festina lente." At the bottom are the words, "Unity is strength and the Goal for those who strive the hardest." Of all the sporting trophies in existence to-day, the oldest is the Bulawayo First League Cup, which dates back to 1895. In that year and for many seasons after, Queen's Club were far too good for the B.A.C. and Police teams. Later on B.A.C. and King's often beat Queen's; then Raylton revived and sprang to the fore, and in 1934 the virile Old Miltonians' Club carried all before it. A trophy remembered by the older players is the shield donated by the Board of the Memorial Hospital. Proceeds from matches were given to the Hospital, but when this became a Government institution the competition was abandoned.

Mr. Frank McGregor's fine shield replaced the Hospital Charity Shield, the only difference in the conditions of competition being that the proceeds from McGregor Shield matches are placed in the McGregor Fund from which, as occasion arises, injured rugger players, at the Rugby Board's discretion, may receive financial assistance. Many are the deserving cases that have received timely aid from this fund. The trophy is played for on the knock-out principle.

The principal trophy in Salisbury is the cup given by H. Edwards for the Senior League competition. In 1912 the Deputy Mayor, Councillor James Lawson, presented a shield, also for senior competition, on which is inscribed: "For the Love of God is broader than the measure of man's mind, and the heart of the Eternal is most wonderfully kind." For the juniors, a Greek enthusiast gave the present Demos Cup. An interesting annual fixture is that between Mashonaland and Nyasaland for the Rodwell Cup, presented by the late Governor of Southern Rhodesia, who was a keen follower of rugby. For this game, which is played alternately in each centre, a motor car journey of 800 miles, there and back, is involved. The principal Salisbury clubs are: Salisbury, Alexandra, B.S.A. Police and Old Hararians. The last name is derived from A'Rari Kop, the native name of

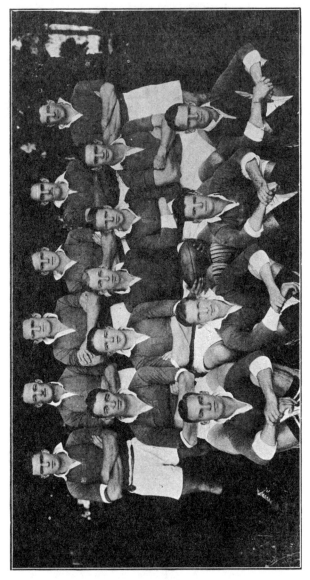

MASHONALAND RUGBY TEAM, 1933.

Back row: Arthur, Elley, Joelson, Gafney, Addecott, Robinson. Centre row: Cluff, Morgan, Wood (Captain), Belton, Scott. Front row: Bloom, Gould, Lardant, Cornell.

the kopje overlooking Salisbury, on which the Pioneer Column planted the Union Jack in October, 1890.

In Manicaland, rugby has been played since the earliest days, but the game has suffered from the isolation of this centre and the difficulty in obtaining variety of opposition. In Umtali there are three clubs, Territorials, Umtali Town and Old Borderers, though for some years there were many more clubs, such as Railways, Umtali School Old Boys, Penhalonga, Melsetter, Chipinga, Rusape and also Inyazura, until the Romsley Tobacco Company closed down. As the population increases, so will the game grow, because there is no lack of enthusiasm in Manicaland. An annual fixture is with Beira for the Lawley Cup, which must be played for in Beira. Manicaland have won it on most occasions. A big step in the development of the game is the establishment of· a turf ground in Umtali, which is expected to be ready in 1936.

The province in which rugby has made the biggest strides in recent years is the Midlands, and this despite the fact that each club is separated from its neighbours by many miles. Reference to a map would best convey the difficulties of the Midlands sportsmen. Gwelo is the district's headquarters, with Selukwe just 23 miles away. South of Gwelo, 72 miles away, is Shabani, while south-east of Gwelo is Fort Victoria, 114 miles distant, Shabani being 67 miles from Fort Victoria. Que Que is 40 miles north of Gwelo, with Eiffel Flats 50 miles beyond Que Que. As the roads between the northern and southern clubs pass through Gwelo, and as various competitions are played on the "home" and "away" principle, a Fort Victoria—Eiffel Flats match involves a journey of 408 miles, there and back! There are several competitions, each of which is keenly contested, so it is small wonder Midlands' enthusiasm is a household word in rugger circles.

The Rhodesia Rugby Football Union, which is affiliated to the S.A.R.F. Board, was formed in 1895, and to-day it controls the game throughout the Colony. Each of the four provincial boards nominates two delegates to the Union, and the different clubs affiliate to their respective boards. The game has been fortunate in its servers on the Union. Sir William Milton was president for fourteen years, during

SHABANI, 1932.

Reading from left to
right.

Back row:
E. DE KOCK,
W. MAXWELL,
N. CARPENTER.

Centre Row:
L. W. HANSON,
D. HOBKIRK,
S. HATFIELD,
S. MORRIS,
W. H. LEONARD,
K. N. BOARDMAN.

Front Row:
F. W. SIMMONDS,
F. N. VAN RYNEVELD,
C. J. C. FLEMING,
Dr. A. J. IRELAND,
A. HOGG,
C. R. VAN LENNEP,
E. LAMOND.

which time he gave the game every encouragement. No record would be complete without mention of W. G. Swanson. "Daddy," as he was affectionately known to all sportsmen, was a useful half-back in his day, and during twenty years as Chairman of the Union his enthusiasm was unabated. He was a great Queen's Club supporter. Lieut.-Col. A. C. L. ("Sonny") Webb has been Chairman of the governing body for ten years, a position he has filled with dignity and efficiency. A really splendid all-round sportsman in his day, he has, on the administrative side, rendered, not only to rugby, but to all sport, service in its highest degree. The affairs of the game have seldom been in such capable hands as when Lynden Webber was honorary secretary. His high standard was maintained by Noel Cranswick, who was subsequently president of the Matabeleland Board for many years. "Spratt" was a fine footballer and cricketer, and captained Bulawayo teams at both games. Among others deserving of the thanks of those who follow the game are the honorary treasurers, C. Davis and T. M. Fairlamb, the latter an ex-Matabeleland player, A. C. Amyot and F. Howe-Ely. On the S.A.R.F. Board, Rhodesia has been ably represented by H. A. Solomon who, during the years he spent in Rhodesia, played centre-three-quarter for Matabeleland against Mashonaland from 1903 to 1905.

Of the four provincial boards, the strongest, financially, is Matabeleland, and there is a long list of enthusiasts who guided the Board to its present sound position. Among these are F. McGregor, R. H. Hart, Chairman of the Referees' Society, B. N. Eckard, an ex-Hamilton, F. St. J. Bromehead, an ex-Villager, and Dr. G. R. Ross, the present Chairman. In Mashonaland there are few who have done as much for the game as Mr. Justice J. P. F. Watermeyer, C. E. Duff, P. H. Gifford, F. E. J. Rosselli, and that indefatigable worker in the interests of both rugger and cricket, Capt. A. H. Bowker. Great Midlands enthusiasts are Dr. A. J. Ireland of Shabani, E. Mannix, H. A. Cripwell and L. R. Tarr, while in Umtali the young Manicaland Board, after being given a good start by B. L. King, President, and D. M. Livingston, Chairman, is now in the safe hands of A. F. Ternouth, with A. H. van Coller as secretary.

MATABELELAND RUGBY FOOTBALL BOARD, 1933.

Reading from left to
right.

Back row:
E. SCOT-RUSSELL,
A. D. CAMPBELL,
R. W. BARBOUR,
F. BROMEHEAD,
B. W. BLAND.

Centre Row:
B. J. CARNEGIE
(Hon. Sec.),
J. L. VEALE,
T. M. DAVIES,
J. de L. THOMPSON,
H. JARVIS,
P. K. LOUW.

Front Row:
Col. J. B. BRADY, D.S.O.,
M.P.
R. H. HART,
Dr. G. R. ROSS
(Chairman),
F. McGREGOR,
A. N. CRANSWICK.

The Hon. H. U. Moffat, C.M.G.   T. M. Fairlamb.

A. N. Cranswick.   Dr. G. R. Ross.

THE CURRIE CUP TOURNAMENT.

1898 (CAPE TOWN).

Rhodesia: T. B. Hepburn (Captain), W. Jackson, H. Forbes, C. E. Duff, E. W. Graham, M. G. Linnell, D. I. C. Montgomerie, G. F. Scott, D. W. Hook, B. E. Dugmore, B. de V. Heatlie, W. S. Spain, Mather, D. Davis, C. Brown, G. N. Fleming, M. Spence, L. Phillipson, H. B. Douslin, R. Mackendrick, F. A. Hodson, M. Giles. Manager, E. St. M. Hutchinson.

Opponents.		Results.	
Griqualand West	(lost)	13 —	8

Hepburn, 2 tries; Scott, 1 conversion.

| Transvaal | (drew) | 8 — | 8 |

Hepburn, 1 try converted by Duff; Linnell, 1 try.

| Eastern Province | (won) | 3 — | 0 |

Forbes, 1 try.

| Western Province | (lost) | 11 — | 0 |
| Orange Free State | (won) | 25 — | 0 |

Hepburn, 1 goal 2 tries; Linnell, 2 tries; Forbes, 1 try; Duff, 1 penalty goal; Scott, 1 conversion.

1899 (KIMBERLEY).

Rhodesia: T. B. Hepburn (Captain), C. E. Duff, G. Fussell, A. L. Jones, M. G. Linnell, R. Heard, H. B. Douslin, B. E. Dugmore, B. A. Helm, W. F. Alexander, A. H. Newton, L. P. Ashburnham, F. Hopley, P. C. Farquharson, G. Hepburn, S. Arthur, R. Mackendrick, T. S. Cloete, G. D. O'Leary, H. G. Morris, G. F. Scott. Manager, C. S. Gill.

Opponents.		Results.	
Eastern Province	(lost)	11 —	9

Hepburn, 1 goal; Duff, 1 drop-goal in play.

| Border | (won) | 31 — | 0 |

Hepburn, 3 goals; Duff, 4 drop-goals in play.

| Griqualand West | (drew) | 0 — | 0 |

1906 (JOHANNESBURG).

Rhodesia: T. B. Hepburn (Captain), J. V. McCormack, F. G. Brooks, P. J. le Cordeur, G. M. Tait, F. W. Taylor, C. E. Duff, J. P. Kennedy, C. Blackwell, H. C. Thwaits, H. S. Keigwin, F. J. Gater, W. van der Spuy, H. T. Almond, A. R. Gillett, H. A. Cloete, H. O. Coker, A. Ford, J. J. Dobson, S. D. Evans, G. van der Byl.

Opponents.		Results.	
Griqualand West	(won)	10 —	9

Brooks, 2 tries, converted by Keigwin.

Western Province	(lost)	35 —	0
Eastern Province	(lost)	8 —	0
Orange Free State	(lost)	19 —	6

Taylor, 1 try; Coker, 1 try.

| Transvaal | (lost) | 33 — | 0 |
| Border | (lost) | 15 — | 14 |

Brooks, 2 tries; Duff, 2 penalty goals; Almond, 1 conversion.

| Natal | (lost) | 12 — | 7 |

Gillett, 1 drop-goal in play; Keigwin, 1 penalty goal.

1908 (PORT ELIZABETH).

Rhodesia: F. G. Brooks (Captain), G. P. L. Matthews, W. T. Urquhart, L. A. N. Brooks, V. Devine, A. J. Bradley, H. T. Shone, C. Devitt, C. von Levitzow, A. von Levitzow, H. O. Coker, C. von T. Helm, A. Ford, T. E. Wylde, K. M. Webb, H. D. Monk, G. Hughes, S. D. Evans, W. van der Spuy, J. C. Taylor, E. H. Clothier, G. E. Henderson. Manager, H. A. Cloete.

Opponents.		Results.
Natal	(lost)	19 — 0
North-Easterns	(won)	6 — 5

F. G. Brooks, 1 try; Urquhart, 1 penalty goal.

Orange River Colony	(lost)	13 — 0
Eastern Province	(lost)	25 — 0
Western Province	(lost)	48 — 0
Borner	(lost)	34 — 0
Transvaal	(lost)	12 — 5

Bradley, 1 try, coverted by Urquhart.

Griqualand West	(lost)	11 — 9

Bradley, 1 try, converted by Urquhart; Devine, 1 drop-goal in play.

1914 (DURBAN).

Rhodesia: S. Ashley (Captain), L. Rabinson, W. C. Robertson, B. Rabinson, P. Rabinson, R. A. Gower, E. A. Green, A. B. Morton, F. J. V. Hopley, P. A. Bolus, C. D. Ferris, W. H. Brooks, J. J. Phillips, W. M. Attwell, D. T. Koch, G. A. P. Thomas, A. F. B. Curran, V. R. C. Hoets, J. F. S. Curtis, E. E. Wright, E. Hare, E. W. Eyles, H. T. Moll, J. C. Elsworth, E. H. Beck, G. Blackbeard. Manager, T. B. Hepburn.

Opponents.		Results.
Orange Free State	(lost)	13 — 5

B. Rabinson, 1 try, converted by Koch.

Griqualand West	(lost)	8 — 3

L. Rabinson, 1 penalty goal.

Natal	(lost)	13 — 3

B. Rabinson, 1 try.

Border	(drew)	13 — 13

Moll, 2 tries; P. Rabinson, 1 try; L. Rabinson, 2 conversions.

South-Westerns	(lost)	5 — 0
Eastern Province	(lost)	6 — 0
Western Province	(lost)	45 — 0
Transvaal	(lost)	33 — 6

P. Rabinson, 1 try; L. Rabinson, 1 penalty goal.

North-Easterns	(lost)	13 — 5

P. Rabinson, 1 try, converted by L. Rabinson.

F

THE 1923 TOUR

Rhodesia: W. E. Thomas (Captain), R. A. Gower, J. C. Coaton, A. McIntyre, J. Hardman, S. J. D. Longden, P. G. Peiser, J. A. G. Kirstein, T. C. Ricketts, C. H. Steele, F. Holland, A. H. Ling, J. R. Mitchell, L. R. Bentley, V. Morkel, I. H. Salonika, E. J. Bushell, E. W. White, J. G. Lewis, L. J. Hancock, W. H. Stead, J. Carmichael, A. L. Reynolds, R. W. Brown, R. G. Davies. Manager, T. M. Fairlamb.

Opponents.		Results.
Transvaal	(lost)	22 — 5
Peiser, 1 try, converted by Ling.		
Western Transvaal	(lost)	19 — 5
Longden, 1 try, converted by Ling.		
Griqualand West	(lost)	5 — 0
Orange Free State	(lost)	12 — 3
Mitchell, 1 try.		
Natal	(lost)	19 — 3
Peiser, 1 try.		
Natal	(lost)	36 — 7
Coaton, 1 drop-goal in play; Gower, 1 try.		
Transvaal	(lost)	30 — 5
Gower, 1 try, converted by Coaton.		

TWO MASHONALAND REPRESENTATIVES.

J. C. Elsworth.   The Hon. V. A. Lewis, M.C., K.C., Minister of Justice and Internal Affairs.

BRITAIN v.
RHODESIA, 1910.

Standing—

T. E. WYLDE.
F. B. BROOKS.
W. E. THOMAS.
W. L. JENKINS.
A. B. POCKLING-
TON.

G. A. P. THOMAS.
A. J. BRADLEY.
VAN NIEKERK.
F. W. WUNDER.

Sitting—

C. DEVITT.
BEN RABINSON.
C. HORNE.
H. O. COKER
(Capt.)
SIR Wm. MILTON.
A. C. HOARE.
P. J. le CORDEUR.
J. C. TAYLOR.
W. G. SWANSON.

1910.

Great Britain: A. N. McClinton, A. M. Baker, J. P. Jones, C. G. Timms, R. C. S. Plummer, E. Milroy, N. F. Humphreys, J. Webb, H. Jarman, T. J. Richards, D. F. Smith, F. G. Handford, O. J. S. Piper, P. D. Waller, W. H. Tyrrell.

Rhodesia: H. O. Coker (Captain), P. J. le Cordeur, C. Horne, A. J. Bradley, F. B. Brooks, B. Rabinson, C. Devitt, F. W. Wunder, J. C. Taylor, A. C. Hoare, W. E. Thomas, A. B. Pocklington, G. A P. Thomas, W. L. Jenkins, Van Niekerk. Referee: B. A. Helm.

Result: Great Britain, 24 points; Rhodesia, 11 points.

1924.

Great Britain: J. D. Clinch, I. S. Smith, R. Kinnear, R. B. Maxwell, W. Rowe-Harding, H. Waddell, A. T. Young, N. McPherson (Captain), A. T. Voyce, Dr. J. Roche, D. S. Davies, M. Bradley, A. Brand, A. Ross, J. M. McVicker.

Rhodesia: W. E. Thomas (Captain), J. C. Coaton, S. J. D. Longden, H. Longden, A. McIntyre, J. Hardman, C. H. Steele, E. A. Green, H. Robinson, N. E. Brooks, D. Farquharson, L. T. Huxtable, R. W. Brown, A. D. Campbell, B. Norton. Referee, C. F. Cranswick.

Result: Great Britain, 16 points; Rhodesia, 3 points.

1928.

New Zealand: D. Lindsay, R. Rushbrooke, F. W. Lucas, A. C. C. Robilliard, H. Lilburne, L. Johnson, W. C. Dalley, M. Brownlie (Captain), I. Finlayson, E. Snow, G. T. Alley, J. Hore, G. Scrimshaw, J. P. Swain, W. E. Hazlett.

Rhodesia: G. J. Smith (Captain), J. de L. Thompson, F. H. Yates, D. McIntosh, J. W. Rackham, A. Gardiner, W. A. Cunningham, V. Crowther, A. G. E. Speight, G. F. A. Aston, H. P. Charles, D. Farquharson, L. J. Hancock, L. Rae, E. Meikle, and W. H. S. Cary who, by courtesy of the All Blacks, replaced Rae (injured). Referee, A. N. Cranswick.

Result: New Zealand, 44 points; Rhodesia, 8 points.

1933.

Wallabies: A. W. Ross (Captain), F. McPhillips, M. Grace, A. D. McLean, J. D. Kelaher, W. J. Warlow, J. C. Steggall, D. L. Cowper, G. Sturtridge, J. B. Young, R. Bilman, C. N. Campbell, S. Malcolm, W. G. Bennett, W. H. Cerutti, M. F. Morton, E. T. Bonis, J. B. Doneley, W. Ritter, E. W. Love, G. Bland, W. G. White, G. M. Cooke, A. J. Hodgson, M. C. White, W. A. Mackney, R. B. Loudon, O. L. Bridle, J. G. Clarke.

Rhodesia: P. K. Louw (Captain), R. L. Robinson, G. A. Cunningham, J. D. Crowther, R. H. P. Cornell, A. P. Wheeler, M. Napier, J. J. Lardant, F. M. Royston, J. N. Morgan, W. W. Cluff, M. Rest, E. W. Dicks, J. F. Gallimore, T. R. H. Gaffney, S. L. Wolffe, E. Maytham, S. H. Compton, H. P. Charles.   Referees: P. G. Morkel and P. Rabinson.

Results:—

At Salisbury: Wallabies, 24 points; Rhodesia, 5 points.

At Bulawayo: Wallabies, 33 points; Rhodesia, nil.

BRITISH TEAM
(1924)
v. RHODESIA.

Standing: J. W. Roche, R. Kinnear, A. MacIntyre, Rowe Harding, R. W. Brown, I. S. Smith, D. Farquharson, R. D. Maxwell, A. D. Campbell, B. Norton. R. Cove-Smith.

Middle row: N. Brooks, H. Longden, I. McVicker, J. C. Coaton, A. Ross, W. E. Thomas (captain), N. McPherson, E. A. Green, M. Bradley, S. J. D. Longden, D. S. McPherson Davies

Front row: H. Robinson, A. T. Voyce, L. T. Huxtable, A. T. Young, J. D. Clinch, C. H. Steele, A. Brand, J. Hardman, H. Waddell.

SOUTH AFRICAN COLLEGE VISIT, 1912.

The results were:—

Versus King's Club at Bulawayo	won	13 —	0
Versus Alexandra Club at Salisbury	won	30 —	0
Versus Combined Salisbury Clubs at Salisbury	won	13 —	3
Versus Hartley District at Gatooma	won	23 —	0
Versus Midlands at Gwelo	won	12 —	4
Versus Combined Bulawayo Clubs at Bulawayo	won	19 —	0
Versus Combined Bulawayo Clubs at Bulawayo	won	32 —	0

Bulawayo: D. Elliott, L. Rabinson, P. Rabinson, R. H. Hart. F. Bromehead, E. A. Green, Whales, H. Moll (Captain), G. Otterson, T. Taylor, C. L. Burrows, J. F. S. Curtis, L. Handley, F. Woods. W. W. Bamberger, Wright, Myburgh and C. B. Sauerman.

King's: P. J. le Cordeur, C. B. Sauerman, B. Rabinson (Captain), P. Rabinson, F. Bromehead, E. A. Green, L. Rabinson, L. Handley, W. Harvey, W. Bamberger, J. Baker, B. Knoeson, V. Davis, T. Barrow, F. Woods.

Salisbury: A. C. Hoare (Captain), V. A. Lewis, C. C. D. Ferris, W. B. Nicol, H. O. Coker, J. M. Scallan, W. E. Thomas, J. J. Phillips, F. W. Wunder, Walsh, C. Pfaff, E. H. Beck, J. C. Elsworth. G. P. L. Matthews, R. A. Gower. Referee, C. E. Duff.

Alexandra: A. C. Hoare (Captain), H. H. Henwood, D. Fraser, Carney, W. B. Nicol, Pascoe, C. Maritz, J. J. Phillips, F. W. Wunder, T. Fisher, C. Pfaff, McTavish, Johnston, Bowley, R. A. Gower. Referee, C. E. Duff.

Midlands: J. Curtis, H. Bradley, V. Eriksen, G. P. L. Matthews, Wagner, Wright, Black, Hughes, Fawcett, Wathes, Johns, Legiste, Cranswick, Horne, H. Spargo.

S.A.C.S.: S. Malan, B. G. Melle, P. F. Roux, R. Macdonald, E. Theunissen, H. Marchand, C. Basset, M. Wundie, F. Malder, C. Steyn (Captain), W. Allen, E. van Dyk, J. Versveld, A. Bayly, A. McGregor, J. P. Roux, Nicholson, Neser, Dunvan, D. Steyn.

WESTERN PROVINCE COUNTRY CLUB VISIT, 1922.

The results were:—

Versus Bulawayo at Bulawayo	drew	9 —	9
Versus Bulawayo at Bulawayo	won	15 —	0
Versus Salisbury at Salisbury	lost	8 —	9
Versus Salisbury at Salisbury	won	9 —	0
Versus Gatooma at Gatooma	won	31 —	0
Versus Midlands at Que Que	won	11 —	5
Versus Rhodesia at Bulawayo	won	3 —	0

Rhodesia: W. E. Thomas (Captain), F. J. du Plessis, P. G. Peiser, R. A. Gower, K. Carstens, J. V. Kerr, D. V. Scully, D. Huddy, I. H. Salonika, C. C. D. Ferris, J. Barrett, E. J. Bushell, I. D. MacGillivray, R. J. Lucas, J. Carmichael. Referee, A. N. Cranswick.

Bulawayo: R. W. Brown, B. Melville, P. Peiser, S. J. D. Longden, Meyer, Smith, C. H. Steele, R. J. Lucas, I. MacGillivray, L. R. Bentley, A. McLaren, H. N. Titterton, I. H. Salonika (Captain), G. A. P. Thomas, E. J. Bushell, Kerr.

Midlands: J. C. Coaton, J. Murray, H. Bradley, V. Eriksen, Niebuhr, Swan, Swan, Reynolds, R. Biffen, H. A. Cripwell, Windsor, H. Arzt, Smith, J. Carmichael, S. Hurrell.

Gatooma: G. Brewster, W. Poley, W. Thane, Rynd, A. McMasters, Price, Burton, McGregor, Theal, Bryant, Slott, Levin, Ulyett. Ogilvie, Gibb.

Salisbury: F. J. du Plessis, J. W. Leach, K. Carstens, R. A. Gower, Kerr, D. V. Scully, D. Huddy, W. E. Thomas (Captain), C. C. D. Ferris, H. Robinson, E. Hockey, Pascoe, Helm, J. Barrett, Van der Spuy, D. C. Cowan, W. G. Phillips.

TRANSVAAL UNIVERSITY COLLEGE VISIT, 1925.

The results were:—

Versus Bulawayo at Bulawayo	won	9 —	6
Versus Bulawayo at Bulawayo	won	18 —	0
Versus Salisbury at Salisbury	won	12 —	8
Versus Salisbury at Salisbury	won	33 —	0
Versus Eiffel Flats	won	39 —	3
Versus Midlands at Que Que	won	34 —	13
Versus Midlands at Gwelo	won	37 —	0
Versus Livingstone at Livingstone	won	27 —	3

Midlands: W. A. Shackleton, A. M. Kuys, R. Biffen, J. E. Hogg, D. Victor, H. C. Fletcher (Captain), J. M. Fox, J. Carmichael (Captain), F. A. H. Greenfield, J. E. S. Bradford, A. Simpson, Williams, E. Simpson, A. McLaren, C. Mills, D. J. Avery, J. Cowie, Brooks.

Eiffel Flats: W. Poley, W. Thane, A. McCallum, D. Olver, W. Black, G. Long, A. McMasters, A. Birnie, A. Scrutton, A. Hunt, J. Fitt, D. Clark, Farquharson, Du Preez, Coetzee.

Bulawayo: J. de L. Thompson, A. C. Burgess, J. W. Rackham, J. A. Kirstein, J. D. Crowther, C. H. Steele, E. A. Green (Captain), P. Basson, R. W. Brown, A. D. Campbell, B. Norton, L. J. Hancock, J. Thompson, L. Rae, J. G. Lewis, H. J. Smith, I. H. Salonika (Captain), T. H. Dyke.

Salisbury: D. Newman, H. Lovemore, R. A. Gower (Captain), P. Power, McChlery, Gordon, Huddy, H. Robinson, C. S. Style, J. Collard, Reynolds, Brooks, H. Steyn, L. Hill, G. Hodgson, Green, F. Alcock, Roberts, R. Mitchell, Wells, Siebert, Tainton, Walton, Butler.

T.U.C.: Fourie, Dames, Zwarenstein, Lund, Smit, Nel, Alexander, Mare, Glatthaar, Starke, Neethling, Van der Berg, Wilson, Quinn, Van der Spuy, Smith, Visser, Kruger, Reid.

WITWATERSRAND UNIVERSITY VISIT, 1928.

The results were:—

Versus Umtali at Umtali	won	16 —	8
Versus a Rhodesian XV at Salisbury	won	16 —	6
Versus Salisbury at Salisbury	lost	0 —	10
Versus Midlands at Gwelo	won	30 —	11
Versus Bulawayo at Bulawayo	won	9 —	7
Versus a Rhodesian XV at Bulawayo	lost	9 —	19

Midlands: A. M. Kuys, A. J. Liebenberg, J. R. Franks, D. Homan, Langridge, C. M. Hunt, W. A. Cunningham (Captain), E. Williams, C. P. Louwrens, Van Reenen, W. F. Cunningham, B. J. McGuire, R. H. Waghorn, Bartlett, Coventry.

Bulawayo: J. de L. Thompson, F. H. Yates, E. A. Barbour, J. D. Crowther, G. A. Cunningham, J. W. Rackham, C. H. Steele, D. Farquharson (Captain), L. J. Hancock, J. H. van Niekerk, J. G. Lewis, P. Siebert, K. T. Widdicombe-Smith, C. le Cordeur, L. Rae.

Umtali: J. C. Coaton, J. Livingston, D. Meikle, S. J. D. Longden, L. B. Ade, Mason, D. Killen, Rolfe, Clements, E. Meikle, E. Palmer, T. Hulley, J. Ward, J. Harrison, Beynon.

Salisbury: T. M. Davies, A. C. Burgess, A. Gardiner, A. L. Fielding, D. Mackintosh, Lambert, V. Crowther, G. J. Smith (Captain), A. G. E. Speight, Meyer, H. P. Charles, J. Collard, G. F. A. Aston, King, W. H. S. Cary.

Varsity: B. Sieff (Captain), J. G. Kneen, P. Kirsch, R. Brinton, T. Kneen, E. A. Faber, F. A. Brandt, T. Richardt, Dr. H. Heydenreich, R. G. Weavind, F. Uys, L. van Flynen, G. Mynhardt, P. van der Lith, Q. Ochse, W. Heines, M. A. Cooper, A. D. Proudfoot, A. H. van Wyk, G. L. Burger, A. N. Sandenbergh, C. J. Claassen, H. Michalow, J. Freislich.

GRIQUALAND WEST RUGBY UNION TEAM VISIT, 1930.

The results were:—

Versus Bulawayo at Bulawayo	lost	14 — 15
Versus Bulawayo at Bulawayo	won	8 — 5
Versus Midlands at Gwelo	won	16 — 0
Versus Eiffel Flats at Gatooma	won	27 — 3
Versus Salisbury at Salisbury	lost	3 — 11
Versus Mashonaland at Salisbury	won	24 — 11
Versus Manicaland at Umtali	won	27 — 5

Midlands: H. C. Quinn, E. M. Kenny, J. Johnstone, Jackson, Fowler, C. J. Fleming, D. Kirstein, G. J. Smith (Captain), W. H. Leonard, A. Hogg, Penrose, M. Kenny, P. M. Jackson, C. F. Parker, D. Furse.

Umtali: T. Viljoen, H. van der Linden, McCarthy, P. Edwards, C. E. White, J. Livingston (Captain), D. Killen, E. Meikle, P. Taylor, S. Burnett, J. Ward, D. Barry, W. E. Baugh, R. Fulton, J. Sutherland.

Bulawayo: T. M. Davies, G. A. Cunningham, J. D. Crowther, W. F. Bromehead, D. M. Ross, J. W. Rackham, N. I. Boast, J. H. van Niekerk (Captain), A. Matthews, E. W. Dicks, K. T. Widdicombe-Smith, J. G. Lewis, C. H. Steele, L. Rae, L. J. Hancock, W. W. Acutt, J. Gazet.

Salisbury: L. J. Coley, W. F. S. Belton, A. L. Fielding, E. J. B. Shaw, I. S. Evans, H. W. Driver, V. Crowther, H. P. Charles (Captain), G. F. A. Aston, J. P. Kruger, F. Olver, I. Potgieter, P. P. van Wyk, H. N. Morgan, W. W. Cluff, Halse, B. Joelson, H. Steyn.

Eiffel Flats: Raebow, Nixon, Pattinson, McCallum, Viljoen, Bell, Dillon, Maeyer, du Preez, Winther, Taylor, Simpson, Boddington, Weatherhead, D. J. Avery.

Griqualand West: F. Awerbuck, R. Addison, R. Babb, H. Dickson, E. Jostling, H. Marvel, L. Marvel, E. Billing, C. P. Buitendag, A. Gericke, J. Hogg, J. J. Kipling (Captain), H. Kipling, T. Waddington, G. McCarthy, W. Rousseau, P. McCurrie, W. Clark, H. Reid, P. McRae, A. Butler, C. Moult.

UNIVERSITY OF CAPE TOWN VISIT, 1934.

Versus Matabeleland at Bulawayo	lost	9 — 13
Versus Midlands at Gwelo	won	23 — 6
Versus Salisbury at Salisbury	lost	5 — 6
Versus Mashonaland at Salisbury	won	20 — 9
Versus Manicaland at Umtali	won	14 — 10
Versus Matabeleland at Bulawayo	won	9 — 8
Versus Livingstone at Livingstone	won	47 — 8
Versus a Matabeleland XV at Bulawayo	won	27 — 5

Varsity: G. Dommissee, G. J. Luyt, M. Zimmerman, P. W. Gerber, R. MacDonald, L. Babrow, E. Tucker, S. Lawton, J. Weir, D. S. Theron (Captain), A. Kruger, D. Adler, M. C. Marais, H. van Hoogstraten, O. Gordon, P. Duvenage, J. Coppens, H. A. Kent, G. Osler, J. Albers, D. Kotze.

Matabeleland: L. J. Coley, A. P. Wheeler, J. D. Crowther, J. H. Charsley, W. E. C. Atherstone, M. Napier, L. Gruber, A. Matthews (Captain), E. W. Dicks, H. Fox, F. M. Royston, I. P. Potgieter, J. Birnie, D. L. Burke, R. A. G. Stupart.

Midlands: G. Baker, J. B. Longhurst, E. M. Kenny (Captain), B. van der Kooi, T. Nielson, A. W. Rose, F. Phillips, J. F. Gallimore, Waghorn, W. B. Daniel, R. Wharton, C. F. Parker, E. T. Lines, I. L. Mitchell, J. Ward.

Salisbury: R. L. Robinson, H. M. M. McKenzie, W. Belton, F. McChlery, I. S. Evans, J. D. Burne, J. Lardant, L. C. O'Donohoe (Captain), J. Winter, J. A. du Plessis, L. Lewis, W. Cluff, Moir, Nimmo, Beukes.

Umtali: P. O'Leary, P. Edwards, A. van Heerden, E. Livingston, R. Longhurst, R. Crowther, W. Myburgh, G. F. A. Aston, W. E. Baugh, A. S. Fulton, G. C. Digweed, A. Mackintosh, V. H. Abrams, H. Myburgh, R. Fulton.

Matabeleland XV: W. Logan, H. Streak, W. van Blerk, L. R. Gordon, B. McWilliams, G. Burne, R. E. Brooke-Sumner, R. McVey, A. Sarif, M. Radue, A. Garside, R. E. Walker, W. ·Howe, K. Sinclair, N. Longhurst (Captain).

MR. L. RABINSON'S TRANSVAAL TEAM, 1935.

Versus Livingstone at Livingstone ... ... won   25 —   5
Versus Matabeleland at Bulawayo ... ... won   19 —ˑ 8
Versus Combined Midlands and Matabeleland at

Bulawayo ... ... won   11 —   6
Versus Manicaland at Umtali ... ... won   13 —   0
Versus Salisbury at Salisbury ... ... won   8 —   3
Versus Mashonaland at Salisbury ... ... won   12 —   6
Versus Que Que at Que Que ... ... won   18 —   6

Transvaal: C. Steyn, G. Sennet, Ben Olivier, W. Kriel, F. W. Waring (Captain), W. Campher, T. Barlow, Beyers Olivier, J. Segal, W. K. Carter, C. Kohler, T. R. van Wyk, J. Bakkes, W. P. Stork, D. Ryan, W. Gunning, J. Wilson, H. C. Steyn, R. Talken, A. G. Ingram, I. Donaldson.

Matabeleland: F. D. W. Payne, G. Cunningham, S. L. Wolffe, B. W. Bland, L. Taylor, L. B. Codd, J. H. Fuller, D. L. Burke (Captain), H. Fo, H. Meyers, R. L. Murray, R. E. Walker, J. Bamberger, S. E. D. Brown, F. S. Haslett.

Combined Midlands and Matabeleland: L. J. Coley, G. Cunningham, L. Taylor, S. L. Wolffe, D. Baker, S. Elley, I. Gruber, W. H. Leonard (Captain), H. Fox, D. L. Burke, S. E. D. Brown, W. Milton, A. Fitzstephens, R. E. Walker, L. E. May.

Manicaland: Edwards, Brown, Herbst Longhurst (Captain), G. Gammon, Livingston, E. Meikle, A. Mackintosh, H. Myburgh, Baugh, Schempers, Van Gran, Henderson, G. F. A. Aston.

Salisbury: R. L. Robinson, H. Mackenzie, R. Cornell, Reid, I. S. Evans, Payne, J. J. Lardant, O'Donohoe, McVey, Cowie, W. Cluff (Captain), Watson, Nimmo, Moir, Hearne.

Mashonaland: Robinson, Mackenzie, Cornell, Reid, Hill, Payne, Scott, Cowie, Hards, Parker, Cluff (Captain), Watson, Mitchell, Nimmo, Lines.

Que Que: J. S. Robertson, R. Landsberg, K. Wood, D. Baker, K. L. Jackson, N. A. Shackleton, F. D. Phillips, R. McCabe, R. H. C. Waghorn, C. Mildred, V. Godden, L. E. May, D. Billing, J. du Toit, L. H. Smit.

INTER-PROVINCE MATCHES.

Year.	Winners.	Points.	Year.	Winners.	Points.
1901	Matabeleland	16— 0	1905 (1)	Matabeleland	9— 8
1903 (1)	Mashonaland	9— 3	(2)	Drawn	0— 0
(2)	Mashonaland	11— 9	1907	Mashonaland	3— 0
1904 (1)	Mashonaland	8— 3	1909	Matabeleland	11— 0
(2)	Drawn	3— 3			

RUSSELL CUP.

Year.	Winners.	Points.	Year.	Winners.	Points.
1910	Mashonaland	6— 5	1924 (1)	Matabeleland	12— 3
1911	Mashonaland	23— 3	(2)	Matabeleland	12— 4
1912	Matabeleland	21— 9	1925	Matabeleland	11— 8
1913 (1)	Mashonaland	10— 7	1926	Mashonaland	13— 3
(2)	Drawn	7— 7	1927	Mashonaland	9— 8
1914 (1)	Matabeleland	4— 3	1928	Matabeleland	22— 3
(2)	Mashonaland	8— 3	1929	Matabeleland	19— 3
1920 (1)	Drawn	9— 9	1930	Matabeleland	15— 0
(2)	Mashonaland	6— 3	1931	Mashonaland	13— 8
1921 (1)	Matabeleland	3— 0	1932	Mashonaland	17— 9
(2)	Mashonaland	8— 0	1933	Midlands	12— 9
1922 (1)	Mashonaland	5— 3	1934	Midlands	19—16
(2)	Mashonaland	4— 0	1935	Mashonaland	12— 8
1923 (1)	Matabeleland	12— 0			
(2)	Matabeleland	9— 0			

INTER-TOWN (" BLACK AND WHITE " CUP).

Year.	Winners.	Points.	Year.	Winners.	Points.
1925	Bulawayo	12— 6	1931	Bulawayo	18— 0
1926	Salisbury	7— 3	1932	Bulawayo	10— 8
1927	Bulawayo	21— 6	1933	Bulawayo	9— 5
1928	Bulawayo	13—10	1934	Bulawayo	13—10
1929	Salisbury	13— 9	1935	Gwelo	11— 3
1930	Salisbury	17— 5			

THE TOD SUTTIE CUP.

This trophy was presented in 1923 by Mr. J. Tod Suttie, for competition between Bulawayo and the Midlands.

Results:—

Year.	Winners.	Points.	Year.	Winners.	Points.
1923	Bulawayo	10— 3	1930	Bulawayo	11— 9
1924	Bulawayo	9— 0	1931	Midlands	18—15
1925	Bulawayo	34— 0	1932	Midlands	9— 3
1926	Bulawayo	20— 8	1933	Bulawayo	13— 3
1927	Bulawayo	31— 0	1934	Bulawayo	13— 6
1928	Bulawayo	29— 5	1935	Midlands	14— 6
1929	Bulawayo	29— 3			

THE GLOBE AND PHOENIX SHIELD.

Presented by the Globe and Phoenix Gold Mining Company, Limited, to the Midlands Rugby Football Board, for competition between clubs in Rhodesia. The semi-finals and final must take place in Que Que.

Results:—

1926	Raylton, Bulawayo.	1933	Salisbury Club.
1927	B.A.C., Bulawayo.	1934	Old Miltonians, Byo.
1928-30	Raylton, Bulawayo.	1935	Que Que.
1931-32	B.S.A.P., Salisbury.		

JUNIOR INTER-PROVINCE.

1913 Winner: Matabeleland (20—3).

VAN DER BYL SHIELD.

Year.	Winners.	Points.	Year.	Winners.	Points.
1914	Matabeleland	32— 0	1928	Mashonaland	12— 3
1921 (1)	Mashonaland	6— 3	1929	Mashonaland	3— 0
(2)	Mashonaland	8— 5	1931	Matabeleland	9— 6
1922	Matabeleland	14—10	1932	Matabeleland	18—11
1923	Drawn	0— 0	1933	Mashonaland	19—12
1924	Mashonaland	12— 6	1934	Mashonaland	24—13
1925	Matabeleland	5— 3	1935	Mashonaland	14— 5
1926	Matabeleland	6— 5			

THE BULAWAYO MEMORIAL HOSPITAL SHIELD.

1898	Queen's	1910-14	King's
1901-04	Queen's	1919	Queen's and B.A.C.
1905	Raylton	1920	King's
1906-08	Queen's	1921	B.A.C.
1909	B.A.C.	1923	Queen's

THE McGREGOR SHIELD.

1925	B.A.C.	1931	Old Miltonians
1926	Raylton	1932	Queen's
1927	Queen's	1933	B.A.C.
1928	Raylton	1934	Old Miltonians
1929	B.A.C.	1935	Raylton
1930	Raylton		

The McGregor Shield.

BULAWAYO FIRST LEAGUE CUP.

The Bulawayo First League Cup was presented by the Rhodesia Rugby Football Union.

1895	Queen's	1925-26	Raylton
1897-99	Queen's	1927	B.A.C.
1901-07	Queen's	1928-29	Raylton
1908-09	B.A.C.	1930	B.A.C.
1910-14	King's	1931	Queen's
1919-20	King's	1932	B.A.C.
1921	B.A.C.	1933	Raylton
1922	King's	1934	Old Miltonians
1923	Raylton	1935	Raylton
1924	B.A.C.		

THE LAWSON SHIELD (SALISBURY).

Presented by the Deputy-Mayor, Councillor James Lawson, 1910-1912.

1912	Salisbury	1928-29	Alexandra
1913	Alexandra	1930	B.S.A.P.
1914	Salisbury	1931	Salisbury
1921	Salisbury	1932	Alexandra
1922-25	Alexandra	1933	Salisbury
1926	B.S.A.P.	1934	B.S.A.P.
1927	Salisbury		

THE EDWARDS CUP.

1901-04	Salisbury	1924	B.S.A.P.
1905	Alexandra	1925	Salisbury
1906	United Police	1926	Alexandra
1907	Salisbury	1927	Salisbury
1908	Alexandra	1928	Alexandra
1909	Salisbury	1929-30	B.S.A.P.
1910	Alexandra	1931-32	Salisbury
1911	Salisbury	1933-34	B.S.A.P.

INTER-PROVINCIAL CAPTAINS.

Matabeleland.		Mashonaland.	
1901-05	T. B. Hepburn	1901	A. E. Fitzgerald
1907	G. P. L. Matthews	1903	P. C. Farquharson
1909	W. van der Spuy	1904-05	F. G. Brooks
1910	F. B. Brooks	1907-10	H. O. Coker
1911-12	H. T. Moll	1911	G. A. P. Thomas
1913	V. R. C. Hoets	1912	A. C. Hoare
1914	S. Ashley	1913	J. M. Scallan
1920-21	G. A. P. Thomas	1914	C. C. D. Ferris
1922-23	I. H. Salonika	1920-24	W. E. Thomas
1924	J. C. Coaton	1925	R. A. Gower
1925	A. D. Campbell	1926	P. G. Morkel
1926	S. J. D. Longden	1927	G. J. Smith
1927	D. Farquharson	1928	A. G. E. Speight
1928	J. de L. Thompson	1929-33	H. P. Charles
1929	J. W. Rackham	1934	L. C. O'Donohoe
1930	J. H. van Niekerk	1935	W. W. Cluff
1931	P. K. Louw		
1932	C. H. Frielick		
1933	T. M. Davies		
1934	A. Matthews		
1935	D. L. Burke		

Midlands.		Manicaland.	
1927	B. Norton	1927	D. Meikle
1928	J. R. Franks	1928	S. J. D. Longden
1929-30	G. J. Smith	1929	D. Meikle
1931	J. B. Johnstone	1930	J. Livingston
1932	W. H. Leonard	1931	W. Myburgh
1933	A. F. Holmes	1932	E. Meikle
1934	E. M. Kenny	1933-35	W. Myburgh
1935	W. H. Leonard		

OFFICERS, PAST AND PRESENT, OF THE RHODESIA RUGBY FOOTBALL UNION.

Presidents: Col. H. Melville Heyman, 1895-1896; the Hon. Sir Arthur Lawley, 1897-1900; H. H. Sir Wm. Milton, 1900-1914; H.H. Sir Drummond Chaplin, 1915-1924; H.E. Sir John Chancellor, 1925-1927; H. E. Sir Cecil Hunter Rodwell, 1928 to 1935.

Vice-Presidents: Col. J. A. Spreckley, 1895-1896; Clarkson Tredgold, Esq., 1897-1903; W. G. Swanson, Esq., 1904-1924; Capt. R. E. Murray, 1908; T. B. Hepburn, Esq., 1915-1920; C. E. Duff, Esq., 1921 to date; Lieut.-Col. A. C. L. Webb, 1925 to date.

Hon. Vice-Presidents: Messrs. V. A. Lewis, W. G. Swanson, E. Mannix, T. B. Hepburn and W. E. Thomas, jnr.

Hon. Secretaries: W. Dempster, 1895-1896; D. Christopherson, 1897-1898; Q.M. Sergt. F. A. Hodson, 1899-1900; C. W. Cosnett, 1901; B. A. Helm, 1902-1903; C. P. Goldsmith, 1904-1905; J. E. Thomas, 1906-1907; T. A. Sidgreaves, 1908; T. E. Wylde, 1909-1910; Lynden Webber, 1914; A. N. Cranswick, 1915, 1919-1925; A. Randall, 1916-1918; H. N. Titterton, 1926-1927; A. C. Amyot, 1927-1929; E. R. M. Manning, 1930-1931; W. E. Scot-Russell, 1931-1932; W. A. Carnegie, 1933 to date.

Hon. Treasurers: N. Platnauer, 1895-1896; K. B. Gloag, 1897-1900; C. W. Cosnett, 1901-1905; C. Burrows, 1906-1909; J. C. Cowley, 1910-1911; C. Davis, 1911-1925; T. M. Fairlamb, 1926 to date.

Present Delegates to S.A. Board: Messrs. E. Allen and H. A. Solomon. Past Delegates were Messrs. J. D. de Villiers, M. J. Louw, S. J. Oliphant and Bevill G. Rudd.

MATABELELAND, 1932.

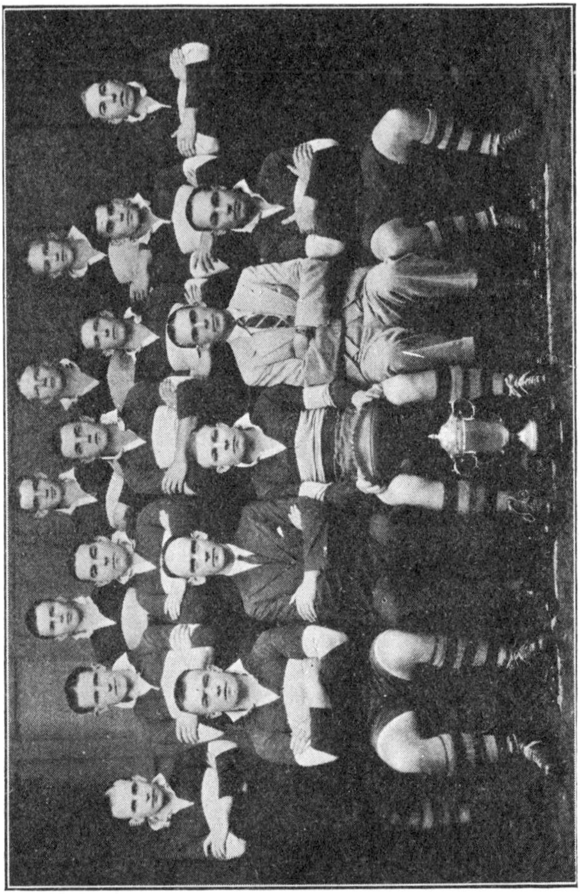

Reading from left to right.

Back row:
W. ATHERSTONE,
J. H. CHARSLEY,
A. E. WALKER,
S. L. WOLFFE.

Centre Row:
B. N. GELDENHUYS,
E. W. DICKS,
K. T. WIDDICOMBE-
SMITH,
W. HOWE,
N. LONGHURST,
N. E. SCOTT,
M. NAPIER.

Front Row:
S. COMPTON,
Dr. G. R. ROSS,
P. K. LOUW,
J. de L. THOMPSON,
J. M. FOX.

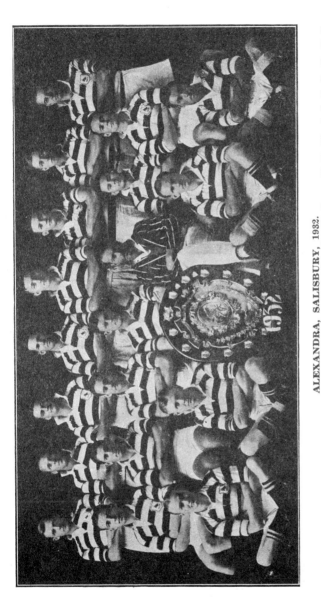

ALEXANDRA, SALISBURY, 1932.

Back row: F. H. Bowman, G. van der Westhuizen, H. J. C. Schultz, H. Steyn, K. T. Wood, J. B. Scott, N. C. Wood, D. H. Cummings.

Middle row: N. D. W. Scott, W. E. Cawood, H. G. Addecott, A. L. Fielding (Capt.), R. C. MacFarlane, (Hon. Secretary), I. S. Evans, R. H. P. Cornell.*

Front row: O. Shepherd, R. McVey, T. A. Patterson, V. du Toit.   * Selected against Wallabies.

B.A.C., BULAWAYO.

Reading from left to
right.

Back row:
M. DANNAHER,
D. BURGER,
A. ROBERTSON,
K. T. WIDDICOMBE-
          SMITH,
H. FOX.

Centre Row:
M. RADUE,
A. K. CAMPBELL,
A. V. ZEEDERBERG,
A. HOWARD,
N. E. SCOTT,
R. J DICKINSON,

Front Row:
E. GREEN (Coach),
P. K. LOUW,
J. M. FOX,
M. NAPIER.

On Floor:
R. E. BROOKE-SUMNER,
B. LEWIS.

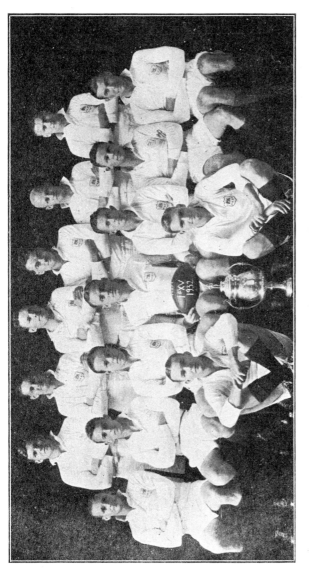

SALISBURY CLUB, 1932.

Back row: T. R. H. Gafney, G. M. Moir, R. M. G. Warton, B. J. MacGuire, H. A. M. Kufal, G. Symons.
Centre row: H. M. M. MacKenzie, M. B. Benoy, J. N. Morgan, H. W. Driver (Captain), E. G. Gould,
A. P. Wheeler, W. D. Mills.

Front row: F. C. Wisdom and R. R. Lancaster.

OLD MILTONIANS, BULAWAYO.

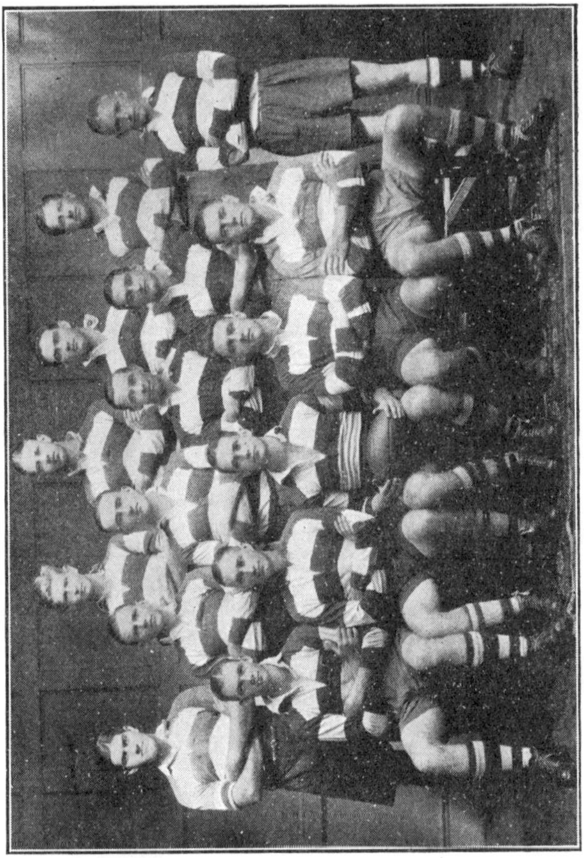

Reading from left to right.

Back Row:

F. HASLETT,
A. GARSIDE,
W. ACUTT.
N. LONGHURST.

Centre Row:

S. FISHER.
W. ATHERSTONE.
R. HAMMOND.
R. BRAGGE.
L. GRUBER,
S. L. WOLFFE.

Front Row:

J. H. CHARSLEY,
C. B. STREAK,
A. M. PERRY,
W. WILSON,
W. HOWE.

SALISBURY B.S.A. POLICE, 1932.

Back Row: Troopers Gallimore, Bridger, Burne, Constable Robinson, Troopers Gordon, Long, and Constable O'Reilly.

Centre Row: Trooper Betts, Constables Cluff, Taylor, Smith, Troopers Brown and Booth, and Constable Elley.

Front Row: Cpl. Belton, Maj. J. S. Morris (Commissioner), Sgt. Charles, Lt. H. G. Seward and Capt. J. M. Parr.

On ground: Constable Arthur and Trooper Walshaw.

QUEEN'S, BULAWAYO.

Reading from left
right.

Back Row::
—. FOURIE,
P. MARTIN,
R. HENWOOD
(Hon. Sec.)
—. MITCHELL,
W. WALLACE.

Centre Row:
P. BUTCHER,
E. T. HEPBURN,
K. A. SINCLAIR,
—. DOUGLAS,
E. W. DICKS,
A. J. DAVIES,
D. MURRAY,
A. E. WALKER.

Front Row:
F. V. CLARANCE,
E. W. WRIGHT
(President),
S. COMPTON,
T. M. DAVIES,
K. O. GOLDHAWK,
E. BURTON (Coach),
B. W. BLAND.

On Floor:
A. E. KLUCKOW,
—. HOGAN.

ATHLETICS

SPORT finds a footing in strange places and holds its own in diverse circumstances. Long before the clash with the fighting Mashonas was over, the early Rhodesian Pioneers began their first athletic contests in a rough stone enclosure, known as Johnson's yard, situated below Fort Salisbury at the foot of A'Rari Kop. It is doubtful whether they were in actual danger of attack at the time but the ancient spirit of Francis Drake persists and it is with thoughts of that famous game of bowls that one pictures the Pioneers throwing the quoit and breasting the tape while the wily Mashonas sharpened their assegais no great distance from the settlement. The Fort itself was built on top of A'Rari Kop, and below it, in Johnson's yard, were sheltered all the discarded wagons and transport equipment of the Johnson, Heany and Borrow pioneer expedition. In the north-east corner of the yard, now crossed by Pioneer and Raleigh Streets, James ("Friday") Wallace had his smithy and worked day and night repairing the wagons after their long treks, and later converting some of them into Scotch carts for the use of the prospecting parties that went out from Salisbury after the pioneer force was disbanded. "Friday" Wallace himself was killed on the Umsweswe River in the 1896 Rebellion. Little remains of the old yard but the Pioneer Store still stands and is now used as a stable.

Quoits was a favourite pastime of the pioneers and some fine games were played in the yard between Chris Human and Jim Sweetman.

The first real sports meeting was held in Salisbury at Christmas, 1891. By that time Bobbie (later Colonel) Beal, Piet Kolbe and Jack Carruthers had set out Salisbury's first racecourse and built the stand enclosures, and in the space encircled by the course the first running track was laid. At this first meeting the high jump was won with 4 ft. 10 ins. and W. Swanepoel won the long jump with 18 ft. 3 ins. George Dinsdale, of De Beer's party, won all the short events and Bly Hopley the half-mile and the mile, against such fine distance men as Ferreira, Christian MacGear who was killed on the Mazoe Patrol in 1896, and "Sally" Nunn, a former 4-mile champion in England. Boyes Moodie put the shot

Capt. C. F. Lendy,
who commanded the Artillery of the
Victoria Column and to whose
memory the Lendy Memorial in
Bulawayo is dedicated.

J. P. Richardson.   J. Carruthers.

36 ft. 4 ins. and another athlete who featured in this meet was Snodgrass, one time a champion wrestler in South America.

In 1894, with the return of those who had taken part in the Matabele war, a renewed interest in sport of every kind brought into existence a gymkhana ground which was laid out where the Girls' High School and the Drill Hall now stand. The field did service also for cricket and rugby matches, which, for the most, appear to have been exciting " national " contests between the English, Scots and Irish, with the Civilians and Police joining in. Some fine athletic meetings were held on this gymkhana ground and an event which invariably evoked great enthusiasm was the tug-o'-war, usually won by the Scots with hefty John McChlery on the end of the rope.

On Queen Victoria's birthday in 1894, a particularly successful meeting was held, interest being added by the recent arrival of Toogood of the Standard Bank, and Sid Fichat, both fine athletes. There was much speculation and betting as to whether Toogood or Jack Carruthers would be the better man over the 100 yards and excitement ran high. On the day of the race Carruthers got up from an attack of malaria, drank half a bottle of champagne and toed the line to win. Later he was beaten in the 120 yards hurdles by Sid Fichat but succeeded in putting the 16lb. shot just over 37 feet. During these years Carruthers was only once beaten in the shot putt event, and that was by Capt. C. F. Lendy with 40 ft. 10 ins. The half-mile flat was a remarkable event, S. Dalton and Bly Hopley running home shoulder to shoulder to tie for first place, with the other competitors far behind.

Bulawayo's first athletic efforts were centred in the Bulawayo Athletic Club which came into existence in 1895, the sports ground being situated where the present Railway Administrative Offices now stand. With the extension of the railways in 1897, Mr. Rhodes took in that site and in exchange gave the present B.A.C. sports ground. At the first meeting in September, 1895, G. B. Peiser, H. G. M. Huntley and W. E. Biddulph proved themselves first-class sprinters, J. P. Richardson shone as a quarter-miler and Percy Ross won the mile and excelled at the long jump. The meeting also included a quoit competition—a favourite sport of the early days.

This meeting was held under the auspices of the Queen's Athletic Club and Dr. John A. Wilson presented a cup for the best all-round athlete which was won by Percy H. Ross. This fine silver trophy, believed to be the first of its kind in Rhodesia, is now among the collection of Rhodesiana in the Bulawayo Museum.

Later additions in the athletic world were Shergold and G. M. Tait, the latter a splendid all-rounder. He and G. P. L. ("Pondo") Matthews are the only men who have represented Rhodesia at both rugby and soccer.

The first echoes of athletics in the districts came in 1897 when Queen Victoria's 78th birthday in the year of her Diamond Jubilee was celebrated at Fort Soluse in right royal fashion. The 200 yards flat race was run in top-boots, in very slow time! and was won by Trooper Payne (B.S.A.P.), who also distinguished himself in the sack and blindfold races. The ponderous Corporal Harris won the cock-fighting, and the shooting, at empty whisky bottles, was won by Mr. Greene who never missed once from about 120 yards! Corporal Harris's team beat Corporal Woollacott's in the ever popular tug-o'-war and Troopers Smuts and Cornell won the three-legged race easily. In the wheelbarrow race, Troopers Jurish and Payne got away quickly but unfortunately the former placed his hand on a cactus plant. He stopped to comment and Troopers Smuts and Cornell dashed ahead and won by half a barrow's length. The sports provided a welcome respite from the rigours of fighting the Matabele and a great day was ended by a bonfire concert in the evening.

After the Boer War athletics resumed popularity and in the Capital claimed such enthusiasts as F. G. Brooks, W. S. Taberer, Bobbie Bain (a Canadian Scout in '93), D. Bruce of the B.S.A. Police, a fine sprinter, Jim Hazelhurst and Ironsides.

In 1903, C. Maritz, A. Welensky and P. J. de Stadler, one-time long jump champion of South Africa, came to the fore. De Stadler's career was full of incident and on one occasion he took part in a curious race, for a big wager, against a man on horseback, over a distance of one hundred yards, fifty yards there and fifty yards back. De Stadler won!

In 1903, F. G. Brooks went to Umtali and won the 100 yards Manicaland championship from E. P. Gubb, the high jump at 5 ft. 1 in. from H. Formby, and the long jump with

20 ft. 5 ins. H. Allen won the 220 yards championship. Other notables were the Southeys, E. R. and Corney, who, with C. Swift, were a trio of fine half-milers, and W. Hill, long-jumper and champion walker. Generally athletics were at a very high standard during this 'tween wars period. D. W. Smith's ten seconds for the 100 yards is still unbeaten, and D. R. McLachlan, a " quarter " man, J. W. Elsworth, over the mile, J. C. Ferreira, a great ten-miler, and C. Pfaff in the long jump all performed creditably. Other distance men of note were R. A. Gower and A. Hampson, and the Mazoe district claimed great runners in C. Horne, W. J. Smith and E. W. Eyles.

In Bulawayo, too, the sports were flourishing. First there was W. H. Trott, now Major, a sprinter of class who returned excellent times on the old tracks. Then came Frank Bromehead, a real flier, whose 75 yards Rhodesian record still holds after 27 years.

At a sports meeting held in Bulawayo on May 24, 1900, to celebrate the Relief of Mafeking, the first prizes were procured from a curious source. A detachment of the Diamond Fields Horse was stationed in the town and this regiment was very handsomely appointed. The browpiece of each bridle was embossed with two silver medallions and a number of these were used as prize medals. A ring for a ribbon was soldered on to each medal and, there being none of the present up-to-date machinery available, the engraving on the back of the medals was done by hand. The medal shown to me by A. M. Cumming, a crack cyclist in those early days, who treasures this quaint trophy more than any in his numerous collection, has in it the four holes through which tiny rivets fastened the ornament to the harness.

At the 1907 Christmas sports in Que Que the crack runner was J. G. Austen. F. Drake, the famous hunter and runner, though well past his prime then, won the 100 yards handicap. A. Haddon won the high jump with 4ft. 9 ins. and Conway the long jump with 15 ft. 7 ins. W. B. Sutton did the 440 yards in 56 4-5 seconds, E. E. Somerset the 120 yards hurdles in 19 4-5 secs. and J. Forrester put the shot 32 ft. 7 ins.

On New Year's Day, 1909, at Umtali, Frank Bromehead created a sensation by winning the 100, 220 and 440 yards handicaps in addition to the 100 and 220 yards Manicaland championships. There were crack runners in Umtali then

A. F. H. NEWTON.

in Geoff. Huxtable and Percy Harvey. The latter held the 120 yards Manicaland championship four times between 1906 and 1912 and in 1908 went to Macequece and won the Portuguese Blue Riband for the Governor's Cup for the 100 yards. W. Ernest Harvey, father of Percy, and now aged 77, took part in veterans' races until fifteen years ago and generally won. A. St. J. Harvey, the rugger player, is also a son of "W.E." In Bulawayo at that time, W. H. Griffiths was a good distance man. The longer distances were covered by P. J. Kealy, a grand runner, who won the first 10 miles cross-country championship. Others of his calibre were W. G. Walton, F. McCarthy, A. H. Knoesen, of walking fame, and Freddy Peters, a fine miler.

In 1911 the crack sprinter, A. N. Hutchinson, came to Bulawayo, and drew into competition a batch of fine runners from St. George's School, among whom was Briggs Campbell, reckoned the best over the 100 yards this country has produced. Others were his brother, A. Campbell, now Doctor, who has held several Matabeleland, Midlands and Rhodesian championships, Pat Walsh, A. Carroll, and fine athletes in the Stuttaford and Rabinson brothers.

In 1912 the Celtic Harriers Club, the first of its kind, was formed in Bulawayo and enjoyed a brief but flourishing existence until the Great War broke out.

Prominent athletes in the post-war period were the Old Georgians, T. A. Hubbard, sprinter, D. G. Blackbeard, who won the high jump championship eight times, and C. Schultz; the Milton schoolboy, J. G. W. Baggott, the Old Miltonian, Andrew Ross, E. F. Harris, A. H. Minter, who had run at the Crystal Palace, G. L. Yeats, C. E. Nevett and E. R. Tamblyn, two sprinters, and A. W. McKenzie, who won the shot put championship 10 times and throwing the hammer seven times. There was, however, a considerable falling away at this time and the advent of A. F. H. Newton in 1926 gave athletics a much needed fillip. Marathon running, his special forte, became popular, and while he was in Bulawayo Newton broke the world's records for the 100 miles and the 60 miles so that, in 1927, he held the world's records for all distances from 30 to 100 miles. In that same year he won the Comrades' Marathon, Maritzburg-Durban, 54¾ miles, in 6 hours 40 minutes 56 2-5 seconds. F. C. M. Watkins also ran in this gruelling race and gained eighth place with a time of 9 hours 18 minutes—a creditable performance.

Arthur Newton's best work for Rhodesian athletics was the formation of the Bulawayo Harriers Club. This club has done a great deal for all branches of athletics and has in turn been well served by J. Cowden, M.P., president since its inception and N. S. Ferris, now Colonel.

Names that have figured prominently in the records of the Harriers' Club are R. P. Wilson, a crack runner over middle distances, H. E. F. Mathews, C. Bissett, F. C. M. Watkins, J. J. Ronan and G. A. Zamek, the latter a great marathon runner. Other notable long distance men are A. B. Scott, J. B. Playford, J. C. Rutherford, C. W. Hall and M. L. Edmunds.

Among the sprinters of recent times are O. Connolly, J. Dodd, M. Meltzer, who won open championships while still at Milton School, I. S. Evans, H. M. Botha, G. J. W. Hartwell and C. A. Wootton, who has a splendid athletic record. It is interesting to note that the 440 yards record was created by W. F. Bromehead, son of the great sprinter. Other good men over this distance are E. J. Smith, A. R. Kerr, G. T. Crispin and H. R. Bragge.

F. St. J. Bromehead.

W. F. Bromehead.

Two jumping records stand in the name of J. H. Galvin who, before he had reached his prime unfortunately damaged both his ankles. P. Kileff, R. L. Harper, a fine hurdler, A. J. Bell, the Springbok cricketer and a splendid athlete, A. M. Perry, a stylish exponent of the pole vault, F. E. McChlery and B. C. Ledeboer, son of " George " and I. M. Barratt are a group of fine jumpers. Quite recently H. P. McCay has come to the fore in the field events at which A. J. Bell and I. McChlery are also first class exponents.

B. C. Ledeboer.   G. W. Ledeboer.

In recent years athletics have grown in popularity with women and credit for this must go to Mr. A. F. H. Newton and the Bulawayo Harriers. Rhodesia's outstanding woman performer is Miss M. G. Bragge, while others who have shown athletic prowess include Miss J. Capstick, Miss M. Mayes, Miss B. Musgrove, Miss M. Douglas, Miss D. Miller and Miss E. Wilson.

W. H. TROTT.

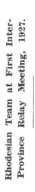

Rhodesian Team at First Inter-
Province Relay Meeting, 1927.

F. C. M. Watkins, J. J. Ronan,
H. E. F. Mathews, R. P. Wilson.

In 1927 the first team of athletes to visit Rhodesia came from Natal. S. J. M. Atkinson was the outstanding performer of the visitors, E. M. Bayley and D. Parrott were two fine sprinters, V. C. Welman did the middle distances and A. J. Bell, who later made his home in Rhodesia, excelled in the field events. Two ladies were included in the visiting team, Miss A. Marcovitch and Miss M. Freeman, sprinter and jumper respectively. The Rhodesian championships were thrown open to the visitors and they bettered several Rhodesian records as well as winning most of the championships.

In 1930 the R.A.A. and C.U. brought up five athletes from the Wanderer's Club, Johannesburg. The visitors ran in sports meetings at Gwelo, Umtali, Bulawayo and Salisbury and several Rhodesian records went by the board. The Wanderers men were G. G. Dustan, Trevor Jones, G. L. Hartman, R. M. Evans and N. G. Meyer. An outstanding performer was the Milton schoolboy, M. Meltzer, who won the 100 and 220 yards events from the visitors in Bulawayo.

In Bulawayo, in 1932, the Bloemfontein Harriers beat the local Harriers by 69 points to 40 points and won 11 of the 13 events. The outstanding performances were Miss M. G. Bragge's equalling the then South African record of 11 2-5 secs. for the 100 yards and A. W. Wright's four victories for the visitors.

In the same year a Rhodes University College athletic team toured the Colony.

The first representative Rhodesian athlete was W. H. Trott who, in 1908, competed in the South African trials for the first Olympic Games held in England. He then proceeded to England and ran in the English trials at the White City and in several centres in England where he did very well.

In 1924, R. P. Wilson and E. R. Tamblyn wore Rhodesian colours at the South African championships. In the mile, Wilson ran fourth with the Eastern Province representative, Dr. R. B. Hoole, now of Bulawayo, fifth.

In 1927, a Rhodesian team consisting of R. P. Wilson, F. C. M. Watkins, J. J. Ronan and H. E. F. Mathews, proceeded to Kimberley and participated in the first South African inter-province relay meeting. Rhodesia was placed third. J. J. Ronan obtained second place in the one mile championship and in the 7 miles race the second and third places were filled by F. C. M. Watkins and R. P. Wilson respectively.

The second South African inter-provincial relay meeting was held at Kimberley in 1928. Our representatives, J. Dodd, A. N. Cross, J. H. Galvin and C. Weinberg, competed in the quarter and half-mile relay and were third in each event.

Rhodesian Team at Second Inter-Province Relay Meeting, 1928.
J. Dodd, A. N. Cross, C. Weinberg, J. H. Galvin.
Inset: I. S. Evans.

In 1928 at the South African championships and Olympic trials, Rhodesia was represented at Paarl by G. A. Zamek who finished third in the marathon and at Newlands by A. M. Perry in the hurdles and pole vault, with H. L. Caryer for the half-mile.

In 1933 C. A. Wootton and P. Kileff competed in the South African championships at Cape Town, the latter taking second place in the pole vault with 11 ft. 2 ins.

Rhodesia's Empire Games team in 1934 consisted of Miss M. G. Bragge, Miss D. Ballantyne, Miss C. Keay, G. T. Crispin and G. J. W. Hartwell, with Mr. W. C. Robertson as manager. In the women's relay event Rhodesia gained third place which carried with it a bronze medal for each of the three runners. Of the 19 countries represented Rhodesia came sixth, and were awarded one of the Lonsdale Cups.

A. K. Young,
who represented Rhodesia
in the wrestling.

The Lonsdale Cup.

The first and only Rhodesian inter-province athletic contest was staged in Bulawayo in 1931 when Mashonaland (whose captain, C. A. Wootton, won three events) beat Matabeleland by six events to five and so won the R.A.A. and C.U. floating trophy which had been donated that year for inter-province competition. This competition has not been held since for financial reasons, but is likely to be revived in 1936.

The first attempt to control cycling and athletics in Rhodesia was the formation, in 1896, of the Bulawayo Amateur Athletic Club with Major Maurice Heany as president and W. Dempster as its hon. secretary. The club was affiliated to the Transvaal Athletic Union until 1901 when it was felt that headquarters were too far away and so a Rhodesian centre was formed. The Rev. J. G. Aldridge was chairman of the new council and J. E. Jelks, hon. secretary. These men did great work during their term of office. In

1903 there were negotiations with the National Cyclists' Union in England resulting in a further change of title to Rhodesia Cyclists' Union and A.A.A.

Under the aegis of this association annual championships were held throughout the Colony and every encouragement was given to the two sports. The Association has been well served since its inception. A long and meritorious record stands to the credit of Major W. Baxendale, chairman for ten years, and to Lieut.-Col. A. C. L. Webb, who held office for a similar period. The sports owe much also to Capt. A. G. Hendrie, M.C., honorary secretary for 15 years, and to R. P. Wilson who, in this capacity, still serves athletics so well. As auditor, C. Davis put in a long term of voluntary service, while this year D. E. Downing completed his tenth year as honorary auditor.

For many years, there were no clubs, other than in Bulawayo, that existed solely for the fostering of cycling and athletics and the governing body would have encountered great difficulty in arranging its championship meetings but for the assistance of the various Caledonian Societies. Each year these latter hold Highland Games in Bulawayo, Umtali and Salisbury, and championships are often included in the programmes. But for these Caledonian sports it is doubtful whether Rhodesian cycling and athletics would have attained to their present high standard.

Most of the cycling and athletic meetings in the Midlands have been under the auspices of the Gwelo Sons of England Society. H. Munro Samuel played a large part in the organising of these meetings. One of the best athletes from the Midlands was J. J. de C. Walsh, a sprinter. He was also proficient at most other sports. To-day he is a shrewd judge of form and, gifted with a rare humour, Jack Walsh is popular with all sportsmen.

With so few clubs devoted to the furtherance of the two sports it is fortunate that the schools produce such fine athletes. They do this chiefly through the annual inter-school sports, the original organiser of which, in 1912, was Lieut.-Col. J. B. Brady, D.S.O., M.P., who is now vice-president of the Union.

The coming of A. F. H. Newton in 1927 gave athletics throughout the Colony a fresh impetus. This famous runner's best work here was the formation of the Bulawayo Harriers' Club, which is to-day the stronghold of athletic activity in Rhodesia.

Among those deserving of special mention for their service to athletics are A. H. MacDonald, a splendid organiser of sports gatherings, G. W. Ledeboer, T. G. Standing, C. Dodd, R. L. Hardy, Major C. Duly, D.S.O., who may be styled the " G.O.M. " of cycling in Rhodesia, J. J. Sloman, and G. D. Smith. The latter, who is the sports editor on " The Bulawayo Chronicle," has, in fact, done much for all sports here and gratitude is due to him and his paper.

Rhodesia has produced some splendid athletes who have performed very creditably against runners and jumpers both in and out of the Colony. The cyclists, however, have earned the highest honours and numerous South African champion- ship titles have been won by Rhodesians.

H. P. McKay.   J. H. Galvin.

THE NATAL VISIT, 1927.

75 yards: Atkinson (N.), 7 4-5 secs.
100 yards: Atkinson, 10 secs.
120 yards: Atkinson, 11 4-5 secs.
220 yards: Bayley (N.), 23 2-5 secs.
440 yards, Bayley, 52 secs.
880 yards: R. P. Wilson, 2 mins. 5 1-5 secs.
1 mile: R. P. Wilson, 4 mins. 49 secs.
120 yards hurdles: Atkinson, 15 4-5 secs.
High Jump: Bell (N.), 5ft. 10ins.
Long Jump: Atkinson, 21ft. 7ins.
Hop, step and jump: T. Viljoen (N.), 39ft. 1½ins.
Shot put: Bell, 38ft.

THE WANDERERS CLUB VISIT, 1930.

AT UMTALI.

220 yards: Duston (W.), 22 4-5 secs.

AT SALISBURY.

220 yards: Duston, 22 2-5 secs.
220 yards (heats): Hartman (W.), 22 1-5 secs.
880 yards: Jones (W.), 1 min 57 2-5 secs.

AT BULAWAYO.

100 yards: M. Meltzer (Milton School), 10 secs.
220 yards: M. Meltzer, 22 3-5 secs.
440 yards: Jones, 51 secs.
Long jump: Evans (W.), 22ft. 11ins.
Long jump: J. H. Galvin (Byo.), 22ft. 2ins.

THE BLOEMFONTEIN HARRIERS' VISIT, 1932.

Women's Events.

100 yards: Miss M. G. Bragge (Bulawayo) 11 2-5 secs.
220 yards: Miss Pretorius (Bloemfontein), 27 2-5 secs.
440 yards relay: Bloemfontein, 54 secs.
High jump: Miss A. Weaver (Bloemfontein), 4ft. 11ins.

Men's Events.

100 yards: J. de Klerk (Bloemfontein), 10 secs.
220 yards: J. de Klerk (Bloemfontein), 23 secs.
440 yards: M. Botha (Bloemfontein), 54 1-5 secs.
880 yards: A. W. Wright (Bloemfontein), 2 mins. 1 3-5 secs.
1 mile: A. W. Wright (Bloemfontein), 5 mins. 44 secs.
2 miles: A. W. Wright (Bloemfontein), 12 mins 7 secs.
4 miles: A. W. Wright (Bloemfontein), 23 mins. 20 secs.
Long jump: G. J. W. Hartwell (Bulawayo), 21ft. 5ins.
1 mile relay: Bloemfontein Harriers, 3 mins. 54 secs.

MASHONALAND ATHLETIC TEAM, 1932. *Beat Rhodes University by 19 points to 17.*

Standing: G. C. Maltas, E. A. J. Smith, I. McChlery, L. R. Carruthers, H. P. McCay, C. B. Richards.

G Howat, D. A. Ewing.

Sitting: E. Drakes, H. M. Botha, C. A. Wootton (capt.), I. S. Evans, J. B. Playford.

G. Harris.

A. Cook.

THE RHODES UNIVERSITY VISIT, 1932.

There was a triangular contest at Gwelo at which the Varsity scored 24 points, Gwelo 6 and Bulawayo 5 points.

(R. signifies the Varsity, B. Bulawayo, and G. Gwelo.)

100 yards: M. Meltzer (B.), 10 1-5 secs.
220 yards: E. Q. Davies (R.), 23 2-5 secs.
440 yards: J. H. Ingham (R.), 54 secs.
880 yards: M. L. Edmunds (B.), 2 mins 7 4-5 secs.
1 mile: G. Leach (R.), 4 mins. 43 secs.
2 miles: J. Ormond (R.), 10 mins 23 2-5 secs.
120 yards hurdles: Ingham (R.), 17 secs.
High jump: Davies (R.), 5ft. 9ins.
Jong jump: Davies (R.), 20ft. 3ins.
Shot put: Davies (R.), 35ft. 10ins.

In Salisbury the visitors were defeated by a Mashonaland team by 19 points to 17.

(M. Mashonaland.)

100 yards: C. A. Wootton (M.), 10 2-5 secs.
220 yards: Wootton, 22 4-5 secs.
440 yards: Wootton 52 2-5 secs.
880 yards: Leach (R.), 2 mins. 1 sec.
1 mile: Leach, 4 mins. 50 4-5 secs.
4 miles: J. B. Playford (M.), 22 mins. 22 secs.
120 yards hurdles: Davies (R.), 16 2-5 secs.
High jump: P. Kileff (M.), 5ft. 9½ins.
Long jump: I. S. Evans (M.), 20ft. 0½ins.
Pole vault: Leach, 11ft. 2ins.
Shot put: H. P. McCay (M.), 37ft. 3ins.
Javelin throw: P. Blakeway (R.), 173ft. 9ins.

THE INTER-PROVINCIAL MEETING, 1931.

Mashonaland: A. R. Kerr, A. W. McKenzie, A. B. Scott, J. B. Playford, H. M. Botha, C. A. Wootton, R. L. Harper, R. B. N. Wetmore, H. P. McCay.

Matabeleland: C. Dodd, W. F. Bromehead, H. R. Bragge, G. A. Zamek, J. C. Rutherford, A. N. Cross, P. MacDonald, C. W. Hall, G. J. W. Hartwell, A. M. Perry, J. H. Galvin, D. G. Blackbeard, J. W. Willing.

Results:

100 yards: Wootton, 10 3-5 secs.
220 yards: Wootton, 22 4-5 secs.
440 yards: Wootton, 52½ secs.
880 yards: Bragge, 2 mins. 7 1-5 secs.
1 mile: Hall, 4 mins 45 secs.
4 miles: Zamek, 23 mins. 15 3-5 secs.
120 yards hurdles: Harper, 16 4-5 secs.   (Equal to his own Rhodesian record).
High jump: Blackbeard, 5ft. 5ins.
Long jump: Galvin, 21ft. 2ins.
Shot put: McKenzie: 38ft. 0½ins.
Hammer throw: McKenzie, 93ft.

RHODESIAN RECORDS.

30/5/08.—75 yards flat ... ... F. St. J. Bromehead.
(7 1-5 secs.)

1/1/13.—100 yards flat ... ... D.W. Smith.

27/5/33.—100 yards flat ... ... G. J. W. Hartwell.
(10 secs.)

30/5/08.—120 yards flat ... ... F. St. J. Bromehead.

25/5/26.—120 yards flat ... ... O. Conolly.
(12 1-5 secs.)

5/7/30.—220 yards flat ... ... I. S. Evans.
(22 3-5 secs.)

16/5/31.—440 yards flat ... ... W. F. Bromehead.

3/5/35.—440 yards flat ... ... L. Archell.
(51 1-5 secs.)

18/3/26.—880 yards flat ... ... R. P. Wilson.
(2 mins. 0 3-5 secs.)

3/6/25.—1 mile flat ... ... R. P. Wilson.
(4 mins. 34 3-5 secs.)

16/10/30.—120 yards hurdles ... ... R. L. Harper.
(16 4-5 secs.)

4/5/35.—High jump ... ... B. C. Ledeboer.
(5ft. 11¼ins.)

13/7/31.—Long jump ... ... J. H. Galvin.
(22ft. 5½ins.)

25/5/28.—Hop, step and jump ... ... J. H. Galvin.
(41ft. 11ins.)

4/5/35.—Pole vault ... ... I. M. Barratt.
(12ft.)

4/5/35.—Putting the shot ... ... H. P. McKay.
(42ft. 4¾ins.)

3/6/24.—Throwing the hammer ... ... A. W. McKenzie.
(117ft. 10ins.)

27/8/32.—4 miles track ... ... G. A. Zamek.
(22 mins. 42 2-5 secs.)

10/6/28.—10 miles cross country ... ... R. P. Wilson.
(1 hr. 0 min. 29 secs.)

4/3/28.—Marathon (26 miles 385 yards) ... ... R. P. Wilson.
(2 hrs. 46mins. 50 secs.)

15/8/27.—60 miles road race ... ... A. F. H. Newton.
(7 hrs. 35 mins. 55 secs.)

10/7/27.—100 miles road race ... ... A. F. H. Newton.
(14 hrs. 43 mins.)

2/7/32.—100 yards flat (ladies) ... ... Miss M. G. Bragge.
(11 2-5 secs.)

5/7/30.—High jump (ladies) ... ... Miss M. G. Bragge.
(4ft. 11ins.)

27/5/33.—Throwing the discus ... ... A. J. Bell
(110ft. 2½ins.)

21/5/34.—Throwing the javelin ... ... A. J. Bell.
(169ft. 10ins.)

RHODESIAN CHAMPIONSHIP WINNERS.

1903.
440 yards flat.—W. H. Trott ... ... 53 4-5 secs.
1904.
220 yards flat.—W. H. Trott ... ... 23 4-5 secs.
440 yards flat.—W. H. Trott ... ... 51 secs.
Long jump.—F. G. Brooks ... ... 19ft. 9½ins.
1905.
120 yards flat.—F. G. Brooks ... ... 12 4-5 secs.
220 yards flat.—W. H. Trott ... ... 23 secs.
440 yards flat.—W. H. Trott ... ... 53 secs.
880 yards flat.—H. Carr ... ... 2 mins. 27 1-5 secs.
1 mile.—R. A. Gower ... ... 5 mins.
1906.
100 yards flat.—W. Greathead ... ... 11 secs.
220 yards flat.—W. H. Trott ... ... 23 1-5 secs.
440 yards flat.—W. H. Trott ... ... 52 secs.
High jump.—J. P. Purcell ... ... 5ft. 3ins.
1907.
220 yards flat.—W. H. Trott ... ... 23 3-5 secs.
440 yards flat.—J. Lea ... ... 58 secs.
120 yards hurdles.—H. van der Struys ... ... 19 secs.
1908.
75 yards flat.—F. St. J. Bromehead ... ... 7 1-5 secs.
100 yards flat.—F. G. Brooks ... ... 10 2-5 secs.
120 yards flat.—F. St. J. Bromehead ... ... 12 1-5 secs.
120 yards hurdles.—H. van der Struys ... ... 18 2-5 secs.
1909.
100 yards flat.—F. G. Brooks ... ... 10 3-5 secs.
220 yards flat.—W. H. Griffiths ... ... 25 1-5 secs.
1 mile.—W. H. Griffiths ... ... 5 mins. 4 4-5 secs.
120 yards hurdles.—T. E. Wylde ... ... 17 secs.
1910.
100 yards flat.—F. St. J. Bromehead ... ... 10 1-5 secs.
440 yards flat.—N. W. Eastwood ... ... 49 3-5 secs.
1 mile flat.—W. H. Griffiths ... ... 5 mins. 0 1-5 secs.
120 yards hurdles.—T. E. Wylde ... ... 17 1-5 secs.
High Jump.—W. X. Stuttaford ... ... 5ft. 3½ins.
1911.
100 yards flat.—A. N. Hutchinson ... ... 10 4-5 secs.
440 yards flat.—A. N. Hutchinson ... ... 52 secs.
880 yards flat.—A. N. Hutchinson ... ... 2 mins. 12 secs.
1 mile flat.—J. Abrams ... ... 4 mins. 58 2-5 secs.
1912.
75 yards flat.—A. N. Hutchinson ... ... 8 3-5 secs.
100 yards flat.—A. N. Hutchinson ... ... 11 secs.
120 yards flat.—A. N. Hutchinson ... ... 12 3-5 secs.
220 yards flat.—F. St. J. Bromehead ... ... 24 3-5 secs.
440 yards flat.—D. R. McLachlan ... ... 54 2-5 secs.
880 yards flat.—W. H. Griffiths ... ... 2 mins. 12 secs.
1 mile flat.—J. W. Elsworth ... ... 5 mins. 13 secs.
High jump.—J. P. Purcell ... ... 5ft. 5ins.
High jump (standing).—J. P. Purcell ... ... 4ft. 8 1-16ins.
Long jump.—A. Loggie ... ... 21ft. 0½ins.
10 miles cross country.—P. J. Kealy ... ... 1 hr. 10 mins. 54 4-5 secs.

1913.

100 yards flat.—D. W. Smith ... ... 10 secs.
120 yards flat.—A. Campbell ... ... 13 secs.
440 yards flat.—A. N. Hutchinson ... ... 53 2-5 secs.
880 yards flat.—H. E. Cohen ... ... 2 mins. 14 4-5 secs.
1 mile flat.—A. Hampson ... ... 5 mins. 23 secs.
High jump.—J. P. Purcell ... ... 5ft. 4ins.
Long jump.—C. Pfaff ... ... 20ft. 1in.
Putting the shot (16lb.).—W. S. Wood ... ... 36ft. 6½ins.
Throwing the hammer.—A. Loggie ... ... 84ft. 1in.

1914.

100 yards flat.—D. W. Smith ... ... 10 1-5 secs.
120 yards flat.—A. H. Minter ... ... 13 1-5 secs.
880 yards flat.—W. H. Griffiths ... ... 2 mins. 19 4-5 secs.
1 mile flat.—W. G. Walton ... ... 5 mins. 1 1-5 secs.
High jump.—E. W. Eyles ... ... 5ft. 8½ins.
Long jump.—T. Wilson ... ... 20ft. 7ins.
Putting the 16lb. shot.—W. S. Wood ... ... 37ft.
Throwing the 16lb. hammer.—J. Robertson ... ... 93ft. 8ins.

1919.

75 yards flat.—A. Ross ... ... 8 1-5 secs.
100 yards flat.—A. Ross ... ... 10 3-5 secs.
120 yards flat.—A. Ross ... ... 13 secs.
220 yards flat.—A. Ross ... ... 23 4-5 secs.
440 yards flat.—C. Schultz ... ... 53 4-5 secs.
880 yards flat.—C. Schultz ... ... 2 mins. 8 2-5 secs.
High jump.—D. G. Blackbeard ... ... 5ft. 6ins.
Long jump.—C. R. Rouncivell ... ... 18ft. 7ins.
Putting the 16lb. shot.—D. McLean ... ... 38ft. 11ins.
Throwing the 16lb. hammer.—W. F. Sutherland ... ... 86ft. 10½ins.

1920.

75 yards flat.—M. Iverson ... ... 8 2-5 secs.
100 yards flat.—T. P. Leach ... ... 11 secs.
120 yards flat.—T. A. Hubbard ... ... 13 secs.
220 yards flat.—T. A. Hubbard ... ... 24 1-5 secs.
440 yards flat.—C. H. Schultz ... ... 55 1-5 secs.
880 yards flat.—H. S. Walker ... ... 2 mins. 13 secs.
1 mile flat.—J. Ashwin ... ... 5 mins. 3 secs.
120 yards hurdles. J. Hazelhurst ... ... 17 3-5 secs.
High jump.—D. G. Blackbeard ... ... 5ft. 9ins.
Long jump.—J. G. W. Baggott ... ... 21ft. 7ins.
Hop, step and jump.—C. R. Deary ... ... 41ft. 5ins.
Putting the 16lb. shot.—D. McLean ... ... 36ft. 10½ins.
Throwing the 16lb. hammer.—D. McLean ... ... 109ft. 0ins.

1921.

75 yards flat.—E. Nevett ... ... 8 2-5 secs.
100 yards flat.—C. E. Nevett ... ... 10 4-5 secs.
120 yards flat.—S. Hepker ... ... 12 4-5 secs.
220 yards flat.—E. Nevett ... ... 23 2-5 secs.
440 yards flat.—C. Schultz ... ... 54 3-5 secs.
880 yards flat.—H. S. Walker ... ... 2 mins. 10 3-5 secs.
1 mile flat.—J. Ashwin ... ... 4 mins. 50 secs.
120 yards hurdles.—D. G. Blackbeard ... ... 20 1-5 secs.
High jump.—D. G. Blackbeard ... ... 5ft. 8½ins.
Long jump.—L. H. Waring ... ... 19ft.
Hop, step and jump.—J. G. W. Baggott ... ... 40ft. 6ins.
Putting the shot.—A. W. McKenzie ... ... 35ft. 1in.

1922.

75 yards flat.—C. E. Nevett ... ... 8 secs.
100 yards flat.—C. E. Nevett ... ... 10 3-5 secs.
120 yards flat.—G. Fletcher ... ... 12 3-5 secs.
220 yards flat.—C. E. Nevett ... ... 23 2-5 secs.
440 yards flat.—G. E. Fletcher ... ... 55 4-5 secs.
880 yards flat.—H. S. Walker ... ... 2 mins. 10 2-5 secs.
High jump.—D. G. Blackbeard ... ... 5ft. 4¾ins.
Long jump.—J. G. W. Baggott ... ... 20ft. 4ins.
Putting the shot.—A. W. McKenzie ... ... 37ft. 2ins.
Throwing the 16lb. hammer.—A. W. McKenzie ... ... 115ft. 1½ins.

1923.

75 yards flat.—E. R. Tamblyn ... ... 8 1-5 secs.
100 yards flat.—E. Nevett ... ... 10 4-5 secs.
220 yards flat.—R. R. Tamblyn ... ... 23 1-5 secs.
880 yards flat.—R. P. Wilson ... ... 2 mins. 5 3-5 secs.
High jump.—D. G. Blackbeard ... ... 5ft. 8ins.
Long jump.—J. G. W. Baggott ... ... 20ft. 5½ins.
Putting the shot.—A. W. McKenzie ... ... 39ft. 5½ins.
Throwing 16lb. hammer.—A. W. McKenzie ... ... 102ft. 3ins.

1924.

100 yards flat.—J. Markham ... ... 10 1-5 secs.
120 yards flat.—E. R. Tamblyn ... ... 12 2-5 secs.
220 yards flat.—E. R. Tamblyn ... ... 23 4-5 secs.
440 yards flat.—E. R. Tamblyn ... ... 54 secs.
880 yards flat.—W. R. Nelson ... ... 2 mins. 9 2-5 secs.
120 yards hurdles.—J. Hazelhurst ... ... 17 4-5 secs.
High jump.—D. G. Blackbeard ... ... 5ft. 4½ins.
Long jump.—D. G. Blackbeard ... ... 19ft. 5ins.
Hop, step and jump.—J. G. W. Baggott ... ... 41ft. 8ins.
Putting the shot.—A. W. McKenzie ... ... 37ft. 4ins.
Throwing the 16lb. hammer.—A. W. McKenzie ... ... 117ft. 10ins.

1925.

75 yards flat.—O. Conolly ... ... 8 1-5 secs.
100 yards flat.—E. R. Tamblyn ... ... 10 1-5 secs.
120 yards flat.—O. Conolly ... ... 12 4-5 secs.
220 yards flat.—F. Parks ... ... 23 2-5 secs.
440 yards flat.—W. R. Nelson ... ... 53 secs.
880 yards flat.—R. P. Wilson ... ... 2 mins. 6 secs.
1 mile.—R. P. Wilson ... ... 4 mins. 34 3-5 secs.
120 yards hurdles.—W. R. Nelson ... ... 18 secs.
High jump.—D. G. Blackbeard ... ... 5ft. 6ins.
Long jump.—R. J. Perrott ... ... 20ft. 5ins.
Putting the shot.—A. W. McKenzie ... ... 37ft. 4ins.
Throwing 16lb. hammer.—F. Chalmers ... ... 96ft. 8ins.

1926.

100 yards flat.—O. Conolly ... ... 10 4-5 secs.
120 yards flat.—O. Conolly ... ... 12 1-5 secs.
220 yards flat.—T. H. Martin ... ... 23 secs.
440 yards flat.—R. P. Wilson ... ... 52 1-5 secs.
880 yards flat.—R. P. Wilson ... ... 2 mins. 1 2-5 secs.
1 mile flat.—W. R. Nelson ... ... 4 mins. 46 secs.
High jump.—D. G. Blackbeard ... ... 5ft. 5ins.
Long jump.—J. H. Steyn ... ... 19ft. 1in.
Hop, step and jump.—R. J. Perrott ... ... 40ft. 4½ins.
Putting the shot.—A. W. McKenzie ... ... 38ft.

1927.

880 yards flat.—R. P. Wilson ... ... 2 mins. 5 1-5 secs.
1 mile flat.—R. P. Wilson ... ... 4 mins. 49 secs.
Hop, step and jump.—T. Viljoen ... ... 39ft. 1½ins.
4 miles track.—F. C. M. Watkins ... ... 23 mins. 9 2-5 secs.
10 miles cross country.—R. P. Wilson ... ... 1 hr. 0 mins. 51 2-5 secs.
Marathon (26 miles 385 yards).—A. F. H. Newton ... 2 hrs. 55 mins.
60 miles road race.—A. F. H. Newton ... ... 7 hrs. 35 mins. 33 secs.
100 miles road race.—A. F. H. Newton ... ... 14 hrs. 43 mins.

1928.

75 yards flat.—J. Dodd ... ... 8 2-5 secs.
100 yards flat.—I. S. Evans ... ... 10 2-5 secs.
120 yards flat.—L. McDowell ... ... 12 3-5 secs.
220 yards flat.—J. Dodd ... ... 23 4-5 secs.
440 yards flat.—J. Dodd ... ... 53 secs.
880 yards flat.—H. E. F. Mathews ... ... 2 mins. 13 1-5 secs.
1 mile flat.—S. G. E. Allnutt ... ... 4 mins. 51 2-5 secs.
120 yards hurdles.—A. S. Haslam ... ... 20 3-5 secs.
High jump.—D. A. R. Arnold ... ... 5ft. 1¾ins.
Long jump.—J. H. Galvin ... ... 21ft. 2ins.
Hop, step and jump.—J. H. Galvin ... ... 41ft. 11ins.
Putting the shot.—F. Gill ... ... 38ft.
Throwing 16lb. hammer.—A. W. McKenzie ... ... 108ft. 9ins.
10 miles cross country.—R. P. Wilson ... ... 1 hr. 0 mins. 29 secs.
Marathon (26 miles 385 yds.).—R. P. Wilson ...2 hrs. 46 mins. 50 secs.

1929.

75 yards flat.—M. Meltzer ... ... 7 3-5 secs.
100 yards flat.—M. Meltzer ... ... 10 2-5 secs.
220 yards flat.—J. Dodd ... ... 23 4-5 secs.
440 yards flat.—J. Dodd ... ... 54 secs.
880 yards flat.—E. Smith ... ... 2 mins. 5 3-5 secs.
1 mile flat.—M. L. Edmunds ... ... 4 mins. 55 1-5 secs.
120 yards hurdles.—R. L. Harper ... ... 17 secs.
High jump.—A. M. Perry ... ... 5ft. 6ins.
Long jump.—J. H. Galvin ... ... 21ft. 6½ins.
Hop, step and jump.—D. G. Blackbeard ... ... 39ft. 11½ins.
Putting the shot.—A. W. McKenzie ... ... 35ft. 3½ins.
Throwing 16lb. hammer.—A. W. McKenzie ... ... 104ft. 2ins.
4 miles track.—R. Wetmore ... ... 23 mins. 44 secs.
10 miles cross country.—G. A. Zamek ... ... 1 hr. 1 min. 20 secs.
Marathon (26 miles 385 yards).—G. A. Zamek, 3 hrs. 28 mins. 30 secs.

1930.

100 yards flat.—M. Meltzer ... ... 10 1-5 secs.
220 yards flat.—I. S. Evans ... ... 22 3-5 secs.
440 yards flat.—A. R. Kerr ... ... 53 1-5 secs.
880 yards flat.—A. R. Kerr ... ... 2 mins. 3 4-5 secs.
1 mile flat.—M. L. Edmunds ... ... 4 mins. 54 3-5 secs.
120 yards hurdles.—R. L. Harper ... ... 16 4-5 secs.
High jump.—P. Kileff ... ... 5ft. 7ins.
Long jump.—J. H. Galvin ... ... 22ft. 2ins.
Hop, step and jump.—J. H. Galvin ... ... 39ft. 10½ins.
Putting the shot.—A. W. McKenzie ... ... 37ft. 3½ins.
Throwing 16lb. hammer.—A. W. McKenzie ... ... 105ft. 6ins.
4 miles track.—J. B. Playford ... ... 22 mins. 44 4-5 secs.
100 yards (ladies).—Miss M. G. Bragge ... ... 12 secs.
High jump (ladies).—Miss M. G. Bragge ... ... 4ft. 11ins.

1931.

100 yards flat.—C. A. Wootton ... ... 10 2-5 secs.
220 yards flat.—H. M. Botha ... ... 23 3-5 secs.
440 yards flat.—W. F. Bromehead ... ... 51 1-5 secs.
880 yards flat.—C. W. Hall ... ... 2 mins. 11 4-5 secs.
1 mile flat.—C. W. Hall ... ... 4 mins. 50 4-5 secs.
120 yards hurdles.—R. L. Harper ... ... 17 4-5 secs.
High jump.—P. Kileff ... ... 5ft. 8ins.
Long jump.—J. H. Galvin ... ... 22ft. 5½ins.
Hop, step and jump.—J. H. Galvin ... ... 39ft. 10½ins.
Putting the shot.—A. W. McKenzie ... ... 36ft. 1in.
Throwing 16lb. hammer.—A. W. McKenzie ... ... 96ft. 5ins.
4 miles flat.—G. A. Zamek ... ... 23 mins. 39 2-5 secs.
10 miles cross country.—G. A. Zamek ... ... 1 hr. 1 min. 29 secs.
Marathon (26 miles 385 yards).—G. A. Zamek—
3 hrs. 0 mins. 25 2-5 secs.
100 yards (ladies).—Miss M. G. Bragge ... ... 12 4-5 secs.
220 yards (ladies).—Miss M. G. Bragge ... ... 27 3-5 secs.
High jump (ladies).—Miss B. Musgrove ... ... 4ft. 5ins.

1932.

100 yards flat.—C. A. Wootton ... ... 10 1-5 secs.
220 yards flat.—C. A. Wootton ... ... 22 4-5 secs.
440 yards flat.—H. R. Bragge ... ... 52 4-5 secs.
880 yards flat.—H. R. Bragge ... ... 2 mins. 5 secs.
1 mile flat.—M. L. Edmunds ... ... 4 mins. 54 2-5 secs.
High jump.—P. Kileff ... ... 5ft. 9½ins.
Long jump.—J. H. Galvin ... ... 21ft. 1in.
Hop, step and jump.—J. H. Galvin ... ... 39ft.
Pole vault.—G. Leach ... ... 11ft. 2ins.
Putting the shot.—A. W. McKenzie ... ... 37ft. 1in.
4 miles flat.—G. A. Zamek ... ... 22 mins. 42 2-5 secs.
10 miles cross country.—G. A. Zamek ... ... 1 hr. 5 mins. 30 4-5 secs.
100 yards (ladies).—Miss M. G. Bragge ... ... 11 2-5 secs.
220 yards (ladies).—Miss M. G. Bragge ... ... 29 4-5 secs.
High jump (ladies).—Miss M. G. Bragge ... ... 4ft. 8ins.

1933.

100 yards flat.—G. J. W. Hartwell ... ... 10 1-5 secs.
220 yards flat.—H. M. Botha ... ... 22 2-5 secs.
440 yards flat.—E. J. Smith ... ... 51 3-5 secs.
880 yards flat.—H. R. Bragge ... ... 2 mins. 2 4-5 secs.
1 mile flat.—A. B. Scott ... ... 4 mins. 47 4-5 secs.
120 yards hurdles.—I. McChlery ... ... 16 1-5 secs.
High jump.—P. Kileff ... ... 5ft. 10ins.
Long jump.—I. S. Evans ... ... 21ft.
Hop, step and jump.—F. E. McChlery ... ... 41ft. 7ins.
Pole vault.—P. Kileff ... ... 10ft. 2ins.
Putting the shot.—A. J. Bell ... ... 38ft. 5ins.
Throwing 16lb. hammer.—G. Howat ... ... 91ft. 3½ins.
Throwing the Javelin.—I. McChlery ... ... 164ft. 1in.
4 miles flat.—A. B. Scott ... ... 22 mins. 58 secs.
100 yards (ladies).—Miss M. Bragge ... ... 11 4-5 secs.
220 yards (ladies).—Miss D. Ballantyne ... ... 27 secs.
High jump (ladies).—Miss M. Bragge ... ... 4ft. 6½ins.
Throwing the discus.—A. J. Bell ... ... 110ft. 2½ins.

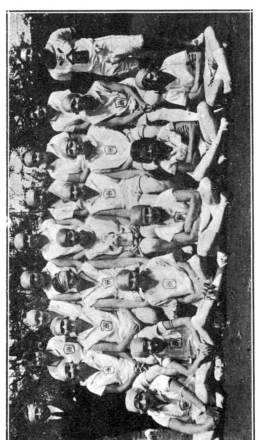

BULAWAYO HARRIERS LADIES SECTION, 1927.

Standing: A. H. MacDonald (Coach), ————, A. O'Connor, A. Wilson, D. Preece,
G. Bull, N. Stanbury, G. Brown, A. F. H. Newton (Trainer).

Sitting: R. Mail, G. Cooper, E. Cooper, D. Miller (Capt.), N. Jevons, P. Lynch,
D. Hartwell.

Bottom row: M. Montgomery, M. Trott, J. Payne, D. Miller, E. Botton, H. Hill.

1934.

100 yards flat.—G. J. W. Hartwell ... ... 10 secs.
220 yards flat.—G. J. W. Hartwell ... ... 22 3-5 secs.
440 yards flat.—G. T. Crispin ... ... 51 2-5 secs.
880 yards flat.—G. W. Harris ... ... 2 mins. 5 secs.
1 mile flat.—A. B. Scott ... ... 4 mins. 42 2-5 secs.
4 miles.—A. B. Scott ... ... 22 mins. 42 3-5 secs.
10 miles.—G. A. Zamek ... ... 1 hr. 5 mins. 30 4-5 secs.
Shot put.—H. P. McCay ... ... 42ft. 2¼ins.
Hop, step and jump.—F. E. McChlery ... ... 40ft. 3ins.
High jump.—B. C. Ledeboer ... ... 5ft. 10ins.
Long jump.—B. C. Ledeboer ... ... 22ft. 2½ins.
120 yards hurdles.—B. C. Ledeboer ... ... 16 2-5 secs.
Throwing the javelin.—A. J. Bell ... ... 169ft. 10ins.
Throwing the discus.—A. J. Bell ... ... 106ft. 7ins.
Pole vault.—P. Kileff ... ...10ft.
100 yards (ladies).—Miss I. S. Ballantyne ... ... 11 4-5 secs.
220 yards (ladies).—Miss I. S. Ballantyne ... ... 26 2-5 secs.
High jump (ladies).—Miss M. Bragge ... ... 4ft. 10ins.
80 metres hurdles (ladies).—Miss M. Bragge ... ... 14 3-5 secs.

1935.

100 yards flat.—G. J. W. Hartwell ... ... 10 secs.
220 yards flat.—G. J. W. Hartwell ... ... 22 4-5 secs.
440 yards flat.—L. Archell ... ... 51 1-5 secs.
880 yards flat.—G. W. Harris ... ... 2 mins. 1 sec.
1 mile flat.—A. B. Scott ... ... 4 mins. 45 2-5 secs.
4 miles flat.—A. B. Scott ... ... 23 mins. 27 4-5 secs.
Shot put.—E. D. K. Maclean ... ... 36ft. 2ins.
Hop, step and jump.—F. E. McChlery ... ... 39ft.
High jump.—F. E. McChlery ... ... 5ft. 7¼ins.
Long jump.—I. S. Evans ... ... 19ft. 11ins.
120 yards hurdles.—F. Brown ... ... 18 secs.
Throwing the javelin.—A. F. Bennett ... ... 132ft. 2ins.
Throwing the discus.—E. D. K. Maclean ... ... 104ft.
Throwing the hammer.—G. Howat ... ... 90ft. 10ins.
Pole vault.—I. M. Barratt ... ... 11ft. 7ins.
100 yards (ladies).—Miss C. Keay ... ... 11 3-5 secs.
220 yards (ladies).—Miss C. Keay ... ... 26 3-5 secs.
High jump (ladies).—Miss N. Westergaard ... ... 4ft. 7ins.

MAJOR MAURICE HEANY

Took part in the raising and equipping of the Salisbury Horse, and was
appointed to Command "A" Troop.

CYCLING

THIS sport has always been popular in Rhodesia and though it is not so general among the young men of to-day, there was a time when everyone who could afford to rode a bicycle. Mr. Rhodes was the only exception. Nothing could persuade him to give up his beloved pony for the iron contraption on wheels. In those days a roadster cost £45 and a racing bike a good deal more! The enthusiasm of those early cyclists may be measured by the fact that to-day their interest is unabated. To mention only two, Major C. Duly, D.S.O., and Capt. A. G. Hendrie, M.C., both of whom biked 600 miles to Rhodesia, have been prominent in the country's sporting activities for nearly 40 years, during which time they have built up a record of service that will never be forgotten.

It is a curious fact that the country's cycling activities have been confined almost entirely to Bulawayo. The first cycle race in Bulawayo was in 1895 on the original B.A.C. ground. The distance was a mile. The scratch man was N. Platnauer, a German, and a fine rider. C. Duly, with 100 yards start, won by a 200 yards margin. After this he rode from scratch and remained on that mark for over six years when he retired. During 1895 cycle racing had become so popular that in 1896 the Bulawayo Amateur Athletic Club was formed with a very strong membership. Major M. Heany was its president and "Billie" Dempster its secretary. In 1896 the Queens Club built a cycle track which will remain forever in the memories of the old riders. It was, to all intents and purposes, square, and four and one-eighth laps to the mile. It was banked on the "home" corner only, with the result that the riders often went over the top into Grey Street. In spite of many disadvantages, however, some exciting events took place on this track and, comparatively speaking, excellent times were made.

It soon became obvious, however, that a proper cycle track was needed. The sport had become so popular that monthly competitions were being held and, in addition to the fact that these clashed with the football and cricket fixtures, the small, shapeless Queen's track was a perpetual handicap to the development of the sport. So, in 1901, the B.A.A.C. changed its name to the Kings A.A. Club and the recently-formed Municipal Council granted it the present King's Ground. The men trained hard and racing was very keen so that the meetings always drew big gates. Prominent early cyclists were Davy Coutts, I. Nicholson, a long distance man, C. Duly, up to ten miles, H. F. Sherry, Dan Gow, J. L. Johnstone, who in 1894 in the South African Championships won the mile in 2 mins. 29 4-5 secs. and the five miles in 13 mins. 43 secs., W. Henderson, H. E. Jackson who rode up from the Rand on the first tandem ever seen in Rhodesia, and J. Cowden, a fine rider who, however, paced rather than raced. The team for pacing in the 25 miles, triplet and tandem, was Cowden and Barrett, with H. R. Webb, Bowman and W. E. Say. Nicholson and Duly did 25 miles in under the hour, good going on the old track. The new club held social outings when about a hundred cyclists would turn out. They formed two groups, the fast squad who put their heads down and raced for the picnic spot, and the " steadies " who did the journey in comfort. Cape carts used to follow and Crombie's was a favourite spot for picnicking and sports.

Major C. Duly, D.S.O., V.D.

J. Cowden, M.P.

This Bulawayo Amateur Cycling Club had a fine war record. During the '96 Rebellion many of them, prominent among whom were Duly and Armstrong, rode despatches between Bulawayo and the outlying laagers, performing very valuable and dangerous work. At the outbreak of the Boer War the cyclists of the B.A.A.C. formed the " E " Troop or Cycle Corps under Plumer. They went through the campaign with great credit. At one juncture the Bulawayo cyclists kept the line of communication open along seventy miles, mostly by intrepid night riding.

Extract from Special General Brigade Orders by Major R. S. S. Baden-Powell, Commanding Frontier Force, Rustenburg, 9th July, 1900:

" The General Officer Commanding desires to place on record his appreciation of the valuable services which have very frequently been rendered of late by the Cyclists under Lieut. Duly and Sergeant-Major H. R. Webb. Lieut. Duly's ride, 140 miles, from Rustenburg to Pretoria and back, while the intermediate country was in the hands of the enemy, was ably seconded on Friday last by the ride of Troopers Pearson and Barrett from our Headquarters Camp to Rustenburg and back when the road traversed was in possession of the enemy."

Further orders mentioned MacDonald and Gold for breaking through the Boer investment of the Eland's River garrison and then through Boer lines to Pretoria.

While the decade following the Boer War saw an abatement of the earlier general enthusiasm, there were some fine riders in H. F. Sherry, whose 25 miles (paced) record created in 1903 was only beaten in 1927 by F. C. Bennett, H. W. Heekes, Ben Wilson, the Davies brothers, A. M. Cummings, many times Rhodesian champion, and J. S. Kritzinger, another great rider. The little cycling that was done in Salisbury was fostered by the Alexandra Club and J. B. Hamilton, M. E. Bain, W. H. and F. C. Flanagan, were excellent wheelers. In Que Que there was a crack cyclist in F. Holborn, who, at the sports in 1907, won the half-mile, the mile, the two miles and the five miles, all from scratch.

After the Great War there flourished the redoubtable R. J. Wentzel, who in 1924 represented Rhodesia at S.A. Championships and Olympic Trials at Durban, F. S. C. Seaborn and J. van Rooyen. Then in 1925, came that great enthusiast, R. C. Branfield, who did so much to put local

F. C. Bennett.   D. H. B. McKenzie.

J. van Rooyen.

cycling on the map. His keenness led to the discovery of
talent such as J. H. Carlsson, T. H. Dyke, B. H. Theron,
R. J. Potterton, J. A. Rolfe, J. P. D. van Heerden, F. C.
Bennett and D. H. B. McKenzie, with the gratifying result
that the three last named have gathered numerous South
African championship honours. Almost all of these riders
are members of the Bulawayo Harriers cycling section with
its headquarters at King's which is the real home of cycling
in Rhodesia. Other fine riders include I. H. Robertson, A.
Watt and A. V. Carver.

Challengers from the south came up here as early as
1897, but the local men proved too good for them. Thirty
years later, in 1927, A. J. Gibbs, the Natal crack, rode in
the Rhodesian championships and won the quarter-mile in
32 1-5 secs., the mile in 2 mins. 25 1-5 secs., the two miles
in 5 mins. 20 4-5 secs., and the five miles in 13 mins. 47 secs.
F. C. Bennett took the half mile in 75 4-5 secs. while the three
miles provided an all-Salisbury finish, L. Nel, S. du T.
Dreyer and J. F. Salmon taking the first three places in the
order named, Nel's time being 8 mins. 17 1-5 secs. In 1928
three Rhodesians rode in the South African Championships
and Olympic Trials at Paarl, R. C. Branfield and B. H.
Theron in the 100 miles and F. C. Bennett in the other
events. Shortly afterwards Branfield retired from the track,
but in 1934 staged a come-back and performed the remarkable feat of breaking the Rhodesian record for 25 miles
motor-paced, covering the distance in 47 mins. 39 1-5 secs.
and doing 31 miles, 472 yards in the hour.

When the Wanderers Club, Johannesburg, toured here
in 1930, they were accompanied by two Natal cyclists. In
a quarter-mile heat L. W. Moody's time was 31 4-5 secs.,
while the other visitor, J. C. Geoghegan, won the mile in 2
mins. 11 3-5 secs. In all other scratch events the Natalians
were beaten by local men.

In 1930 a team of local cyclists, captained by A. F. Bennett, went north to the Exposition at Elizabethville, where
Bennett won the 25 kilometre championship of the Belgian
Congo. Bennett crashed during the race, changed a wheel,
caught up the leaders despite the fact that they were fighting
for several lap prizes, and won.

The riding of Rhodesians has commanded so much
recognition in South Africa in recent years that in 1931 the
South African Championships were held in this country, F.

A. F. Bennett.

P. H. Gifford.

Lieut.-Col. J. B. Brady, D.S.O.,
M.P.

C. Bennett, D. H. B. McKenzie and A. F. Bennett representing Rhodesia. All six events were won by Rhodesians,
F. C. Bennett carrying off four of them.

In 1934, D. H. B. McKenzie represented Rhodesia at the
Empire Games. This splendid rider has held several South
African titles.

At the 1935 South African Championships, R. C. Branfield rode second in the 25 miles motor-paced event. D. H.
B. McKenzie was second in the 5 miles event and third in
two others, the 1,000 metres and the 1-mile race.

In 1935 McKenzie established himself as Rhodesia's
premier cyclist by winning all the local championships and
at present six of the Colony's records stand in his name.

Major R. Gordon, D.S.O., O.B.E.

OFFICERS PAST AND PRESENT OF THE RHODESIA AMATEUR ATHLETIC AND CYCLING UNION.

Patrons: Sir William Milton, 1901/14; Sir Drummond Chaplin, 1919/23; Sir John Chancellor, 1924/28; Sir Cecil Rodwell, 1929/34.

Presidents: Rev. J. G. Aldridge, 1901/2; Capt. W. Baxendale, 1903/13; Lt. Col. A. C. L. Webb, 1917/22, 1926/32; T. P. Gilbert, 1923/25; Capt. A. G. Hendrie, M. C., 1933; Lt.-Col. J. B. Brady, D.S.O., M.P., 1934; P. H. Gifford, 1935.

Vice-Presidents: C. Davis, 1917/20; Capt. A. G. Hendrie, M.C., 1921, 1923/25, 1929/32; Major C. Duly, D.S.O., 1933/34; Lt.-Col. J. B. Brady, D.S.O., M.P., 1935.

Hon. Secretaries and Treasurers: J. E. Jelks, 1901/2; Rev. J. G. Aldridge, 1903/4; A. G. Hendrie, 1905/20; D. G. Blackbeard, 1921/25; R. P. Wilson, 1926/32; J. Dodd, 1931; C. Dodd, 1933/34; R. P. Wilson, 1935.

Asst. Hon. Secretary and Treasurer: P. W. Hendrie, 1913/17.

Hon. Auditors: W. H. Trott, 1908/12; C. Davis and A. Ruxton, 1913; C. Davis and J. Fettes, 1919/20; C. Davis 1921/23; T. A. Ness, 1924; D. E. Downing, 1925 to date.

Delegates to S.A.A. and C.A.: D. W. E. Watkeys, 1926/27; Gordon Smith, 1926/28; F. A. Nicolai, 1928; W. J. Atkinson, 1929/32; F. R. Zurcher, 1929/35.

RHODESIAN RECORDS.

8/10/32.—Quarter Mile ... ... D. H. B. McKenzie.
(30 1-5 secs.)

1/8/25.—Half Mile ... ... R. J. Wentzel.
(1 min. 0 3-5 secs.)

12/8/33.—One Mile ... ... D. H. B. McKenzie.
(2 mins 11 secs.)

27/5/33.—Two Miles ... ... D. H. B. McKenzie.
(4 mins 4 2-5 secs.)

1/8/25.—Three Miles ... ... R. J. Wentzel.
(7 mins. 11 secs.)

21/5/34.—Five Miles ... ... D. H. B. McKenzie.
(11 mins. 57 4-5 secs.)

21/5/34.—Ten Miles ... ... D. H. B. McKenzie.
(24 mins. 20 secs.)

8/11/34.—25 Miles M.P. ... ... R. C. Branfield.
(31 miles, 472 yards in the hour) (47 mins. 39 1-5 secs.)

21/5/34.—1000 Metres ... ... D. H. B. McKenzie.
(1 min. 19 4-5 secs.)

16/7/33.—100 Miles ... ... J. A. Rolfe.
(5 hrs. 15 mins. 42 2-5 secs.)

RHODESIAN CHAMPIONSHIP WINNERS.
1903.

5 Miles.—H. F. Sherry ... ... 10 mins. 38 secs.
10 Miles.—H. F. Sherry ... ... 21 mins. 33 secs.
15 Miles.—H. F. Sherry ... ... 32 mins. 43 4-5 secs.
20 Miles.—H. F. Sherry ... ... 43 mins. 17 1-5 secs.
25 Miles.—H. F. Sherry ... ... 53 mins. 57 secs.
(27 miles, 630 yards 1ft. in the hour.)
25 Miles (unpaced).—H. F. Sherry ... ... 1 hr. 10 mins. 0 4-5 secs.

1904.

½ Mile.—J. B. Hamilton .... 1 min. 20 secs.
3 Miles.—W. H. Flanagan .... 8 mins. 23 2-5 secs.

1905.

¼ Mile.—M. E. Bain .... 38 3-5 secs.
3 Miles.—A. M. Cummings .... 8 mins. 7 4-5 secs.
5 Miles.—W. H. Flanagan .... 13 mins. 40 2-5 secs.

1906.

1 Mile.—W. G. Bayles .... 2 mins. 30 secs.
5 Miles.—A. M. Cummings .... 14 mins.

1907.

10 Miles.—E. V. Davies .... 29 mins. 13 secs.

1908.

10 Miles.—M. B. Davies (Hepworth Cup) ...... 27 mins. 40 secs.
25 Miles.—Ben Wilson (Dunlop Trophy) ... 1 hr. 10 mins. 44 secs.

1909.

1 Mile.—A. M. Cummings .... 2 mins. 24 1-5 secs.
3 Miles.—M. E. Bain .... 8 mins. 32 secs.
10 Miles.—M. B. Davies (Hepworth Cup) ...... 27 mins. 33 4-5 secs.
25 Miles.—A. M. Cummings (Dunlop Trophy)—
1 hr. 12 mins. 41 4-5 secs.

1910.

2 Miles.—J. S. Voster .... 5 mins. 48 3-5 secs.
5 Miles.—W. H. Flanagan .... 15 mins. 15 secs.
10 Miles.—J. S. Kritzinger (Hepworth Cup) ... 27 mins. 16 4-5 secs.
25 Miles.—J. S. Kritzinger .... 1 hr. 14 mins. 52 4-5 secs.

1911.

10 Miles.—J. S. Kritzinger .... 28 mins. 52 secs.
25 Miles.—J. S. Kritzinger (Dunlop Trophy)—
1 hr. 7 mins. 36 3-5 secs.

1912.

½ Mile.—H. A. Oberholster .... 1 min. 9 3-5 secs.
1 Mile.—J. S. Kritzinger .... 2 mins. 42 3-5 secs.
25 Miles.—J. S. Kritzinger .... 1 hr. 15 mins. 49 2-5 secs.

1913.

2 Miles.—R. L. Barratt .... 5 mins. 29 2-5 secs.
5 Miles.—R. D. Gracie .... 14 mins. 20 secs.
10 Miles.—J. A. Haarhoff .... 29 mins. 40 secs.

1914.

½ Mile.—R. C. J. Voster .... 1 min. 12 secs.
10 Miles.—R. D. Gracie .... 27 mins. 25 secs.

1921.

3 Miles.—F. S. C. Seaborn .... 8 mins. 22 2-5 secs.
5 Miles.—F. S. C. Seaborn .... 15 mins. 35 2-5 secs.

1922.

½ Mile.—R. J. Wentzel .... 1 min. 6 4-5 secs.
3 Miles.—R. J. Wentzel .... 8 mins 0 2-5 secs.
10 Miles.—R. J. Wentzel .... 28 mins. 51 3-5 secs.

1923.

½ Mile.—R. J. Wentzel .... 1 min. 27 1-5 secs.
1 Mile.—R. J. Wentzel .... 2mins. 40 secs.
5 Miles.—N. Erasmus .... 13 mins. 47 2-5 secs.
10 Miles.—R. J. Wentzel .... 29 mins. 2 secs.

1924.

½ Mile.—F. S. C. Seaborn .... 1 min. 14 secs.
2 Miles.—P. C. J. van Rooyen .... 6 mins. 56 secs.
10 Miles.—F. S. C. Seaborn.

1925.

¼ Mile.—J. van Rooyen ... ... 34 4-5 secs.
½ Mile.—R. J. Wentzel ... ... 1 min. 0 3-5 secs.
1 Mile.—R. C. Branfield ... ... 2 mins. 28 3-5 secs.
2 Miles.—R. J. Wentzel ... ... 5 mins. 21 secs.
3 Miles.—R. J. Wentzel ... ... 7 mins. 11 secs.
4 Miles.—J. van Rooyen ... ... 11 mins. 26 2-5 secs.
5 Miles.—F. J. Nel ... ... 14 mins. 53 3-5 secs.
10 Miles.—F. J. Nel ... ... 29 mins. 58 secs.

1926.

2 Miles.—A. F. Bennett ... ... 5 mins. 11½ secs.
5 Miles.—J. F. Salmon ... ... 14 mins. 3 2-5 secs.
10 Miles.—A. F. Bennett ... ... 28 mins. 58 secs.

1927.

¼ Mile.—F. C. Bennett ... ... 32 secs.
½ Mile.—F. C. Bennett ... ... 1 min. 15 4-5 secs.
3 Miles.—L. Nel ... ... 8 mins. 17 1-5 secs.
10 Miles.—F. C. Bennett ... ... 28 mins. 56 secs.
25 Miles M.P.—F. C. Bennett ... ... 50 mins. 56 secs.
(29 miles 204 yards in the hour)

1928.

¼ Mile.—R. C. Branfield ... ... 33 1-5 secs.
½ Mile.—A. Watt ... ... 1 min. 6 3-5 secs.
1 Mile.—J. A. Rolfe ... ... 2 mins. 25 2-5 secs.
2 Miles.—J. van Rooyen ... ... 4 mins. 51 4-5 secs.
3 Miles.—F. C. Bennett ... ... 7 mins. 38 secs.
5 Miles.—J. van Rooyen ... ... 12 mins. 43 4-5 secs.
10 Miles.—R. J. Potterton ... ... 26 mins. 18 2-5 secs.
20 Miles M.P.—F. C. Bennett ... ... 53 mins. 25 secs.

1929.

¼ Mile.—R. C. Branfield ... ... 33 1-5 secs.
½ Mile.—J. Rolfe ... ... 1 min. 3 secs.
1 Mile.—F. C. Bennett ... ... 2 mins. 26 secs.
2 Miles.—F. C. Bennett ... ... 4 mins. 58 1-5 secs.
3 Miles.—F. C. Bennett ... ... 7 mins. 43 4-5 secs.
5 Miles.—F. C. Bennett ... ... 12 mins. 14 2-5 secs.
10 Miles.—F. C. Bennett ... ... 26 mins. 52 2-5 secs.
25 Miles M.P.—F. C. Bennett ... ... 53 mins. 3 secs.

1930.

¼ Mile.—A. F. Bennett ... ... 33 4-5 secs.
½ Mile.—F. C. Bennett ... ... 1 min. 8 1-5 secs.
1 Mile.—F. C. Bennett ... ... 2 mins. 19 3-5 secs.
2 Miles.—D. H. B. McKenzie ... ... 5 mins. 2 3-5 secs.
3 Miles.—A. F. Bennett ... ... 7 mins. 41 3-5 secs.
5 Miles.—F. C. Bennett ... ... 13 mins. 9 secs.
10 Miles.—F. C. Bennett ... ... 25 mins. 36 3-5 secs.

1931.

¼ Mile.—D. H. B. McKenzie ... ... 32 4-5 secs.
½ Mile.—F. C. Bennett ... ... 1 min. 5 2-5 secs.
1 Mile.—F. C. Bennett ... ... 2 mins. 43 2-5 secs.
2 Miles.—F. C. Bennett ... ... 4 mins. 52 1-5 secs.
3 Miles.—F. C. Bennett ... ... 7 mins. 49 2-5 secs.
5 Miles.—F. C. Bennett ... ... 12 mins. 42 secs.
10 Miles.—D. H. B. McKenzie ... ... 26 mins. 25 secs.

1932.

¼ Mile.—D. H. B. McKenzie ... ... 30 1-5 secs.
½ Mile.—D. H. B. McKenzie ... ... 1 min. 12 2-5 secs.
1 Mile.—D. H. B. McKenzie ... ... 2 mins. 15 secs.
5 Miles.—D. H. B. McKenzie ... ... 12 mins. 9 4-5 secs.
10 Miles.—D. H. B. McKenzie ... ... 26 mins. 34 1-5 secs.

1933.

¼ Mile.—D. H. B. McKenzie ... ... 31 4-5 secs.
½ Mile.—D. H. B. McKenzie ... ... 1 min. 8 3-5 secs.
1 Mile.—D. H. B. McKenzie ... ... 2 mins. 11 secs.
2 Miles.—D. H. B. McKenzie ... ... 4 mins. 4 2-5 secs.
5 Miles.—W. A. Lieberman ... ... 12 mins. 22 2-5 secs.
10 Miles.—D. H. B. McKenzie ... ... 25 mins. 46 3-5 secs.
100 Miles.—J. A. Rolfe ... ... 5 hrs. 15 mins. 42 2-5 secs.

1934.

¼ Mile.—A. Watt ... ... 33 1-5 secs.
½ Mile.—W. A. Lieberman ... ... 1 min. 7 secs.
1 Mile.—E. J. MacKay ... ... 2 mins. 22 secs.
5 Miles.—A. Watt ... ... 12 mins. 38 secs.
10 Miles.—A. Watt ... ... 26 mins. 32 secs.
100 Miles.—A. V. Carver ... ... 5 hrs. 17 mins. 53 secs.
25 Miles M.P.—R. C. Branfield ... ... 47 mins. 39 1-5 secs.
(31 miles 472 yards in the hour.)

1935.

¼ Mile.—D. H. B. McKenzie ... ... 31 4-5 secs.
½ Mile.—D. H. B. McKenzie ... ... 1 min. 11 secs.
1 Mile.—D. H. B. McKenzie ... ... 2mins. 34 3-5 secs.
5 Miles.—D. H. B. McKenzie ... ... 13 mins. 26 3-5 secs.
10 Miles.—D. H. B. McKenzie ... ... 26 mins. 21 4-5 secs.

RHODESIAN WINNERS OF S.A. CHAMPIONSHIPS.

1929.

½ Mile.—F. C. Bennett ... ... 1 min. 17 1-5 secs.
1 Mile.—F. C. Bennett ... ... 2 mins. 45 2-5 secs.
10 Miles.—F. C. Bennett ... ... 26 mins. 24 secs.

1930.

½ Mile.—F. C. Bennett ... ... 1 min. 4 3-5 secs.
1 Mile.—F. C. Bennett ... ... 2 mins. 30 4-5 secs.
5 Miles.—F. C. Bennett ... ... 12 mins. 28 3-5 secs.

1931.

¼ Mile.—F. C. Bennett ... ... 31 1-5 secs.
½ Mile.—F. C. Bennett ... ... 1 min. 3 1-5 secs.
1 Mile.—F. C. Bennett ... ... 2 mins. 25 1-5 secs.
5 miles.—D. H. B. McKenzie ... ... 12 mins. 41 secs.
10 Miles.—F. C. Bennett ... ... 25 mins. 53 2-5 secs.
100 Miles.—J. P. D. van Heerden ... ... 5 hrs. 42 mins.

1932.

½ Mile.—F. C. Bennett ... ... 1 min. 8 1-5 secs.
1 Mile.—D. H. B. McKenzie ... ... 2 mins. 52 3-5 secs.
5 Miles.—F. C. Bennett ... ... 12 mins. 32 2-5 secs.
10 Miles.—D. H. B. McKenzie ... ... 24 mins. 3 secs.
100 Miles.—J. P. D. van Heerden ... ... 4 hrs. 53 mins. 7 2-5 secs.

1934.

½ Mile.—D. H. B. McKenzie ... ... 1 min. 13 3-10 secs.
10 Miles.—D. H. B. McKenzie ... ... 25 mins. 20 secs.

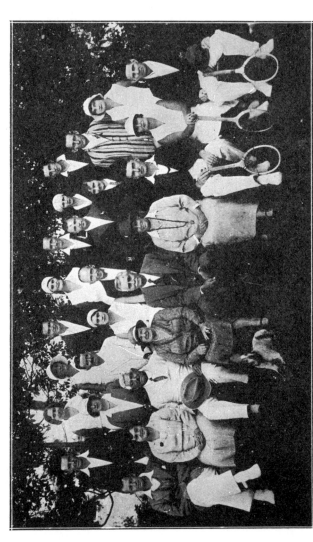

A GROUP OF PAST AND PRESENT CHAMPIONS.

Back Row: Mrs. Treloar, Miss E. McManus, A. P. Shone, Miss J. Standen (Mrs. Vallaro), D. P. C. Gumpertz, Mrs. Gumpertz, F. B. Brooks.

Middle Row: D. G. Blackbeard, Mrs. Pulbrook, J. McLoughlin, Mrs. Style, A. T. Tait, E. E. Cross, Mrs. Webb, C. S. Style, Mrs. Mail.

Sitting: H. Cross, Mrs. Jearey, W. S. Taberer, Mrs. Kennedy, Sir Percy Fynn, Mrs. A. M. Fleming, R. Vincent, Mrs. Griffin, F. G. Brooks.

TENNIS

BECAUSE of its simple equipment and the easy preparation of hard courts (there being no grass courts in Rhodesia) tennis was one of the first games to be played by the early settlers.

The first court was laid at Fort Victoria in 1893 by the enterprising proprietor of the Standard Hotel. Umtali saw the formation of the country's first club in December of 1893, as a result of the efforts of J. B. Taylor, the honorary secretary. The original Umtali court is now owned by the Park Club. Among the early Umtali players George Carey, who died recently in Salisbury, J. B. and T. P. Gilbert, Johnny Holland, Frank Myburgh, Chas. Eickhoff, Teddy Lamport and Mrs. J. Meikle were outstanding. In the following year, 1894, the Queen's and then the B.A.C. opened courts in Bulawayo, with P. T. Neve, first singles champion of Bulawayo, and other fine exponents. H. B. Douslin, Major R. M. Poore and J. Barry, among the first players. Gwelo followed suit in November, 1894, with the inauguration of a recreation club for tennis and cricket.

In Salisbury the first tennis court was laid out at the foot of A'Rari Kop, just behind the old Pioneer Store. Mrs. Cowan, Mrs. Caldicott and her sister were the first ladies to play on this court, and later they were joined by Mrs. Greenfield and her sister, Miss Cynthia Stockley, the novelist. The sport flourished under the aegis of the Salisbury Lawn Tennis Club, which was formed in 1894.

Within a year or two the game achieved a universal popularity, which it has maintained ever since, both socially and competitively, but as yet Rhodesia has produced no players of a standard comparable with the world's best.

Competitions began in Salisbury in 1897, when the first Rhodesian Championship meeting was organised by the Salisbury Lawn Tennis Club in September during a three weeks' carnival held throughout the country to celebrate the opening of the Railway from Vryburg to Bulawayo. A prime mover in the organisation of the tournament was G. N. Fleming, who can be called the doyen of Rhodesian tennis. To meet the long list of entries, three courts were hastily constructed, and these formed the nucleus of the present Salisbury Lawn Tennis Club. There were four championship events: gentlemen's and ladies' singles, gentlemen's doubles, and mixed doubles. There was no ladies' doubles event until 1920. In the final of the first event, for which there were ten entries, P. D. L. Fynn (now Sir Percy) beat G. C. Candler in straight sets, 6—1, 6—2, 6—2. Seven couples competed in the gentlemen's doubles, the final match being won by P. D. L. Fynn and W. S. Taberer who beat E. W. Graham and W. P. Grimmer, 6—4, 5—7, 11—9, 5—7, 6—4, a real marathon! There were only two entries for the ladies' event, Mrs. A. M. Fleming defeating Miss Coleman, 6—4, 6—3, the former also sharing with Grimmer the honour of winning the mixed doubles from Miss Coleman and Taberer, 7—5, 6—4. Four couples entered. The tournament was a great social event, and it is recorded that the fine band of the B.S.A. Police, conducted by Mr. Hinds, contributed greatly to the enjoyment of the spectators. What the competitors thought of the music is *not* recorded.

A team from Beira played Salisbury at this time and were well beaten. Two years later Salisbury returned the visit. Through the kindness of Mr. A. L. Lawley, then Administrator, free passes were granted on the railways. The Salisbury team consisted of Mr. and Mrs. W. S. Honey, Miss Candler (afterwards Mrs. Fynn) and Messrs. Graham, Fynn, Flanagan, Lingard and Morris. Salisbury won a close match by 161 games 18 sets, to 146 games 14 sets.

The Salisbury Lawn Tennis Club at this time had official control of the game, managing and advertising tournaments and conferring Rhodesian championship titles. In 1900 a curious condition was laid down: "The holder, in the case of being beaten by the challenger, to play the second player in the final event for second prize"!

In 1901 the Right Hon. Cecil John Rhodes gave two cups, one for each of the singles championships.

The annual open meetings continued to attract the best players from such centres as Bulawayo, Beira, Gwelo and Umtali, inspiring "Half-Volley" to write the following in the *Rhodesian Times*:

"A tennis court, some pretty sport, the lawn is bright with gazers,
And pouring tea so daintily, are pretty girls in 'blazers.' "

In 1905 the Salisbury Lawn Tennis Club, at the suggestion of the South African Lawn Tennis Union, undertook the formation of a Rhodesian Lawn Tennis Association. The following clubs affiliated: Salisbury and Alexandra, of Salisbury; Queen's, B.A.C. and the Suburban, of Bulawayo; Gwelo, Marandellas, Beira, and the Maramba, of Livingstone.

In 1906 Mr. G. N. Fleming presented a floating trophy for annual inter-club competition, teams to comprise four gentlemen players. In 1912 the competition became intertown. Mr. Fleming donated a second cup in 1933 under the same conditions as the first, but for women only. This was an inter-provincial trophy, and in 1934 the men's cup was also raised to inter-provincial status. The Fleming Cup encounters are to-day the most important in local tennis, and they have done much to maintain a high standard in the game.

The Association, from its inception, has been alive to the benefit of visits from touring teams, and Rhodesia has at various times had opportunities of trying conclusions with some of the world's best players, including Miss Kitty McKane and Miss Bobby Heine.

Four teams from England have toured Rhodesia.

The first was in 1909, led by Commander G. W. Hillyard, R.N., who was then Secretary of the Lawn Tennis Association (England). He was accompanied by Dr. W. V. Eaves, M. M. Woods and H. W. Sevenoaks. The two latter were Transvaal players who had replaced R. F. Doherty and L. H. Escombe who were unable, owing to ill-health, to visit Rhodesia. In Salisbury F. G. Brooks, P. D. L. Fynn, H. J. K. Brereton, and in Bulawayo, A. C. L. Webb and A. R. Welsh, all put up a good opposition against the visitors. The only Rhodesian win was secured by W. S. Taberer in Salisbury, and when two Bulawayo players combined with Salisbury to form a Rhodesian team, the Bulawayo couple, F. B. Brooks and E. Youatt, took a set off Woods and Sevenoaks.

The second English team toured Rhodesia early in 1911. It consisted of A. Wallis Myers (captain), C. P. Dixon, A. E. Beamish, R. B. Powell and F. G. Lowe. The Bulawayo match gave the visitors an easy victory, but in Salisbury their win was not so easily earned, by reason of the excellent play of P. D. L. Fynn and H. J. K. Brereton. This pair combined splendidly, Brereton breaking up the combination of the Englishmen with well-judged lobs, while Fynn brought

off many fine cross-court shots. They succeeded in beating
first Myers and Powell, and later Dixon and Lowe, the latter
couple in a tough tussle. The score in the first set at one
time read four all, and in the second eight all.

In March, 1912, a British mixed doubles team of two
couples, captained by A. D. Prebble, was due to come here,
but the men fell out and were replaced by two members of
the Wanderers' Club, Johannesburg. These were F. E.
Cochran and C. N. Davis, who partnered the English
women, Miss M. Coles and Miss E. G. Johnson. Rhodesia
achieved two singles wins, F. G. Brooks (Salisbury) defeating
Davis, and Mrs. A. L. Baker (Salisbury) inflicting on Miss
Coles her first defeat in South Africa. In a return match
Miss Coles emerged victorious from a very keen contest after
Mrs. Baker had won the first set. At Gwelo, Mrs. Shand
and Mrs. Peel played well to take a set off the visiting ladies.
No matches were played against Matabeleland. Miss Coles
and Davis remained for the Rhodesian championships at
Easter. They won the singles titles and, in partnership, the
mixed doubles title.

In January, 1926, Rhodesia saw the first complete
English mixed doubles team. In Salisbury the appearance
of Miss K. McKane, holder of the world's singles title, was
greeted with loud and prolonged applause. She was, however, unable to play in Bulawayo on account of indisposition.
The visitors, although never extended, won every match,
with one exception, when Andrew Ross (Bulawayo) defeated
G. R. O. Crole-Rees in straight sets.

Transvaal, our nearest neighbours, have sent up three
teams. The first came in 1921. Louis Raymond, holder of
the South African Men's Singles title, and Miss Edwards,
South African Women's Champion, were the two stars, while
Mr. and Mrs. Winslow, Mrs. McLaren, Mrs. Harding, Rex
Tucker and J. C. le Sueur made up the balance of a splendid
array of talent. In an exhibition game, Andrew Ross, of
Bulawayo, beat C. L. Winslow after a great struggle. In
Salisbury, F. G. Brooks defeated Tucker, the Brooks brothers
beat Tucker and le Sueur, Mrs. Ellis and Mrs. Jearey beat
Mrs. Winslow and Miss Edwards, and Mrs. Ellis and F. G.
Brooks won from Mr. and Mrs. Winslow.

Transvaal came up again in 1923 and played three
matches. As a team they were everywhere victorious, but
Rhodesia scored some noteworthy individual triumphs. In

Bulawayo Miss I. Gradwell defeated Miss Hopkins and A. Ross gained two victories, the first over C. R. Blackbeard and the other over A. W. Kirby. In the Capital the only local win was that of the Brooks brothers (F. G. and F.B.), who beat Kirby and M. J. Connor. At Gwelo, the veteran H. J. K. Brereton provided the strongest opposition in his singles match, but Kirby's youth eventually won the day. Mr. Victor R. Gauntlet, manager of the team and Rhodesia's councillor on the South African Lawn Tennis Union, made many friends here, and his willingness to officiate as umpire was much appreciated by the local officials.

In 1927 we welcomed the third Transvaal team, who gave us a very fine exhibition of the game. Salisbury won only two matches, when F. B. Brooks and H. S. Cross beat Rex Tucker and C. L. Winslow, and F. B. Brooks, after a keen singles tussle, defeated Rex Tucker. At Bulawayo Andrew Ross scored a great win over Winslow, and Mrs. Mail and E. A. Barbour beat Miss Cole and T. D. Green. Against Midlands the Transvaal lost two games, Evans and Geard beating G. D. Dodd and Green, while Mrs. Baker and Geard defeated Mrs. Neave and Dodd.

The first team from Natal paid a visit in September and October of 1926. Miss Bobbie Heine was the "star," and her performances at Bulawayo, Gwelo and Salisbury delighted the spectators. The only Rhodesian win was in the Capital, when F. G. Brooks and H. S. Cross won their match in straight sets from F. Wells and W. Pittaway. In a friendly match J. McLoughlin, of Salisbury, defeated L. Hatton. In many other matches, notably mixed doubies, the visitors were given a severe battle.

In 1931 the first overseas team to visit Rhodesia consisted of four men from Czecho-Slovakia, M. Soyka (captain), Jan Kozeluh, P. Macenauer, and F. Marsalek. The Matabeleland team scored three splendid victories, but the tourists had five wins to their credit and so won the match, Midlands were beaten decisively, winning only one set, which V. H. van Breda took from M. Soyka. At Salisbury the visitors likewise lost only one set, but the match had to be abandoned owing to heavy rain.

There have also been visits from individuals of note, and on each occasion the Association has arranged for coaching and exhibitions in order to improve the game under their jurisdiction.

H

RHODESIA v. NATAL, 1935.

M. H. Quinn, W. G. Wood, Mrs. C. Taberer, R. Vincent (capt.),
Mrs. Gumpertz, C. S. Style.

Miss N. Dugmore.

In December, 1911, the German star, F. W. Rahe, came to Salisbury on a visit of many weeks' duration to his sister, Mrs. Thierfelder, and advantage was taken of his stay to arrange several matches on the Salisbury courts, Rahe demonstrating his superiority throughout.

In 1932, George Demasius, the German professional, visited Rhodesia and was asked to coach at the various schools.

The Association has always given every encouragement to the youth of the Colony, and there are several inter-school as well as junior championships. Those who have donated floating trophies for these competitions are the late J. P. du Toit who, in 1926, represented Rhodesia on the South African Lawn Tennis Union Council, Sir Percy Fynn, A. Sanders, the Hon. A. R. Welsh, M.P., and Capt. C. E. Wells.

In May of 1932, Norman Farquharson, South African Singles Champion, gave exhibition matches during a business visit to Rhodesia, in the four principal towns, where his game was much admired. Except in Bulawayo, where he was beaten by Ralph Vincent, himself in the South African ranking list before he came to Rhodesia, Farquharson won all his matches.

This year, 1935, a Natal team has made an extensive tour of the Colony. The visitors were F. H. Lowe (captain) and Mrs. Lowe, holders of the South African Mixed Doubles Championship, Mrs. R. Hathorn, C. H. Robbs, who has represented Transvaal, E. Fannin, aged 19 and winner of the S.A. Junior Championship in 1933, and E. Getaz, who has represented South Africa against overseas teams.

Against Matabeleland the visitors won all their matches except one, when H. H. Davies defeated Getaz in straight sets. Natal also beat Rhodesia decisively, the only local victory being in the men's doubles, R. Vincent and M. H. Quinn beating Lowe and Robbs. In his singles against Lowe, Vincent gave a fine exhibition and was only narrowly beaten.

After a comfortable win over Midlands, the Natal team played in the Rhodesian Championships at Salisbury, which were thrown open to them by the Rhodesia Lawn Tennis Association. They annexed all five titles. They also won all nine matches against Mashonaland, the latter taking only two sets. Towards the end of the afternoon poor light stopped play in two sets.

RHODESIA INTER-PROVINCIAL TEAM (Bloemfontein), 1924.

A. Ross (Capt.), E. A. Barbour, L. G. Morgenrood, D. G. Blackbeard.

In their second match against Rhodesia, at Salisbury, the visitors won fourteen of the fifteen matches, the only local winner being Vincent.

In addition to receiving visiting teams, Rhodesia has also gone touring.

In 1921 a strong team was sent to Bloemfontein to compete in the Inter-Provincial Shield (mixed and men's doubles) " knock-out " competition. The side consisted of F. G. Brooks (captain), V. H. van Breda, B. Howard, F. B. Brooks, Mrs. F. H. Ellis and Miss I. Gradwell. In the mixed doubles Rhodesia was unfortunate in drawing, in the first round, Natal the ultimate winners, who beat the Colony soundly. Rhodesia, in the men's doubles, however, beat what was considered the strongest team, Southern Transvaal, but lost by one set to Natal. The Rhodesians then participated in the South African Championships. These showed our singles and mixed doubles play as being very weak, but the men's and ladies' doubles combinations could hold their own with all but a few of the outstanding pairs. Mrs. Ellis and Miss Gradwell were beaten only in the final of their event.

In 1924 Rhodesia again entered for the Inter-Provincial Shield competitions. On this occasion each team was required to play every other team, and Rhodesia played five matches and lost them all. The team was: A. Ross (captain), E. A. Barbour, D. G. Blackbeard, L. G. Morgenrood, Miss I. Gradwell and Miss J. Standen. In the first match Ross and Blackbeard, who played well throughout the tournament, created a sensation by defeating the Blackbeard brothers who were the South African doubles champions. The younger pair, Barbour and Morgenrood, also did quite well and gained some valuable experience. Miss Gradwell was consistent throughout and as a mixed doubles player there was hardly anyone better than she. Miss Standen, brilliant at times, was poor at others. She was considered the hardest hitter among the ladies. After the inter-provincial matches Ross won the Orange Free State and Basutoland Singles Championship.

At the invitation of the Southern Transvaal, a team visited Johannesburg and Pretoria in 1928. The team comprised Mrs. Griffin, women's singles champion, Mrs. F. H. Ellis, Mrs. Gumpertz, Miss Clemo, A. Ross (holder of the men's singles title), F. B. Brooks (captain), J. H. Holding

RHODESIA v. TRANSVAAL, 1928.

Mrs. Ellis, Mrs. Griffin, Mrs. Gumpertz, Miss Clemo.

J. H. Holding, A. Ross, D. P. C. Gumpertz, F. B. Brooks.

and D. P. C. Gumpertz, and the manager, Mr. G. N. Fleming, then President of the Rhodesia Lawn Tennis Association. The tour was an instructive one, and the players acquitted themselves well. A. Ross achieved two personal triumphs by defeating C. R. Blackbeard and C. H. Winslow. This year, 1935, R. Vincent and M. H. Quinn, holders of the Rhodesian men's doubles title, represented the Colony in the South African Championships.

On the administrative side of the game, the outstanding personality is Mr. G. N. Fleming. He is the G.O.M. of our tennis, and his initiative, resource and powers of organisation are unequalled. He has also been a fine player and, on more than one occasion, just missed becoming a champion of Rhodesia. Others deserving of mention in the management of the game are the late Hon. Mr. Justice J. P. F. Watermeyer, Sir Clarkson Tredgold, Sir Percy Fynn, C.M.G., G. Duthie, Lieut.-Col. A. C. L. Webb, A. Sanders, a very good player, N. F. Shillingford, H. B. Capstick, another useful man on the court, Wm. Smith, A. W. Beadle, A. I. Aitken, W. R. D. Lewis, " Lex " Love, J. H. Downing, E. B. Shepherd and J. S. Blackwell, who is the present President of the Rhodesia Lawn Tennis Association and who has given over thirty years of service to Rhodesian tennis. I am indebted to Mr. Blackwell for a large supply of the material for this chapter.

Of players the outstanding is F. G. Brooks. He figures in the championships no less than twenty-one times, six of which include the singles title, and he has been triple champion three times. Sir Percy Fynn, the first singles champion, has held the title on six occasions, and W. S. Taberer, another fine player, has shared the men's doubles title with F. G. Brooks on seven occasions. A. Ross, Rhodesian-born, has won the singles seven times. His tennis is unattractive but, in his heyday, he had a faculty of beating players who were regarded as better than he. His ball-control, agility and court-craft were wonderful. Tommy Atkins used to say of the late Lord Roberts: " He's little but he's wise, he's a terror for his size!" and the same may be said of Andrew Ross on the tennis court. Ralph Vincent, ex-South African representative, was triple champion in 1933 and 1934. He is a fine exponent, and in 1932 he was ranked tenth in South Africa.

BRITISH TEAM v. RHODESIA, 1909.

Standing: F. G. Brooks, W. S. Taberer, L. L. J. Orpen, E. Youatt.
Sitting: H. W. Sevenoaks, H. J. K. Brereton, G. W. Hillyard, P. D. L.
Fynn, Dr. W. V. Evans, M. L. Woods.

COMMITTEE OF R.L.T.A., 1908.

Back Row: H. J. K. Brereton, Sir Wm. Milton, The Hon. Mr. Justice
Watermeyer (President), B. G. Derry, J. W. Downie.
Front Row: John Milton, J. S. Blackwell (Hon. Sec.), C. H. Tredgold,
P. D. L. Fynn, F. de Stadler, G. Duthie.

The standard of play of Rhodesian women has never reached that to which the men have attained. There have been individual triumphs over visitors of repute, but we have had no great all-rounder of the Wimbledon standard. In the local records Mrs. S. J. Oliphant is unrivalled with her seven successive singles wins, and Mrs. Griffin is next with five wins to her credit. In the mixed doubles Mrs. J. H. Kennedy and Mrs. J. G. Jearey share the honours with five victories each, four of the former's wins being in partnership with F. G. Brooks. ·

Since the formation of the R.L.T.A. in 1905, the constitution of the Association has undergone many changes. To-day over thirty clubs are represented on the Association through the four provincial Boards. A levy of two shillings per annum per player is raised, of which sixpence is retained by the Boards and one shilling and sixpence is paid to the Association towards a guarantee fund, to be used for such purposes as the Association may decide. It is by this means that touring teams are financed. In 1932 Rhodesia seceded from the South African Lawn Tennis Union, and is now affiliated directly to the Lawn Tennis Association in England.

THE ENGLISH VISIT, 1909.

v. MASHONALAND, at Salisbury.

Hillyard and Eaves beat P. D. L. Fynn and H. J. K. Brereton 6—3, 7—5, after a match lasting 45 minutes.
Sevenoaks and Woods beat F. G. Brooks and W. S. Taberer 6—4, 6—4.
Sevenoaks beat Brooks 6—3, 4—6, 6—4.
Woods lost to Taberer 6—3, 7—5.
Hillyard beat Brereton 6—0, 6—4.
Eaves Beat Fynn 6—1, 6—4.

v. RHODESIA, at Salisbury.

Hillyard and Eaves beat F. B. Brooks and E. Youatt 6—0, 6—3; beat F. G. Brooks and Taberer 6—8, 6—1, 7—5.
Sevenoaks and Woods beat F. B. Brooks and Youatt 4—6, 6—2, 6—2.
Sevenoaks beat Fynn, 6—4, 6—2.
Woods beat Brereton 6—3, 5—7, 6—3.
Eaves beat Taberer 6—0, 6—1.
Hillyard beat F. G. Brooks 7—5, 6—1.

v. MATABELELAND, at Bulawayo.

Sevenoaks and Woods beat A. R. Welsh and A. C. L. Webb 6—3, 6—3; beat F. B. Brooks and E. Youatt 6—4, 6—3.
Hillyard and Eaves beat Brooks and Youatt 6—2, 6—1; beat J. P Furber and G. Young 6—0, 6—3.
Eaves beat Furber 6—1, 6—0.
Hillyard beat Young 6—1, 6—0.
Sevenoaks beat P. J. le Cordeur 6—0, 6—2.

THE ENGLISH VISIT, 1911.

v. SALISBURY, at Salisbury.

Myers and Powell beat L. A. N. Brooks and A. C. Bagshawe 10—8, 7—5; lost to H. J. K. Brereton and P. D. L. Fynn 5—7, 2—6; beat Brereton and Fynn in straight sets.

Beamish and Dixon beat F. G. Brooks and W. S. Taberer 6—4, 6—4; beat L. A. N. Brooks and Bagshawe 6—3, 6—4.

Dixon and Lowe beat F. G. Brooks and Taberer 4—6, 11—9, 6—3; lost to Brereton and Fynn 4—6, 8—10.

Myers and Lowe beat F. G. Brooks and Taberer 6—3, 6—2.

Lowe beat W. S. Taberer 6—4, 6—4; beat Brereton 6—0, 6—4.

Myers beat Fynn 7—5, 1—6, 6—2; beat W. Smith 6—2, 6—4.

Powell beat L. Brooks 6—1, 6—1. Beamish beat Brereton 7—5, 6—3.

v. BULAWAYO, at Bulawayo.

Myers and Powell beat A. C. L. Webb and R. J. Hudson 6—0, 9—7; beat Furber and A. R. Welsh 4—6, 7—5, 8—6; beat Webb and Welsh 6—2, 6—3.

Dixon and Beamish beat Hudson and G. J. McLoughlin 6—1, 6—1.

Lowe and Beamish beat E. Youatt and G. Matthews 3—6, 6—1, 6—0.

Dixon and Lowe beat Webb and Youatt 6—3, 5—7, 6—3.

Beamish beat Youatt 6—1, 5—7, 6—3; beat Webb 6—1, 6—2.

Myers beat McLoughlin 2—6, 6—3, 11—9.

Lowe beat Welsh 6—2, 6—2; beat Youatt 7—5. 6—3.

Powell beat Hudson 6—2. 6—2; beat Welsh 6—3, 6—1.

Dixon beat McLoughlin 6—2, 6—1.

THE BRITISH TEAM, 1912.

v. MASHONALAND, at Salisbury.

Miss Coles and Cochran beat Mrs. Fraser and A. C. Bagshawe 6—1, 6—0; beat Mrs. Kennedy and F. G..Brooks 6—2, 3—6, 6—3; beat Mrs. Baker and W. S. Taberer 6—2, 6—3.

Miss Johnson and Davis beat Mrs. Baker and Taberer 6—1, 6—2; beat Mrs. Fraser and Bagshawe 6—0, 6—3.

Miss Johnson and Cochran beat Mrs. Kennedy and Taberer 6—4, 6—4.

Cochran and Davis beat F. G. Brooks and Taberer 6—3, 6—4; beat L. A. N. Brooks and Bagshawe 6—4, 6—2.

Miss Coles lost to Mrs. A. L. Baker 6—3, 2—6, 0—6; then won 7—9, 6—3, 6—2.

Miss Johnson beat Mrs. Taberer 6—1, 6—0; beat Mrs. Baker 6—1, 6—1.

Davis beat L. A. N. Brooks 6—3, 8—6; lost to F. G. Brooks 6—4, 3—6, 4—6.

Cochran beat F. G. Brooks 6—0, 6—1; beat W. Smith 6—3, 6—1.

v. MIDLANDS, at Gwelo.

Miss Coles and Cochran beat Mr. and Mrs. Norris 6—0, 6—2; beat Mrs. Hogg and Haddon 6—0, 6—1.

Miss Johnson and Davis beat Mrs. Peel and Morgan 6—0, 6—1; beat Mr. and Mrs. Norris 6—0, 6—0.

Miss Johnson and Miss Coles beat Mrs. Shand and Mrs. Peel 7—5, 4—6, 6—2; beat Mrs. Norris and Mrs. Hogg 6—0, 6—1.

Cochran and Davis beat Pringle and Wright 6—2, 8—6; beat Haddon and Wright 6—2, 6—1.

Miss Johnson beat Mrs. Shand 6—2, 6—1.

Miss Coles beat Mrs. Peel 6—4, 6—1.

Davis beat Cox 6—2, 6—1. Cochran beat Haddon 6—1, 6—4.

THE ENGLISH VISIT, 1926.

v. MASHONALAND, at Salisbury.

G. R. O. Crole-Rees and M. V. Summerson beat F. B. Brooks and
L. A. N. Brooks 6—2, 6—3.
Miss K. McKane and L. A. Godfree beat Miss Maytham and L.
Powys-Jones 7—5, 6—0.
Miss Joan Ridley beat Mrs. Jearey 6—3, 6—0.
Summerson beat G. Davies 6—2, 7—5.
Miss E. Colyer and C. G. Eames beat Miss D. Purdon and D. P .C.
Gumpertz 6—1, 6—2.
Mrs. M. Watson beat Miss Maytham 6—0, 6—0.
Godfree and Eames beat L. G. Morgenrood and C. H. Boshoff
6—2, 6—3.
Miss McKane and Miss Colyer beat Mrs. Jearey and Mrs. Webb
6—2, 6—0.

v. MATABELELAND, at Bulawayo.

Mrs. Watson beat Mrs. Ellis 7—5, 6—2.
Summerson beat D. G .Blackbeard 6—4, 6—2.
Crole-Rees lost to A. Ross 3—6, 3—6.
Mrs. Watson and Miss Colyer beat Mrs. Ellis and Mrs. Bennie
6—3, 6—1.
Miss Colyer and Miss Ridley beat Miss I. Gradwell and Miss R.
Botton 6—3, 6—3.
Miss Colyer and Eames beat Mrs. Ellis and Ross 6—2, 7—5.
Miss Colyer and Godfree beat Mr. and Mrs. R. M. Price 6—0, 6—1.
Crole-Rees and Summerson beat A. T. Tait and A. Sarsons 6—1, 6—1.
Godfree and Eames beat Ross and Blackbeard 6—3, 6—4.

THE TRANSVAAL VISIT, 1921.

v. MASHONALAND, at Salisbury.

Winslow beat B. Howard 9—7, 6—0.
Tucker lost to F. G. Brooks 6—4, 1—6, 2—6.
Raymond beat Cross 6—0, 6—2.
Mrs. Winslow beat Mrs. Jearey 6—4, 6—3.
Mrs. McLaren beat Miss Whiley 6—2, 6—2.
Raymond and Winslow beat Brooks Bros. 6—3, 2—6, 8—6; beat
Howard and Cross 6—4, 7—5.
Tucker and Le Sueur beat Howard and Cross 6—2, 5—7, 7—5; lost
to Brooks Bros. 1—6, 4—6.
Mrs. Winslow and Miss Edwards lost to Mrs. Ellis and Mrs. Jearey
4—6, 4—6; beat Mrs. Jennings and Miss Whiley 7—5, 6—3.
Mrs. McLaren and Mrs. Harding beat Mrs. Jennings and Miss
Whiley 6—3, 7—5; beat Mrs. Ellis and Mrs. Jearey 6—2, 6—4.
Miss Edwards and Raymond beat Mrs. Ellis and F. G. Brooks 7—9,
6—2, 6—3; beat Miss Whiley and Cross 6—4, 6—1.
Mrs. Winslow and Winslow beat Miss Whiley and Cross 7—5, 7—5;
lost to Mrs. Ellis and F. G. Brooks, 3—6, 6—4, 1—6.
Mrs. McLaren and Tucker beat Mrs. Jearey and F. B. Brooks 6—1,
6—2; beat Mrs. Jennings and Howard 6—3, 6—1.
Mrs. Harding and Le Sueur beat Mrs. Jearey and F. B. Brooks 3—6.
6—4, 6—4; beat Mrs. Jennings and Howard 11—9, 6—0.

v. MATABELELAND, at Bulawayo.

Raymond beat A. Ross 6—3, 7—9, 6—0.

Winslow beat V. H. van Breda 6—1, 6—2.

Miss Edwards beat Miss Standen 8—6, 6—4.

Mrs. Winslow beat Miss I. Gradwell 6—3, 6—1.

Mrs. McLaren beat Mrs. Jacques 6—2, 6—4.

Winslow lost to Ross 6—0, 3—6, 3—6 in an exhibition match.

Tucker and Le Sueur beat A. C. L. Webb and R. J. Hudson 8—6, 6—0; beat Ross and Tait 6—0, 6—1.

Raymond and Winslow beat Van Breda and Brooks 6—8, 6—4, 6—4; beat Webb and Hudson 6—2, 6—2; beat Ross and Tait 6—0, 6—3.

Mrs. Winslow and Miss Edwards beat Mrs. Brooks and Miss I. Gradwell 7—5, 6—4; beat Miss Standen and Miss de Beer 6—3, 6—1.

Mrs. McLaren and Mrs. Harding beat Miss Standen and Miss de Beer 6—2, 6—1; beat Mrs. Brooks and Miss Gradwell 7—5, 3—6, 6—2.

Mrs. Winslow and Winslow beat Miss de Beer and Hudson 6—3, 6—4; beat Miss Gradwell and Van Breda 6—3, 6—1.

Miss Edwards and Raymond beat Miss Standen and Tait 6—1, 6—2; beat Mr. and Mrs. Brooks 6—1, 6—0.

Mrs. Harding and Le Sueur beat Mrs. Boyes and Webb 6—4, 6—4; beat Mr. and Mrs. Brooks 6—4, 6—3; beat Miss de Beer and Hudson 6—1, 8—6.

Miss McLaren and Tucker beat Mrs. Boyes and Webb 7—5, 7—5; beat Miss Standen and Tait 6—0, 6—2; beat Mrs. Jacques and Ross 6—0, 6—2.

THE TRANSVAAL VISIT, 1923.

v. MATABELELAND, at Bulawayo.

C. R. Blackbeard lost to A. Ross 3—6, 6—4, 4—6.

G. H. Dodd beat D. G. Blackbeard 6—1, 6—3; beat Ross 6—0, 7—5.

Mrs. Moore beat Miss J. Standen 7—5, 3—6, 6—3.

Kirby lost to Ross 4—6, 6—4, 0—6.

Miss Hopkins lost to Miss I. Gradwell 3—6, 1—6.

Dodd and Blackbeard beat Ross and L. A. N. Brooks 6—4, 6—1; beat Tait and Blackbeard 6—1, 4—6, 6—3.

Kirby and Connor beat A. T. Tait and Blackbeard 6—2, 6—2; beat Ross and Brooks 7—9, 6—3, 6—4; beat A. C. L. Webb and D. G. Lewis 6—1, 6—1.

Mrs. Moore and Miss Murray beat Mrs. Petley and Miss Standen 6—2, 6—4.

Miss Hopkins and Miss Murray beat Mrs. Boyes and Miss Gradwell 8—6, 6—1.

Miss Hopkins and Kirby beat Miss Gradwell and Webb 7—9, 6—2, 6—0.

Mrs. Moore and Blackbeard beat Mrs. Boyes and Ross 6—1, 6—4; beat Miss Gradwell and Webb 6—2, 6—1.

Miss Murray and Connor beat Mrs. Petley and Brooks 6—1, 6—2; beat Miss Standen and Tait 6—2, 5—7, 6—1.

v. MIDLANDS, at Gwelo.

Blackbeard beat V. H. van Breda 6—2, 6—3.
Mrs. Moore beat Mrs. Baker 6—3, 6—3.
Connor beat L. T. Powys-Jones 6—1, 8—10, 6—3.
Dodd beat W. C. W. Pringle 6—3, 6—2.
Kirby beat H. J. K. Brereton 6—4, 4—6, 6—4.
Connor and Kirby beat Powys-Jones and Pringle 8—6, 6—4.
Blackbeard and Dodd beat Van Breda and Brereton 6—3, 6—4.
Mrs. Moore and Miss Murray beat Mrs. Baker and Mrs. Wood
    6—4, 6—3.
Mrs. Moore and Blackbeard beat Mrs. Baker and Powys-Jones
    6—4, 6—4.
Miss Hopkins and Kirby beat Miss Stevens and Van Breda 6—1, 6—3.
Miss Hopkins and Dodd beat Miss Stevens and Brereton 6—1, 6—4.
Miss Murray and Connor beat Mrs. Wood and Pringle 6—2, 6—3.

v. MASHONALAND, at Salisbury.

Blackbeard beat F. B. Brooks 6—4, 6—2.
Dodd beat F. G. Brooks 6—4, 6—1.
Miss Murray beat Mrs. Bowley 6—2, 6—0.
Connor beat C. H. Boshoff 6—1, 3—6, 6—3.
Miss Hopkins beat Mrs. F. G. Smith 6—3, 6—2.
Mrs. Moore beat Mrs. Jearey 6—1 (unfinished).
Blackbeard and Dodd beat Brooks Bros. 6—2, 6—8, 6—3; beat H. S
    Cross and E. Cross 6—4, 4—6, 6—4.
Mrs. Moore and Miss Murray beat Mrs. Jearey and Mrs. Bowley
    6—3, 6—1.
Kirby and Connor beat Cross Bros. 7—5, 6—3; lost to Brooks Bros.
    5—7, 7—5, 4—6.
Miss Murray and Miss Hopkins beat Mrs. Mackenzie and Mrs. F. G.
    Smith 6—3, 6—3.
Mrs. Moore and Blackbeard beat Mrs. Jearey and H. S. Cross 6—1,
    6—2; beat Mrs. F. G. Smith and F. B .Brooks 4—6, 7—5,
    6—2.
Miss Murray and Connor beat Mrs. F. G. Smith and F. B. Brooks
    6—4, 6—3; beat Mrs. Maasdorp and F. G. Brooks 6—2, 6—3.
Miss Hopkins and Kirby beat Mrs. Maasdorp and F. G. Brooks 6—3,
    6—1; beat Mrs. Jearey and H. S. Cross 6—1, 4—6, 8—6.

THE TRANSVAAL VISIT, 1927.

v. MASHONALAND, at Salisbury.

C. L. Winslow beat H. S. Cross 6—2, 6—2.
T. D. Green beat D. P. C. Gumpertz 4—6, 6—2, 6—1.
Mrs. Neave beat Mrs. Webb 6—4, 6—3.
Mrs. Winslow beat Mrs. Jearey 6—2, 6—2.
G. H. Dodd beat C. S. Style 2—6, 6—2, 6—1.
R. Tucker lost to F. B. Brooks 2—6, 6—2, 4—6.
Mrs. Everett beat Mrs. Humphreys 6—1, 6—2.
Miss D. Cole beat Miss McChlery 6—4, 6—2, 6—2.

Tucker and Winslow beat Style and E. E. Cross 6—3, 6—0; beat
  Gumpertz and L. G. Morgenrood 6—4, 10—8; lost to F. B.
  Brooks and H. S. Cross 7—5, 4—6, 5—7.
Dodd and Green beat F. G. and F. B. Brooks 6—4, 1—6, 6—1; beat
  H. S .Cross and W. H. S. Cary 6—2, 8—6; lost to Style and
Gumpertz 6—4, 1—6, 2—6.
Mrs. Everett and Miss Cole beat Mrs. Webb and Mrs. Humphreys
  6—1, 6—1; beat Mrs. Jearey and Miss McChlery 6—2, 6—1.
Mrs. Winslow and Mrs. Neave beat Mrs. Webb and Mrs. Humphreys
  10—8, 7—5; beat Mrs. Jearey and Miss McChlery 6—3, 6—3.
Miss Cole and Tucker beat Mrs. Jearey and H. S. Cross 6—4, 6—2.
Mrs. Neave and Winslow beat Mrs. Hardy and Cary 6—2, 6—2.
Mrs. Winslow and Dodd beat Mrs. Webb and E. E. Cross 4—6, 6—4,
  7—5.
Mrs. Everett and Green beat Miss Purdon and Gumpertz 6—4, 6—3.

v. BULAWAYO, at Bulawayo.

Tucker and Winslow beat Ross and A. Sarsons 4—6, 6—4, 6—4;
  beat Owens and E. Barbour 6—4, 6—4.
Dodd and Green beat Ross and Sarsons 6—0, 6—4; beat Owens and
  Barbour 8—10, 6—4, 6—2.
Mrs. Everett and Miss Cole beat Miss Miller and Miss V. Godbolt
  6—3, 6—2; Mrs. Mail and Mrs. Bennie 7—5 (unfinished).
Mrs. Winslow and Mrs. Neave beat Mrs. Mail and Mrs. Bennie 6—2.
  6—3; beat Miss Miller and Miss Godbolt 6—4, 6—1.
Mrs. Everett and Tucker beat Mrs. Bennie and Ross 9—7, 6—1.
Mr. and Mrs. Winslow beat Miss Miller and Sarsons 6—4, 6—4.
Miss Cole and Green lost to Mrs. Mail and Barbour 4—6, 7—5, 1—6.
Mrs. Neave and Dodd beat Miss Godbolt and Owens 6—2, 10—8.
Winslow lost to Ross 9—7, 7—9, 2—6.
Dodd beat Owens 6—3, 6—4.
Mrs. Neave beat Mrs. Mail 9—7, 8—6.
Mrs. Everett beat Mrs. Bennie 6—2, 6—2.

v. MIDLANDS, at Gwelo.

Mrs. Neave beat Mrs. Griffin 6—2, 6—2.
Winslow beat Evans 9—7, 7—5.
Tucker and Winslow beat Evans and R. G. Geard 6—2, 9—7; beat
  Appleby and Pringle 6—3, 4—6, 6—4.
Dodd and Green beat Appleby and Pringle 6—1, 6—2; lost to Evans
  and Geard 4—6, 4—6.
Mrs. Winslow and Mrs. Neave beat Mrs. Griffin and Mrs. Lewin
  6—1, 6—4.
Mrs. Everett and Miss Cole beat Mrs. Baker and Mrs. Price 6—2, 6—3
Mrs. Everett and Tucker beat Mrs. Price and Appleby 6—1, 6—3;
  beat Mrs. Lewin and Pringle 6—1, 4—6, 6—1.
Miss Cole and Green beat Mrs. Price and Appleby 6—4, 6—4; beat
  Mrs. Baker and Geard 6—1, 6—4.
Mrs. Neave and Dodd lost to Mrs. Baker and Geard 4—6, 2—6; beat
  Mrs. Griffin and Evans 4—6, 6—4, 6—3.
Mrs. Winslow and Winslow beat Mrs. Lewin and Pringle 6—1, 6—2;
  beat Mrs. Griffin and Evans 6—3, 7—5.

THE NATAL VISIT, 1926.
v. BULAWAYO, at Bulawayo.

G. Eaglestone beat Ross 6—4, 6—4.

W. Pittaway and F. Wells beat Owens and Blackbeard 6—3, 9—7.

Miss J. Parker and Pittaway beat Miss Gradwell and Owens 6—3, 6—4.

Miss E. L. Heine beat Mrs. J. D. Mail 6—0, 6—1.

L. Hatton and Eaglestone beat Ross and Holding 6—0, 6—1.

Miss Parker and Miss Heine beat Miss Gradwell and Mrs. Mail 6—4, 6—0.

Wells beat Blackbeard 7—5, 9—7.

Hatton and Pittaway beat Ross and Holding 4—6, 6—4, 6—0.

Hatton and Eaglestone beat Owens and Blackbeard 6—3, 6—3.

Miss Parker and Eaglestone beat Mrs. Mail and Ross 6—0, 6—2.

Miss Heine and Wells beat Miss Gradwell and Holding 6—4, 7—5.

Miss Heine beat Miss Gradwell 6—1, 6—3.

v. MIDLANDS, at Gwelo.

Wells beat H. J. K. Brereton 6—3, 8—6.

Hatton beat Eriksen 6—1, 6—0.

Eaglestone beat Geard 6—2, 6—0.

Pittaway beat W. C. W. Pringle 6—1, 4—6, 6—3.

Miss Parker beat Mrs. A. L. Baker 6—1, 6—0.

Miss Heine beat Mrs. Griffin 6—1, 6—3.

Hatton and Eaglestone beat Pringle and Eriksen 6—1, 7—5.

Pittaway and Wells beat Brereton and Geard 6—3, 6—3.

Eaglestone and Miss Parker beat Mrs. Griffin and Pringle 6—0, 6—3.

Hatton and Miss Heine beat Mrs. Baker and Geard 6—2, 6—4.

Miss Parker and Miss Heine beat Mrs. Baker and Mrs. Griffin 6—1, 6—1.

v. MASHONALAND, at Salisbury.

Wells beat F. G. Brooks 2—6, 6—2, 6—2.

Pittaway beat D. P. C. Gumpertz 6—2, 6—2.

Eaglestone beat H. S. Cross 6—3, 8—6.

Miss Heine beat Miss Burdett 6—1, 6—1.

Miss Parker beat Mrs. Webb 6—4, 6—4.

Hatton and Eaglestone beat F. B. Brooks and Gumpertz 6—4, 6—2; beat F. G. Brooks and Cross 6—2, 6—1.

Wells and Pittaway lost to F. G. Brooks and Cross 5—7, 2—6; beat F. B. Brooks and Gumpertz 4—6, 6—4, 7—5.

Miss Parker and Miss Heine beat Mrs. Webb and Miss Burdett 6—1, 6—0.

Miss Parker and Eaglestone beat Miss Burdett and F. B. Brooks 7—5, 6—3.

Miss Heine and Hatton beat Mrs. Webb and Cross 10—8, 6—3.

THE CZECHO-SLOVAKIAN VISIT, 1931.
v. MATABELELAND, at Bulawayo.

F. Marsalek lost to A. Ross 4—6, 1—6.

J. Kozeluh lost to R. Vincent 1—6, 7—9; beat Ross 6—4, 5—7, 6—3.

M. Soyka and Marsalek lost to R. Vincent and D. G. Blackbeard 5—7, 6—4, 2—6; beat Ross and J. Brown 6—1, 6—4.

Kozeluh and P. Macenauer beat Brown and Ross 6—2, 6—1; beat Vincent and Blackbeard 6—4, 6—3.

Macenauer beat Vincent 6—2, 7—5.

v. MIDLANDS, at Gwelo.

Soyka beat Van Breda 7—5, 1—6, 6—2.

Marsalek beat Roux 6—0, 7—5.

Kozeluh and Macenauer beat Evans and Coventry 6—2, 6—2; beat
    Evans and Van Breda 6—0, 6—1.

Marsalek and Soyka beat Pringle and Carey 6—3, 7—5.

v. MASHONALAND, at Salisbury.

Macenauer beat D. P. C. Gumpertz 6—1, 6—2.

Kozeluh beat C. S. Style 10—8, 6—3.

Marsalek and Soyka beat L. Powys-Jones and A. B. Spurling 6—3,
    6—1; beat J. R. D. Evans and Gumpertz 6—4, 1—6, 6—0.

Kozeluh and Macenauer beat F. B. Brooks and Style 7—5, 6—3.

Soyka v. K. Grainger 6—4, 1—1 (unfinished).

INTER-PROVINCIAL SHIELD COMPETITION, 1921.

RHODESIA v. NATAL.

Mrs. Reid and Upton beat Mrs. F. H. Ellis and F. G. Brooks 4—6,
    6—3, 6—3; beat Miss I. Gradwell and V. H. van Breda 6—1,
    6—0.

Miss Parker and Goldborn beat Mrs. Ellis and Brooks 6—4, 6—1;
    beat Miss Gradwell and Van Breda 6—4, 6—1.

RHODESIA v. TRANSVAAL.

Raymond and Richardson lost to Van Breda and B. Howard 2—6,
    6—2, 4—6; lost to Brooks Brothers 8—10, 2—6.

Tucker and Van Ryn beat Van Breda and Howard 6—3, 1—6, 6—3;
    v. Brooks Brothers 2—6, 6—4. (This match was unfinished
    as Rhodesia had won on sets.)

RHODESIA v. NATAL.

Goldborn and Upton beat Brooks Brothers 6—1, 10—8; beat Van
    Breda and Howard 6—2, 6—3.

Whitley and Eaglestone lost to Brooks Brothers 5—7, 4—6; lost to
    Van Breda and Howard 6—3, 2—6, 5—7.

INTER-PROVINCIAL SHIELD COMPETITION, 1924.

v. NORTHERN TRANSVAAL.

Leach and Taylor-Taswell beat Ross and Barbour 6—3, 4—6, 6—1;
    beat Blackbeard and Morgenrood 6—3, 6—4.

Van Duyn and Norgarb beat Blackbeard and Morgenrood 6—3, 4—6,
    6—1; beat Ross and Barbour 6—4, 2—6, 6—3.

Mrs. McArthur and Borchers beat Miss Gradwell and Ross 6—3, 7—5;
    beat Miss J. Standen and Blackbeard 7—5, 6—2.

Mrs. Wood and Leach beat Miss Standen and Blackbeard 7—5, 6—2;
    beat Miss Gradwell and Ross 6—3, 7—5.

v. ORANGE FREE STATE.

Symonds and Van der Walt beat Barbour and Morgenrood 9—7,
    6—2; lost to Ross and Blackbeard 4—6, 2—6.

F. Gray and A. Gray lost to Ross and Blackbeard 6—2, 5—7, 3—6;
    beat Barbour and Morgenrood 6—1, 7—5.

Mrs. W. F. du Plessis and P. M. Dixon beat Miss Standen and Black-
    beard 6—2, 6—4; beat Miss Gradwell and Ross 6—4, 9—7.

Mrs. J. Reid and G. T. Welsford beat Miss Gradwell and Ross 4—6,
    6—2, 6—3; lost to Miss Standen and Blackbeard 6—1, 4—6,
    1—6.

v. SOUTHERN TRANSVAAL.

Blackbeard Brothers beat Barbour and Morgenrood 6—2, 7—5; lost to Ross and Blackbeard 6—3, 1—6, 3—6.

Winslow and Kirby beat Ross and Blackbeard 6—3, 6—2; beat Barbour and Morgenrood 6—2, 7—5.

Mrs. Peacock and Hillier beat Miss Standen and Blackbeard 6—0, 6—0; beat Miss Gradwell and Ross 6—0, 6—1.

Mrs. Moore and G. Dodd beat Miss Gradwell and Ross 6—3, 6—2; beat Miss Standen and Blackbeard 7—5, 9—7.

v. NATAL.

Hatton and Eaglestone beat Barbour and Morgenrood 6—0, 6—4; beat Ross and Blackbeard 7—5, 6—2.

Peacock and Hurst beat Ross and Blackbeard 6—4, 6—4; beat Barbour and Morgenrood 6—1, 6—3.

Miss Parker and Eaglestone beat Miss Gradwell and Ross 6—0, 6—2; beat Miss Standen and Blackbeard 6—0, 6—3.

Miss Brown and Hatton beat Miss Standen and Blackbeard 6—2, 11—9; beat Miss Gradwell and Ross 6—8, 6—4, 6—3.

v. BORDER.

Frolich and Bowes beat Blackbeard and Morgenrood 9—7, 6—3· beat Ross and Barbour 4—6, 6—4, 6—3.

King and Carrington beat Ross and Barbour 10—8, 6—8, 7—5; beat Blackbeard and Morgenrood 6—4, 6—4.

Mrs. Newman and King beat Miss Gradwell and Ross 6—1, 6—4; beat Miss Standen and Blackbeard 6—3, 6—3.

Mrs. Hodgson and Carrington beat Miss Standen and Blackbeard 6—3, 8—6; beat Miss Gradwell and Ross 0—6, 6—4, 10—8.

Eastern Province scratched to Rhodesia.

THE TRANSVAAL TOUR, 1928.
v. SOUTHERN TRANSVAAL.

Mrs. Everett beat Mrs. Griffin 6—3, 6—1.

Miss Cole beat Mrs. Ellis 8—6, 6—3.   Raymond beat Ross 6—4, 7—5.

Mrs. Peacock and Miss McCann beat Mrs. Griffin and Mrs. Ellis 6—1, 6—3.

Mrs. Everett and Miss Hopkins beat Mrs. Gumpertz and Miss Clemo 6—0, 6—3.

Dodd and Miss McCann beat Mr. and Mrs. Gumpertz 6—2, 6—1.

Malcolm and Robbs lost to Ross and Holding 6—4, 4—6, 2—6.

Blackbeard and Winslow lost to Brooks and Gumpertz 6—8, 4—6.

v. BEREA CLUB.

Dodds and Vincent beat Brooks and Gumpertz 6—1, 6—3.

Badham and C. Jones lost to Ross and Holding 6—4, 4—6, 4—6.

Miss Webber and Miss McNiece lost to Mrs. Gumpertz and Miss Clemo 2—6, 6—8.

Mrs. Everett and Miss Hopkins beat Mrs. Ellis and Mrs. Griffin 6—2, 3—6, 6—4.

Miss Hopkins and Brown beat Mrs. Griffin and Brooks 6—4, 6—4; beat Miss Clemo and Ross 6—3, 4—6, 7—5.

Mrs. W. Green and Vincent beat Mrs. Griffin and Brooks 5—7, 6—1. 6—3; beat Mrs. Ellis and Ross 6—2, 6—2.

Mrs. Everett and C. Jones lost to Mrs. Ellis and Ross 2—6, 6—4, 2—6.

Miss Webber and Badham lost to Mr. and Mrs. Gumpertz 5—7, 6—4, 2—6.

Dodd and Miss McNiece beat Miss Clemo and Holding 6—4, 6—3; lost to Mr. and Mrs. Gumpertz 10—12, 7—5, 3—6.

v. SOUTHERN TRANSVAAL.

Malcolm beat Ross 4—6, 6—0, 6—0.

C. R. Blackbeard lost to Ross 2—6, 3—6.

Miss Cole beat Mrs. Griffin 6—2, 0—6, 6—3.

Miss McCann beat Mrs. Gumpertz 6—3, 6—2.

Mrs. Peacock and Mrs. Wood beat Mrs. Griffin and Mrs. Ellis 6—1, 6—0.

Miss McCann and Miss Cole beat Mrs. Gumpertz and Miss Clemo 6—2, 6—2.

Raymond and Malcolm beat Gumpertz and Brooks 6—3, 6—2.

Rhodesia lost by 6 matches to 1.

v. NORTHERN TRANSVAAL, at Pretoria.

Connor lost to Ross 2—6, 5—7.

Mrs. Wilson and Miss Hook beat Mrs. Griffin and Mrs. Ellis 6—2, 6—4.

Borchers and Connor beat Gumpertz and Brooks 6—1, 6—4.

Daniel and O'Shea lost to Ross and Holding 6—3, 3—6, 6—8.

Mrs. Adkins and Buchanan beat Mrs. Gumperts and Miss Clemo 4—6, 6—3, 6—2.

Mrs. Wilson and Borchers lost to Mrs. Griffin and Brooks 6—8, 1—6.

Miss Hook and Daniel lost to Mrs. Ellis and Ross 6—8, 6—4, 3—6.

Mrs. Adkins and Connor beat Mr. and Mrs. Gumpertz 7—5, 6—4.

v. WANDERERS.

C. H. Winslow lost to Ross 4—6, 4—6.

Hilson lost to Gumpertz 4—6, 6—3, 4—6.

H. A. Kitson and Dr. S. Hewitt beat Ross and Holding 4—6, 6—1, 7—5.

Brash and Heeley lost to Brooks and Gumpertz 4—6, 2—6.

Mrs. Winslow beat Mrs. Ellis 6—4, 6—4.

Miss McCann beat Mrs. Griffin 3—6, 6—0, 6—4.

Miss McCann and Winslow lost to Mrs. Griffin and Brooks 2—6, 0—6.

Mrs. Hall and Mrs .Hurley beat Mrs .Gumpertz and Miss Clemo 6—1, 6—3.

Mrs. Peacock and Miss McCann beat Mrs. Griffin and Mrs. Ellis 6—1, 6—3.

Mrs. Simmonds and Hall beat Miss Clemo and Holding 4—6, 6—3, 6—3.

Mrs. Lowe and Mrs. Winslow beat Mrs. Gumpertz and Miss Clemo 6—3, 6—3.

Mrs. Hurley and Stuart lost to Mr. and Mrs. Gumpertz 4—6, 4—6.

Mrs. Jones and Tennant lost to Ross and Mrs. Ellis 8—10, 5—7.

THE NATAL VISIT, 1935.

v. MATABELELAND.

Mrs. Lowe beat Mrs. D. Mail 6—1, 6—1.

Robbs beat W. G. Wood 6—2, 6—4.

Lowe beat R. Vincent 7—5, 6—4.

Getaz lost to H. H. Davies 4—6, 3—6.

Mrs. Lowe and Mrs. Hathorn beat Mrs. Mail and Miss M. Hopley 6—1, 6—2.

Fannin and Getaz beat Davies and H. Kelly 9—7, 6—3.

Lowe and Robbs beat Vincent and Wood, 6—3, 9—7.

Mrs. Hathorn and Getaz beat Mrs. Mail and Wood 6—2, 4—6, 6—4.

Mrs. Lowe and Fannin beat Miss Hopley and Vincent 6—4, 7—5.

TENNIS.   251

v. RHODESIA, at Bulawayo.

Mrs. Lowe beat Mrs. D. P. C. Gumpertz 6—3, 6—2.
Mrs. Hathorn beat Mrs. C. B. Taberer 6—2, 6—2.
Getaz beat Wood 6—4, 6—3.
Fannin beat M. H. Quinn 7—5, 7—5.
Lowe beat Vincent 6—4, 4—6, 7—5.
Robbs beat C. S. Style 6—1, 6—2.
Mrs. Lowe and Mrs. Hathorn beat Mrs. Gumpertz and Mrs. Taberer
    6—1, 6—4.
Fannin and Getaz beat Vincent and Quinn 6—3, 8—6; beat Style
    and Wood 4—6, 6—0, 6—4.
Lowe and Robbs beat Style and Wood 1—6, 6—4, 12—10; lost to
    Vincent and Quinn 3—6, 3—6.
Mrs. Hathorn and Robbs beat Mrs. Taberer and Style 6—3, 3—6,
    6—3.
Mr. and Mrs. Lowe beat Mrs. Gumpertz and Vincent 6—3, 4—6, 6—3.
Mrs. Hathorn and Getaz beat Mrs. Gumpertz and Vincent 6—1,
    6—8, 6—3.
Mrs. Lowe and Fannin beat Mrs. Taberer and Quinn 6—2, 7—9, 6—3.

v. MIDLANDS.

Lowe beat Roux 6—3, 6—8.
Lowe and Getaz beat Quinn and W. C. Pringle 6—4, 6—4.
Lowe and Robbs beat Roux and Quinn 6—3, 3—6, 6—1.
Mrs. Hathorn and Lowe beat Miss Franklin and Pringle 6—4, 6—1.
Mrs. Lowe and Fannin beat Mrs. Sutcliffe and Tedder 6—1, 4—6,
    6—2.
Mrs. Lowe and Mrs. Hathorn beat Miss MacGillivray and Miss Pils-
    worth 6—0, 6—1.
Fannin and Getaz beat O'Reilly and Tedder 6—0, 6—4.

v. MASHONALAND.

Robbs beat A. P. Shone 6—4, 6—1.
Fannin beat Palmer 6—2, 7—5.
Mrs. Hathorn beat Mrs. Taberer 6—4, 6—4.
Getaz beat Greenfield 6—4, 5—7, 6—4.
Mrs. Lowe and Mrs. Hathorn beat Mrs. Webb and Mrs. Browne
    6—1, 6—1.
Lowe and Getaz beat Botha and Style 6—1, 3—6, 6—4.
Mrs. Hathorn and Fannin v. Mrs. Webb and Gumpertz 6—2 (play
    stopped).
Robbs and Fannin beat Morris and Gumpertz 6—3, 7—5.
Mr. and Mrs. Lowe v. Mrs. Gumpertz and Style 6—2 (play stopped).

v. RHODESIA, at Salisbury.

Getaz beat D. P. C. Gumpertz 6—4, 6—2.
Robbs beat Quinn 6—2, 6—4.
Mrs. Lowe beat Mrs. Gumpertz 6—2, 6—2.
Mrs. Hathorn beat Miss N. Dugmore 6—0, 6—4.
Lowe beat Style 6—3, 6—3.
Fannin lost to Vincent 6—8, 2—6.
Lowe and Getaz beat Vincent and Quinn 7—5, 6—4; beat Style and
    Gumpertz 6—1, 8—6.
Robbs and Fannin beat Style and Gumpertz 6—8, 6—3, 6—3; beat
    Vincent and Quinn 6—4, 9—7.

Mrs. Lowe and Mrs. Hathorn beat Mrs. Gumpertz and Miss Dug-
     more 6—3, 6—2.
Mr. and Mrs. Lowe beat Miss Dugmore and Vincent 6—2, 6—3.
Mrs. Hathorn and Fannin beat Mrs. Taberer and Quinn 6—1, 6—3.
Mrs. Lowe and Robbs beat Mrs. Gumpertz and Style 8—6, 6—3.
Mrs. Hathorn and Getaz beat Mrs. Taberer and Gumpertz 8—6, 6—8,
     10—8.

v. MANICALAND.

Fannin beat R. H. Cazalet 6—2, 6—3.
Getaz beat D. Meikle 6—0, 6—1.
Mrs. Hathorn beat Mrs. L. B. Ade 6—0, 6—0.
Mr. and Mrs. Lowe beat Mrs. Ade and R. A. Yates, 6—1, 6—1.
Fannin and Getaz beat Meikle and Dednam 6—1, 6—1.
Robbs and Getaz beat Cazalet and Yates 6—2, 6—0.
Mrs. Hathorn and Robb beat Mrs. J. Mares and Dednam 6—1, 6—1.
Mrs. Lowe and Mrs. Hathorn beat Mrs. Ade and Mrs. Mares
     6—2, 6—1.

THE FLEMING CUP COMPETITIONS.

It is a great pity that, in common with those of most
other sports, the earlier records of this series are so incom-
plete. True it is, though, that when these inter-town matches
first started there was an imposing array of talent in the
Colony. This will have been seen from the excellent performances of Rhodesians against the early visiting teams.
Apart from those already mentioned, there is a long list of
players whose names are equally well known in local tennis.
L. A. N. (" Paddy ") Brooks, brother of F. G. and F. B., has
represented both Bulawayo and Salisbury, and so has J.
O'C. McLoughlin. A. C. Bagshawe and Dr. L. L. J. Orpen
were a strong pair from Salisbury. Two Bulawayo stalwarts
for many years were T. J. Tiernan and A. T. Tait. The
latter first played for Bulawayo in 1912, and his cheery personality is well known on local courts even to-day. Judge
Hudson was a splendid player in his day, and two more
notables are A. E. Boyton and G. M. Tait.

In 1922 Shamva produced a first-class player in D. V.
Scully, and in the next season D. G. Blackbeard started on
his long career in Rhodesian tennis. W. C. W. Pringle was
for many years a Midlands stalwart. In 1924 Bulawayo
exhibited two fine young players in D. G. (" Tommy ") Lewis
and A. Sarsons, while Salisbury produced C. Boshoff and
that splendid exponent, D. P. C. Gumpertz. In 1926 two
newcomers to Bulawayo were R. Owens, a Transvaal-seeded
player, and a fine stylist in G. A. E. Norgarb. In recent
year C. S. Style and C. A. Lilford, H. S. Cross, A. P. Shone
and K. R. C. Grainger have figured prominently in Salisbury,

while Bulawayo has known a fine succession of players in I. Campbell-Rodger, an Oxford Blue, T. C. de Klerk, M. H. Quinn, one-time Western Province champion, H. H. Davies, W. Musgrove, who is now doing well in the Transvaal and made a European tour this year, and W. G. Wood, a young player who has rapidly come into the front rank of local tennis.

The institution in 1933 of the Fleming Cup competitions for women has already made for an improvement in the standard of the women's play. The Salisbury couple, Mrs. Webb and Mrs. Gumpertz, are a very strong doubles combination. Two more good players from the East are Mrs. C. B. Taberer and Mrs. Barbour. In Bulawayo are Mrs. F. K. Taylor, the 1934 singles champion, and Miss Elliott, who shared the mixed doubles title with R. Vincent in the same year. Mrs. D. Mail, Miss F. Sherry, Miss E. Hunt, Miss N. Dugmore and Miss J. Capstick are other prominent players among the women.

FLEMING CUP.

This Challenge Cup was presented to The Rhodesian Lawn Tennis Association by G. N. Fleming, Esq., on the 14th April, 1906. The records to date are:—

MEN.

1909:	Salisbury L.T.C.	1925:	Bulawayo.
1910:	Queens L.T.C.	1926:	Salisbury.
1912-14:	Bulawayo.	1927-28:	Bulawayo.
1915:	Salisbury.	1929:	Salisbury.
1919:	Bulawayo.	1930-31:	Bulawayo.
1920·	Salisbury.	1932:	Salisbury.
1921-23:	Bulawayo.	1933:	Bulawayo.
1924:	Salisbury.	1934-35:	Matabeleland .

WOMEN.
1934-35: Mashonaland.

FLEMING CUP.

(Players of winning team named first in each case.)

1909.

SALISBURY L.T.C. v. QUEENS L.T.C.

Final at Salisbury. Salisbury L.T.C. won.

Salisbury: F. G. Brooks, W. S. Taberer. P. D. L. Fynn, H. J. K. Brereton.
Queens: A. C. L. Webb, A. R. Welsh, J. P. Furber, E. Youatt.

The Hon. A. R. Welsh, M.P.   Sir Percy Fynn, C.M.G., M.P.

H. B. Capstick.   Mr. Justice Hudson, K. C., M.C.

1910.

QUEENS. L.T.C. v. SALISBURY L.T.C.

Final at Bulawayo.   Queens L.T.C. won.

Queens: E. Youatt, F. B. Brooks, H. Mansergh, A. C. L. Webb.
Salisbury: Dr. Orpen, W. S. Taberer, H. J. K. Brereton, L. A. N.
Brooks.

1912.

BULAWAYO. v. SALISBURY.

Final at Bulawayo.   Bulawayo won by 7 games.

F. B. Brooks and E. Youatt beat P. D. L. Fynn and W. S. Taberer
9—6; beat L. A. N. Brooks and A. C. Bagshawe 8—7.
A. C. L. Webb and A. T. Tait beat L. Brooks and Bagshawe 9—6;
lost to Fynn and Taberer 7—8.
Youatt beat Taberer 8—7.
F. Brooks v. L. Brooks 5—5 (unfinished).

1913.

BULAWAYO v. SALISBURY.

Final at Salisbury.   Bulawayo won by 7 games.

V. H. Collins and R. J. Hudson lost to A. C. Bagshawe and F. G.
Brooks 7—8; beat W. S. Taberer and G. P. L. Matthews 8—7.
A. T. Tait and D. H. Lindsay beat Taberer and Matthews 9—6; lost
to Bagshawe and Brooks 5—10.
Collins beat Brooks 8—7.
Tait v. Matthews 9—1 (unfinished).

1914.

BULAWAYO v. SALISBURY.

Final at Bulawayo.   Bulawayo won by 15 games.

A. T. Tait and J. O'C. McLoughlin beat G. P. L. Matthews and
W. S. Taberer 10—5; lost to L. A. N. Brooks and A. C.
Bagshawe 7—8.
V. H. Collins and F. B. Brooks beat Matthews and Taberer 10—5;
lost to Brooks and Bagshawe 7—8.
Collins beat Bagshawe 8—7.
Tait v. Brooks 8—2 (unfinished).

1915.

SALISBURY v. BULAWAYO.

Final at Salisbury.   Salisbury won by 2 matches.

L. A. N. Brooks and V. H. van Breda beat F. B. Brooks and A. T.
Tait 6—3, 6—4; beat A. C. L. Webb and T. J. Tiernan 2—6,
6—2, 6—3.
F. G. Brooks and A. C. Bagshawe beat Webb and Tiernan 6—8,
6—3, 6—3; lost to Brooks and Tait 4—6, 5—7.
Van Breda lost to F. B. Brooks 2—6, 0—6.
F. G. Brooks beat Webb 6—1, 6—2.
Bagshawe lost to Tiernan 3—6, 4—6.
L. A. N. Brooks beat Tait 7—5, 6—0.

1919.
BULAWAYO v. SALISBURY
Final at Bulawayo.   Bulawayo won by 2 matches.

F. B. Brooks and T. J. Tiernan beat F. G. Brooks and W. S. Taberer
6—4, 6—4; beat A. C. Bagshawe and Carlton 6—2, 6—0.

A. C. L. Webb and A. Ross beat Bagshawe and Carlton 1—6, 9—7,
6—4; beat Brooks and Taberer 6—4, 6—4.

Brooks lost to Brooks 4—6, 6—3, 7—9.

Tiernan lost to Bagshawe 5—7, 6—1, 3—6.

Webb lost to Taberer 2—6, 6—3, 6—8. Ross beat Carlton 6—2, 6—2.

1920.
SALISBURY v. BULAWAYO.
Final at Salisbury.   Salisbury won by 6 matches.

A. C. Bagshawe and J. O'C. McLoughlin beat A. T. Tait and A. C. L.
Webb 6—2, 6—1; beat L. A. N. Brooks and T. J. Tiernan
6—0, 6—2.

F. G. and F. B. Brooks beat Tait and Webb 6—2, 6—2; beat Brooks
and Tiernan 6—3, 6—2.

Bagshawe beat Tiernan 6—2. McLoughlin beat Tait 6—1.

1921.
BULAWAYO v. SALISBURY.

In 1921 the two finalists were Bulawayo and Salisbury.   The
latter scratched and Bulawayo won by default .

1922.
BULAWAYO. v. SHAMVA.
Final at Salisbury.   Bulawayo won by 3 sets.

Bulawayo: A. Ross, F. B. Brooks, A. E. Boyton.

Shamva: D. V. Scully, Kelly, Burger.

1923.
BULAWAYO v. FORT VICTORIA.
Final at Bulawayo.   Bulawayo won.

Bulawayo: A. Ross, L. A. N. Brooks, D. G. Blackbeard, A. C. L.
Webb.

Fort Victoria: V. H. van Breda, G. M. Tait, H. J. K. Brereton, J.
Appleby.

1924.
SALISBURY v. BULAWAYO.
Final at Salisbury.   Salisbury won by 6 matches.

F. B. and F. G. Brooks beat D. G. Blackbeard and A. Sanders
6—1, 6—3; beat E. A. Barbour and D. G. Lewis 6—1, 6—1.

C. H. Boshoff and G. M. Tait beat Barbour and Lewis 9—7, 6—2;
beat Blackbeard and Sanders 6—3, 7—5.

F. B. Brooks beat Blackbeard 6—1, 6—2.

Boshoff beat Lewis 6—1, 6—1.

1925.
BULAWAYO v. GWELO.
Final at Gwelo.   Bulawayo won.

Bulawayo won easily, losing only one singles match to W. C. W.
Pringle of Gwelo.

Bulawayo: A. Ross, A. Sarsons, D. G. Blackbeard, E. A. Barbour.

1926.
SALISBURY v. BULAWAYO.
Final at Bulawayo. Salisbury won by 4 sets.

F. B. Brooks and D. P. C. Gumpertz lost to A. Ross and R. Owens
3—6, 7—5, 4—6; v. A. Sarsons and G. A. E. Norgarb 6—2
(Match abandoned).

C. H. Boshoff and J. O'C McLoughlin beat Ross and Owens 7—5,
6—2; beat Sarsons and Norgarb 6—4, 6—4.

Brooks beat Ross 6—3, 6—1.

McLoughlin lost to Sarsons 5—7, 6—2, 3—6.

Boshoff lost to Owens 6—2, 1—6, 0—6.

Gumpertz beat Norgarb 6—8, 6—4, 6—4.

1927.
BULAWAYO v. SALISBURY.
Final at Salisbury. Bulawayo won by 2 matches.

A. Ross and R. Owens lost to D. P. C. Gumpertz and C. S. Style
2—6, 4—6; beat D. G. Steyn and G. Davies 6—3, 6—3.

D. G. Blackbeard and E. A. Barbour beat Steyn and Davies 6—1,
6—3; lost to Gumpertz and Style 10—8, 4—6, 3—6.

Ross beat Gumpertz 6—4, 6—1. Owens beat Style 4—6, 6—4, 6—1.

Blackbeard beat Steyn 6—4, 6—4. Barbour lost to Davies 7—5,
1—6, 4—6.

1928.
BULAWAYO. v. SALISBURY.
Final at Bulawayo. Bulawayo won by one set.

A. Ross and A. Sarsons lost to F. B. Brooks and H. S. Cross 3—6,
2—6; beat C. S. Style and D. P. C. Gumpertz 2—6, 10—8, 6—1.

E. A. Barbour and D. G. Blackbeard lost to Style and Gumpertz
4—6, 6—4, 8—10; lost to Brooks and Cross 2—6, 8—6, 3—6.

Barbour beat Cross 6—0, 6—2. Ross beat Style 6—2, 6—2.

Sarsons beat Brooks 6—1, 6—1.

Blackbeard lost to Gumpertz 2—6, 2—6.

1929.
SALISBURY v. BULAWAYO.
Final at Salisbury. Salisbury won by one set.

G. Davies and C. P. Lilford beat D. G. Blackbeard and I. Campbell-
Rodger 1—6, 6—4, 7—5.; lost to A. Ross and A. Sarsons 3—6,
4—6.

C. S. Style and D. P. C. Gumpertz beat Blackbeard and Campbell-
Rodger 6—4, 6—4; lost to Ross and Sarsons 6—2, 2—6, 4—6.

Gumpertz beat Sarsons 6—0, 6—0. Style lost to Ross 3—6, 8—10.

Lilford lost to Campbell-Rodger 7—5.

Davies beat Blackbeard 7—5, 6—1.

1930.
BULAWAYO v. SALISBURY.
Final at Bulawayo. Bulawayo won by 2 matches.

A. Ross and A. Sarsons beat D. P. C. Gumpertz and A. P. Shone
4—6, 6—4, 6—3; beat C. P. Lilford and G. Davies 2—6, 6—4,
6—2.

D. G. Blackbeard and H. S. Cross lost to Gumpertz and Shone 2—6,
6—2, 6—8; lost to Lilford and Davies 3—6, 4—6.

Ross beat Gumpertz 6—1, 6—1. Blackbeard beat Davies 6—1, 6—1.

Sarsons beat Lilford 7—5, 9—7. Cross lost to Shone 6—4, 1—6, 5—7.

1931.
BULAWAYO v. SALISBURY.
Final at Salisbury.   Bulawayo won by 2 matches.

W. Musgrove and T. C. de Klerk beat J. R. D. Evans and K. R. C.
Grainger 6—1, 6—4; v. D. P. C. Gumpertz and A. P. Shone
6—2, 7—9 (unfinished).

R. Vincent and D. G. Blackbeard lost to Gumpertz and Shone 5—7,
6—4, 1—6; v. Evans and Grainger 6—8, 6—1, 3—0 (unfinished).

De Klerk lost to Grainger 6—8, 6—2, 4—6.

Vincent beat Gumpertz 3—6, 6—0, 6—1.

Musgrove beat Shone 6—0, 6—4.

Blackbeard beat Evans 6—3, 6—3.

1932.
SALISBURY v. BULAWAYO.
Final at Bulawayo.   Salisbury won by 6 matches.

A. P. Shone and C. S. Style beat A. Ross and H. Davies 6—2, 6—2;
beat D. G. Blackbeard and E. A. Barbour 6—2, 6—1.

K. R. C. Grainger and C. P. Lilford beat Blackbeard and Barbour
4—6, 6—4, 6—1; beat Ross and Davies 3—6, 6—2, 9—7.

Style beat Davies 3—6, 6—3, 6—2.

Grainger beat Blackbeard 6—3, 6—1.

Lilford lost to Ross 3—6, 2—6.

Shone beat Barbour 6—1, 7—5.

1933.
BULAWAYO. v. SALISBURY
Final at Gwelo.   Bulawayo won by 4 matches.

R. Vincent and M. Quinn beat K. R. C. Grainger and C. S. Style
6—1, 6—2.

W. Musgrove and T. C. de Klerk beat D. P. C. Gumpertz and C. P.
Lilford 3—6, 6—3, 9—7.

Vincent beat Gumpertz 7—5, 6—1.

Quinn beat Grainger 6—4, 10—8.

Musgrove beat Lilford 6—4, 6—3.

De Klerk lost to Style 4—6, 5—7.

1934.
MATABELELAND v. MASHONALAND
Mashonaland won by 2 sets.
WOMEN.

Mrs. Gumpertz and Mrs. Webb beat Miss Capstick and Mrs. Mail
8—6, 8—6; beat Miss Hunt and Miss Elliott 6—1, 6—2.

Mrs. Taberer and Mrs. Barbour beat Miss Hunt and Miss Elliott
6—0, 1—6, 6—3; lost to Miss Capstick and Mrs. Mail 6—4,
3—6, 6—8.

Mrs. Gumpertz lost to Miss Elliott 6—8, 7—5, 4—6.

Mrs. Taberer lost to Mrs. Mail 1—6, 3—6.

Mrs. Webb beat Miss Hunt 6—1, 6—2.

Mrs. Barbour lost to Miss Capstick 4—6, 6—3, 5—7.

MATABELELAND v. MASHONALAND.
Matabeleland won by 4 matches.
MEN.

R. Vincent and M. H. Quinn beat D. P. C. Gumpertz and A. P
Shone 6—4, 6—4; beat A. Ross and K. R. C. Grainger 6—3,
6—4.

W. G. Wood and D. G. Blackbeard beat Ross and Grainger 6—2, 8—6; beat Gumpertz and Shone 5—7, 6—3, 8—6.
Vincent lost to Ross 2—6, 6—3, 4—6. Wood beat Grainger 6—3, 6—4.
Quinn beat Shone 6—3, 6—2. Blackbeard lost to Gumpertz 1—6, 4—6.

1935.
MASHONALAND v. MATABELELAND.
Mashonaland won by 3 matches (one not played).
WOMEN.

Mrs. Webb beat Miss Elliott 10—8, 0—6, 6—1.
Mrs. Barbour beat Miss Dugmore 3—6, 7—5, 7—5.
Mrs. Style lost to Miss Capstick 3—6, 3—6.
Mrs. Lewin lost to Miss Hopley 6—4, 5—7, 1—6.
Mrs. Lewin and Mrs. Barbour beat Miss Capstick and Miss Hopley 6—1, 6—4; beat Miss Dugmore and Miss Elliott 6—4, 1—6, 6—2.
Mrs. Webb and Mrs. Style beat Miss Capstick and Miss Hopley 6—1, 8—6.

MATABELELAND v. MASHONALAND.
Matabeleland won by 2 matches.
MEN.

R. Vincent beat D. P. C. Gumpertz 6—4, 6—0.
W. G. Wood beat Morris 7—9, 6—3, 6—3.
Kelly lost to Roberts 4—6, 5—7.
H. H. Davies beat Palmer 6—3, 7—5.
Vincent and Wood beat Gumpertz and Morris 1—6, 6—3, 6—3; beat Palmer and Roberts 7—5, 6—2.
Kelly and Davies lost to Palmer and Roberts 6—1, 8—10, 2—6; lost to Gumpertz and Morris 6—4, 1—6, 2—6.

J. S. Blackwell.   G. N. Fleming.

RHODESIAN CHAMPIONSHIPS.

MEN'S SINGLES.

1897: P. D. L. Fynn.
1899: W. S. Taberer.
1900: P. D. L. Fynn.
1901: D. W. Hook.
1902: H. J. K. Brereton.
1903: P. D. L. Fynn.
1904: P. D. L. Fynn.
1905: F. G. Brooks.
1906: P. D. L. Fynn.
1907: P. D. L. Fynn.
1908: F. G. Brooks.
1909: F. G. Brooks.
1910: H. J. K. Brereton.
1911: F. G. Brooks.
1912: C. N. Davis (Transvaal).
1913: J. McLoughlin.
1914: V. Collins.
1915: F. G. Brooks.

1919: V. H. van Breda.
1920: F. G. Brooks.
1921: A. Ross.
1922: A. Ross.
1923: A. Ross.
1924: F. B. Brooks.
1925: H. S. Cross
　　　 D. G. Blackbeard.
1926: D. G. Blackbeard.
1927: R. Owens.
1928: A. Ross.
1929: A. Ross.
1930: A. Ross.
1931: R. Vincent.
1932: A. Ross.
1933: R. Vincent.
1934: R. Vincent.
1935: F. H. Lowe (Natal).

LADIES' SINGLES.

1897: Mrs. A. M. Fleming.
1898: Mrs. A. M. Fleming.
1899: Mrs. A. M. Fleming.
1900: Mrs. A. M. Fleming.
1901: Mrs. S. J. Oliphant.
1902: Mrs. S. J. Oliphant.
1903: Mrs. S. J. Oliphant.
1904: Mrs. S. J. Oliphant.
1905: Mrs. S. J. Oliphant.
1906: Mrs. S. J. Oliphant.
1907: Mrs. S. J. Oliphant.
1908: Mrs. J. H. Kennedy.
1909: Miss F. Braddon.
1910: Mrs. C. A. Shaw.
1911: Mrs. C. A. Shaw.
1912: Miss Coles (England).
1913: Mrs. Baker.
1914: Mrs. K. Peel.

1915: Mrs. A. L. Baker.
1919: Miss F. Standen.
1920: Mrs. F. H. Ellis.
1921: Miss J. F. Standen.
1922: Mrs. F. H. Ellis.
1923: Mrs. Griffin.
1924: Miss I. Gradwell.
1925: Mrs. Griffin.
1926: Mrs. Griffin.
1927: Mrs. D. Mail.
1928: Mrs. Griffin.
1929: Mrs. Ellis.
1930: Miss F. Sherry.
1931: Mrs. D. P. C. Gumpertz.
1932: Mrs. D. P. C. Gumpertz.
1933: Mrs. D. P. C. Gumpertz.
1934: Mrs. R. Taylor.
1935: Mrs. F. H. Lowe (Natal).

MEN'S DOUBLES.

1897: P. D. L. Fynn and W. S. Taberer.
1902: W. S. Taberer and D. W. Hook.
1903: H. B. Douslin and L. P. Ashburnham.
1904: P. D. L. Fynn and E. W. Graham.
1905: W. S. Taberer and F. G. Brooks.
1906: W. S. Taberer and F. G. Brooks.
1907: W. S. Taberer and F. G. Brooks.
1908: W. S. Taberer and F. G. Brooks.
1909: W. S. Taberer and F. G. Brooks.
1910: F. B. Brooks and E. Youatt.
1911: H. J. K. Brereton and P. D. L. Fynn.
1912: Watson and J. McLoughlin.
1913: L. Brooks and A. C. Bagshawe.
1914: F. B. Brooks and V. Collins.

Tennis.

1915 and 1919: W. S. Taberer and F. G. Brooks.
1920: F. B. and L. A. N. Brooks.
1921: A. Ross and A. E. Boyton.
1922: H. S. and E. E. Cross.
1923-1924: F. G. and F. B. Brooks.
1925: A. Ross and L. A. N. Brooks.
1926: F. B. Brooks and D. P. C. Gumpertz.
1927: C. S. Style and E. E. Cross.
1928: D. G. Blackbeard and J. H. Holding.
1929: C. S. Style and Brooks.
1930-1931: C. S. Style and F. B. Brooks.
1932: D. Gumpertz and A. P. Shone.
1933-1934: R. Vincent and M. H. Quinn.
1935: F. H. Lowe and E. Getaz (Natal).

MIXED DOUBLES.

1897: Mrs. A. M. Fleming and W. P. Grimmer.
1903: Miss Fynn and P. D. L. Fynn.
1904: Mrs S. J. Oliphant and P. D. L. Fynn.
1905-1906: Mrs. J. H. Kennedy and F. G. Brooks.
1907: Miss Pett and W. S. Taberer.
1908-1909: Mrs. J. H. Kennedy and F. G. Brooks.
1910: Mrs. C. A. Shaw and H. J. K. Brereton.
1911: Mrs. Baker and C. H. Webb.
1912: Miss Coles and C. N. Davis.
1913: Mrs. J. H. Kennedy and P. D. L. Fynn.
1914: Miss N. de Villiers and L. A. N. Brooks.
1915: Miss I. Gradwell and V. H. van Breda.
1919: Mrs. Ellman Brown and F. G. Brooks.
1920: Mrs. Ellis and F. G. Brooks.
1921: Miss J. F. Standen and A. T. Tait.
1922-1923-1924-1925: Mrs. Jearey and H. S. Cross.
1926: Miss J. F. Standen and F. B. Brooks.
1927: Mrs. Jearey and H. S. Cross.
1928: Mrs. Mail and E. Barbour.
1929: Mrs. Ellis and I. Campbell-Rodger.
1930: Mrs. Gumpertz and C. S. Style.
1931: Mrs. Mail and R. Vincent.
1932: Mrs. Webb and D. Gumpertz.
1933-1934: Miss Elliott and R. Vincent.
1935: Mr. and Mrs. F. H. Lowe (Natal).

LADIES' DOUBLES.

1920: Mrs. L. A. N. Brooks and Miss I. Gradwell.
1921: Miss J. F. Standen and Miss D. de Beer.
1922-1924: Mrs. Boyes and Miss Gradwell.
1925: Mrs. Bennie and Mrs. Taylor.
1926: Mrs. Ellis and Miss Gradwell.
1927-1928: Mrs. Mail and Mrs. Bennie.
1929: Mrs. Webb and Miss McChlery.
1930: Mrs. Mail and Mrs. Jennings.
1931: Mrs. Webb and Mrs. Gumpertz.
1932: Miss McManus and Miss Harper.
1933: Mrs. Mail and Mrs. Griffin.
1934: Mrs. Webb and Mrs. Gumpertz.
1935: Mrs. Lowe and Mrs. Hathorn (Natal).

SQUASH RACKETS

Major-General H. M. G. Watson,
C.M.G., D.S.O.

Lieut. Col. C. F. Birney, D.S.O.

Captain Gregory Smith.

SQUASH RACKETS

HE Bulawayo Club holds the distinction of possessing the first squash court laid down in South Africa. This was presented to the club in 1898 by Col. J. S. Nicholson, Commandant-General of the Matabeleland Forces. It was of the size of the old court at Lords, 42 feet by 25 feet, but four years ago it was rebuilt to conform with the standard measurements of 32 feet by 21 feet.

Among distinguished players who have used this court is the Prince of Wales, who is no mean exponent of the game. Others include Capt. T. O. Jameson, who was here with Solly Joel's cricket side in 1924, and Capt. V. Cazalet, each of whom have held the All-England amateur championship.

There was great enthusiasm over squash from '98 onwards and of the prominent early players were E. H. Cooper, who was outstanding; Piper; the two cricketers, M. H. Routledge and H. Hallward; Popham, Simon and T. H. Cooke. Numerous tournaments were held and a high standard obtained. As there was no other court in the Colony these games were confined to the Bulawayo Club.

In the first tournament after the Great War, Bulawayo saw many good players in Col. C. F. Birney, D.S.O., A. B. Pocklington, MacDonagh, Ludlow, R. L. Hardy, B. L. Gardiner, the three Bourdillons, Tom, a fine stylist, Victor and Theo.

In Salisbury squash owes a great deal to Major A. L. Cooper, D.S.O., who set the game going when he built a private court in 1924. Several sportsmen became keen and Major Cooper allowed them to form a club and use his court. When the Prince of Wales visited Rhodesia in 1926 he played on this court which he allowed to be named "Prince's Court." H.R.H. Prince George also played on the court during his tour of Rhodesia in 1934. In 1928 the Salisbury Club built a squash court.

Among Salisbury's best are Capt. Gregory-Smith, F. G. Brooks, Col. (now Major-Géneral) Hugo Watson, C.M.G., D.S.O., Pat Power, P. C. Kent, a Charterhouse player, D. A. Saunder of Marlborough, Roger Howman, Major Cooper, "Cherry" Reynolds, the Rt. Rev. E. F. Paget, Bishop of Southern Rhodesia, the Marquis of Graham, Col. T. E.

T. H. COOKE   **1933.**   A. G. COWLING
(Singles Champion).   (Capt. of Bulawayo Club Team).

1935.
Standing: R. Howman, B. R. W. Johnson, Capt. Reynolds, R. Johnson.
T. H. Cooke, D. Sander.
P. J. Power (Singles Champion), B. Johnson.

Robins and W. C. Robertson. There are two outstanding women players who are in a class by themselves, Mrs. A. MacEwan, of Darwendale, and Mrs. Baillie. Capt. Cazalet spoke very highly of the latter's play.

The first inter-town competition was in 1930 when Bulawayo scored a narrow victory over Salisbury, thanks to some fine play by T. H. Cooke and P. H. Gifford. In 1932, H.E. the Governor, Sir Cecil Hunter Rodwell, a keen player and one-time champion of the Rand, presented a cup for an inter-town series and in that year it was won by Salisbury whose win was largely due to Pat Power and Alex Howard. The latter also won the singles championship and the cup donated by Col. C. F. Birney, D.S.O., himself a prominent squash player. Howard was one-time Public Schools champion and a half-blue at Cambridge.

In 1933, for the inter-town cup, Bulawayo beat Salisbury very decisively. The singles honours went to T. H. Cooke, by far the oldest active player in the territory and one who has done more for the game in Rhodesia than anyone. He is a fine exponent of squash and a few years ago, when in Cape Town, was invited to play in some exhibition matches at the opening by the Governor-General of the Kelvin Grove courts. He gave a good account of himself against such players as Capt. Hegearty, first string for the R.A.F. Club and inter-services champion, and Bevill Rudd.

Last year, Bulawayo again won the inter-town cup while the singles title was annexed by Brian Johnson, also of Bulawayo. This town at the present time is rich in talent, with A. G. Cowling, who gave Cazalet his toughest game when the latter visited here in 1932, H. G. Livingston, two good young players in the brothers Dick and Brian Johnson, P. H. Gifford, H. S. Sly, Bertram Johnson and T. E. S. (Tim) Francis, the Cambridge Double Blue (rugger and cricket) and England rugger international who since his arrival in Bulawayo a few years ago has identified himself closely with, and to the advantage of, all sport, particularly rugby.

Squash rackets has become increasingly popular in recent years and additional courts are now being prepared in Bulawayo.

A prime mover in the acquisition of these is Mr. T. H. Cooke and he is supported by a large number of younger sportsmen. The excellence of squash needs no extolling here and when more of the younger generation have tried it the game will be assured of an extended popularity. In con-

I

clusion it is desired to correct the general impression that squash is an expensive game. On the contrary, it is far less expensive than most of the sports played in the Colony.

INTER-TOWN CONTESTS, 1930.
Bulawayo v. Salisbury.

T. H. Cooke beat F. G. Brooks, 2—1; beat Col. H. W. M. Watson, 2—1.
Col. C. F. Birney lost to Brooks, 1—2; lost to Watson, 1—2.
P. H. Gifford beat Major Blackburn, 2—0.

Bulawayo won by 3 matches to 2.

RODWELL CUP.
1932.
Salisbury v. Bulawayo.

A. Howard beat T. H. Cooke, 3—2; beat A. G. Cowling, 3—2.
P. J. Power beat Cooke, 3—1; beat Cowling, 3—0.
W. C. Robertson beat P. H. Gifford, 3—0; lost to T. E. S. Francis, 0—3.
H. C. Reynolds lost to Gifford, 1—3; lost to Francis, 0—3.

Salisbury won by 5 matches to 3.

1933.
Bulawayo v. Salisbury.

T. H. Cooke beat D. A. Saunder, 3—1; beat P. C. Kent, 3—0.
W. C. Robertson beat Bishop Paget, 3—0; beat The Marquis of Graham, 3—0.
R. Johnson beat Bishop Paget, 3—1; beat The Marquis of Graham, 3—1.
B. R. W. Johnson beat H. C. Reynolds, 3—1; beat Capt. Cherry, 3—0.
A. G. Cowling lost to Saunder, 1—3; lost to Kent, 1—3.
J. H. Sly lost to Reynolds, 1—3; lost to Cherry, 2—3.

Bulawayo won by 8 matches to 4.

1934.
Bulawayo v. Salisbury.

B. R. W. Johnson beat P. J. Power, 3—1; beat H. R. G. Howman, 3—1.
T. H. Cooke beat D. A. Saunder, 3—0; beat P. C. Kent, 3—1.
T. E. S. Francis beat Kent, 3—1; lost to Saunder, 1—3.
P. H. Gifford beat S. Morgenrood, 3—0.
H. S. Sly lost to Power, 1—3; lost to Howman, 2—3.

Bulawayo won by 6 matches to 3.

1935.
Salisbury v. Bulawayo.

P. J. Power beat B. R. W. Johnson, 3—0; beat B. Johnson, 3—0.
R. Johnson beat B. R. W. Johnson, 3—0; beat B. Johnson, 3—1.
H. R. G. Howman lost to T. H. Cooke, 2—3.
H. C. Reynolds lost to T. H. Cooke, 1—3.

Salisbury won by 4 matches to 2.

SOUTHERN RHODESIA SINGLES CHAMPIONSHIP (Birney Cup).
1932.

T. E. S. Francis beat W. C. Robertson, 3—0.
T. H. Cooke beat Major A. L. Cooper, 3—0; beat Francis, 3—2.
A. Howard (champion) beat P. J. Power, 3—1; beat A. G. Cowling, 3—1; beat Cooke, 3—1.

1933.

A. G. Cowling beat D. A. Saunder, 3—1; R. Johnson beat H. C. Reynolds, 3—0.

W. C. Robertson beat P. C. Kent, 3—0; beat Cowling, 3—1.

T. H. Cooke (champion) beat Mrs. Baillie, 3—0; beat Johnson, 3—1; beat Robertson, 3—0.

1934.

P. J. Power beat H. R. G. Howman, 3—0.

D. A. Saunder beat P. C. Kent, 3—2.

T. H. Cooke beat S. Morgenrood, 3—1; beat Saunder, 3—1.

B. R. W. Johnson (champion) beat H. S. Sly, 3—1; beat Power, 3—0; beat Cooke 3—1.

1935.

B. R. W. Johnson beat R. Johnson, 3—2; Howman beat B. Johnson, 3—1.

Power (champion) beat Cooke, 3—0; beat B. R. W. Johnson, 3—1; beat Howman, 3—0.

BADMINTON

IN Bulawayo this game was first played in 1922 by the staff of the Milton School in the Beit Hall of the present Junior School. H. G. Houlding and Capt. G. T. I. Leonard, the latter a fine player, were the prime movers. Later on, courts were marked out in the Drill Hall, and to-day an active club is fostering the game there. Among Bulawayo's best players are Major N. E. Creasy, Capt. E. R. Day, A. Utterton, J. H. Downing, Sergeant T. T. G. Race and Mrs. Race, R. H. Ely, E. Price, F. V. Clarance and Mr. and Mrs. H. G. Pritchard.

The game spread to the Drill Halls in Gwelo, Salisbury, and Umtali. and has become very popular.

Umtali took up badminton in 1931 and, of a fairly large number of enthusiasts, the best are L. E. Creasy, C. S. Davies, H. Mason, G. Muir, Sergeant H. Crossland, Mrs. Hiller and the Misses Webb, Ternouth and Brunton.

E. G. Howman encouraged the game at Sinoia, where it is now played chiefly at the Kutama Mission.

Badminton in the Colony is still in its infancy, and the standard of play is not very high. It is, however, improving steadily, and should go ahead rapidly if the proposed inter-town tournaments eventuate.

SHOOTING

R HODESIA has always been a great country for the shooting man, whether he fancies the range or veld, or both. It is not surprising, therefore, that the standard of shooting in the Colony is high and that its representatives can hold their own at the chief of all shooting festivals, the English Bisley. Judging from the standard of shooting in the Colony to-day Rhodesia will continue to maintain this wonted high level.

On March 17, 1890, a little band of Irishmen were gathered together on the outskirts of Gubulawayo, not far from Lobengula's royal kraal where Government House now stands. It was decided that the day should not pass without the customary celebrations in honour of St. Patrick and the anniversary is still remembered as one of the most riotous ever spent in Rhodesia. It began with a visit to Lobengula when, armed with bottles of champagne, the Irishmen descended on the old chief and impressed him mightily with tales of Ireland's patron saint, making much of his curious power over snakes. Lobengula needed no encouragement to drink St. Patrick's health in the visitors' champagne and carefully passed on the heel taps to two of his dusky queens. The party left him in a rare good humour and, returning to camp, spent the rest of St. Patrick's Day in a rifle shooting match. A high standard of marksmanship was shown but unfortunately no records exist of what must surely have been the first shooting contest in Rhodesia.

The day ended with a sumptuous dinner given by Major Maxwell and a smoking concert at which one of the artistes was the hunter, Selous, whose graphic coster recitation brought down the house.

The first record of a shooting competition in the Colony is in April, 1893, when at Victoria a team from the Mashonaland Horse scored 772 points against 730 points by a team chosen from the Victoria Rangers.

In Bulawayo a volunteer corps was formed called the Rhodesia Horse which in turn became the Bulawayo Field Force at the time of the '96 Rebellion. The only shooting done in their time was practice at the week-ends. Rifles and ammunition were drawn from an armoury in the form of a large wood and iron shed between what are now the

Municipal Offices and the Bulawayo Club. The Bulawayo Field Force was disbanded after the Rebellion and some of its members formed a local rifle club. The first range was laid out in 1894 and competition for the monthly medals awarded by the B.S.A. Company was very keen.

Similar shoots were conducted by a rifle club in Salisbury where the first range stretched from about where the grand stand is now on the race course to the back of the Kopje. The government afterwards gave this land to the Turf Club and the rifle range was then taken across the Makabusi to where the brickfields are to-day. The 600 yards firing point was where the Magistrate's courthouse or the railway station now stands. With the coming of the railways the present range was laid out by Col. Beal and F. Newman.

The first prize meeting of the Salisbury Rifle Club took place in 1895 when a large silver goblet presented by Dr. Jameson was won by F. Newman. The shoot was under the Queen's Prize, Wimbledon, conditions, i.e., 200, 500 and 600 yards, which to-day constitute the first stage of the King's Prize shot for at the English Bisley.

The rifles used by the early shottists were mostly Lee Metfords, although there was a large number of Martini Henri's in use. The first ammunition was very poor. There was sometimes cordite, sometimes pellet powder, and later a smokeless powder caused bullets to drop between the firing mound and the target. In one instance a shottist fired and was signalled a miss. So positive was he that he had not missed that he challenged the signal. It was repeated. Then he happened to remove his bolt and there was the bullet stuck up the barrel! On such weapons did the Pioneers have to rely, not only for target shooting, but also for protection against the natives. During the Boer War the long Lee Enfield rifles were issued and very much better ammunition.

In 1897 the B.S.A. Company presented a shield for annual competition between teams of ten of the Police and Rifle Clubs. The shoot was held in Salisbury during the September celebrations and was won by the Salisbury Rifle Club from teams representing Bulawayo, Umtali, Victoria and Gwelo, the B.S.A. Police and the 7th Hussars. The winning team consisted of F. Newman (captain), now over eighty years old, affectionately known as " Pa " and still resident near Salisbury, N. McGlashan, J. Hamilton, G. B.

Hovel, Major Carnac, J. McIlwraith, G. Southey, N. Gilmer, H. Ross and J. Taute. Twelve men travelled by mule-coach from Bulawayo, viz., M. Blunt (captain), C. J. A. Blackler, W. Clouston, Bolt, T. W. Davey, Dr. E. Head, A. E. Marris, W. K. Thompson, Walker, Woods, F. R. Williams, Van Blerk. The journey lasted nearly a week and on the way the team indulged in some game shooting. Near Salisbury a reed-buck was shot and brought on to the coach. Much to the disgust of the shottists it was treated as excess luggage and charged for but fortunately meat was at a premium in Salisbury, fetching as much as 4s. 6d. per lb., and on their arrival they disposed of the buck at a figure which still gave them a reasonable profit.

Owing to the difficulty of transport the Salisbury Rifle Club did not compete when the B.S.A. Company's Shield was shot for in Bulawayo in 1898 and the Bulawayo Club won from the B.S.A. Police.

The lack of travelling facilities in those days presented a problem to Rhodesian sportsmen and even when the railway first opened a Salisbury shooting team travelled to Bulawayo in an open mail van with eighteen passengers all sitting on top of the mail bags for 72 hours!

One of the best of the stories that crop up in the shooting records relates to a meeting in Salisbury when a Bulawayo team had been celebrating victory in a rather Bacchanalian manner. One of the survivors, when the rest were under the table, was the Colony's crack shot, now a very well-known all-round sportsman in Bulawayo. He emerged from the " pub," imagined he saw a lighted tram-car travelling down the street, sprinted as if the devil were at his heels and caught the tram just in time to fling himself on and land among a pile of sanitary buckets!

In 1899 the Southern Rhodesia Volunteers were formed and shooting in the country was given a great impetus. In Bulawayo " G " Troop (S.R.V.) was the recognised Bulawayo rifle club unit and it won most of the shooting trophies. The Volunteer training ground was near the Old Nick Mine where " F " Troop, commanded by a fine old Scotsman, Sandy Butters, put up a target and started musketry. Most of his gallant warriors had never fired a rifle and the red flag was waving most of the time. Capt. Butters became exasperated and sent for Sergeant Robb who was a reputed shot (his own statement) and told him to show the " pink loons " how it was done. Sergeant Robb, a little

1902 BISLEY TEAM.

Back Row:

Troop Sgt.-Major D. McDonald, Cpl. J. Huntly, Cpl. W. K. Thompson, Sgt. C. J. A. Blackler, Sgt. T. W. Davey.

Middle Row:

Tpr. C. B. Fox, Sgt. E. E. Templar, Troop Sgt.-Major J. Mac-Namara, Capt. W. Baxendale (capt.), Lt. A. C. L. Webb.

In Front:

Sgt. H. Lucas, Tpr. G. W. Gibbings.

fat man, lay down, made himself comfortable a la the
crack Bisley men, and fired. Result . . . red flag. A
long explanation followed and then shot No. 2 and another
red Lincoln with a further explanation. Shot No. 3, red
flag, and so on to shot No. 7 and still a red flag. Collapse
of O.C. and Sergeant Robb and cheers from the firer "loons."
Sergeant Robb was never asked again to show his ability.

Immediately after the Boer War shooting was very
popular. Col. Raleigh Grey and Col. Ramsay, commanding
the Eastern and Western Divisions, respectively, of the
S.R.V., gave shooting every encouragement and it was their
idea, supported by the Administrator Sir William Milton
and Mr. Rhodes, that enabled the first Rhodesian team to
take part in the English Bisley in 1902. The team of twelve
consisted of Capt. W. Baxendale, Lt. A. C. L. Webb, Sgt.
H. Lucas, Sgt. T. W. Davey, Troop Sgt.-Major J. Mac-
Namara, Troop Sgt.-Major (now Colonel) D. McDonald,
Cpl. W. K. Thompson, Sgt. C. J. A. Blackler, Cpl. J.
Huntly, Tpr. G. W. Gibbings, Tpr. C. B. Fox and Sgt.
E. E. Templar. The prime object of the team was to try
to secure the trophy open to Colonial teams, i.e., the Rajah
of Kolapore's Cup. The other objective was necessarily that
of individuals in the King's Prize, the Grand Aggregate and
other events. Australia won the Kolapore Cup and Rhodesia
was placed second with a score of 758 points, only 12 behind
the winning score. It was a splendid achievement on
Rhodesia's part. The team returned an average of 94.75 points
per man. In the individual events J. MacNamara with a
score of 101 was second in the Coronation Prize shoot and
second in the All-comer's Aggregate.

In 1906, two Rhodesians, Capt. J. MacDonald and Lt.
W. S. Craster, on leave in the old country, shot at the Bisley
and did remarkably well. Craster in particular caused a
sensation in the King's Prize when he came second with
a score of 323 which was only one point behind the winning
total.

Rhodesia was represented again at Bisley in 1909. The
team was: Capt. E. Hope Carson, Lt. F. T. Stephens, Lt.
J. B. Sybray, Squadron Sgt. Major J. G. Jearey, Sgt. Fowler,
Sgt. J. Steel, Band Sgt. R. P. Arnold, Cpl. J. Rock, Tpr. G.
Link, Tpr. Harper, Tpr. O. Cartwright and Constable
Miller.

1909 BISLEY TEAM.

Standing:

Tpr. G. Link, Band-
Sgt. R. P. Arnold, Cpl.
J. Rock, Constable Mil-
ler, Tpr. Harper, Tpr.
O. Cartwright.

Sitting:

S.Sgt.-Major J. G.
Jearey, Lt. F. T.
Stephens, Capt. E.
Hope Carson, Lt. J. B.
Sybray, Sgt. J. Steel.

Sgt. Fowler.

Photo by Gale and Polden, Aldershot.

1925 **BISLEY TEAM.**

Standing: Sgt. Major E. G. Browne, Cpl. N. A. Fereday, Rfm. V. G. Phipps, Rfm. W. F. Smith, Sgt. J. W. Watson, Sgt. J. Lea, Sub. Inspr. R. Walker.

Sitting: Cpl. R. E. Neville, Lt. J. W. Rayner, Col. Ffennell, Capt. W. C. Hoaten (capt.), Capt. W. R. Benzies.

In Front: Rfm. F. H. Morgan, Sgt.-Major P. M. Fallon.

There was a close finish in the Kolapore Cup shoot which was won by Canada with 765 points, Rhodesia finishing sixth with 730 points. The best Rhodesian score was Trooper Harper's 95. Canada also won the Mackinnon Cup with a total of 1616 points. Rhodesia's 1422 points earned her eighth place and Trooper Harper (136) was again the Colony's top scorer. The Canadian team used the Rose rifle against which a protest was lodged but which was overruled by the Bisley committee.

In the shoot for the "Daily Graphic" Cup, Lt. Sybray and Trooper Harper, with possibles, tied with twenty others. Harper was placed fourth in the shoot-off. Corporal Rock came second in the Salutaris competition (200 yards) after an unprecedented double tie in which he repeated his possibles. There were many other individual successes and although the Rhodesians were disappointed with their own efforts in the team shoots, their shooting evoked very favourable comment in the Home press which gave great publicity to the Colony.

The third Rhodesian team to compete at Bisley went over in 1925, when the Colony was conspicuous in the various team and individual events. The team consisted of Capt. W. C. Hoaten, team captain, Capt. W. R. Benzies, Lt. J. W. Rayner, Sgt.-Major P. M. Fallon, Sgt.-Major E. G. Browne, Sub.-Inspr. R. Walker, Sgt. (now Major) J. W. Watson, Sgt. J. Lea, Cpl. R. E. Neville, Cpl. N. A. Fereday, Rfm. F. H. Morgan, Rfm. W. F. Smith and Rfm. V. G. Phipps. In the great team event for the Kolapore Cup, Canada won with an aggregate score of 1099. The Mother Country was second with 1097 and Rhodesia a proud third with 1089 points. In the second stage of the King's Prize, Rfm. Morgan, who in 1920 won this most important of the individual events, tied with a Canadian with a possible at 300 yards. No team trophies came Rhodesia's way but there were numerous individual successes. Cpl. Neville won the Stock Exchange competition and tied with four others for the "Graphic" Cup but lost the shoot-off. Cpl. Fereday also lost the shoot-off when he tied with two others for the Prince of Wales' Prize. Lt. Rayner was another Rhodesian who figured in a tie, in the squadded competition. The St. George's challenge trophy was won by Sgt.-Major Browne while Sgt. Lea created a sensation with two possibles that won him the "Daily Telegraph" Cup.

Photo by Gale and Polden, Aldershot.

1930 BISLEY TEAM.

Standing: C.S. Major F. H. Morgan, Sgt. N. A. Fereday, Sgt. Major E. G. Browne, Sub. Inspr. R. Walker, Sgt. W. F. Smith, Sgt. T. Forbes, Sgt. A. M. Cumming, C.Q.M. Sgt. W. E. C. Owen
Sitting: Lt. J. W. Rayner, Lt. L. M. McBean, Lt. Col. E. Hope Carson, D.S.O., M.C., Lt.-Col. C. M. Newman, M.C., Lt. D. J. Wilson, Lt. A. G Healey.

The results of the 1925 visit were considered so satisfactory, not only from the point of view of good shooting, but also because of the immense value of the publicity which the visit gave to Southern Rhodesia that, on the recommendation of the High Commissioner, backed up by the Minister of Defence and the Commandant of the S.R. Forces, the Government generously granted £1,000 towards the cost of sending another team in 1930. This team consisted of Lt.-Col. E. Hope Carson, D.S.O., M.C., V.D., Commandant of team, Lt.-Col. C. M. Newman, M.C., Lt. J. W. Rayner, Lt. A. G. Healey, Lt. L. M. McBean, Lt. D. J. Wilson, Sgt.-Major E. G. Browne, Sub.-Inspr. R. Walker, C.Q.M.-Sgt. W. E. C. Owen, Coy. Sgt.-Major F. H. Morgan, Sgt. A. M. Cumming, Sgt. W. F. Smith, Sgt. N. A. Fereday and Sgt. T. Forbes.

The Mother Country, which includes the whole of the British Isles, won the Kolapore Cup, registering its 35th win out of 56 contests to that time. The conditions are eight in a team and ten shots to count at each of the distances of 300, 500 and 600 yards. At 300 yards the Mother Country established a lead of 5 points over Canada and 6 points over Southern Rhodesia. At 500 yards some remarkable shooting by the leading team gave them a lead of 15 points over Canada who were only 2 points ahead of Southern Rhodesia. Then came the battle royal at 600 yards. India and the others were forgotten while all eyes watched the targets of the three leaders. Every shot was vital; the silence was intense and broken only by the " crack " of the rifles. With a point here and a point there the Dominion and the Colony crept up on the Mother Country but, though Canada had 369 and Rhodesia 367 to the Mother Country's 361, the previous lead proved too much and the final places were left unchanged. The winning score was 1122, with Canada's 1115 second and Rhodesia's 1111 third. The Rhodesian team, with scores, was Fereday (142), Rayner (141), McBean (140), Forbes (139), Browne (138), Cumming (138), Morgan (137), Owen (136).

The Mackinnon Cup, in which the Mother Country is split up into her component parts of England, Scotland, Ireland and Wales, is shot for at 900 and 1,000 yards. This trophy was secured by Canada with 1076 points, with S. Rhodesia second. The Rhodesian team, with scores, was: Morgan (96), Healey (94), Browne (88), Cumming (88), Rayner (87), McBean (87), Walker (85), Wilson (83), Forbes

(82), Fereday (80), Owen (80), Smith (75), total 1025 points. A feature of the two cup shoots was the excellent coaching of Lt.-Col. Newman to whom most of the credit was given for S. Rhodesia's success.

Among the minor team events the 2nd Battalion, The Rhodesia Regiment, put in a team of four in the Cheylesmore competition, which is a service event over a run of approximately 100 to 150 yards and the knocking over of tiles. The team knocking over the greatest number of tiles with the fewest rounds expended, automatically puts its opposite number out of the competition. No overseas team had ever before had the effrontery to compete with the regular units of both the Army and Navy who regard this class of work as peculiarly their own. Nevertheless the 2nd Battalion survived three heats and was beaten only in the semi-final by the 4th Battalion R.W. Kents. Among the notable teams that failed to reach the semi-final were: H.M.S. Victory, 2nd Rifle Brigade, 1st Scots Guards, 1st K.O.Y.L.I., Royal Marines (Chatham), H.M.S. Vivid, H.M.S. Excellent, 2nd Grenadier Guards, Small Arms School, Royal Marines (Plymouth), 1st Manchester Regiment, 1st The Suffolk Regiment, H.M.S. Emperor of India and H.M.S. Courageous.

The most notable of the individual successes were notched by Coy. Sgt.-Major Morgan. He obtained first place in the 1st Stage King's, the Loder Cup and the Secretary for State for War shoots as well as being well up in numerous other competitions. Sgt. Fereday took high honours in the Grand Aggregate and in most of the Service events, particularly the "Queen Mary's." Altogether the visit was an outstanding success.

It might here be noted as a point of interest that during the visit of this 1930 team to England the premier event, the King's Prize, was won by a woman competitor, Miss Foster, whose unique performance greatly disturbed some of the hard-bitten old shooting men. In this connection the following authentic story is told by one of the Rhodesian competitors. As he left Bisley station by train after the meeting, two elderly petty officers of the Royal Navy, bearded and stout, one from H.M.S. Pembroke and one from H.M.S. Excellent, who had forgathered at Bisley meetings for many years, were saying "goodbye." This was the manner of their leave taking.

First Petty Officer: Well, goodbye Bill! See you next year!

Second Petty Officer: No damn fear! I'm sending the missus!

In 1904 and for some years after the Southern Rhodesia Volunteers (Western Division) sent teams to compete in the Transvaal Bisley. On the first occasion Capt. A. C. L. Webb won the Grand Aggregate and with it a cup and the National Rifle Association medal. He also won the Johannesburg Cup and was placed second in the President's Cup and Mappin Cup shoots. His brother, Cadet Lt. K. M. Webb, of St. George's School, carried off the Cadet's Cup.

In 1905 the Western Division finished 13th out of 20 entrants for the Schumacher Cup. This was shot for over long ranges, 800, 900 and 1,000 yards and among the competing teams were many representing the various Imperial regiments in South Africa at that time. Tpr. L. Babb and one other tied with a top score of 98. In the inter-regimental shoot for the Hamilton Cup the S.R.V. were fourth. The meeting was a triumph for Cadet Lt. K. M. Webb who won the Strange Cup, the Belgravia Cup, and the Troyeville Cup, the latter open to Volunteers as well as cadets. He also won the Grand Aggregate but in the excitement of his win and with men crowding round to congratulate the young marksman, he failed to hand in his card within the time allotted after the shoot and was disqualified, the prize being given for the next best score.

In 1906, Tpr. D. Drummond won the highest individual honour when he annexed the Lieutenant Governor's Cup. His aggregate score was 102.

In 1907, the S.R.V. (W.D.) came third in the Schumacher Cup and fourth in the Hamilton Cup, two team achievements that were highly satisfactory. In the Mappin Cup shoot, Cpl. T. Forbes was counted out and therefore came second. Tpr. W. Burnett also took second place in the Boxburg shoots.

In 1908 another team visited the Transvaal but met with only minor individual successes.

In 1913 the S.R.V. (W.D.) paid their first visit to a Cape Bisley where Reg. Sgt.-Major W. C. Hoaten was runner-up in the King's Prize, 5 points behind the winner who returned an aggregate of 321. Other Rhodesians distinguished themselves in this, the premier individual event; Bandmaster

Arnold was third with 314; Tpr. Evans was first in the first stage, and Sgt. Panton second.

In 1922 a team chosen from Bulawayo and Salisbury went down to the Cape Bisley. Many of the team distinguished themselves, particularly Rfm. Tiffin, who won the B.S.A. competition after a tie with another competitor, and Rfm. J. G. Jearey, who figured prominently in the prize list. In the Inter-Province Grand Challenge competition the Cape Province was first with 1795 points and Rhodesia second with 1720 points. The following was the Rhodesian team: Major W. Hill, Capt. W. C. Hoaten, C.S.-Major R. Krienke, Sgt. J. C. Smith, and Riflemen N. A. Fereday, L. B. Fereday, J. Steel, W. F. Smith, J. W. Rayner, J. Mackay, F. Kenworthy, S. C. Small, F. C. Croxford, J. G. Jearey, P. McKie, J. Hawkey, F. R. McLellan, J. Perks, J. Tiffin and J. Cumming.

In 1935 a team from the 2nd Battalion, The Rhodesia Regiment, went to Booysens (Transvaal) to shoot in the All-South Africa Bisley.

The Rhodesian contingent was not large but its lack of numerical strength was countered by the quality of its marksmanship. Lt. F. H. Morgan tied with one other in the O.F.S. Cup with a score of 103 out of a possible 105, and then won the shoot-off. He also won the President's Cup and in the Long Range competition, for which ten shots are fired at 900 and 1,000 yards, he won with a possible 100, a remarkable performance. Many of the Rhodesians figured well up in the prize lists although in the Hamilton Cup shoot the 2nd Battalion, The Rhodesia Regiment, came last.

In 1934 Southern Rhodesia came fourth in the list of twenty entries in the overseas .303 full range postal match shot under the auspices of the National Rifle Association, scoring 1088 points out of a highest possible of 1200. Kenya was first with 1137 points, Barbados second, and the Federated Malay States third. The competition was open to teams of eight, resident or stationed in the colonies, protectorates and countries of the Empire and the conditions were similar to those of the "Morning Post" (Junior Kolapore) match, that is, 10 shots a man at 300, 500 and 600 yards. Shooting could take place on any one day between January 1 and December 31, 1934, on any range in the competing country. This novel correspondence shoot attracted, in addition to those mentioned, teams from the Gold Coast, China (Shanghai), Ceylon, Falkland Islands, British Guiana,

Sierra Leone, Jamaica, Trinidad, Tanganyika, Fiji, Anglo-Egyptian Sudan, Nyasaland, Straits Settlements, Mauritius, Gibraltar and Cyprus. The Southern Rhodesia team was: Lt.-Col. C. M. Newman, M.C., V.D. (team captain), Lt. L. M. McBean, Lt. F. H. Morgan, Coy. Sgt.-Major N. A. Fereday, Sgt.-Major E. G. Browne, Reg. Q.M.-Sgt. W. E. C. Owen, Sgt. D. Devine, Cpl. W. L. Smith, Cpl. T. A. Robbins. The coach was Sgt. W. F. Smith.

In 1935 in the Empire Postal Shoot, which corresponds to the 2nd Stage King's, the Rhodesian team established a record score with 1138 points out of a possible 1200 points. Credit is due to Lt.-Col. C. M. Newman, M.C., V.D., the coach, for his expert advice in conditions which, though excellent on the whole, were at times very tricky. The scores were: Lt. F. H. Morgan 146, Capt. L. M. McBean 145, Sgt. A. M. Cumming 144, Lt. N. A. Fereday 144, R.Q.M.-Sgt. W. E. C. Owen 141, Cpl. C. Watkins 140, Sgt. W. L. Smith 139, and Lt. J. B. Lombard 139. The team captain was Sgt. L. B. Fereday.

Shooting in Rhodesia has not been confined to the men and there have been various women's rifle and revolver clubs in which the standard of shooting has been excellent. Women have also done remarkably well at the annual Bisleys although they have not competed as regularly as could be wished. At the first meeting in 1909, Miss Mac-Namara won the women's principal competition with a score of 87. In 1913, Mrs. W. Ross was top scorer with 90. In 1914 this record was equalled by Mrs. Hope Carson who also won in 1922 with an aggregate of 88. The last women's competition was in 1924 when it was won by Mrs. W. Hill with a score of 89.

Shooting was first brought under a central controlling body in 1908 when the Southern Rhodesia Rifle Association was formed. Prior to this the commanding officers, Col. Raleigh Grey and Col. Ramsay of the Eastern and Western Divisions, respectively, of the Southern Rhodesia Volunteers, were responsible for the shooting in their districts. At the first meeting of the S.R.R.A. Council there were present Lt.-Col. J. W. Fuller, B.S.A.P. (chairman), Major W. Baxendale, S.R.V. (W.D.), Major G. V. Drury, S.R. Constabulary, Capt. E. Hope-Carson, S.R.V. (E.D.), and Lt. F. T. Stephens, B.S.A.P. A draft constitution and rules and regulations were drawn up and these were finally approved and published under Government Notice No. 331, 1908. Some alterations

BULAWAYO WOMEN'S RIFLE CLUB, 1910.

Bandsman Greening, R.S.M. W. C. Hoaten, Major MacQueen, Capt. W. Ross, Bandmaster R. Arnold.
Mrs. Osborn, Mrs. Baxendale, Mrs. E. Strong, Mrs. W. Ross, Mrs. L. Woods, Mrs. Arnold.

and additions were published in Government Notice No. 39, 1910.

The S.R.R.A., supported and subsidised by the Government, was responsible for the conduct and encouragement of shooting throughout the country and from 1909 to 1931, with the exception of the war period, it conducted the annual national bisleys at which a very high standard of shooting has always been maintained.

The necessity for better control saw the abolition in 1932 of the S.R.R.A. and in its stead there was formed the S.R. National Rifle Association, with Colonel G. Parson, C.B.E., D.S.O., as its president, and Capt. A. C. Walker as its very able and energetic secretary.

In 1930, Major R. A. C. Radcliffe, Brigade Major in Southern Rhodesia, organised and placed the district weapon meetings on their present basis. It is doubtful whether Major Radcliffe himself imagined the extent to which success would crown his endeavours. The weapon meeting to-day is looked forward to in each military district as the peak of the shooting year and the steady increase in the numbers attending these meetings is evidence of their popularity. In 1934 there were 1491 competitors at the weapon meetings organised by the S.R.N.R.A. and the 23 military districts.

The premier shoot of the year, under purely Bisley conditions, is for the Governor's Cup. In the days before Southern Rhodesia became a Colony the cup was presented by the Administrator. The severest test under service conditions is the King's Medal shoot which has done a great deal to popularise service shooting. The conditions are:—10 rounds "deliberate" at 600 yards, 10 rounds "fire with movement" from 600 yards to 100 yards, 10 rounds "snap" at 300 yards, and 10 rounds "rapid" at 300 yards. The following is an extract from Army Order No. 12 of 1926: "His Majesty the King has been graciously pleased to approve of the grant of the King's Medal to be awarded annually to the champion shot of the military forces of Southern Rhodesia." During the ten years in which this coveted prize has been shot for Lt. F. H. Morgan and Coy. Sgt.-Mjr. N. A. Fereday have each won the medal four times.

The oldest trophy is the shield presented by the directors of the B.S.A. Company in 1897. Then Earl Grey in 1903 and Lord Dewar in 1904 each presented a valuable floating trophy. The "Grey" is open to teams of six members firing 15 shots each at 900 yards and the "Dewar" for teams of six firing 10 shots each at 600 yards. Another old trophy is the cup donated by the Municipality of Salisbury. Prior to 1921 the competition was confined to teams from the Salisbury district. In 1928, Messrs. Kynoch, Ltd., presented a cup for competition between the provinces of the Colony. The conditions are:—Teams of twelve and distances as for the Kolapore and Mackinnon Cup shoots combined, i.e., 300, 500, 600, 900, and 1,000 yards. There are numerous other important and handsome trophies.

From the earliest days to the time of his death in the East African campaign in 1916, Lt.-Col. W. Baxendale, D.S.O., was the inspiration of the shooting men and he maintained his interest right up to the last. He was a splendid shot. Lt.-Col. E. Hope Carson, D.S.O., M.C., V.D., is another who has done a great deal for shooting and in fact was the prime mover in the formation of the S.R.R.A. Among a large number who served on this Association those deserving of special mention are the late Major W. Hill, V.D., Major W. C. (Bill) Hoaten and Major H. Harnell. More recently a great deal has been done for shooting by Col. J. S. Morris, Lt.-Col. N. S. Ferris, Lt.-Col. T. Baker, E.D., Major W. H. Power, Capt. A. V. Adams, and Capt. D. M. Ross, who gave welcomed assistance with this record.

Rifle shooting receives every encouragement in the schools and for many years Rhodesian teams have performed with credit in the Schools Empire Competition. It is a great pity, however, that shooting does not claim the attention of more of these young Rhodesians after they leave school because it is the one sport at which it has been proved that Rhodesia can hold her own with, and sometimes beat, the world's best.

CLASSES OF COMPETITORS.

For competition purposes competitors are divided into classes as under.

For Bisley shooting:—

Class " A " (a) Any competitor who obtains or has obtained a place in the first twelve (twenty prior to 1935) in the Governor's Aggregate at a Rhodesian Bisley.

Should any competitor so classified subsequently fail to obtain a place in the first twelve (twenty prior to 1935) of the Governor's Aggre-

gate on three successive occasions of entering for
that competition at any Rhodesian Bisley, he shall
revert to Class " B."

(b) Any competitor who has qualified for the
third stage of a competition comprising the three
stages of the King's at a Bisley of a similar status
to the Rhodesian Bisley.

Class " B " Any other competitor.

The following are thus classified Class " A ": —

Rfm. A. Alexander, Cpl. A. Bagnall, Lt. A. E. Banning,
Major J. S. Bridger, Sgt.-Major E. G. Browne, Capt. H.
Bugler, Rfm. A. M. Butcher, Cpl. G. R. Butcher, Rfm. R. S.
Carlisle, Rfm. H. A. Clarke, Cpl. S. A. Cole, Sgt. W. D.
Cook, Sgt. A. M. Cumming, Mr. D. M. Dall, Sgt. D. Devine,
Cpl. T. A. Driver, Rfm. R. K. Edwards, Sgt.-Major F. G.
Elliot, C.S.-Major P. M. Fallon, Sgt. L. B. Fereday, C.S.-
Major N. A. Fereday, Sgt. R. H. Fitt, Sgt. T. Forbes, Cpl.
J. W. Frost, Sgt-Major D. Graham, Rfm. E. Hallauer, Cpl.
S. H. Harrison, Sgt. J. Hawkey, Lt. A. G. Healey, Sgt. S.
Hearnah, Cpl. L. R. S. Hill, Major W. C. Hoaten, Mr. J.
G. Jearey, Lt. L. S. Jenkins, Sgt. G. S. Joss, Mr. W. R.
Kiley, Sgt. J. Lea, Lance-Cpl. D. C. Lilford, Lt. G. E. R.
Lock, Lt. J. B. Lombard, Rfm. H. Lucas, Pipe-Major A.
MacBean, Rfm. R. D. MacLennan, Rfm. H. J. Main, Sgt. R.
H. Malt, Capt. L. M. McBean, Rfm. A. R. Metelerkamp,
Lt. F. H. Morgan, Lt. R. E. Neville, Lt.-Col. C. M. New-
man, M.C., V.D., C.Q.M.-Sgt. W. E. C. Owen, Sgt. S. H.
Park, Cpl. C. E. R. Payne, Sgt. V. G. Phipps, Cpl. L. A.
Pocket, Major W. H. Power, Mr. J. W. Rayner, Lt. J. Reid
Rowland, Sgt. T. A. Robbins, Lt. J. S. S. Russell, Capt. S.
C. Small, Capt. F. Smith, C.Sgt.-Major W. F. Smith, Sgt.
W. L. Smith, Rfm. L. R. Tarr, Rfm. S. P. Tarr, C.S.-Major
C. H. Thorne, Sgt. A. S. Tod, Mr. R. Walker, Sgt. J. Water-
worth, Cpl. C. Watkins, Major J. W. Watson, Lt. D. J.
Wilson.

For Service Shooting : —

Class I (a) Any competitor who gains or has gained one
of the first 20 places in the Service Rifle Championship.

Should any competitor so classified subsequently fail to obtain a place in the first 20 in
the final of the Service Rifle Championship on
three successive occasions of entering for that competition he shall revert to Class II.

BULAWAYO DEFENCE FORCE RIFLE CLUB TEAMS, 1927.

Standing: Sgt. D. Welsh, Cpl. T. Driver, Sgt. T. Forbes, C.Q.M. Sgt. F. H. Morgan, Cpl. A. M. Cumming, Rfm.
C. Payne, Lt. A. G. Healey, Lt. D. J. Wilson, Sgt.-Major A. Utterton, M.B.E. (Hon. Sec.).
Seated: Lt. R. E. Neville, Capt. W. C. Hoaten, Major C. M. Newman, M.C., C.S. Major G. MacLennan (Coach).
In Front: C.Q.M. Sgt. W. E. C. Owen, Sgt. J. Waterworth.

(b) Any Class " A " competitor.

Class II Any other competitor irrespective of age.
The following are thus classified Class I : —

Lt. J. Appleby, Sgt. C. M. Baldwin, Rfm. R. D. Bean, Tpr. B. E. Bulstrode, Tpr. C. L. Cable, Cpl. A. W. Crombie, Rfm. P. J. Cumming, Sgt. N. T. Deacon, Rfm. J. B. Dougherty, Rfm. J. A. Dowell, C.S.-Major R. F. Dowell, Sgt. M. E. Edgar, Lt.-Col. N. S. Ferris, Sgt. N. Fouche, Cpl. C. Glover, Cpl. R. H. Jordan, Lt. R. H. Kirkman, Tpr. A. G. Lanning, Capt. E. H. Lindsell, Cpl. F. Littleton, Cpl. J. I. Logan, Rfm. A. Mackenzie, Cpl. G. Milford, Lt. D. A. B. Moodie, Sgt. C. H. Muller, Sgt. T. T. G. Race, Rfm. H. L. S. Rainer, Rfm. D. Robbie, Sgt. H. R. Robson, Rfm. T. H. Scorror, Sgt. R. H. Smith, Lt. B. G. Spurling, Mr. H. A. Stidolph, Tpr. G. L. Sturrock, Lt. J. G. Thurlow, Capt. R. H. von Broembsen, Cpl. W. H. D. Walker.

(Note : This list includes only those who are not shown in Class " A.").

THE ADMINISTRATOR'S CUP.
1909	... ...	Tpr. T. W. Davey, S.R.V. (W.D.)
1910	... ...	Capt. W. E. Haworth, S.R.V. (E.D.)
1911	... ...	Capt. W. E. Haworth, S.R.V. (E.D.)
1912	... ...	Lt. W. S. Craster, S.R.V. (E.D.)
1913	... ...	Mt. T. W. Davey, Byo. Rifle Club.
1914	... ...	Sgt. H. W. Winward, B.S.A.P.
1921	... ...	Rfm. N. A. Fereday, S'by. Rifle Coy.
1922	... ...	Capt. W. C. Hoaten, B.S.A.P.
1923	... ...	Capt. W. C. Hoaten, B.S.A.P.
1924	... ...	Rfm. F. H. Morgan, Byo. Rifle Club.
1925	... ...	Rfm. F. H. Morgan, Byo. Rifle Club.

THE GOVERNOR'S CUP.
1926	....	S.I. R. Walker, B.S.A.P.
1927	... ...	Lt. R. E. Neville, 2nd Bn., R.R.
1928	... ...	Sgt. N. A. Fereday, T.F.R., Sby.
1929	... ...	C.S.-M. F. H. Morgan, Byo. Rifle Club.
1930	... ...	C.S.-M. F. H. Morgan, Byo. Rifle Club.
1931	... ...	S.-I. R. Walker, B.S.A.P.
1932	... ...	Sgt. N. A. Fereday, 1st Bn., R.R.
1933	... ...	Lt. L. M. McBean, 1st Bn., R.R.
1934	... ...	Lt. L. M. McBean, 1st Bn., R.R.
1935	... ...	Lt. F. H. Morgan, 2nd Bn., R.R.

H.M. THE KING'S MEDAL.
1926	... ...	Sgt. F. G. Elliot, B.S.A.P.
1927	... ...	C.S.-M. F. H. Morgan, T.F., Byo.
1928	... ...	C.S.-M. F. H. Morgan, T.F., Bulawayo.
1929	... ...	C.S.-M. F. H. Morgan, T.F., Byo.
1930	... ...	Sgt. N. A. Fereday, T.F., Sby.
1931	... ...	Sgt. N. A. Fereday, T.F., Sby.

1932 ... ... C.S.-M. F. H. Morgan, 2nd Bt., R.R.
1933 ... ... C.Q.M. Sgt. N. A. Fereday, 1st Bn., R.R.
1934 ... ... C.Q.M. Sgt. N. A. Fereday, 1t Bn., R.R.
1935 ... ... Rfm. D. F. Butcher, 2nd Bn., R.R.

KYNOCH CUP.

Year:	Winner.	Points:	Year:	Winner.	Points:
1928—Mashonaland	... ...	2861	1932—Matabeleland	... ...	2561
1929—Matabeleland	... ...	2646	1933—Mashonaland	... ...	2084
1930—Mashonaland	... ...	2624	1934—Matabeleland	... ...	2149
1931—Matabeleland	... ...	2607	1935—Matabeleland	... ...	2141

THE B.S.A. COMPANY'S SHIELD.

1897—Salisbury Rifle Club.
1898—Bulawayo Rifle Club.
1899—Salisbury Rifle Club.
1900—Salisbury Rifle Club.
1901—S.R.C. (W.D.)
1902—S.R.V. (E.D.)
1903—S.R.V. (W.D.)
1904—S.R.V. (W.D.)
1905—S.R.V. (W.D.)
1906—S.R.V. (E.D.)
1908—S.R.V. (W.D.)
1909—S.R.V. (W.D.)
1910—Salisbury Rifle Club.
1911—S.R.V. (E.D.)
1912—B.S.A. Police.
1913—S.R.V. (W.D.)
1914—S.R.V. (E.D.)

1921—Salisbury Rifle Club.
1922—Sby. Military District.
1923—Midlands Military Dist.
1924—Salisbury Rifle Coy.
1925—Bulawayo Rifle Coy.
1926—Salisbury Rifle Platoon.
1927—Byo. Military District.
1928—Byo. Military District.
1929—Byo. Military District.
1930—Permanent Force Rifle
        Club.
1931—Bulawayo Rifle Club.
1932—1st Bn., R.R.
1933—2nd Bn., R.R.
1934—1st Bn., R.R.
1935—2nd Bn., R.R.

DEWAR CHALLENGE SHIELD.

1904—S.R.V. (W.D.)
1905—S.R.V. (W.D.)
1906—S.R.V. (W.D.)
1908—S.R.V. (W.D.)
1909—S.R.V. (W.D.)
1910—S.R.V. (W.D.)
1911—S.R.V. (E.D.)
1912—B.S.A. Police
1913—S.R.V. (W.D.)
1914—S.R.V. (W.D.)
1921—Sby. Military District.
1922—Sby. Military District.
1923—Midlands Military District.

1924—Salisbury Rifle Coy.
1925—Bulawayo Rifle Coy.
1926—Salisbury Rifle Platoon.
1927—Byo. Military District.
1928—Byo. Military District.
1929—Byo. Military District.
1930—Permanent Force Rifle
        Club.
1931—Bulawayo Rifle Club.
1932—1st Bn., R.R.
1933—2nd Bn., R.R.
1934—1st Bn., R.R.
1935—2nd Bn., R.R.

GREY CHALLENGE SHIELD.

1903—S.R.V. (W.D.)
1904—S.R.V. (W.D.)
1905—S.R.V. (W.D.)
1906—S.R.V. (W.D.)
1908—Bulawayo Rifle Club.
1909—S.R.V. (E.D.)
1910—S.R.V. (W.D.)
1911—S.R.V. (W.D.)
1912—S.R.V. (E.D.)
1913—S.R.V. (W.D.)
1914—S.R.V. (W.D.)
1921—Gwelo Military District.
1922—Sby. Military District.
1923—Byo. Military District.

1924—Salisbury Rifle Coy.
1925—B.S.A. Police.
1926—Byo. Military District.
1927—Byo. Military District.
1928—Salisbury Rifle Club.
1929—Sby. Military District.
1930—Permanent Force Rifle
        Club.
1931—Bulawayo Rifle Club.
1932—1st Bn., R.R.
1933—2nd Bn., R.R.
1934—1st Bn., R.R.
1935—1st Bn., R.R.

MUNICIPAL CUP.

1902—Salisbury Rifle Club.
1903-1905—S.R.V. (E.D.).
1906—B.S.A. Police.
1907-1909—Salisbury Rifle Club.
1910-1913—S.R.V. (E.D.).
1921-1924—Salisbury Rifle Coy.

1925—B.S.A. Police.
1926—Bulawayo Rifle Club.
1927-1929—Byo. Military District.
1930-1931—Bulawayo Rifle Club.
1932-1934—2nd Bn., R.R.
1935—1st Bn., R.R.

HILL MEMORIAL CUP.

1931—2nd Bn., R.R.
1932—1st Bn., R.R.
1933—B.S.A.P.

1934—B.S.A.P.
1935—1st Bn., R.R.

CASTLE BREWERY CUP.

1912—Lonely Mine Rifle Coy.
1922-1923—Salisbury Rifle Coy.
1924—Bulawayo Rifle Coy.
1925—Salisbury Rifle Coy.
1926—Salisbury Rifle Platoons.
1927-1929—Byo. Military District.

1930—Salisbury Rifle Club.
1931—Bulawayo Rifle Club.
1932—2nd Bn., R.R.
1933—1st Bn., R.R.
1934-1935—2nd Bn., R.R.

ZEEDERBERG CUP.

1931—2nd Bn., R.R.
1932—1st Bn., R.R.

1933—Chipinga.
1934-1935—Inyati.

SERVICE RIFLE CHAMPIONSHIP (Kirschbaum Cup).

1932—S.-M. F. G. Elliot, Permanent Staff Corps.
1933—Lt. F. H. Morgan, 2nd Bn., R.R.
1934—C.S.-M. N. A. Fereday, 1st Bn., R.R.
1935—Corpl. D. G. Lamont, Cam & Motor.

MERCHANTS' CUP.

1932—Shamva.

1933-1935—1st Bn., R.R.

TERRITORIAL CUP.

1932—1st Bn., R.R.
1933—B.S.A.P.

1934—B.S.A.P.
1935—1st Bn., R.R.

From 1909 Major P. S. Inskipp, O.B.E., Rhodesian Manager of the B.S.A. Company, presented a cup each year for the winner of Military Aggregate. His successor, Lt.-Col. T. E. Robins, D.S.O., E.D., has presented the trophy from 1927. Since 1932 a cup has been awarded for Class II. shots in the Military Aggregate by Lt.-Col. E. Hope Carson, D.S.O., M.C., V.D.

WINNERS OF INSKIPP CUP AND ROBINS CUP.

1909—Mr. C. J. A. Blackler, Byo. Rifle Club.
1910—Tpr. J. J. Bain, S.R.V. (E.D.)
1911—Lt. W. Ross, S.R.V. (W.D.).
1912—Capt. A. C. L. Webb, S.R.V. (W.D.)
1913—Tpr. J. J. Bain, S.R.V. (E.D.)
1914—Tpr. L. B. Fereday, S.R.V. (E.D.)
1921—Sgt. J. J. Bain, Salisbury Rifle Coy.
1922—Rfm. L. B. Fereday, Salisbury Rifle Coy.
1923—Rfm. S. Tarr, Gwelo.
1924—S/I. R. Walker, B.S.A.P.
1925—Lt. D. J. Wilson, Bulawayo Rifle Coy.

1926—Sgt. F. G. Elliot, Staff.
1927-1929—C.S.-M. F. H. Morgan, T.F., Bulawayo.
1930—Sgt. N. A. Fereday.
1931—Lt. A. G. Healey, Bulawayo.
1932—Stg.-Major F. G. Elliot, P.S. Corp.
1933—Lt. F. H. Morgan, 2nd Bn., R.R.
1934—C.S.-M. N. A. Fereday, 1st Bn., R.R.
1935—Cpl. Jordan, B.S.A.P.

CARSON CUP.

1932—C.S.-M. R. F. Dowell, 2nd Bn., R.R.
1933—Rfm. W. H. Dowell, Shabani.
1934—Cpl. W. L. Smith, 1st Bn., R.R.
1935—Cpl. C. C. Glover, 2nd Bn., R.R.

The National Rifle Association's Silver Medal is highly prized because it entitles the holder to compete for the Prince of Wales Prize at Bisley. Each winner of the N.R.A. competition secures one medal only and each year the award goes to the holder of the highest score who is not already a medallist.

Medal awarded to and place on Prize List.	Competition won by
1909—Tpr T. W. Davey	Tpr. T. W. Davey.
1910—Capt. W. E. Haworth	Capt. W. E. Haworth.
1911—Sgt. T. Forbes (2nd)	1. Capt. W. E. Haworth.
1912—Lt. W. S. Craster	W. S. Craster.
1913—S.S.-Mjr. J. Tiffin	S.S.-Mjr. J. Tiffin.
1914—Tpr. L. B. Fereday	Tpr. L. B. Fereday.
1921—Capt. W. C. Hoaten	Capt. W. C. Hoaten.
1922—Cpl. N. A. Fereday (2nd)	1. Capt. W. C. Hoaten.
(Shoot-off with Sgt. L. B. Fereday)	
1923—Rfm. S. Tarr	Rfm. S. Tarr.
1924—S/I. R. Walker	S/I. R. Walker.
1925—Lt. D. J. Wilson (2nd)	1. Rfm. F. H. Morgan.
1926—Lt. R. E. Neville	Lt. R. E. Neville.
1927—Cpl. A. M. Cumming (2nd) ...	1. C.Q.M. Sgt. F. H. Morgan.
1928—Capt. J. W. Watson	Capt. J. W. Watson.
1929—Lt. A. G. Healey (3rd)	1. C.Q.M. Sgt. F. H. Morgan.
	2. Capt. W. C. Hoaten.
1930—Lt.-Col. C. M. Newman, M.C. V.D. (3rd).	1. Sgt. N. A. Fereday.
	2. Sgt. L. B. Fereday.
1931—Lt. L. M. McBean (5th)	1. Lt. A. G. Healey.
	2. Sgt. N. A. Fereday.
	3. Insp. R. Walker.
	4. C.S.-M. F. H. Morgan.
1932—Rfm. R. H. Fitt (3rd)	1. C.Q.M. Sgt. N. A. Fereday.
	2. Lt. F. H. Morgan.
1933—Capt. S. C. Small (4th)	1. C.Q.M. Sgt. N. A. Fereday
	2. Lt. F. H. Morgan.
	3. Lt. L. M. McBean.
1934—C.Q.M. Sgt. W. E. C. Owen (5th)	1. Lt. L. M. McBean.
	2. Lt. F. H. Morgan.
	3. C.S.-M. N. A. Fereday.
	4. Lt.-Col. C. M. Newman.
1935—Cpl. C. Watkins	Cpl. C. Watkins.

HOCKEY

HE first organised games were played after the Anglo-Boer War when clubs were formed in Salisbury, Umtali and Hartley. In the latter district, E. E. F. Blackwell set the game going in 1902 and Eiffel Flats and Gatooma soon formed more enthusiastic teams. The first clubs in Salisbury were formed in 1903. F. H. S. Lee was a moving factor and strong teams were fielded by the Salisbury, Alexandra, and B.S.A. Police Clubs. A popular innovation was the five-a-side league won by an Old Bedfordians' team consisting of two brothers Blackwell and three brothers Brooks, a quintet well known in Rhodesian sporting circles. Other well known players of the early days in Salisbury were A. V. Williams later known as "Father," a fine centre-half who represented Rhodesia in Currie Cup hockey in 1926 and then saw his son in the Rhodesian team in 1929; W. R. Blanckenberg, W. A. Ludgater, Chalmers, E. G. Smith who captained the first Salisbury team to Gwelo, A. W. ("Tim") Whiley, C. Deane-Simmons, O'Farrell, A. M. ("Ginger") Kuys, who was also a fine rugger player and cricketer, and G. B. Jennings

Hockey was first played in Bulawayo in 1900, when Home Born played Colonials in a series of matches. Then the game lapsed until it was revived in 1906. At first there were only two teams, Combined Banks and Rest of Bulawayo. Gwelo took up the game in the same year and the two towns met in July, 1906, on the Queens ground. Gwelo won the first match 4—2, and the second 1—0, and displayed a superior combination and better ball control than the homesters. For the winners, A. E. Speight, who scored three goals in the first game and the only one in the second, J. Watkinson and W. C. Palgrave were outstanding while for Bulawayo the best on view were M. G. Linnell, Schooling, Shipman and G. Payne in goal.

In the same season in Bulawayo the St. John's School ladies' club was formed with some excellent players in the Misses Booth, Chouse, A. Joss and F. Smith. In 1907 the game became more generally popular, with more good players in Scott, Collins, FitzGibbon, Knowles and Dempster to the fore and a hockey league was formed with four teams, Kings. Banks, Queens and S.R. Constabulary. The game was played in the form of rink hockey at the Empire Theatre

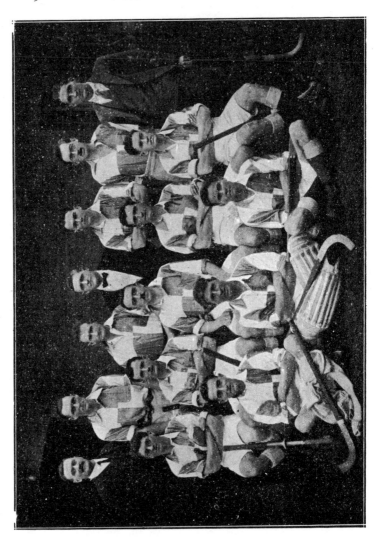

1926.

Standing:

E. E. F. Blackwell
(Manager &
Umpire).

D. McLean.

T. P. Morgan.

J. Carmichael.

C. C. W. Ingham.

E. V. Saunder.

J. E. Hogg.

Sitting:

C. L. Honey.

A. V. Williams.

G. T. I. Leonard
(Capt.)

G. E. Fletcher.

E. A. Barbour.

In Front:

A. Ross.

A. McIntosh.

B. B. Napier.

where competition for the Davis Bowl, a handsome trophy presented by C. Davis, a keen sportsman, was very enthusiastic. The transference of the railways headquarters from Umtali gave hockey in Bulawayo a tremendous fillip at this stage.

Up to 1914 hockey had a very large following. One of the principal reasons for this was the fact that the girls' schools took to the game with great zest. As the scholars left school they imbued the men with an added keenness for the game and naturally it soon commanded a large support! The first Bulawayo teams were Kings, Queens and Police. The latter had such fine exponents as Capt. Bettle, Lieutenants Burton and V. A. New and F. Kettle, the Rhodesian goalie. Other prominent players were George Hopley, Piet le Cordeur, the brothers Tiernan, who were fine full-backs, D. Evans, S. Mitchell, C. A. V. Porter, Reg. Hart, an outstanding goalkeeper, Tom Ely, E. F. Harris, J. Lea, a great centre-forward, Phil Rabinson, A. C. Tomlin, Ben Wilson, E. M. Wells the soccer player, and the popular " Bill " Hoaten. A popular ladies' club in Bulawayo was formed by the Selborne team and when during the Great War men's hockey stopped, these ladies kept the game going at a high standard. Outstanding were the Misses D. B. Dolton, one of the best players the Colony has seen among the women, R. Rackham, now Mrs. F. K. Taylor, Rhodesian tennis champion, the Oakley sisters, the Badham sisters and Miss I. Gradwell, the tennis player.

After the War there was a great revival in the game and in 1922 the first of the inter-town and inter-provincial series took place when teams from Salisbury, Bulawayo and the Midlands met at Gatooma. Since that date these matches, both men's and women's have been played every year and the standard of hockey in these tournaments is always at a high level.

In 1922 the Matabeleland Board was formed with Capt. D. Evans and E. J. Dawson as the first president and secretary respectively. G. T. I. Leonard came to Bulawayo in 1924 and he did for Rhodesian hockey what Arthur Newton did for Rhodesian athletics. With Leonard's coming there was an immediate boom in the game. Bulawayo had four teams, viz.: Town, Raylton, Old Miltonians and Ghosts. In the last named's first season, led by Leonard, it won the Davis Bowl and the Dewar Challenge Shield. These teams had some fine men in Andrew Ross, E. A. Barbour, G. E. Fletcher, Joe

OLD GEORGIANS', BULAWAYO, 1935. WINNERS OF THE SENIOR COMPETITION.

Standing:

R. A. Simpson,
D. P. Hussey,
M. W. Clarke,
D. G. Blackbeard,
N. Crossley,
B. Catella.

In Front:

H. C. Holl,
W. H. Powell,
R. Fredman,
W. V. Holl,
D. Crossley.

Rackham, Bill Ayling and Frank Barbour, two good goalies, Dick Ely and G. Baker. Latterly there have been C. A. Barbour, L. A. Eastwood, B. E. Hays, Harry Collins and the Misses O. Bowley, N. Dromey, the three Botton sisters and Miss J. Capstick. The Harriers, Nondescripts, Eveline Old Girls, Harlequins and Old Georgians' teams have brought many more good players to the fore.

Bulawayo's enthusiasm spread to the capital where, generally speaking, the best hockey in the Colony is played. Post war players of note are Bill Cary, who earned a big reputation down South, A. Holden, an outstanding goalie, B. B. Napier, R. N. Tomlinson, T. L. Hopkins, the Misses Maisie Gordon, now Mrs. Wills, first women's captain of Mashonaland, E. M. Cassells, R. W. du Preez, now Mrs. P. Hinde, E. Burdett, the Bouette sisters, Miss M. Eaton and Mrs. Rule. To-day in Salisbury there are five men's and ten women's teams.

Pre-war hockey in the Midlands was very spasmodic and it was only about 1924 that the game was really established. In the last decade Gatooma, which won the inter-town competition in 1928, and Gwelo have produced numerous good players among whom the following have played for Rhodesia: The Misses Keey and O. S. Jackson, Honorary Secretary of the Midlands Board since its inception in 1932, Mrs. M. Davis, Mrs. E. Ogilvie, Mrs. R. M. Price, J. Carmichael who also played rugby for Rhodesia, A. McIntosh, T. P. Morgan, Dr. R. B. Saunders and A. and E. Blackburn. A great supporter in the Midlands is E. E. F. Blackwell one of the three brothers who have done a great deal for most sports in the Colony. His brother J. S. Blackwell is president of the tennis association, while C. Blackwell, killed in the Great War, played rugger for Rhodesia.

With one exception the visiting teams to the Colony have been women's teams. The first was the Cape Town Gardens Women's team which came here in 1924 and again in 1929. On the first occasion the local teams were well beaten but in 1929 the visitors lost 1—0 in Salisbury and 5—1 in Bulawayo.

In 1925 the All-England women's team played Rhodesia in Bulawayo where the visitors won 9—0. The Rhodesians, whose defence was given no respite, played pluckily but were out-generalled. The local team had only two shots at goal during the whole match.

RHODESIA vs. ENGLAND, 1930.

Standing:

G. T. I. Leonard,
    (Pres., R.H.A.),
Mrs. M. Rule,
    (Capt.),
D. Bouette,
R. du Preez,
D. Woodley,
L. Capstick,
G. Eckersley,
E. M. Cassels,
A. Franceys,
S. L. Williams
    (Hon. Sec.,
    R.H.A.),

In Front:

M. Walkden,
I. Bouette,
D. B. Dolton.

In 1930, teams from England, Scotland and Australia came to Rhodesia for the Empire Women's tournament. Though Rhodesia lost each of the three matches, she played pluckily throughout, improving with each game, and of the local players, Mrs. Rule, the Rhodesian captain, and the Misses D. B. Dolton, A. Franceys and L. Capstick earned warm praise for their displays. Miss R. du Preez was outstanding and after this series was chosen to play for South Africa against the visitors, an honour that carried with it the distinction of her being the first Rhodesian to earn Springbok colours.

In 1931 a Mashonaland team motored eight hundred miles there and back to play Nyasaland who returned the visit in 1933.

The governing body is the Rhodesia Hockey Association of which Capt. G. T. I. Leonard was president for several years. O. B. Guest and W. H. S. Cary have done useful work for the association. The R.H.A. is affiliated to the S.A. Hockey Union which was formed in 1925, and in 1931 Rhodesia was honoured by the election of a Rhodesian, Capt. Leonard, as president. There are four provincial boards that administer the game in Bulawayo, Gwelo, Gatooma, Livingstone, Salisbury and Umtali. Latterly hockey has received comparatively poor support, but in spite of this an exceptionally high standard has been maintained in both the men's and women's competitions.

THE S.A. INTER-PROVINCIAL TOURNAMENTS.

1926 was the first season of the annual inter-provincial tournaments and Rhodesia's participation was an auspicious one. The Colony finished third on the log. The only match lost was that against Transvaal, the ultimate winner of the tournament. Transvaal scored a lucky goal in the first half but there was no question about their superiority in the second spell. Drawn matches were played against Western Province and Orange Free State in both of which Rhodesia had her opponents defending most of the time, but was unable to score the deciding goals. Ross and Leonard were considered two of the best players in the competition.

Rhodesia's second entry in the inter-provincial contest was crowned with success and the team emerged victorious without suffering a single defeat. Rhodesia played really

1929.

Standing:

H. H. Hill.
B. Ulyett.
H. Troughton.
K. F. L. Nanson.
W. H. Williams.
A. Blackburn.
R. W. Hill.
R. N. Seldon.
A. Ross.

Sitting:

R. N. Tomlinson.
W. H. S. Cary.
G. T. I. Leonard
(Capt.)
E. A. Barbour.
R. J. Oliver.

In Front:

A. Holden.

1930.

—

Back Row:

L. G. Morgenrood

A. Blackburn.

C. C. Meadows.

3rd Row:

H. Collins.

T L. Hopkins.

Dr. R. B. Saunders

Rev. T. Pattinson.

B. B. Napier.

H. M. Mackenzie.

Sitting:

W. J. Somerville.

S. L. Williams.

W. H. S. Cary.

R. W. Hill.

R. P. Dereham.

In Front:

A. Holden.

good hockey to win the tournament. The only real opposition was offered by Western Province and a drawn game resulted. Leonard scored 12 of Rhodesia's 23 goals and was a splendid leader of a splendid team.

In 1930, at the conclusion of the third tournament, Rhodesia held second place, but with such a strong team as Transvaal taking first place their performance was, notwithstanding, very creditable. Rhodesia drew with Transvaal but were beaten convincingly by Western Province. Cary and Meadows, and Holden in goal, were outstanding.

In 1932 it was Rhodesia's turn to stage the tournament and the matches were played in Bulawayo. The home team was not very convincing and of five entrants Rhodesia finished third. Eastwood in goal, Cary, Cuerdon and Morgenrood were the best of the Rhodesians.

In the 1933 competition Rhodesia was placed fifth of seven entrants. At times the men played brilliant hockey but at others the combination was poor. Tomlinson, Mackenzie and Cary added to their reputations with some fine play in this series.

The 1935 team went to Cape Town where it tied for fifth place with Orange Free State. Rhodesia started well with a drawn game against the strong Transvaal team but thereafter they rarely played up to form. Going from the hard and fast grounds here on to turf at the Cape was a great handicap. The team was also unfortunate in the number of men who were injured. Despite all this, the Rhodesians put up some excellent performances. Gould was an outstanding player in the tournament.

In 1933 a women's team went South for the S.A. Women's inter-provincial tournament and Rhodesia's representatives did well to gain fourth place in a list of seven competitors. Among the Rhodesians the Misses · Keey, Franceys, Dromey, West and Capstick evoked special praise from the critics in the South. Rhodesia's positional play was a weakness but the side earned a reputation as a team of real triers.

The 1934 venture was far from successful. The Rhodesians never became accustomed to the grass fields and each match, except a drawn one, was lost. Some of the players distinguished themselves, among them being the Misses E. Burdett, M. Davies, O. S. Jackson and O. Bowley.

In 1935 the tournament was staged in Salisbury to which centre over a hundred players came from outside the Colony.

1932.

—

Back Row:

C. Meadows.

M. W. Grant.

Middle Row:

L. G. Morgenrood

H. M. Mackenzie.

W. H. S. Cary.

O. B. Guest.

C. A. Barbour.

A. Bottom.

Sitting:

W. A. Clegg.

H. Collins.

L. A. Eastwood.

A. V. Cuerdon.

J. Foster.

After the fixtures had been drawn up Orange Free State found they were unable to make the journey so a Mashonaland team was allowed to fill the gap. This Mashonaland team did extraordinarily well finishing sixth on the log and only losing 1—0 against Rhodesia. Several ex-Rhodesian representatives were included in the side. E. Maasdorp proved a fine goalkeeper while the stick work of C. Green and K. Birkin was excellent.

The Rhodesian side also played well and V. Foster was an outstanding player in the tournament. M. Eaton was also prominent. Rhodesia came fifth in the final placing.

THE S.A. INTER-PROVINCIAL TOURNAMENTS.

1926.

G. T. I. Leonard (Capt.), A. V. Williams, A. McIntosh, G. E. Fletcher, T. P. Morgan, B. B. Napier, E. A. Barbour, I. MacLean, C. L. Honey, D. A. Saunder, A. Ross, J. Carmichael, J. E. Hogg, C. C. W. Ingham; Manager and Umpire, E. E. F. Blackwell.

Transvaal	Lost	5—	0
Eastern Province	Won	10—	0
(Leonard (6), Ross (2), Saunders, Williams).			
Western Province	Drawn	2—	2
(Leonard, Hogg).			
Natal	Won	3—	0
(Leonard (3).			
Orange Free State	Drawn	2—	2
(Leonard (2).			

1929.

G. T. I. Leonard (Capt), W. H. S. Cary, R. N. Seldon, W. H. Williams, R. W. Hill, K. F. L. Nanson, A.Holden, R. N. Tomlinson, E. A. Barbour, B. Ulyett, A. Blackburn, A. Ross, H. H. Hill, R. J. Oliver, H. Troughton.

Natal	Won	5—	0.
(Leonard (3), Ulyett, Tomlinson).			
Eastern Province	Won	4—	1
(Leonard (2), Seldon, Troughton).			
Transvaal	Won	6—	2
(Leonard (2), Oliver (2), Tomlinson, Troughton).			
Western Province	Drawn	1—	1
(Leonard).			
Orange Free State	Won	1—	0
(Leonard).			
Border	Won	6—	0
(Leonard (3), Oliver (2), Tomlinson).			

1930.

W. H. S. Cary (Capt.), A. Holden, W. J. Somerville, A. Blackburn, B. B. Napier, The Rev. T. Patterson, H. H. Collins, L. G. Morgenrood, T. L. Hopkins, C. C. Meadows, Dr. R. B. Saunders, H. M. Mackenzie, S. L. Williams, R. P. Derham, R. W. Hill.

Border	Won	6—	1
(Hopkins (3).			
Western Province	Lost	3—	2
(Meadows (2).			
Eastern Province	Won	7—	0
(Meadows).			

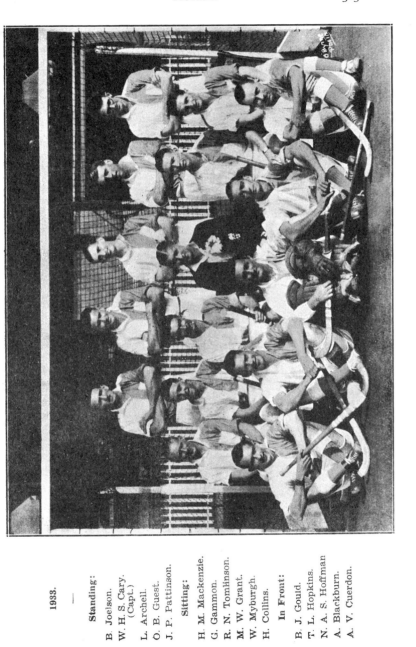

1933.

Standing:
B. Joelson.
W. H. S. Cary.
   (Capt.)
L. Archell.
O. B. Guest.
J. P. Pattinson.

Sitting:
H. M. Mackenzie.
G. Gammon.
R. N. Tomlinson.
M. W. Grant.
W. Myburgh.
H. Collins.

In Front:
B. J. Gould.
T. L. Hopkins.
N. A. S. Hoffman.
A. Blackburn.
A. V. Cuerdon.

| Orange Free State | Won | 2— 0 |
(Meadows, Saunders).
| Transvaal | Drawn | 1— 1 |
(Morgenrood).
| Natal | Won | 4— 1 |

1932.

W. H. S. Cary (Capt.), L. A. Eastwood, J. Foster, O. B. Guest, H. H. Collins, H. M. Mackenzie, A. V. Cuerdon, J. Bartlett, C. Meadows, M. W. Grant, L. G. Morgenrood, C. A. Barbour, W. A. Clegg, A. Bottom.

| Natal | Drawn | 2— 2 |
(Grant, Morgenrood).
| Orange Free State | Lost | 2— 1 |
(Cary).
| Border | Won | 4— 0 |
(Cary (2), Bartlett, Cuerdon).
| Transvaal | Lost | 4— 3 |
(Meadows (2), Morgenrood).

1933.

W. H. S. Cary (Capt.), N. A. S. Hoffman, A. Blackburn, B. Joelson, H. H. Collins, H. M. Mackenzie, R. N. Tomlinson, A. V. Cuerdon, B. J. Gould, T. L. Hopkins, O. B. Guest, W. Myburgh, J. P. Pattinson, G. Gammon, L. Archell; and Manager, M. W. Grant.

| Orange Free State | Lost | 3— 2 |
(Gould, Tomlinson).
| Border | Won | 5— 2 |
(Gammon (2), Archell, Cuerdon, Hopkins).
| Transvaal | Lost | 4— 0 |
| Western Province | Lost | 2— 1 |
(Gammon).
| Natal | Lost | 3— 2 |
(Hopkins, Gammon).
| Eastern Province | Won | 4— 2 |
(Gould, Tomlinson, Blackburn (2).

1935.

E. Roberts (Capt.), A. Holden, J. Cary, S. Gould, A. E. G. Cooney, A. de L. Thompson, I. L. T. Palmer, B. B. Napier, H. M. Mackenzie, J. M. Beveridge, H. Sharwood S. W. Bartlett, H. Evans, W. Myburgh; Manager, O. B. Guest.

| Transvaal | Drawn | 1— 1 |
(Gould).
| Western Province | Lost | 2— 1 |
(Gould).
| Border | Won | 2— 1 |
(Napier, Palmer).
Eastern Province	Lost	1— 0
Natal	Lost	4— 0
Orange Free State	Drawn	0— 0

THE SOUTH AFRICAN WOMEN'S TOURNAMENT.

1933.

The Misses D. Keey (Capt.), J. Arthur, M. Walkden, E. Symons, E. Den, M. E. Duff, G. Eckersley, E. du Preez, N. Dromey, A. Franceys, J. Capstick, J. Goldhawk, G. Brewer, E. Burdett, J. West, Mrs. K. Carey.

| Southern Cape | Won | 3— 1 |
(Mrs. Carey (2), R. due Preez.)
| Western Province | Drawn | 1— 1 |
(Mrs. Carey).
| Northern Transvaal | Drawn | 1— 1 |
(E. Den).

1935.
—

Standing:

J Carey.
S. Gould.
A. E. G. Cooney.
A. de L. Thomp-
    son
I. L. T. Palmer.
B. B. Napier.

Middle Row:

H. M. Mackenzie.
A. Holden.
E Roberts
    (Capt.)
J. M. Beveridge.
H. Sharwood.

In Front:

S. W. Bartlett.
H. Evans.
W. Myburgh.

Griqualand West .... Won   3— 1
    (Mrs. Carey (2), M. E. Duff).

Natal .... Lost   4— 1
    (N. Dromey).

Albany .... Drawn 1— 1
    (Duff).

1934.

The Misses E. Burdett (Capt.), C. Green, M. G. Cary, E. Den, H. Norwood, O. S. Jackson, O. Bowley, M. Den, L. Eckersley, B. Williams, M. Davies, K. Birkin, Mrs. E. Ogilvie and Mrs. M. Davis.

East Griqualand .... Lost   5— 0

North-Eastern Province .... Drawn 2— 2
    (M. Davies 2).

Huguenot .... Lost   3— 2
    (H. Norwood, K. Birkin).

Border .... Lost   4— 1
    (M. Davies).

Natal .... Lost   7— 1
    (B. Williams).

Western Province .... Lost   6— 0

1934.
Standing: E. Den, L. Eckersley, H. Norwood, E. Burdett (capt.),
P. Cary, K. Birkin, B. Williams.
Kneeling: Mrs. M. Davis, M. Den, M. Davies, O. Bowley.
Sitting: O. S. Jackson, Mrs. E. Ogilvie, C. Green.

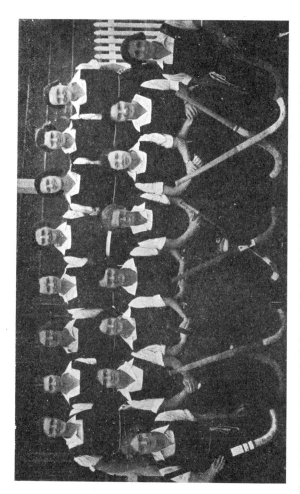

1933 INTERPROVINCIAL TEAM.

Standing: M. Walkden, M. E. Duff, K. Carey, E. Den, J. Arthur, J. Capstick, E. Symons, J. Goldhawk.
Sitting: E. Burdett, J. West, G. Eckersley, A. Franceys, D. Key (Capt.), G. Brewer, N. Dromey, E. du Preez.

1935.

The Misses E. Symons (Capt.), M. Eton, C. Diesel, L. Capstick. M. Davis, M. McGillivray, E. Den, M. Pilsworth, B. Williams, J. Capstick, M. Davies, D. Abrahamson, D. Evans, V. Foster.

Border	Won	3— 1
(B. Williams, D. Abrahamson).		
Southern Transvaal	Lost	8— 3
(M. Davies, D. Evans, V. Foster).		
Northern Transvaal	Lost	2— 1
(V. Foster).		
Bechuanaland	Won	1— 0
(D. Evans).		
Mashonaland	Won	1— 0

Mashonaland (Section B): Mrs. M. Rule (Capt.), the Misses E. Maasdorp, P. Cary, I. Bouette, H. Norwood, D. Mackenzie, C. Green, K. Birkin, L. Harwood, M. Den, M. Williams, E. du Preez, E. Burdett.

Albany	Won	4— 2
(C. Green).		
Western Province	Drawn	1— 1
(C. Green).		
Eastern Province	Won	2— 0
(E. du Preez, 2).		
Natal	Lost	8— 0
Rhodesia	Lost	1— 0
Western Province	Lost	1— 0

THE CAPE TOWN GARDENS LADIES' TEAM, 1929.

Results:—

v. Bulawayo at Bulawayo	Lost	5— 1
v. Salisbury at Salisbury	Lost	1— 0
v. Salisbury at Salisbury	Drawn	1— 1

TEAMS.

Bulawayo: The Misses E. M. Cassels (Captain), Fleetwood, L. Capstick, Leonard, M. Walkden, Kitcat, B. Jacobs, Watt, A. Sherry, D. Woodley, J. Capstick. Umpires: Messrs. G. T. I. Leonard and Henderson.

Salisbury: The Misses M. Gordon (Captain), Symmonds, M. Eaton, Moore, M. Brereton, R. du Preez, E. Shand, M. Hurrell, J. Reid Rowland, K. Underwood. E. Hendriks, H. Pearson, G. Eckersley.

THE ALL-ENGLAND LADIES' VISIT, 1925.

Rhodesia: The Misses M. Gordon (Capt.), R. Botton, S. Cooper, E. Botton, M. Hurrell, R. du Preez, E. Ives, M. Hampton, Mrs. Price (Vice-Capt.), and Mrs. Dean.

THE EMPIRE WOMEN'S TOURNAMENT, 1930.

Rhodesia: Mrs. M. Rule (Capt.), the Misses D. B. Dolton (Vice-Capt.), I. Bouette, L. Capstick, G. Eckersley, M. Walkden, A. Franceys, E. M. Cassels, D. Woodley, D. Bouette, R. du Preez, M. Eaton, B. Jacobs, and Mrs. M. Davis.

Scotland, at Bulawayo	Lost	5— 0
Australia, at Gwelo	Lost	4— 1
(A. Franceys).		
England, at Salisbury	Lost	5— 1
(D. Woodley).		

1935 INTER-PROVINCIAL TEAM.

Standing: B. Williams, M. Davies, J. Capstick, L. Capstick, E. Den, M. Eaton, D. Evans.
Sitting: M. MacGillivray, M. Pilsworth, E. Symons (Capt.), C. Diesel, D. Abrahamson, E. Spears.
In Front: V. Foster, M. Davis.

Mashonaland,
1935.

Standing—
I. Burdette,
E. Maasdorp,
H. Norwood,
D. MacKenzie,
P. Cary,
L. Harwood.

Middle Row—
M. Williams,
I. Bouette,
M. Rule
    (Captain)
E. du Preez,
C. Green.

In Front—
M. Den,
K. Birkin.

Bulawayo Swimming Bath.

**1921 CURRIE
CUP TEAM.**

Standing:

C. Brown.
S. Brooks.
H. Robinson.
T. G. Edmanson.
D. D. Fraser.
N. Fereday.

Sitting:

G. Hodgson.
E. B. Shepherd
(Manager).
J. W. Brown.
A. E. Ward
(Capt.)
A. Wicks.

In Front:

J. T. Brown.
J. Hick.

SWIMMING

HE first acquatic meeting in Rhodesia was held in Salisbury in March, 1891, on a stretch of the Makabusi River. The chief attraction of the day was a diving competition for a bottle of whisky at the bottom of the river. The stream must have been a tricky one and malaria particularly rife at the time, for the meeting filled the four hospital huts and three tents and flattened out many more for whom there was no accommodation.

In 1898 the foundation stone of the Umtali Swimming Bath was laid by Lord Alfred Milner, but the bath was not built until 1925. A Manicaland swimming championship was held, however, a few years after the foundation stone was laid, and the venue of the meeting was a stretch of water on Raheen Farm, known then as Sunnyside, in the possession of Dick Harrison. The principal event was won by Jack Myers, then of the B.S.A.P. He was badly battered in the Great War and died recently at Chipinga.

In Bulawayo the first swimmer in the public eye was Harry Huntley. In 1894 the Matjesumhlope was not graced by any bridges, and one very hot day Mr. Huntley broke a journey to Bulawayo at the present Selborne Avenue crossing. The water was cool and inviting and the traveller plunged in, to be hailed from the bank by a policeman. " You can't bathe here in the town! " said the constable. " Town? " said Huntley, " Where's the town? " or words to that effect, and refused to come ashore. As has been said, it was a *very* hot day, and the temptation was too much for the policeman. He succumbed, threw aside his uniform and joined Mr. Huntley in the river. Several passers-by soon followed suit and a merry bathing party resulted.

On Saturday, January 31st, 1903, mainly through the efforts of Messrs. Knowles and F. L. Lister, the first aquatic sports were held in Bulawayo. They took place in the reservoir of the Electric Light works. There was great enthusiasm all round and as many as twenty entries for most events so that most heats had to be swum off the day before. The first race of two laps, about 86 yards, was won in 1 min. 6 1-5 secs. by Leo. Robinson, who beat Trooper Simpson by nine inches. These two men in the order named were the best swimmers in the town. The Plunging was won by M. Bitter

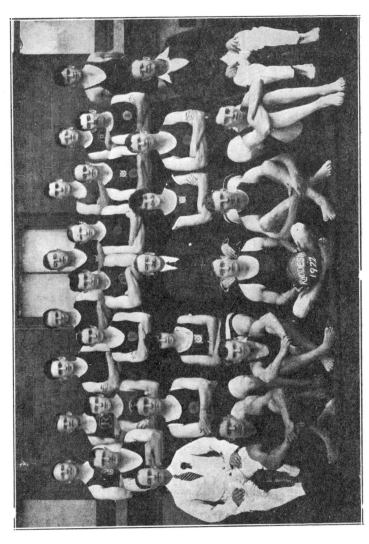

1922 Currie Cup
and S.A.
Championships.

Back Row:

H. C. Finch.
P. Gibbs.
N. Brooks.
G. Hodgson.
F. W. Windsor.
C. W. Littleton.
C. Brown.
S. G. Salmon.

3rd Row:

H. E. Browne.
R. Atkinson.
J. Hick.
H. Robinson.
T. G. Edmanson.
N. Fereday.
D. D. Fraser.

2nd Row:

H. M. Ward.
S. Brooks (capt.)
Miss M. Reid
    Rowland.
J. W. Brown.
Miss I. Burdett.
A. Wicks.
E. B. Shepherd.

In Front:

C. Porter.
F. Flint.
J. T. Brown.
G. Fife.
L. Brown.

Water Polo in the Salisbury Bath.

A view of the swimming bath, Gwelo.

with 44 feet. Much amusement was caused in this event by
some of the competitors who, knowing they could not beat
Bitter, dived low and swam under the water, but, though the
water was too thick to be seen through, the action of the
strokes disturbed it sufficiently to betray them, and they came
up smilingly acknowledging their trick. Simpson won the
four-lap race in 2 mins. 50 secs. from A. R. Garratt. In the
boys' race, in which the competitors were only about ten years
old, and all swam the " dog-paddle," L. Bester was first with
E. Smith second, the latter's large-size costume hampering
him ! In the water-polo, won easily by Police, McGregor, a
non-swimmer who wanted to play goalie, jumped in, thinking
he could stand, and was nearly drowned. Kendle (21) won
the Egg-dive and Kuyper (19) was second. Despite the difficulty of seeing the eggs in the cloudy water they managed to
bring up as many as seven at a time. Two amusing events
were the Tub-race, won by W. Paley, and the Hat and
Umbrella race, won by Simpson. Garratt's team of six won the
Squadron Race. Although the weather was not at its best the
sports were thoroughly enjoyed by a large crowd of spectators.

The first swimming bath in the country was opened in
Salisbury in 1915. Five clubs, namely " Crocodiles," Police,
United Banks, Pirates and Shamrocks (Ladies) were formed
and a large number of fine swimmers soon came to the fore.
The go-ahead policy in the capital has been rewarded by
several South African titles and from Salisbury have come most
of the Colony's best performers, among whom are the brothers
Brown, Freddy Flint, Percy Gibbs, who has held the Rhodesian
diving title on six occasions, Miss I. Burdett, first lady champion, Miss J. Reid Rowland, J. Ledger, W. M. Thomson, triple
champion in 1931, R. W. Atkinson, Norman and Syd Brooks,
the latter a great polo player, J. Hick, a prolific goal-scorer, and
Miss C. Rodwell, daughter of a former Governor, the best
lady swimmer the Colony has produced. Out of the water,
the sport has been well served by Capt. C. Douglas-Jones, E. B.
Shepherd, H. M. Ward, J. C. Smith, A. Pocket, H. G. Bell,
H. L. Kinsey and C. Tyrrell Heaver.

At first the control of swimming was vested in the
Mashonaland Amateur Swimming Association. In 1918 this
body was re-constituted as the Rhodesian Amateur Swimming
Association and affiliated to the South African Amateur Swimming Union.

In 1921 the Gwelo bath was opened and the Gwelo and
District Club joined the Association. In 1926, Umtali affili-

1923 CURRIE CUP TEAM.

Standing:

D. Atkinson.
P. Gibbs.
J. Hick.
A. Wicks.
L. Brown.
N Fereday.
L Morgenrood.
J. Brown.
F. Flint.

Sitting:

S. Brooks.
H. G. Bell.
(Delegate).
H. Robinson
(Capt.)
H. M. Ward
(Manager).
G. Hodgson.

ated. Two strong clubs were formed there, the Railway
Swimming Club and the Umtali A.A.A. Swimming Club,
between whom there was keen rivalry. Under Messrs. R. Y.
Gibbs and F. E. Sayers, life saving classes were formed and
many promising young swimmers received the benefits of
these men's knowledge. P. P. Kelly has also done much
for swimming in Manicaland. Some outstanding swimmers
from this district are Miss M. Loosley, Miss Pat Wallace, H.
Robinson and J. R. Robertson. In 1926, the Wankie Club
and the Bulawayo Clubs, Crusaders and Harriers, joined the
Association, and in 1929 the present system of government
was adopted whereby Salisbury, Bulawayo, Umtali and the
Midlands each has its own Board with two delegates each
on the control body. To-day Bulawayo has several more
clubs, prominent among which is the Old Miltonians', and
the town is a stronghold of swimming. J. B. Gilbert, A. E. W.
Raybould, E. A. Payne, "Curley" Wright and E. R. Davis,
have done much for the sport in Bulawayo and local products of note are Miss H. Henricks, C. N. Foster, A. Painting, W. W. Acutt, Miss D. Wren, Miss G. Chalmers, Miss
P. Butcher, C. H. Frielick, C. Duncombe, and J. Monseair.

The first Rhodesian championships were held in 1916
and confined to juniors, this being the War period. The
principal event, the 100 yards race, was won by J. T. Brown
in 1 min. 13 1-5secs. In 1920 two Rhodesians won S.A.
Championship titles. J. T. Brown won the 100 yards open
and his brother, Leslie, carried off the 100 yards Junior
Championship.   From that year Rhodesian teams have
competed annually in the Currie Cup tournament. In 1922
the Currie Cup meeting was held in Salisbury and this was
the venue again in 1929.

An event of importance was the visit of Miss Hilda
James, the famous English swimmer, in 1925, who gave
some wonderful exhibitions in Salisbury.

In 1929 the Bulawayo Amateur Swimming Board invited
four of the Empire's greatest women swimmers to participate
in a gala in Bulawayo. The four British girls, the Misses
Joyce Cooper, Ellen King, Edith Mayne, and Vera Tanner,
were a great attraction and it was a sheer delight to watch
the way in which these girls, all of whom had world-wide
reputations, swam, dived and turned. In the Ladies' 50
yards open handicap, Miss Cooper won the race from scratch
in 27 4-5secs. The visit ended on a romantic note, for Miss
Mayne shortly afterwards returned to Rhodesia and married
Mr. D. J. Peacock, a keen swimming enthusiast.

1926 CURRIE CUP TEAM.

Standing: J. A. Forbes, S. Brooks, H. M. Ward (Manager), G. E. Wells, R. W. Atkinson.

Kneeling: J. Hick, L. G. Morgenrood.

In Front: E. Porter, F. Flint, C. Porter.

In 1931 a team of Dutch women swimmers visited Rhodesia and performed in Salisbury and Bulawayo. The team consisted of Miss Marie Braun, Miss Cootje Huybers, Miss J. Grendel, and Miss M. P. Oversloot, accompanied by Mrs. Braun as chaperone and manager. In spite of their youth (their ages, respectively, being 19, 16, 17, and 16) they all possessed European reputations as swimmers and had broken many records in their South African tour. Their displays in the two Rhodesian centres were much appreciated by the public and this, together with the excellence of their form, fully justified the policy of the swimming authorities in securing the visit.

In Salisbury, in a ladies' 150 yards handicap, Miss C. Rodwell won by a touch after receiving five seconds start from Miss Oversloot and Miss Grendel, and seven seconds start from Miss Braun. In the team race between the visitors and a Salisbury team of ladies, the visitors conceded six seconds start to the local swimmers (the Misses C. Rodwell, G. C. Chalmers, E. J. Rayner and C. Boshoff), but won the race comfortably.

At Bulawayo Miss Braun and Miss Oversloot attacked the South African record of 1min. 47 1-5secs. for the 150 yards, and Miss Braun successfully lowered it by swimming the distance in 1min. 46 2-5secs. The Hollanders in the team race, conceding nine seconds to the Bulawayo ladies (the Misses D. V. Wren, H. Henricks, P. Butcher, and G. C. Chalmers) won by about sixteen yards.

In 1934 Rhodesia was represented at the Empire Games by C. N. Foster, who did very well indeed. He competed in only two events, gaining a fourth and a fifth place.

Swimming owes much to the keenness of Mr. R. Y. Gibbs, now the Bulawayo Bath Superintendent, who has the distinction of being the first Rhodesian to hold all the awards of the Royal Life Saving Society.

The most important trophy for competition is the Partridge Cup, presented by Mr. A. W. Partridge, in 1920. It was originally donated for inter-club competition, and the Pirates Club, Salisbury, held the cup until 1927. It became an inter-town trophy in 1928, when Salisbury and Umtali competed, but since that date Bulawayo and Salisbury have been the only competitors.

Up to and including 1932, only men's events counted in the competition, but since then ladies' events have also counted. The present allocation of points for individual

1927 CURRIE
CUP TEAM.

Standing:

S. Morgenrood.
P. W. Gibbs.

Middle Row:

C. W. Littleton.
L. G. Morgenrood
(Capt.)
H. G. Bell
(Manager).
J. R. Robertson.
N. Brooks.

In Front:

R. Atkinson.
F. J. Flint.

events is 3, 2, and 1 for first, second and third places respectively; 5, 3, and 1 for the team races, and for the water polo 6 points for a win and three points to each side in a drawn game.

Good work is being done in the various centres by members of the Royal Life Saving Society, and there are numerous swimmers in the Colony who have earned the Society's awards. B. B. Bowley, now President of the Rhodesia Amateur Swimming Association, was the first examiner in Rhodesia, and others connected with this valuable work of teaching life-saving are Major H. Harnell, E. B. Shepherd, R. Y. Gibbs, F. E. Sayers, A. E. W. Raybould and Edgar Jenkins.

THE CURRIE CUP TOURNAMENTS.

The first Rhodesians to participate in South African Championships were the brothers J. T. and L. Brown, who went to Durban in 1920 and won the 100 yards S.A. Championships, Senior and Junior respectively. Their father, Mr. J. Brown, was naturally very interested in swimming, and he has done a great deal to further the sport. The Colony's first appearance as a team was in 1921, when it was seen, among other things, that Rhodesians had a lot to learn about water-polo. Even to-day it is an extraordinary fact that although swimming has reached a high standard and numerous South African titles have come to the Province, water-polo here has not yet attained the level of the game in the other provinces.

The following are details of the various entries:—

1920, at Durban: Championships.
J. T. Brown won the 100 yards open in 64 1-5secs., and the 50 yards scratch event in 27 1-5secs. L. Brown won the 100 yards Junior title in 73 2-5secs.

1921.—AT PORT ELIZABETH.
Water Polo.
H. Robinson, A. E. Wicks, S. G. Brooks, A. E. Ward (Captain), D. D. Fraser, J. Hick, J. T. Brown G. Hodgson, T. G. Edmanson, N. A. Fereday, E. B. Shepherd, C. Brown, E. B. Shepherd.

Border	Lost	6 — 0
Eastern Province	Lost	6 — 1
(Edmanson).		
Transvaal	Lost	6 — 0
Natal	Lost	6 — 0
Western Province	Lost	4 — 0

Championships.
J. T. Brown ,holder of the 100 Yards Championship, was successful in retaining his title, covering the distance in 63 secs.

1929 CURRIE CUP.

Standing:

S. Morgenrood.
G. R. L. Edwards,
S. Sumption,
W. Masters,
G. H. Melville,
R. W. Atkinson,
W. M. Thomson,
L. Dewar.

Sitting:

F. Flint,
Miss B. Redmond,
Miss J. Reid-
    Rowland
L. Brown (Capt.),
Miss C. Wright
Miss M. Reid-
    Rowland,
S. G. Brooks

1922.—AT SALISBURY.
Water Polo.

H. Robinson, A. Wicks, S. G. Salmon, S. G. Brooks, C. W. Littleton, G. Hodgson, J. Hick, T. G. Edmanson, N. E. Brooks, V. A. Lewis, H. E. Browne, H. C. Finch, F. W. Windsor, C. Brown, N. Fereday, D. Fraser, C. Porter, G. Fife, L. Brown.

Eastern Province	Lost	3 — 2	
(Hick, Hodgson).			
Border	Lost	3 — 2	
(Hick, Littleton).			
Transvaal	Lost	7 — 0	
Natal	Lost	6 — 1	
(Hick).			
Orange Free State	Won	4 — 1	
(Lewis 2, Hodgson 2).			

Championships.

J. T. Brown lost his title for the 100 yards, but F. J. Flint, aged 15 years, won the 220 yards race in 2mins. 47 2-5secs. In this latter race, R. W. Atkinson also competed.

N. V. Oxenden (Marandellas), gave a brilliant display to win the Diving, with P. W. Gibbs third.

In the Ladies' Diving, Mrs. N. T. Smith was placed third, and in the Ladies' 100 Yards, Miss M. Reid Rowland swam third, and Miss I. Burdett fourth.

1923.—AT CAPE TOWN.
Water Polo.

N. A. Fereday, S. G. Brooks, H .Robinson, R. W. Atkinson, L. G. Morgenrood, J. Hick, G. Hodgson, A. E. Wicks, J. T. Brown. C. Brown, F. J. Flint, P. W. Gibbs; Manager, H. M. Ward.

Natal	Lost	7 — 1	
(Hodgson).			
Transvaal	Lost	6 — 0	
Western Province	Lost	3 — 1	
(Hodgson).			
South Westerns	Won	3 — 1	
Border	Lost	5 — 1	
(Hodgson).			
Eastern Province	Lost	7 — 4	
(Brown 2, Atkinson, Hodgson).			
Orange Free State	Won	5 — 0	
(Hick 2, Wicks 2, Atkinson).			

1924.—AT PRETORIA.

F. J. Flint and L. Brown were unplaced in the 100 and 220 Yards Championships, and R. W. Atkinson failed to gain a place in his event. No water-polo team competed.

1925.

F. J. Flint and P. W. Gibbs were Rhodesia's only representatives.

1926.—AT PORT ELIZABETH.
Water Polo.

J. A. Forbes, H. Robinson, S. G. Brooks, R. W. Atkinson, L. G. Morgenrood E. Porter C. W. Porter, G. E. Wells, J. Hick.

Western Province	Lost	6 — 1	
(An opponent).			
Eastern Province	Won	4 — 3	
Natal	Lost	4 — 3	
(Morgenrood).			
Transvaal	Lost	7 — 0	
Orange Free State	Lost	1 — 0	

Championships.

In the 100 Yards F. J. Flint won his heat but was unplaced in the final.

1930 CURRIE CUP TEAM.

—

Back Row:

J. R. Robertson.
G. Edwards.
C. H. Frielick.
J. A. Forbes.

Middle Row:

A. L. Dewar.
W. M. Thomson.
S. Turner.
A. J. Ledger.
F. J. Flint.

Front Row:

P. W. Gibbs.
C. W. Littleton.
S. G. Brooks (Capt.)
Miss H. Henricks
J. B. Gilbert (Manager).
C. W. Duncombe.

1927.—AT EAST LONDON.
Water Polo.
F. J. Flint, R. W. Atkinson, P. W. Gibbs, S. Morgenrood, J. R. Robertson, L. G. Morgenrood, N. E. Brooks, and H. G. Bell (Manager).

Natal	Lost	11 — 0	
Transvaal	Lost	6 — 0	
Border	Lost	3 — 2	
(Morgenrood 2)			
Orange Free State	Lost	2 — 0	
Eastern Province	Won	3 — 2	
(Atkinson 2, Morgenrood).			
Western Province	Lost	6 — 0	

1928.
The only Rhodesian competitor at the S.A. Championships was M. Bentley.

1929.—AT SALISBURY.
Water Polo.
F. J. Flint, L. Brown, G. R. L. Edwards, C. H. Frielick, G. H. Melville, L. G. Morgenrood, E. T. Douglas, W. F. Boyd, J. A. Forbes, R. W. Atkinson, S. G. Brooks, S. Morgenrood, C. W. Littleton, S. C. Geyle, A. L. Dewar, S. Sumption, W. Masters, W. M. Thomson.

Transvaal	Lost	7 — 0	
Griqualand West	Won	4 — 1	
(Atkinson 3, Brown).			
Border	Drawn	2 — 2	
(Dewar, Sumption).			
Natal	Lost	5 — 1	
(Dewar).			
Western Province	Drawn	2 — 2	
(Brown, Dewar).			
Eastern Province	Won	3 — 1	
(Brown 2, L. G. Morgenrood).			
Orange Free State	Lost	5 — 1	
(Brown).			

Championships.
In the 100 Yards L. Brown won in 61 3-5secs., with F. J. Flint third.

P. W. Gibbs won the Diving, and Miss M. Loosley was third in the Ladies' Diving.

1930.—AT BLOEMFONTEIN.
Water Polo.
J. A. Forbes, C. W. Duncombe, S. G. Brooks, A. L. Dewar, S. Turner, C. H. Frielick, J. Ledger, J. R. Robertson, C. W. Littleton, P. W. Gibbs, F. J. Flint, W. M. Thomson. Manager, J. B. Gilbert.

Griqualand West	Won	4 — 0	
(Frielick 2, Turner 2).			
Transvaal	Lost	8 — 2	
(Duncombe, Frielick).			
Northern Transvaal	Lost	6 — 0	
Natal	Lost	6 — 1	
(Frielick).			
Western Province	Lost	3 — 2	
(Frielick, Dewar).			
Orange Free State	Lost	4 — 1	
(Frielick).			

Championships.
In the Women's Diving, Miss H. Henricks gained third place, and in the Men's Diving, P. W. Gibbs was beaten into second place and so lost his title.

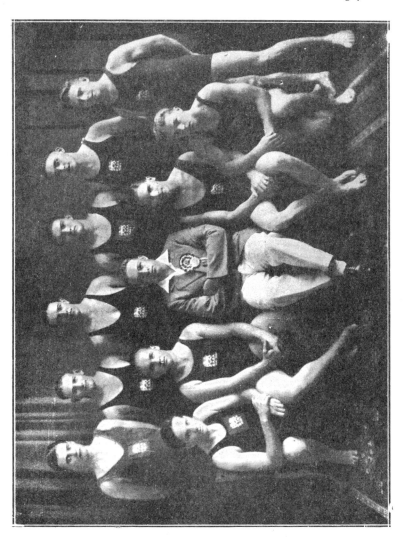

CURRIE CUP
TEAM, 1931.

Back Row:
W. M. Thomson.
J. S. Rowbotham.
M. Walker.
W. W. Acutt.
W J. Morris.
R. Penfold.

Front Row:
A. Vincent.
J. R. Robertson
(Capt.)
C H. Zeederberg
(Manager).
S. Morgenrood.
L. Bater.

1931.—AT CAPE TOWN.

Water Polo.

A. Bater, S. Morgenrood, J. Morris, J. R. Robertson, J. Rowbotham, A. Vincent, R. J. Penfold, W. W. Acutt, M. Walker. Manager, C. Zeederberg.

Northern Transvaal	Lost	7 — 0
Western Province	Lost	12 — 2
(Robertson, Rowbotham).		
Border	Lost	6 — 3
(Walker 2, Robertson).		
Griqualand West	Lost	8 — 0
Transvaal	Lost	7 — 1
(Robertson).		
Natal	Lost	8 — 0
Orange Free State	Lost	7 — 1
(Robertson).		

Championships.

J. R. Robertson competed in the Men's Diving, but was unplaced .

1932.—AT KIMBERLEY.

Water Polo.

J. Monseair, R. J. Penfold, S. Turner, C. W. Duncombe, A. L. Dewar, J. R. Robertson, W. W. Acutt, J. Rowbotham. Manager, B. B. Bowley.

Natal	Won	3 — 2
(Turner 2, Penfold).		
Western Province	Lost	8 — 3
(Dewar, Duncombe, Penfold).		
Transvaal	Lost	9 — 1
(Dewar).		
Northern Transvaal	Lost	9 — 0
Border	Drawn	4 — 4
(Robertson 3, Rowbotham).		
Orange Free State	Lost	6 — 0

Championships.

In the Diving events, Miss Henricks and J. R. Robertson competed.

1933.—AT DURBAN.

Water Polo.

N. A. Fereday, J. R. Robertson, C. W. Duncombe, A. Vincent, D. Black, R. Chalmers, S. Morgenrood, A. Painting. Manager, L. Brown.

Transvaal	Lost	5 — 1
(Robertson).		
Natal	Lost	7 — 1
(Robertson).		
Griqualand West	Lost	4 — 3
(Black 2, Brown).		
Northern Transvaal	Lost	6 — 0
Western Province	Lost	7 — 0
Border	Lost	6 — 2
(Robertson, Chalmers).		
Eastern Province	Won	7 — 3
Brown 5, Morgenrood, Robertson).		

Championships.

J. R. Robertson competed in the Diving, but was unplaced.

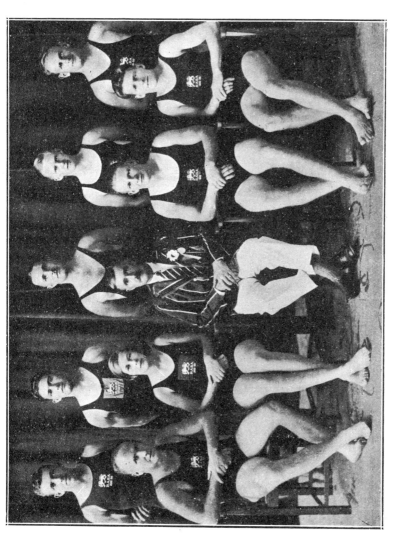

CURRIE CUP
TEAM, 1932.

———

Back Row:
J. Monseair.
W. W. Acutt.
C. W. Duncombe.
S. Turner.
J. Rowbotham.

Front Row:
J. R. Robertson.
Miss H. Henricks.
B. B. Bowley
(Manager).
A. L. Dewar
(Capt.)
R. F. Penfold.

K

1933 CURRIE CUP.

Standing: D. Black, R. S. Chalmers, C. Duncombe, S. Morgen-
rood, H. Maltas.
In Front: A. Vincent, J. R. Robertson (Capt.), L. Brown
(Manager), N. A. Fereday, A. Painting.

1934.—AT PRETORIA.

Water Polo.

J. A. Forbes (capt.), S. Morgenrood, H. Maltas, S. Sumption,
G. H. Addecott, G. R. L. Edwards, D. Black, C. N. Foster, A. Nimmo,
S. Fisher.

Natal	Lost	2 — 1
(Foster.)		
Western Province	Lost	10 — 1
(Sumption.)		
Northern Transvaal	Lost	8 — 0
Transvaal	Lost	8 — 0
Border	Lost	4 — 1
(Foster.)		
Griqualand West	Lost	7 — 3
(Maltas, Nimmo, Edwards.)		
Orange Free State	Lost	2 — 1
(Foster.)		

Championships.

C. N. Foster won the 500 yards race in 6 mins 31 2-5 secs.,
and the 880 yards event in 12 mins. 2 1-5 secs.

Miss P. Wallace competed in the Ladies' Diving and G. R. L.
Edwards swam in the 100 yards championship.

CURRIE CUP
TEAM, 1934.

Standing:

S. Fisher.
C. N. Foster.
G. Edwards.
A. Nimmo.

Sitting:

D Black.
S. Morgenrood.
J. 'A. Forbes
(Capt.)
Miss P. Wallace.
S. Sumption.

In Front:

H. L. Maltas.
G. H. Addecott.

1935.—AT PORT ELIZABETH.

Water Polo.

G. R. L. Edwards, A. Calder, G. Harris, R. L. Foster, A. Vincent, S. Fisher, N. Hunt, C. Davison, G. H. Addicott, C. N. Foster.

Western Province	Lost	8 — 1
(Vincent.)		
Eastern Province	Lost	8 — 4
(C. N. Foster (3), R. L. Foster.)		
Northern Transvaal	Lost	6 — 0
Transvaal	Lost	7 — 2
(Calder (2).)		
Natal	Lost	11 — 0
Orange Free State	Lost	7 — 3
(R. L. Foster (2), C. N. Foster.)		

Championships.

C. N. Foster's performances were outstanding. In the 500 yards race he won his heat in 6 mins. 15 1-5 secs. which equalled the South African record, and then created a new record of 6 mins. 9 2-5 secs. in the final. In the half-mile Foster's time for his heat was 14½ secs. better than the South African record, while his time of 11 mins. 18 secs. was 25 1-5 secs. below the previous record. Foster also competed in the 220 yards event, but was unplaced. Miss O. Baker, who swam in the 100 yards girls' junior championship, was placed third, her time being 71 4-5 secs.

RHODESIAN WINNERS OF S.A. CHAMPIONSHIPS.

1920.

100 yards—J. T. Brown ... ... 64 1-5 secs.

1921.

100 yards—J. T. Brown ... ... 63 secs.

1922.

220 yards—F. J. Flint ... ... 2 mins. 47 2-5 secs.
Diving—N. V. Oxenden.

1929.

100 yards—L. Brown ... ... 61 3-5 secs.
Diving—P. W. Gibbs.

1934.

500 yards—C. N. Foster ... ... 6 mins 31 2-5 secs.
880 yards—C. N. Foster ... ... 12 mins. 2 1-5 secs.

1935.

500 yards—C. N. Foster ... ... 6 mins 9 2-5 secs.
880 yards—C. N. Foster ... ... 11 mins. 18 secs.

RHODESIAN RECORDS.

100 yards—F. J. Flint (22/2/27) ... ... 58 secs.
220 yards—F. J. Flint (26/2/27) ... ... 2 mins. 37 secs.
500 yards—C. N. Foster (15/2/35) ... ... 6 mins 30 4-5 secs.
50 yards Ladies—Miss C. Rodwell (20/12/30) ... ... 30 3-5 secs.
100 yards Ladies—Miss C. Rodwell (27/1/34) ... ... 1 min. 12 secs.
220 yards Ladies—Miss O. Baker (15/2/35) ... ... 3 mins. 16 secs.

This splendid bath, with under-water lighting, was opened in Wankie in 1935.

THE PARTRIDGE CUP WINNERS.

Inter-Club.

1920-27: Pirates (Salisbury).

Inter-Town.

1928: Salisbury.	1932: Salisbury.
1929: Salisbury.	1933: Salisbury.
1930: Salisbury.	1934: Salisbury.
1931: Bulawayo.	1935: Bulawayo.

RHODESIAN CHAMPIONSHIP WINNERS.

1920.

100 yards—J. T. Brown ... ... 1 min. 9 secs.

1921.

100 yards—J. T. Brown ... ... 1 min. 6 secs.

220 yards—J. T. Brown ... ... 3 mins. 13 secs.

1922.

100 yards—J. T. Brown ... ... 1 min. 4 secs.

220 yards—F. J. Flint ... ... 2 mins. 54 4-5 secs.

Diving—N. V. Oxenden.

50 yards, Ladies—Miss I. Burdett ... ... 39 3-5 secs.

1923.

100 yards—J. T. Brown ... ... 1 min. 5 4-5 secs.

220 yards—R. W. Atkinson ... ... 2 mins. 51 4-5 secs.

Diving—P. W. Gibbs.

50 yards, Ladies—Miss I. Burdett ... ... 37 2-5 secs.

1924.

100 yards—L. Brown ... ... 1 min. 3 secs.

220 yards—R. W. Atkinson ... ... 2 mins. 47 secs.

Diving—W. F. Boyd.

50 yards, Ladies—Miss I. Burdett ... ... 36 secs.

1925.

100 yards—F. J. Flint ... ... 1 min. 1 4-5 secs.

220 yards—F. J. Flint ... ... 2 mins. 39 secs.

Diving—P. W. Gibbs.

50 yards, Ladies—Miss Hilda James ... ... 31 1-5 secs.

1926.

100 yards—F. J. Flint ... ... 1 min 0 3-5 secs.

220 yards—F. J. Flint ... ... 2 mins. 37 secs.

Diving—W. F. Boyd.

50 yards, Ladies—Miss J. Reid Rowland ... ... 35 4-5 secs.

1927.

100 yards—F. J. Flint ... ... 58 2-5 secs.

220 yards—F. J. Flint ... ... 2 mins. 44 1-5 secs.

Diving—J. R. Robertson.

50 yards, Ladies—Miss J. Reid Rowland ... ... 34 4-5 secs.

Inter-Town Water Polo: Salisbury 6; Bulawayo 1.

Inter-Town Team Race (Men)—Bulawayo A ... ... 3 mins. 7 2-5 secs.

1928.

100 yards—F. J. Flint ... ... 59 3-5 secs.

220 yards—F. J. Flint ... ... 2 mins. 40 2-5 secs.

Diving—P. W .Gibbs.

50 yards, Ladies—Miss J. Reid Rowland ... ... 35 secs.

Inter-Town Water Polo—Salisbury 5; Umtali nil.

Inter-Town Team Race (Men)—Salisbury A ... ... 1 min. 45 1-5 secs.

1929.

100 yards—F. J. Flint ... ... 1 min.
220 yards—L. Brown ... ... 2 mins. 53 3-5 secs.
Diving—P. W. Gibbs.
50 yards, Ladies—Miss B. Redmond ... ... 33 4-5 secs.
Diving, Ladies—Miss M. Loosley.
Inter-Town Water Polo—Salisbury 4; Bulawayo 1.
Inter-Town Team Race (Men)—Salisbury ... ... 2 mins. 51 secs.

1930.

100 yards—W. M. Thomson ... ... 1 min. 0 4-5 secs.
220 yards—W. M. Thomson ... ... 2 mins. 47 secs.
500 yards—G. Edwards ... ... 7 mins. 9 3-5 secs.
Diving— P. W. Gibbs.
50 yards, Ladies—Miss G. Chalmers ... ... 32 3-5 secs.
100 yards, Ladies—Miss G. Chalmers ... ... 1 min. 19 2-5 secs.
Diving, Ladies—Miss H. Henricks.
Inter-Town Water Polo—Salisbury 2; Bulawayo 2.
Inter-Town Team Race (Men)—Salisbury ... ... 1 min. 46 3-5 secs.

1931.

100 yards—W. M. Thomson ... ... 1 min. 2 3-5 secs.
220 yards—W. M. Thomson ... ... 2 mins. 49 secs.
500 yards—W. M. Thomson ... ... 7 mins. 25 3-5 secs.
Diving—J. R. Robertson.
50 yards, Ladies—Miss C. Rodwell ... ... 30 3-5 secs.
100 yards, Ladies—Miss C. Rodwell ... ... 1 min. 13 3-5 secs.
Diving, Ladies—Miss H. Henricks.
Inter-Town Water Polo—Bulawayo 5; Salisbury 3.
Inter-Town Team Race (Men)—Salisbury A ... ... 1 min. 46 3-5 secs.

1932.

100 yards—W. M. Thomson ... ... 1 min. 2 1-5 secs.
220 yards—W. M. Thomson ... ... 2 mins. 42 3-5 secs.
500 yards—G. Edwards ... ... 7 mins. 18 3-5 secs.
Diving—J. R. Robertson.
50 yards, Ladies—Miss C. Rodwell ... ... 33 secs.
100 yards, Ladies—Miss D. Wren ... ... 1 min. 16 2-5 secs.
220 yards, Ladies—Miss M. McGregor ... ... 3 mins. 30 secs.
Diving, Ladies—Miss P. Wallace.
Inter-Town Water Polo—Salisbury 5; Bulawayo 4.
Inter-Town Team Race (Men)—Salisbury A ... ... 1 min.
Inter-Town Team Race (Ladies)—Bulawayo ... ... 1 min. 26 4-5 secs.

1933.

100 yards—W. M. Thomson ... ... 1 min. 1 1-5 secs.
220 yards—A. Painting ... ... 2 mins. 43 3-5 secs.
500 yards—M. Creed ... ... 7 mins. 7 1-5 secs.
Diving—J. R. Robertson.
50 yards, Ladies—Miss C. Rodwell ... ... 31 2-5 secs.
100 yards, Ladies—Miss C. Rodwell ... ... 1 min. 14 2-5 secs.
220 yards, Ladies—Miss C. Rodwell ... ... 3 mins. 25 1-5 secs.
Diving, Ladies—Miss P. Wallace.
Inter-Town Water Polo—Salisbury 4; Bulawayo 1.
Inter-Town Team Race (Men)—Salisbury ... ... 2 mins 50 secs.
Inter-Town Team Race (Ladies)—Salisbury ... 2 mins. 16 1-5 secs.

1934.

100 yards—G. R. L. Edwards ... ... 1 min. 0 3-5 secs.
220 yards—C. N. Foster ... ... 2 mins. 42 1-5 secs.
500 yards—C. N. Foster ... ... 6 mins. 44 secs.
Diving—P. W. Gibbs.
50 yards, Ladies—Miss C. Rodwell ... ... 30 3-5 secs.
100 yards, Ladies—Miss C. Rodwell ... ... 1 min. 12 secs.
220 yards, Ladies—Miss C. Rodwell ... ... 3 mins. 22 3-5 secs.
Diving, Ladies—Miss P. Wallace.
Inter-Town Water Polo—Salisbury 5; Bulawayo 4.
Inter-Town Team Race (Men)—Salisbury A ... ... 1 min. 44 4-5 secs.
Inter-Town Team Race (Ladies)—Salisbury A ... ... 1 min 23 secs.

1935.

100 yards—A. L. Painting ... ... 1 min. 0 1-5 sec.
220 yards—C. N. Foster ... ... 2 mins. 38 1-5 secs.
500 yards—C. N. Foster ... ... 6 mins. 30 4-5 secs.
Diving—A. L. Painting.
50 yards, Ladies—Miss C. Green and Miss O. Baker (tied) 31 4-5 secs.
100 yards, Ladies—Miss O. Baker ... ... 1 min. 15 4-5 secs.
220 yards, Ladies—Miss O. Baker ... ... 3 mins. 16 secs.
Team Race (Men)—Bulawayo A ... ... 2 mins. 52 secs.
Team Race (Ladies)—Bulawayo A ... ... 2 mins. 27 4-5 secs.

Gwelo Amateur Swimming Club's team which competed in the 1935
Rhodesian Championships, taking second place in the team relay
event. Back row (left to right): K. Gower, D. Baker, W. Bester.
Front row: E. Gower, J. Finch, S. Simpson.

**OFFICERS PAST AND PRESENT OF THE RHODESIA
AMATEUR SWIMMING ASSOCIATION.**

Patrons: Sir Drummond Chaplin, 1918-1923; Sir John Chancellor, 1924-1927; Sir Cecil Rodwell, 1928 to date; Capt. C. Douglas Jones, 1925 to date; G. B. Cumming, 1922 to date; F. L. Hadfield, 1927 to date; A. C. Soffe, 1927 to date; P. R. Pomfret, 1930 to date; E. W. Wright, 1932; E. B. Shepherd, N. E. Brooks, H. Chapman, H. G. Bell, Major R. J. Hudson and Lt.-Col. A. C. L. Webb, 1932 to date; Sir Ronald Storrs, H. Allen, D. Macintyre and C. M. Harris, 1933; and the Governors of Southern and Northern Rhodesia.

Presidents: Capt. C. Douglas-Jones, 1918-1923; J. A. Cope-Christie, 1924-1925; Major R. J. Hudson, 1926-1931; E. Jenkins, 1932; E. W. Wright, 1933; B. B. Bowley, 1934-1935.

Vice-Presidents: Dr. F. E. Appleyard, 1918-1920; J. A. Cope-Christie, 1921-1923; H. G. Bell, 1924-1927; E. B. Shepherd, 1928-1931; J. B. Gilbert, 1932; W. P. T. Hancock, 1933; P. R. Moore, 1934.

Hon. Handicappers: A. Hodgson. 1918; D. Elliott, 1919; C. S. Honey, 1920-1922; F. W. Windsor, 1923; H. M. Ward, 1924-1929; S. G. Brooks, 1930-1931; P. Moore, 1932-1933; W. P. T. Hancock, 1932; C. Duncombe, 1933; J. R. Robertson and G. Addecott, 1934.

Hon. Secretaries and Treasurers: E. B. Shepherd, 1918-1927; N. E. Brooks, 1928-1931, D. J. Peacock, 1932; A. E. W. Raybould, 1933; H. J. Theron, 1934.

Asst. Hon. Secretaries: Mrs. D. J. Peacock, 1932; C. Dodd, 1933; G. Addecott, 1934.

Hon. Auditors: J. C. Smith, 1918-1931; E. W. Wright, 1932; H. J. Tilbury, 1933.

Hon. Timekeepers: H. G. Bell, 1918-1933; H. L. Kinsey, 1918-1933; C. Marston, 1918-1921, 1928, 1930, 1932-1933; C. Tyrrell Heaver, 1922-1927, 1929-1933; W. Wooley, 1929-1933; T. Forbes, Snr., 1930-1933; A. E. W. Raybould, T. Forbes, Jnr., J. Grant and J. B. McNeil, 1932-1933.

C. N. FOSTER,
Holder of Rhodesian and South African records.

YACHTING

DESPITE Rhodesia's lack of coastline and natural inland waters, the sea-faring spirit that is latent in every Britisher has made itself manifest on the few reservoirs in the country. As each of these was constructed, quite a number of small rowing boats made their appearance. Then sailing was attempted on the Zambesi and Kafue rivers, but with the small population the craft were too few for the formation of any clubs. In 1929 the Matopos Sailing Club was formed with, as its waterway, the Rhodes Matopos Dam, situate about seventeen miles from Bulawayo. This is a long narrow stretch of water which, when full, is about a mile and a quarter in length. Buoys are placed in the four main bays but, as the level of the dam falls, so the buoys have to be moved in. After three very poor rainy seasons the complete course of the race which was more than twice round the dam was barely over three miles this year. It is always a source of wonder that there should be a sailing club in arid Matabeleland, which has no good rivers, and the founders are to be commended for their courage and vision.

(By courtesy of Lennon, Ltd.)
A Race in Progress on the Matopos Dam.

The pioneer in this movement was the late Colonel W. Arnold, D.S.O., a member of the Royal Ulster Yacht Club. He was supported by M. N. Varvill, M.C., and Captain D. Evans. In 1926 these gentlemen purchased two boats from Durban, *Hallowe'en,* a Bermuda-rigged 20-footer scow, and *Gnat,* a boat of similar dimensions but gaff-rigged. Gradually the sport attracted those who would "go down to the sea in ships," and three additional craft of the same "skimming-dish" type were imported: *Chloe,* gaff-rigged, and two Bermudas, *Skellum* and *Aliceia.* To-day the club has a membership of nearly fifty. It has the sailing rights on the dam on an annual lease with a proviso that no motor-boats are allowed to be used. With commendable enthusiasm the members built a small wooden jetty and a hut for the storage of sails and gear. In 1932 this enterprising little club published its own magazine. It is a most creditable publication and makes very interesting reading. Mention is made of a native who was employed when the first yacht was launched in 1926. At that date this "boy" was quite "raw," but to-day he manipulates the club's dinghy with an ease that is truly astounding. On more than one occasion this native, whose name is "Good-night," has been seen complete with feathered hat "crewing" in races when there has been a shortage of members present!

The Club has two floating trophies, the "Bill Arnold" Challenge Cup, presented by the widow of Colonel Arnold, and Mr. Macdonald's Ladies' Challenge Cup for a race won by a woman skipper, while each year the Commodore presents a cup.

Results to date are:—

"Bill Arnold" Cup:	Commodore's Cup:
1931 ... ... Chloe.	1930-31 ... ... Aliceia.
1932 ... ... Hallowe'en.	1932 ... ... Chloe.
1933 ... ... Skellum.	1933 ... ... Aliceia.
1934 ... ... Hallowe'en.	1934 ... ... Hallowe'en.

Ladies' Challenge Cup:

1932 ... Mrs. M. H. Barry, at tiller of Hallowe'en.

Prominent among the club's members are Mr. Varvill, the first Commodore, a yachtsman of considerable experience, gained largely in the Karachi Sailing Club; Capt. Evans, the present Commodore, an able and practical sailor; an expert helmsman in N. F. Shillingford, Vice-Commodore, and one of the club's keenest members; Capt. A. T. Stephen, another fine yachtsman; and others who handle their craft well are M. H. Barry, P. H. Haviland, M. Chennells, Howard Gott, A. T. C. Sutton, A. D. Cowper, L. R. B. Green, Dr. C. H. Hart and J. Thompson. Among the best of the women at the tiller are Mrs. Shillingford, Mrs. Stephen, Mrs. Barry, Mrs. Gott and Miss A. Stevens.

It is of interest to note that the club has enabled many of the residents of Bulawayo to learn their first sailing lessons.

[This article is reproduced by courtesy of the proprietors of the " British South Africa Annual."]

At the Landing Stage.

N. F. Shillingford, R. H. Roberts, Mrs. Shillingford, Miss Wells. Master and Miss Shillingford.

ROWING

NE of the most surprising things that reveals itself in a research of Rhodesia's sporting history is the fact that the only World Championship that has ever been held in the country was the rowing contest on the Zambesi River in 1910. The course was on that part of the river still known as Regatta Course, between Loando, or Long Island, and the Northern Rhodesian bank. Long Island is roughly two miles in length, with a breadth of a quarter of a mile, and here the broad Zambesi is about a mile across.

The extension of the Railway from Livingstone to Regatta Siding is shown in the sketch on page 346, from which may be guaged the position of the regatta course and its proximity to the Falls.

Even to experienced rowing men the river presented a difficult proposition. The currents varied from day to day, and at certain points the shortest course was not always the quickest. Wind was also most trying, and the hot African sun prevented most of the crews from exerting themselves as in milder climes. No tow-path could be made along the river because of the dense tropical vegetation reaching down to the water's edge. In any case, the Zambesi is not a place where an enthusiastic coach could, in his excitement, dance himself off the tow-path and into the water unless he was taking compassion on the hungry, ever-watchful crocodiles!

The course was first used in 1905, and a Bulawayo Rowing Club was formed to participate in a regatta. At a cost of £40 a boat was brought up from the coast, and Messrs. H. B. Miller, his cousin, E. H. Miller, Ellis Allen, C. Davis and Shade went into training on the Waterworks Dam at Hillside, Bulawayo. Just before the date fixed for the regatta it was found that one member of the crew could not make the trip, and Bulawayo did not compete.

The World Championship took place five years later, when R. Arnst sculled against E. Barry. This event was made the occasion for a big regatta and, encouraged by the British South Africa Company, Southern Rhodesia entered for various events.

Six men were recruited for preliminary training by Jim Chapman, of boxing fame. These were Lieutenant (now Colonel) G. Parson, captain of the side, who had done a great deal of rowing on the Thames at Cooper's Hill; H. Plumb, who had rowed for Clare College, Cambridge; Trooper (now Major) F. R. Lark, one of the Molesey " nest of larks," and a fine oarsman who coached the crew; C. Davis, G. Hill and W. P. T. Hancock, whose rowing had been learnt in Australia. A second-hand " clinker-built four " was purchased from Durban. When launched on the river, the craft leaked, and the blades of the oars were so large that it was imposible to drive them through the water at a satisfactory number of strokes per minute. The crew, however, soon overcame these obstacles.

After a course of vigorous training the selected four were Parson, Lark, Plumb and Hancock. Then came calamity. A Press representative from Australia recognised Hancock as having once taken part in a professional cycle race in Melbourne. Hancock was, unfortunately, not able to produce proof that he had since regained his amateur status and, in the absence of this, the regatta committee ruled him out of the competitions. This left Southern Rhodesia

In the Rhodesian Camp on the Zambesi.

Left to right: J. Chapman, Dreyer, Cordoray, W. Griffiths, E. Barry, Guy Nicholls, Native, " ——? " " Bossy " Phelps (now the King's Bargemaster), H. Plumb, W. Hancock, F. R. Lark, Native.

without a bow. Fortunately Major Drury, of the B.S.A. Police, was able to send up H. A. Knott from Marandellas. He had not done much rowing and was out of training, but in a short time he came on well and only lacked staying power.

The first race was for the Zambesi Challenge Cup, crews of four, for which Cape Town, East London, and Southern Rhodesia entered. Knott was instructed to save himself for the latter half of the race. For three parts of the distance Southern Rhodesia led, followed closely by East London, with Cape Town well behind, until Lark collapsed. He had had to bear practically the full responsibility for his side of the boat, as Knott had failed to pull his weight. Rhodesia finished last. The crew was H. A. Knott (bow), G. Parson, F. R. Lark, H. Plumb (stroke) and W. Griffiths (cox).

An hour later Parson and Lark turned out for the " pair-oared " race for the Robinow Cup, and would have won had their cox not steered an erratic course. They lost by six inches. The other local pair was Plumb and Knott. Six other pairs competed, representing Germiston, Zambesi Boat Club, and two pairs each from Cape Town and East London. An East London boat won the cup.

In the race for the Rhodesian Challenge Cup, Rhodesian crews only, Bulawayo was beaten by Livingstone by two and a half lengths. This trophy was the old Kafue Cup won outright by a Kafue crew in 1905 and put up again by them for competition.

THE RHODESIAN FOUR ON THE ZAMBESI.

W. Griffiths, F. R. Lark, G. Parson, C. Davis, H. Plumb.

The main feature of the regatta was the Arnst-Barry sculling championship (professional). A contingent of supporters from New Zealand were there to see their countryman, Arnst, win; two special cinematograph operators were in attendance, one from Johannesburg and one from the Warwick Company sent from England for the purpose, while special trains conveyed large crowds from Bulawayo and the South for the event. Arnst won fairly easily.

Col. G. Parson, C.B.E., D.S.O.

THE VICTORIA FALLS—A view from the West Bank.

VICTORIA

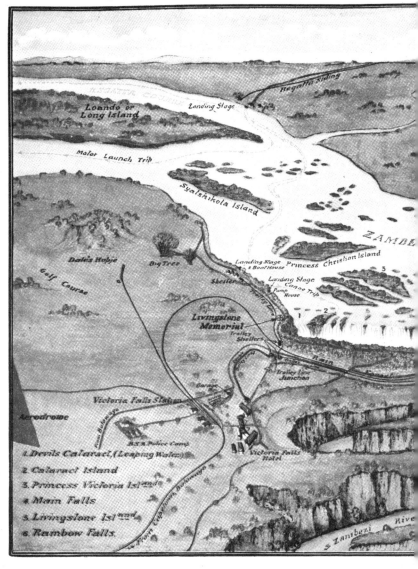

1. *Devils Cataract, (Leaping Water)*
2. *Cataract Island*
3. *Princess Victoria Isl.*
4. *Main Falls*
5. *Livingstone Isl.*
6. *Rainbow Falls.*

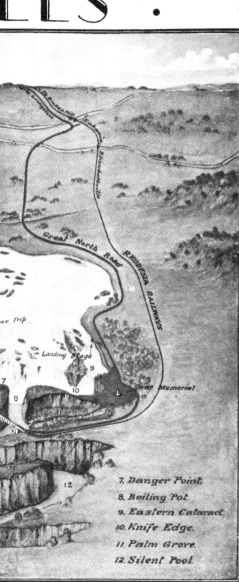

7. Danger Point.
8. Boiling Pot.
9. Eastern Cataract.
10. Knife Edge.
11. Palm Grove.
12. Silent Pool.

"THUS we arrive at the conclusion that, while in secondary features the Zambesi Fall may yield to some of its competitors in other climes, in all those attributes which concern the fall itself, and are of primary value, it is pre-eminent, and may deservedly be called the greatest river-wonder in the world.

Never can there fade

from the mind of one who has seen it the vision of those towers of descending foam, the shouting face of the cataract, the thunder of the watery phalanxes as they charge and reel and are shattered in the bottom of the abyss, or the spray-spumes whizzing upwards like a battery of rockets into the air.

As the train

plunges slowly into the forest and takes us back into the every-day world, the mist-clouds steaming like smoke through the trees and forming a dense white canopy 1,000 feet in height in the sky, and the low thunder, whose reverberations still fill the air, conclude a unique experience and crown an imperishable memory."

These words are part of the late Lord Curzon's description, in his "Tales of Travel," of a visit to the Victoria Falls. A more complete account of his impressions will be found in a booklet obtainable gratis from the Director of Publicity, Salisbury.

SEEING RHODESIA

WHEN Dr. David Livingstone discovered the Victoria Falls in 1855, the journey to this remote part of Africa was one of considerable hardship and took as long as six months to complete. By 1893, however, a start had been made in the penetration of Rhodesia and the iron rails of civilisation were creeping slowly from Beira in the East and Vryburg in the South towards the interior. The Victoria Falls were reached in 1904.

Since those early days, Rhodesia has seen considerable development in transport services. The growth of the country and a rapidly expanding tourist traffic have led to the provision of modern passenger saloons and the introduction of fast and convenient train services. In 1897 "The Bulawayo Chronicle" welcomed the advent of the railway as bringing Bulawayo within four or five days of the sea breezes. This journey is to-day a matter of less than 48 hours in comfortable trains with dining and sleeping accommodation.

The major tourist attractions of Rhodesia are easily accessible by rail. Umtali, the centre for the magnificent mountain scenery of the Eastern Border, is 20 hours' journey from Bulawayo and 12 hours from Beira. A railway motor service operates to Melsetter and Chipinga in the heart of the mountains.

The famous Ruins of Great Zimbabwe lie some 16 miles from Fort Victoria, the terminus of the branch line which runs from Gwelo. Through saloons are operated between Bulawayo and Fort Victoria, most of the journey in both directions being done during the night.

The Victoria Falls are less than 11 hours from Bulawayo and two and a half days from Cape Town by fast train. At the Falls there is a luxurious hotel, with all modern conveniences, including an open-air swimming pool. Launch and canoe trips on the Zambezi are arranged by the hotel management and facilities are available for fishing and golf and for sight-seeing expeditions by car or aeroplane to the game areas.

FISHING

THE Rhodesia Angling Society had its beginning in a Bulawayo Angling Club which was formed in 1925. At the inaugural meeting of the club Mr. J. G. McDonald (now Sir) was elected President, with Dr. G. Arnold, Chairman, R. H. R. Stevenson, Honorary Secretary, and the first members, C. O. V. Owen, H. W. Durrell, D. Francis, H. C. Milton, H. GillBanks, Dr. E. Head and J. Kabot. Those mentioned became the first officials of the Rhodesia Angling Society in 1925. From that date the handful of members has been increased so much that in 1931 the Society had nearly five hundred members, with well-established branches in various centres in the Colony.

The pioneer work of the Rhodesia Angling Society, though arduous, was helped along by the encouragement received from all sides. Messrs. Metcalf Bros., of Kimberley, offered to send carp, free of charge, if the Society would pay the railage and supply the tin containers. Mr. J. Kabot lent a pond for breeding purposes, and in six months fish grew to 3½ lbs. weight. The Railways offered the Society the use of their dam at Khami, and the Rhodes Trustees gave them the fishing rights over the Matopos Dam. Financial assistance was received from the Railways, while the Government made a generous grant each year to the funds.

The first fish imported were 50 Carp and 500 *Barbus Anoplus* (yellow fish). These were immediately successful, and when Mr. P. C. Braybrooke, who was instrumental in the first attempt at importing trout, announced the success of his efforts, fishermen all over the Colony were awakened to the possibilities of Rhodesian waters.

In 1927 the Salisbury branch of the Rhodesia Angling Society was formed, with Major A. L. Cooper as Chairman, T. R. Baxter as Hon. Secretary, and a committee of J. S. Henckel, D. A. McLeod, E. W. Popkiss, J. S. Steele, and Capt. C. E. Wells. Branches were also formed at Filabusi and Chipinga in 1927, and the Society, to encourage these branches, sent 10,000 trout ova to Chipinga and 5,000 to Salisbury. It also placed 575 carp in the Matopos Dam, 40 in the Filabusi Dam, 25 in T. B. Hepburn's pool, and 100 yellow fish in the Mazoe River. Since its formation the Society, at a cost of approximately £400, has introduced into the Colony 2,250 carp, 1,180 yellow fish, 18,000 rainbow trout ova, 1,000 bream (the gift of Mr. F. D. Roscoe) and 100 black bass. By Government Proclamation No. 10 of 1930, the Society has the fishing rights over the Matopos and Criterion dam (Matopos District), Marvel Railway Dam and Hillside Dam (Bulawayo District), Khami Railway Dam (Matopos District), Filabusi Dam (Insiza District), Umfuli Railway Dam and Umsweswe Railway Dam (Hartley District).

Just over two years after carp were introduced in the Matopo Dam, Mr. C. P. Higham (in 1928) landed one of 12lbs. 2ozs., and numbers of 10 lbs. and 8 lbs. were taken. At Rumbavu Park, Salisbury, a privately-owned dam, a 23lb. yellow fish was taken in 1931. In the same year, from the Ingesi River, just outside Bulawayo, bream of 1 lb. in weight were taken in large catches, and excellent bream fishing was reported from the Shangani River and in the Filabusi area.

The first fishing competitions commenced in 1929 and a little later the Rhodesia Angling Society received two handsome championship cups as floating trophies. So far the cups have been won by Bulawayo rods, and in this centre (headquarters of the Society) there is a large number of very keen anglers, men and women.

THE CHAMPIONSHIP CUP.

Presented by C. O. V. Owen, Esq., for the member taking the greatest aggregate weight of sizeable fish in any waters in Southern Rhodesia during the year.

1931—L. Kemp	… … … … … …	60 lbs.
1932—L. Kemp	… … … … … …	49 lbs.
1933—G. Gain	… … … … … …	61 lbs.
1934—G. Gain	… … … … … …	22 lbs.

THE CARP CUP.

Presented by the Bulawayo General Suppliers, Ltd., for the member taking the greatest aggregate weight of sizeable carp during the year.

1930—Jack Moss	… … … …	56 lbs. 6 ozs.
1931—J. E. Cole	… … … … … …	69 lbs.
1932—L. Kemp	… … … …	51 lbs. 12 ozs.
1933—G. Gain	… … … … … …	58 lbs.
1934—G. Gain	… … … … … …	22 lbs.

OFFICERS, PAST AND PRESENT, OF THE RHODESIA ANGLING SOCIETY.

President: Sir J. G. McDonald, O.B.E., 1925-1934 and 1935-1936; C. M. Harris, 1934-1935.

Chairman: Dr. G. Arnold, 1925-1927; C. O. V. Owen, 1928-1931; L. Kemp, 1931-1932; S. Neal, 1932-1934; J. B. Bull, 1934-1936.

Vice-Chairman: H. W. Durrell, 1925-27; W. H. Peard, 1928; D. F. Francis, 1929; L. Kemp, 1930-31; J. B. Bull, 1932-33; L. Kemp, 1933-36.

Hon. Secretary: R. H. R. Stevenson, 1925-27; W. S. Jobson, 1925; Jack Moss, 1928-30; A. H. Futter, 1930-34; H. A. Ketteringham, 1934-35; J. E. Cole, 1935-36.

Hon. Auditor: H. GillBanks, 1925 to date.

TABLE OF MINIMUM SIZES AND WEIGHTS.

Species.	Sizeable.	Competitions.	Carp Cup.	Championships	Specimen.
Tiger Fish	—	—	—	5 lbs.	7 lbs.
Carp	2½ lbs.	2½ lbs.	4 lbs.	5 lbs.	10 lbs.
Bream	1 lb.	1 lb.	—	2 lbs.	3 lbs.
Yellow Fish	12 inches.	12 inches	—	2 lbs.	3 lbs.
Silver Fish	12 inches	12 inches	—	2 lbs.	2½ lbs.
Black Bass	2 lbs.	2 lbs.	—	2 lbs.	3½ lbs.
Barbel	No minimum.	10 lbs.	—	25 lbs.	30 lbs.
		50% of actual weight.		10% of actual weight.	

As far back as 1907 enthusiasts have been concerned with the introduction of trout into Southern Rhodesia. In that year trout fry were distributed in the Gwebi River, near Salisbury, but there is little doubt that the indigenous fish, in particular the Tiger fish, have long since accounted for them. Ova were also put down during the years 1918 to 1923 in the Cleveland Dam, outside Salisbury, but despite good hatchings, the experiment proved abortive, due to high water temperatures, and the attentions of the indigenous fish.

Other attempts were made in the Khami Dam, Bulawayo, and in the Zambesi River above the Falls, but these were also failures. Fortunately the will to succeed was not to be defeated, and in 1929 ova were placed in the hatching boxes at Stapleford on the Odzani River, in the Umtali District. These fry were kept in the stew pens until they reached an average length of 5 inches, then being released to found the beginning of the first successful attempt at trout culture.

The Odzani is more akin to real trout water than any place tried before, being a beautiful stream of clear running water, which is cold the whole year round and practically free from indigenous fish. From this beginning the Umtali and Eastern Districts Piscatorial Society has arisen, with a view to fostering the introduction of trout into all suitable streams in the district.

It was decided that Rainbow trout would be most suitable as they are better able to stand higher temperatures, and therefore be able to spread further downstream than Brown trout.

Stocking of the Odzani was carried on for some years before the fishing was opened. Now, at the end of three seasons' fishing, the hopes held out by the original experiment are definitely justified.

Trout fishing has become a concrete fact in the Umtali district, and no doubt many fly fishermen will make their way to that part of the country in the future. Up to date the best fish captured was one of 4 lbs. 5 ozs., while many of 3 lbs. and over have been taken. The average is about 1 lb.

It is of interest to note that the stream is not kept going entirely by artificial stocking as it has been proved, beyond doubt, that the original fish are spawning in the stream, and it is to be hoped that, at no far distant date, Rhodesia will have its own trout farm at Stapleford.

The Government has proved very generous in donations of ova, which have been distributed in certain streams in Melsetter and Inyanga. So in the near future there will be trout fishing for all.

This year (1935) has been interesting. The Committee of the Umtali and Eastern Districts Piscatorial Society have gone into the question of " open season," in order that everyone in the country may have their opportunity. Trout have been caught throughout the year, and examined to see their condition. From the results obtained the season is now to be from September 1st to April 30th, which will allow of a fishing holiday at Easter, in beautiful surroundings.

Much remains to be done, and it will be many years before all the available waters are stocked, for on the Rhodes Estate (Inyanga) alone there are some 60 to 70 miles of suitable streams. This in itself is no light undertaking, but it is being tackled gradually. At the present time, however, the Odzani is the best water, and no visitor, given the requisite skill, will be disappointed in the quality of the fish.

To help those who may decide to visit the Odzani, a rod of 8 feet to 9 feet is most suitable, and a reel to hold up to 50 yards of line . Flies are more a matter of personal choice, but well-tried favourites can be obtained locally.

For full information, prospective visitors should get into touch with the Secretary of the Society, Mr. G. F. A. Aston, Box 187, Umtali, who will arrange for the necessary permits, etc.

It is well to remember that the Odzani is about 27 miles from Umtali, to the best fishing water, and transport will have to be arranged.

ani Trout Stream, Umtali District.

Rainbow Trout, weight 2 lbs. 12 ozs., length 18 inches, caught in Odzani River, Umtali, by Mrs. W. F. Gray. She and her husband are great fishing enthusiasts.

BOXING

MONG the early Pioneers were numerous boxers of repute. The cream of the collection was in the B.S.A. Company's Police and some grand fights took place in Mafeking while the men were concentrated there for equipment prior to blazing the trail through to Mount Hampden. J. R. Couper was still a power in the land and many of the men in the camp were his pupils. " A " Troop, raised in Johannesburg, contained T. Harris, light-weight champion of South Africa, the two MacMullans and Mulligan, while in "E" Troop was Robertson, a fine boxer from the United States. The redoubtable Billy Martin, who travelled round with Couper as " Little Willie" in the early '80's was in the B.B.P. and later in Salisbury for years. He met his death at sea when the Drummond Castle sank on June 16th, 1896, and when he went down Billy had £500 sewn in his belt, his portion of the sale of the Giant Mine. Another of the early boxers was Dave Morton and then there was Bill Whittaker, a gunner, and the heavyweight champion of his regiment in the Zulu Wars. He showed his worth at the Bembesi Battle on December 1st, 1893, when he saved Kem White from the Matabele.

Early fisticuffs were mostly professional and there were some big fights in the country. Most of the boxers came from the South, and as Bulawayo was their nearest centre it was only natural that this town secured nearly all the contests. Bulawayo boasted three stadiums. One was the Old Maxim's Hotel, now the Savoy; another was the Empire Theatre, but the most popular was the Market Hall, which has since given precedence to the Drill Hall.

The Bulawayo Chronicle of December 7th, 1895, contained the following : " Notice. Percy Carroll has a man who is willing to fight M. Roper for any sum from £50 to £100 a side." Another paragraph in the paper after Christmas reads : " Several pugilisitic encounters came off at the holidays, one of which went into 80 rounds, but none were of special interest " ! In 1899 Jim Holloway fought Malone, ex-Lightweight champion of South Africa, in Bulawayo in Patterson's Ring which was afterwards the old Agricultural Hall in the Show Ground. One of the biggest of those early bouts was between Jones of London and Dunn of New South Wales, in 1900, in the Market Hall for a purse of £500. Dunn won fairly easily.

Known only to a few, a bare-knuckle fight took place in Bulawayo on the Race Course at daybreak one Sunday. Mr. W.P.T. Hancock was the referee and the contest was under the London Prize Ring rules. Bolland, a sailor from Simon's Town and Cunningham, an Australian, were the contestants. With each of them over thirteen stone there was some rather heavy punching and resounding thumps when bare knuckles met bare ribs, and the two men were soon a gory spectacle. Cunningham won after five rounds. In the real English style of that period, many of the spectators turned out in top hats and frock coats.

In 1902 the first amateur contests were held, in which Pat Bland, a first class boxer won the heavyweight and Hancock beat Moss of Manchester, in the final to win the 11-stone weight. Again in 1904, the amateurs appeared in public at a " catchweight " tournament which was won by W. C. Hoaten, now Major, the well-known rugger and tennis player and rifle shot. Other fine boxers in this tournament were J. Knighton, Gillies, Bob Luff, and "Blinder" Evans, an ex-Cardiff forward who played rugby for Rhodesia. Amateur bouts were of rare occurrence, however, but prize fights drew big houses.

There can be few sportsmen in the Colony who have not heard one or more of the exploits of that game fighter, Piet Steyn, who flourished in the decade before the Great War. He would fight anybody and numerous boxers, including several South African champions, were matched against the popular Piet who won the majority of his fights. One of his first encounters was with Barnard of Selukwe who, though the loser, gave Steyn a bad time. In 1902, Esdale and Steyn fought a great draw in the Market Hall. On another occasion Piet fought ' Spider " Kelly all round the ring, then out of it, and finally chased him down the street! Steyn also fought in a bare-knuckle contest against Clay of Australia. It went to 30 or 40 rounds when each lay on the ground unable to continue from sheer exhaustion. The result was a draw and the men spent several weeks in bed recovering.

Early boxing promoters were Bob Climber and Harry Stodel. They were instrumental in getting engagements in Rhodesia for Alf Barnard, the Cast-Iron Jew, Neil Thomson, brother of Lachie Thomson, the Scottish champion, and Jimmy Walker, the South African champion who fought and beat Piet Steyn. Neil Thomson was billed to fight for a big purse in Salisbury, but his opponent failed to turn up. As there was a full house and it was known that Stodel the promoter had a boxing reputation, he was approached to fill the gap and he sportingly agreed. Naturally there was no decision, but the spectators saw no exhibition bout, for it was the " real Mac-Kay " that went the full distance. Stodel opened a school of boxing in Bulawayo and instructed many pupils. His son, who was in Bulawayo in 1933, was also a good boxer. Stodel was once refereeing a match in Bulawayo between two burly policemen who went at it hammer and tongs. At the end of the fourth round one of the boxers was completely out in his corner, and none of the usual restoratives could bring him round. The seconds were crowding round him so that his opponent was not aware of his condition, and there was great amazement when the conscious policeman protested that his opponent was too good for him and refused to continue the fight. Consequently the man who was out got the verdict, although it was fully five minutes before he came round sufficiently to realise that he had won !

In 1911, the famous Jack Lalor came to Rhodesia and fought Piet Steyn. In the third round during a clinch, Steyn bit a piece out of Lalor's shoulder. The champion appealed to the referee, Sam Lewis, who, however, ordered the men to box on. Soon afterwards Steyn was seen going through the air like a comet, no doubt seeing many stars on his way, and that was the end of that fight. Lalor had several fights here and would sometimes take on two and three opponents in an evening. Against " Fireman " Anderson the champion went into the ring with a boil on his neck. The house was crowded and the ringside seats cost two guineas. At the opening of the first round the boxers clinched and Anderson pressed his glove on Lalor's tender spot. Jack drew back, feinted with his left and brought up his right. That was on Saturday night at 9.30, and the fireman only came to next morning at 11 o'clock. Fighting on the same programme that night was Stanley Perry (now Inspector Perry of the C.I.D.), who met Frank Lethaby in what was described as the most appreciated item on the programme. Perry won on points and both men met again on the night that Harry Price drew with Fireman George Anderson over 20 rounds. Perry again won on points and as a result, efforts were made to match him against Piet Steyn for the middleweight championship, but as such a fight meant the loss of his amateur status, Perry was prevailed upon not to fight. The only man here who extended Lalor was Harry Price of Salisbury, whom Lalor beat on points. Price then went overseas and met with a sad end. While boxing

Johnny Basham, the British welterweight champion, Price was knocked down, and his head striking the floor, he never regained consciousness.

One of the cleverest boxers who came to this country was Fred Buckland. As an amateur he had won several competitions in England and on coming to Africa won two more. He then turned professional and after successful tours in England, Australia, the United States and on the Continent, Buckland

Fred Buckland.

R. S. Perry.

settled in Salisbury. He only lost two fights in Rhodesia—one against Harry Price and the other against Piet Steyn. After the Armistice, in 1918, when Buckland was returning to Rhodesia, he was informed in Johannesburg that he was still the holder of the lightweight championship of South Africa, a title he had held for 15 years. He was offered a substantial sum to defend his title, but refused as he was then long past his prime. For many years Buckland coached the schoolboys in Salisbury.

In a fight between Buckland and Billy Fairclough the latter, a splendid boxer, the referee in explaining the conditions to the two men said: "Do you want me to take the knock-out?" and they both replied, "Yes, if one happens." What Teddy Edwards wanted to know was whether he should count the second of grace allowed if either was knocked down. Well, during one mix-up Buckland lashed out at Fairclough and just at that moment the referee's head intervened and he got the blow on the end of his nose. If it had been a couple of inches lower he *would* have taken the knock-out!

Other good boxers were G. A. ("Hacker") Matthews who started the first boxing club in Rhodesia, at Que Que, and trained Jack Ashwin to win the South African middle-weight title; a fine heavyweight in Sergeant Jones, who gave a number of exhibitions; Corporal Anderson, Jim Chapman, Watty Austin, B. Pedder, Mike Williams, Ted Edwards of Wales and Hommell, a coloured boxer. Perhaps the best known was Pat Kealy, an amateur. He never worried if an opponent was heavier and could be frequently seen out-weighed, but always smiling and moving in to his opponent for more. Pat did a lot of good work by coaching in the Police and the schools.

Amateur boxing was first established on a firm basis when the big schools were opened around 1910. Inter-school boxing tournaments are held annually for the floating trophy presented by that fine sportsman, Dr. E. H. Strong, and these contests have revealed some splendid talent in the Colony. St. George's School turned out a long list of good boxers under the training of Mr. W. P. T. Hancock, and during his ten years with them the school lost the Strong Cup only once. For many years that popular sportsman G .W. Ledeboer did much good work for the sport at Milton School.

In recent years there have been very few professional boxers in Rhodesia. Prominent among the amateurs are Sergeant R. Bonnett of the Police, Ted Charsley, Jock Play-ford, the long distance runner, E. Palmer, the five brothers Leach, especially the older three, E. C. Arnold, the brothers Dunlop, Jack Livingston of Umtali, A. E. Walters, the popular "Smiler" Auret of the Police, M. D. McCorkindale, brother of the famous South African boxer, Constable I. P. Potgieter, Rhodesian champion since 1929 and holder of the S.A. heavyweight championship in 1934, J. Ashwin, one of the finest boxers Rhodesia has produced, who won the middle-weight title of South Africa in 1921, the brothers Hyde, W.

G. Walton, H. D. Viljoen, A. Nimmo, L. O'Linn, R. T. Lapham who is now a highly successful professional in the North, A. Calder, L. E. Palmer and N. A. S. Hoffman.

N. A. S. Hoffman was lightweight champion of the Cape Colony in 1909. In March, 1911, he defeated Sam Linsky, the Johannesburg champion in Johannesburg and in September of the same year beat A. McLean, the Transvaal champion, in Germiston. In 1920 and 1921 Hoffman won the heavyweight championship of Rhodesia.

In 1932 Hoffman laid claim to a world's skipping record. Before a committee and a large crowd of spectators he beat the South African record of 4,000 skips per hour. In his first attempt he did 7,862 consecutive skips in sixty-one and a half minutes. The next night, with an average of 132 skips per minute, he did 10,040 in 76 minutes. On the third night he improved on his previous figures, skipping at an average rate of just over 140 per minute and making 8,450 skips in one hour exact.

N. A. S. Hoffman.   E. Charsley.

RHODESIA v. TRANSVAAL, 1931.

Standing:

G. Stumke,

M. McCorkindale,

R. Smith,

R. Emes.

Sitting:

T. Duff,

J. Willing,
(Chairman
M.A.B.A.),

A. W. Crombie
(Hon. Sec.,
M.A.B.A.),

Missing:

I. P. Potgieter.

In 1928 the Witwatersrand University sent up a team of boxers that met first Mashonaland and then Matabeleland. In the Salisbury Drill Hall a large and enthusiastic crowd witnessed one of the best boxing tournaments ever staged in Rhodesia. The meeting ended in a draw, four wins each. The tournament in Bulawayo was also a success. Most of Matabeleland's defeats were by narrow margins, and there were some very interesting bouts. Of the local men the outstanding boxer was Bissett. The visitors won four of the seven contests.

In 1930 a team of Pretoria junior boxers, all weights, and two senior boxers fought against Matabeleland in Bulawayo. A fine exhibition of boxing was seen in which Matabeleland won nine fights to their opponents' four. Perry and Ledeboer of Matabeleland gave convincing displays and clearly demonstrated their superiority. In most of the fights, however, the verdicts were very close.

In 1931 a Transvaal team came up and boxed in Salisbury and Bulawayo. In the Capital Rhodesia's only victory in five contests was V. Hyde's winning of the lightweight. He also won the cup for the best boxer of the tournament. In Bulawayo the visitors won four of the six contests, Stumke and Smith being the only local winners. Transvaal were the stronger team and, particularly as regards speed, they taught the Rhodesians some valuable lessons.

Whenever Rhodesians have gone outside the Colony's borders they have given a good account of themselves. In 1920 J. C. Auret (welter), E. Charsley (feather) and Cpl. Dyer (middle) boxed in the S.A. Championships and Olympic trials and though none got beyond the first round, their boxing called forth good comment from the critics.

In 1921 J. Ashwin (middles), Jordan (welter) and Palmer (fly) went down to the S.A. Championships, where Ashwin won his weight after giving some fine displays. The two other Rhodesians gave good accounts of themselves. In 1928 C. Bissett and Len Hall went to Amsterdam for the Olympic Games and both boxers earned warm praise for their displays. Bissett defeated Orellana, the sturdy Mexican, and was then narrowly beaten on points by Orlandi (Italy), the ultimate winner of the lightweight division, while Hall did well against Usuda, the Japanese welterweight.

In December, 1929, a team of Rhodesian boxers fought in Johannesburg against two Transvaal teams. In the first match the Rhodesian heavyweight, I. P. Potgieter, put out his man in the second round while C. Bissett, lightweight, was far

RHODESIAN TEAM ON THE RAND, 1929.

H. D. Viljoen, V. Hyde, C. Bissett, M. D. McCorkindale, A. E. Walters, I. P. Potgieter.

too good for the Pretoria champion. In the middles, M. Mc-
Corkindale drew with the Transvaal champion after a thrilling
contest. A. E. Walters lost by only a small margin to the
S.A. Olympic light-heavyweight, but the other two Rhodesians
were well beaten. The home team thus won by three matches
to two. In the second series, against a different team, Rhodesia won four of the six bouts. Potgieter again caused a sensation by beating the Transvaal champion. Bissett also impressed
the Rand sportsmen by beating the ex-Scottish welterweight
champion. McCorkindale won decisively and Walters also
won, despite the fact that he broke his arm during the fight and
finished using only his left. V. Hyde (lightweight) and H. D.
Viljoen (bantam) again gave good accounts of themselves but
were out-pointed.

Four Rhodesian boxers fought in the S.A. Championships
in 1931. R. Smith (welter), beat M. Basson of East Rand on
points; scored a spectacular knock-out in his fight against C.
Carroll of Germiston, and then lost in the semi-final. V. Hyde
(light), after beating O'Rell of Kimberley was well beaten by
Laurie Stevens but was a game loser. G. Stumke won a close
fight in the lightweights, but was stopped by Loubscher, a hard
hitting ex-bantam champion. T. E. Duff (fly) lost to Dunn of
Witbank.

In 1934 W. Fulton represented Rhodesia at the Empire
Games and did remarkably well in the featherweight class.
He beat McGregor (Scotland) in the first round; lost by a
narrow margin in the semi-final to Catterall (South Africa), the
winner of the division, and then beat Tomlinson (Canada) in
the fight-off for third place.

The first attempt to control boxing in Rhodesia was made
in Bulawayo in 1911, and the Association organised national
championships up to the middle of 1914. During the war, as
with all other sports in the Colony, there were no senior
competitions and the first enterprising move after the war was
made by Capt. W. C. Hoaten who, in Bulawayo, in company
with several other amateur boxing enthusiasts, formed the Rhodesian Amateur Boxing Association which affiliated to the
South African Amateur Boxing Association. In 1923 the
Mashonaland Amateur Boxing Association was formed in
Salisbury and in 1925 a new Rhodesia Amateur Boxing Association was formed with headquarters in Salisbury.

The defunct body in Bulawayo was resurrected in 1927
mainly through the efforts of R. S. Perry and with its affilia-

tion to the Rhodesian Association, annual championship tournaments were introduced. Strained relations between the two Associations led to disunion a few years ago, but since 1932, with the formation of a Matabeleland Association and a Mashonaland Association, with a Rhodesian Board of Control, matters have worked very satisfactorily.

Some of those who have been responsible for the encouragement of amateur boxing in Rhodesia are Lieut.-Colonel T. Baker, E.D., a useful boxer in his day, Major W. C. Hoaten, Major H. Harnell, J. Symmonds, J. W. Willing, Chairman of the Matabeleland Amateur Boxing Association, Major C. V. Bowles, A. W. Crombie, Hon. Secretary of the Matabeleland Association and a very useful boxer himself, R. S. Perry, Edgar Jenkins, at one time English amateur bantamweight champion, C. Rogers and Neale Taylor.

The following Rhodesians have earned the merit certificates issued by the South African National Amateur Boxing Association : —

Referees: E. Jenkins, J. Symmonds, Neale Taylor and C. Rogers.

Judges: N. C. Innes Baillie, H. G. Bell, A. W. Crombie, H. J. L. Dolan, C. Rogers, J. Willing, Major W. C. Hoaten, J. Knighton and W. P. T. Hancock.

THE WITWATERSRAND UNIVERSITY VISIT, 1928.
AT SALISBURY.

Weight.	University.	Mashonaland.
Bantam	K. Tatz —lost to	S. Hyde.
Feather	A. D. Young —beat	R. Joss.
Light	A. Guard—lost to	H. G. Walton.
	G. Rankin—lost to	V. Hyde.
Welter	O. Schultz—beat	A. Hyde (K.O.).
Middle	G. Dreosti—beat	L. H. Lewis (T.K.O.).
Lightheavy	J. Swartz—lost to	A. E. Walters (K.O.).
Heavy	V. Liebrandt—beat	H. G. Beynon.

IN BULAWAYO.

Weight.	University.	Matabeleland.
Bantam	K. Tatz —lost to	H. Viljoen.
Feather	A. D. Young—beat	A. W. Crombie.
Light	G. Rankin—lost to	C. Bissett (T.K.O.).
Welter	O. Schultz —beat	W. Weight (K.O.).
Middle	G. Dreosti—beat	F. Wolhuter.
Lightheavy	O. Schultz—beat	R. Emes.
Heavy	V. Liebrandt—lost to	A. E. Walters.

THE PRETORIA TEAM'S VISIT, 1930, AT BULAWAYO.
Juniors.

Weight.	Pretoria.	Matabeleland.
Midge	L. Hunter —lost to	W. Treger.
	C. Sagantas —beat	L. Sperring.
Welter	M. G. Smith —lost to	J. van Blerk.
Paper	D. van Vuuren —beat	K. Thal.

Light .... I. Wolson —lost to .... J. Meltzer.
Fly .... N. Hunter —beat .... J. Hall.
Bantam .... R. Kinsella —lost to .... S. Gruber.
Feather .... L. Groce —lost to .... H. Baron.
Middle .... J. O'Connoll —lost to .... G. S. Perry.
Lightheavy .... J. Smith —lost to .... N. Bibra.
Heavy .... H. van der Merwe —lost to .... N. Ledeboer.

Seniors.

Welter .... C. A. Bond —beat .... L. Krell.
Middle .... R. Calemborne —lost to ...... M. D. McCorkindale.

THE TRANSVAAL VISIT, 1931.

In Salisbury.

Weight.	Transvaal.	Rhodesia.
Bantam	A. J. Harvey —beat	A. Calder (K.O.).
Light	W. Sexton —lost to	V. Hyde.
Welter	E. James —beat	H. Hutson.
Lightheavy	T. Porter —beat	J. B. Scott.
Heavy	J. Smit —beat	I. P. Potgieter.

In Bulawayo.

Bantam	A. J. Harvey —beat	T. E. Duff.
Light	W. Sexton —lost to	G. Stumke.
Welter	E. James —lost to	R. Smith.
Middle	E. Pierce —beat	M. D. McCorkindale.
Lightheavy	T. Porter —beat	R. Emes.
Heavy	J. Smit —beat	I. P. Potgieter.

WINNERS OF RHODESIAN CHAMPIONSHIPS.

1920—O. Brown (Bantam), E. Charsley (Feather), C. E. G. Russell (Light), J. C. Auret (Welter), J. Ashwin (Middle), N. A. S. Hoffman (Heavy).

1921—E. J. Palmer (Fly), L. O'Linn (Bantam), Wilson (Feather), E. Charsley (Light), Jordan (Welter), J. Ashwin (Middle), N. A. S. Hoffman (Heavy).

1922—L. O'Linn (Bantam), J. M. Butler (Feather), E. Charsley (Light), B. A. Johnstone (Welter), A. Pickup (Middle), A. Pickup (Heavy).

1923—L. O'Linn (Bantam), Smith (Feather), Leach (Light).

1925—W. G. Walton (Bantam), E. J. Palmer (Feather), A. Hyde (Light), C. V. King (Welter), J. C. Auret (Middle), A. E. Walters (Heavy).

1926—R. M. Crombie (Bantam), W. G. Walton (Feather), A. Hyde (Light), E. C. Arnold (Welter), R. T. Lapham (Middle), A. E. Walters (Heavy).

1927—A. Hyde (Light), L. H. Lewis (Middle), A. E. Walters (Heavy).

1929—A. Calder (Bantam), S. Collins (Feather), V. Hyde (Light), W. Mackinley (Welter), F. C. Perry (Middle), J. Scott (Lightheavy), I. P. Potgieter (Heavy).

1930—T. E. Duff (Fly), A. Calder (Bantam), G. Marshall (Feather), V. Hyde (Light), R. Smith (Welter), M. D. McCorkindale (Middle), R. Emes (Lightheavy), I. P. Potgieter (Heavy).

1933—A. Grieff (Fly), A. Duff (Bantam), V. Edwards (Feather), L. E. Palmer (Light), H. Hutson (Welter), A. Nimmo (Middle), P. Goosen (Lightheavy), I. P. Potgieter (Heavy).

1934—C. Sherwood (Bantam), J. B. Playford (Feather), V. Hyde (Light), L. E. Palmer (Welter), A. Nimmo (Middle), C .R. Lewis (Lightheavy), I. P. Potgieter (Heavy).

1935—R. Payne (Fly), H. Oberholster (Bantam), C. D. Sherwood (Feather), W. Fulton (Light), L. E. Palmer (Welter), A. Nimmo (Middle).

Rhodesia's First Bowling Green, Bulawayo.

BOWLS

T HE pioneer club in Rhodesia—and incidentally the fourth oldest club in South Africa—is the Bulawayo Bowling Club, which was brought into existence chiefly through the efforts of John Langton, the Town Engineer, and Dr. J. W. Wilson. The first meeting was held in the Grand Hotel on June 3, 1899, and was attended by Dr. J. W. Wilson (Chairman), and Messrs. Kiddy, J. A. Robertson, Craggs, Zeederberg, McMillan, F. Scott, B. Jagger, A. Wiles, Raymer, Laughton and Gill. At a subsequent meeting there were, in addition, Messrs. C. R. Edmonds, R. M. Nairn, J. Wightman, G. Stewart and J. H. Ayling. The Boer War was then raging and the green in the North Park was not opened until 1902. The progress made was most gratifying and the game commanded a large following.

In Umtali the first game of bowls was played in the Park. George Lamb, now of Eskbank, Salisbury, and Andrew Howat, were among the players. Conditions were, however, very primitive and it was more than a quarter of a century later that the first real green was laid down by the Umtali Railway Recreation Club.

Meanwhile, in Bulawayo, league and other competitions were played with great enthusiasm and a high standard was attained. The first club champion, 1902, was C. R. Edmonds. In 1907 and 1908 the title was held by J. Main, who was again champion for the four years 1911 to 1914. The first women's championship was in 1921, won by Miss Cowden. To-day there are a large number of very keen women participants.

For over twenty years the Bulawayo Club nursed the game, and then in the next decade bowls really "caught on" in the Colony. Greens were opened in many centres and bowls has now taken its proper place among Rhodesian sports.

In 1923 the Railway Recreation Club, Bulawayo, put down its first green. F. O. John was the moving spirit, supported by J. Denyer, first Chairman of the bowls section, A. E. Clegg, first club champion, and W. Pickard, who in his time acted in a secretarial capacity for more sporting bodies in Bulawayo than anyone else.

THE BRITISH INTERNATIONAL AND BULAWAYO CLUB TEAMS, 1922.

In 1925, the Gwelo bowling green was opened by the Mayor, Major W. Hurrell, a pioneer. R. Barnes was the club's first president, with A. E. Thorne as secretary. F. G. Shaw took a keen interest in laying the foundations of the game and the green in the Midlands and among many other enthusiasts is J. Antoniadis, who has supported most sports in Gwelo.

In 1926 the Salisbury bowling greens were opened and two years later the Salisbury Raylton Club formed a bowls section. The game is played with great enthusiasm in the capital and W. M. Coull has done much useful work. Others who have worked for the game as well as playing for it are A. W. Stodart, P. McKie, J. Irvine, H. S. Taylor, G. Jackman, who was runner-up in the Rhodesian singles this year, C. F. Walton, G. W. Carter, R. B. Mitchell, and A. J. Hodgkinson.

In recent years greens have been opened all over the country—at Que Que (1928), Umtali (1929), Wankie (1931), and Gatooma, Nkana, Luanshya and Broken Hill in 1932. To-day there are nearly thirty greens in the Colony, which is sufficient evidence of the progress and the popularity of bowls. That bowling is not "an old man's game" is borne out by the composition of the rinks that take part in the annual tournament where one finds a judicious blending of old and young. Nor is the game confined to men, for each club has its women's section, and the women's Rhodesian championship events each year are very keenly contested by a large number of competitors whose play is of a high order.

In November, 1922, a British team of international bowlers played two matches against the Bulawayo bowling club. In the first game the visitors won three of the four rinks. The only local victory was won by Cain's team, which beat the four skipped by A. J. Stacey by 19 shots to 17. Cain was in brilliant form. Cowden's team lost by only three shots, but on the other two rinks the British team won easily, although Peter Smith and Tod Suttie both played splendid games.

In the second match the Britishers won all four rinks and beat Bulawayo by 60 shots. The closest game was between Cain's and McLeod's teams, which went to the visitors by a margin of two shots. Cain's team led 7—6 at the ninth end, but were two down, 9—11, at the twelfth. By the fifteenth they led again, 13—12. The three subsequent heads saw the visitors lead by a point, 15—14, and after a great tussle the Britishers finally won 17—15.

Tod Suttie's team led 7—1 after the first three ends, but this opening form did not last and at the sixth end the visitors were two points ahead. At the fifteenth head the Britishers registered 9 and took their total to 27 against the locals' 10. The latter finished well, but the match went to the Britishers, 28—16.

On the other two rinks the Bulawayo teams were well beaten.

The first team of bowlers to visit Rhodesia from the Union was sent by the Central Bowling Association of South Africa in 1926 and consisted of 30 men and 14 women from Kimberley and the Orange Free State. This was the largest number of players of any one sport that had visited the Colony. The visitors played six matches, of which four were won by the local clubs. Against a Rhodesian team the C.B.A. lost by 52 shots, Rhodesia winning four of the six rinks and three of these by a large margin. Cowden's team was in tip-top form. They had a splendid lead in Drummond and won 32—7. Robley's team also won easily, 34—17, and Cain's quartette played in great style to win 26—10. The fourth Rhodesian victory was by one shot, Griffiths' team winning 19—18. The Gwelo team, skipped by Hamilton, did well to lose by only 4 shots. The C.B.A. visit did the game a great deal of good as well as showing that bowls in the Colony was at a high standard.

Within a few weeks of the C.B.A. visit a team representing the Pretoria Railway Bowling Club played a series of matches against the two Bulawayo Clubs. The visitors' men beat Raylton twice by narrow margins and drew twice with Bulawayo, while the visiting women players beat the Raylton women twice and the Bulawayo women once. On the other hand, the Bulawayo Club won four men's and one women's match, and Raylton men registered one win by 16 shots. Taken all round, the play of the local bowlers was far superior to that of the visitors.

A great event for trundlers was the visit in 1929 of the British Bowling Team, which played three matches in Bulawayo. In the first, against Raylton, the visitors won five of the six rinks. Bradley was outstanding and his team registered the only win, 20—16. Vallance's team staged a great recovery, for after being 11 down they pulled up until the score stood at 22 all, the victory eventually going to the visitors by one shot. The Bulawayo Club beat the Britishers by only four shots, 111—107. The decision was in doubt until

the last wood of the last end of the last rink. Britain won
three of the six rinks, one being drawn. In the final match,
Britain v. Rhodesia, the latter won three of the five rinks and
beat Britain by 20 shots, 107 to 87. R. Bradley (skip) gained
the distinction of winning by the greatest margin of the
Rhodesian tour, 18 shots. He and his colleagues played a great
game. Another feature was the recovery of Clegg's team
which, after being 8 down at the 11th end, went on to win
the match 22—15. The victory was largely due to Vallance's
fine play as lead for Clegg. Cain's team won by one shot,
22—21, while Dugmore's rink lost by the same margin, the
score being 19—20. The performances of the clubs' and the
Rhodesian teams against the British players were really
splendid, and as the losers included numerous famous bowlers,
the local achievements prove conclusively that the standard of
play here is indeed high.

In 1931 a strong Kimberley team played in Bulawayo,
Salisbury, Gwelo and Que Que. The Bulawayo Club won
on five rinks out of six, and on the women's green the home
club was also victorious, while the Bulawayo Raylton Club
won one and drew one of the six men's rinks and lost the
women's match. Then the visitors played a combined Bulawayo team which won three of the six rinks and took the
match by a narrow margin of only four shots. The Kimberley
players were given some close games in the other centres,
but they won all with the exception of one, when their
women representatives lost to the Salisbury women. The
visitors presented to the Rhodesia Bowling Association a cup
to be called the Pioneer Cup. In making the presentation
it was remarked that the three men buried at Matopos and
also many of the Pioneers came from Kimberley and the
trophy was to be a link between Kimberley and Rhodesia.

The Rhodesia Bowling Association, formed fifteen years
ago, controls bowls throughout the Colony. The first President of the Association was J. Tod Suttie, who was always
keen to support the cause and give advice, and with his death
the game lost a valuable helper and energetic worker.
Another leading light is F. E. Briers, who held the office
of treasurer for several years. Others who have done good
work are Messrs. S. Philip, J. H. Ayling, J. Cowden, M.P.,
and R. E. Bayliss, while R. A. Cain, for many years honorary
secretary, has been the prompting spirit and guiding star in
all matters relating to the game. For sixteen years he has
been the bowls correspondent of "The Bulawayo Chronicle,"

writing under the pen-name "Trundler." He was the first Rhodesian bowls champion.

The tournaments of the Rhodesia Bowling Association are an annual fixture and have been staged since 1924 at Bulawayo, Salisbury, Gwelo and Umtali. It has been the custom to hold these tournaments at Easter, with as many as 24 men's and 8 women's rinks participating. In addition to the Rhodesian tournaments, bowlers in Southern Rhodesia are entitled, through affiliation with the South African Bowling Association, to participate in the annual tournaments

R. A. Cain.

R. E. Bayliss.

in the Union. The Bulawayo Club has been represented at these tournaments since 1919, whilst the Bulawayo Raylton Club enjoyed its first representation at the Kimberley tournament in 1928. The S.A.B.A. meetings cater for an average of about 120 teams gathered from all corners of the Union, and it speaks well for the ability of the members of the teams representing the two Bulawayo clubs when it is said that both teams have been within an ace of winning their particular sections on several occasions . In 1933 the Bulawayo team was actually successful in winning its section at Johannesburg, a feat of which the club must be justly proud. While not being able to emulate it sister club in the matter of certificates of merit, the Raylton (Bulawayo) Club has enjoyed many creditable victories in the South, some of its notable victims being the Johannesburg Wanderers, Maritzburg Railways and Germiston.

In 1926, J. H. Ayling and F. E. Briers were selected in the S.A. Bowling team that toured Britain.

The first and only team, so far, to represent Rhodesia in an Empire bowling tournament competed at the British Empire Games in England in 1934. The Rhodesian team consisted of A. W. Stodart, J. Houston, C. E. Harrison, H. S. Taylor, G. Baker, G. Evans and G. D. Baxter. There were altogether ten Empire countries in competition.

At the annual general meeting of the Rhodesia Bowling Association at Salisbury in March, 1935, a majority decided to discontinue affiliation with the South African Bowling Association. Feeling in Matabeleland, however, is against this decision and a move is on foot for the formation of a Matabeleland Association to affiliate with the South African Bowling Association direct, with the object of preserving Bulawayo's right to send teams to the annual South African tournament, to share in the visits of overseas teams and to protect Rhodesia's chances of one day staging the South African tournament in this Colony.

THE BRITISH INTERNATIONAL BOWLERS, 1922.

Beat Bulawayo .... 91 — 50
Beat Bulawayo .... 112 — 52

British Internationals: Sir Wm. Don, D. Smallwood, J. Edney, J McLeod (s); I. Thomas, R. Husband, J. Lothian, A. J. Stacey (s); E. H. Pelling, W. Clarke, R. Lawson, A. Malcolm (s); J. Inglis, J. Rice, J. Somerville, W. Smith (s). For the second match D. A. Sutherland and W. Minto replaced W. Smith and J. Lothian respectively.

Bulawayo: P. Smith, A. Keay, J. Webb, J. H. Ayling (s); J. Waterworth, W. McNair, S. Philip, R. A. Cain (s); F. E. Briers, D. Welsh, J. Tod Suttie, T. W. Davey (s); P. Rutherford, J. Gibb, D. Drummond, J. Cowden (s). F. C. Dugmore replaced P. Smith in the second match.

THE CENTRAL BOWLING ASSOCIATION'S VISIT, 1926.

	Men.		Women.	
	C.B.A.	Byo.	C.B.A.	Byo.
v. Bulawayo Club	117	136	36	45
v. Raylton Club	116	112	21	32
v. Combined Bulawayo	106	118	25	30
v. Rhodesia	105	157		
v. Gwelo	C.B.A. won by 25 shots.			
v. Callies (Bulawayo)	C.B.A. won by 27 shots.			

C.B.A.: A. Neale, C. Hogley, J. McKellar, R. Eason, J. Beith, A. Espinasse, A. Laughton, B. P. Jones, R. van Blerk, W. McCall, W. W. Robbins, C. Flockhart, D. Thomson, T. W. McKenzie, S. D. C. Murray, J. B. Dale, A. W. Rolfe, R. Cairncross, J. A. Kruger, L. B. Foster, T. R. Cooke, A. Mason, D. McKay, A. Hove, J. McDonald, H. Gouldie, W. Gouldie, J. Ferguson, W. Gibb, T. Hill, and Mrs. Laughton, Mrs. Robbins, Mrs. Reid. Mrs. Flockhart, Mrs. van Aardt, Mrs. Cairncross, Mrs. Kruger, Mrs. Cooke, Mrs. Foster, Mrs. McCall, Mrs. Thomson, Mrs. McKenzie, Mrs. Dale, and Mrs. Murray.

Bulawayo Club: R. A. Cain (s), F. C. Dugmore, J. Moss, J. Atherton, J. Cowden (s), T. W. Davey, G. Vallance, D. Drummond, A. Keay (s), S. Philip, Reid, Rutherford, Bradley (s), Baker, Leather, A. E. Marris, Waterworth (s), R. E. Pallister, Peard, Granger, Gibb (s), Houston, Cooper, McNair, and Mrs. Griffith (s), Mrs. Dickson, Mrs. Vallance, Mrs. Hounsome, Mrs. Downing (s), Mrs. Batwell, Mrs. Studholme, Mrs. Leather.

Raylton: J. Robley (s), Bradley, Cowell, R. Gloak, A. E. Clegg (s), F. O. John, Evans, Dewar, Smith (s), F. Stripp, T. W. Osterloh, McDougall, F. Barnett (s), Childes, Wilson, R. H. Rayne, Griffith (s), C. F. Burgoyne, Crittall, N. Denyer, C. Myles (s), W. Pickard, Pugh, Robson, and Mrs. Wright (s), Mrs. Clegg, Mrs. Charlton, Mrs. Wilson and Mrs. Childe (s).

Combined Bulawayo: Bradley (s), J. Gibb, Houston, A. Keay, R. A. Cain (s), F. C. Dugmore, S. Philip, J. Atherton, J. Robley (s), Bradley, Robson, T. W. Osterloh, Griffith (s), Crittall, F. Barnett, Smith, J. Cowden (s), T. W. Davey, G. Vallance, A. E. Marris, A. E. Clegg, Inglis, F. O. John, Wilson, and Mrs. Griffith.

Rhodesia: W. A. Hamilton (s), R. Barnes, Capt. H. Harnell, W. H. Williams, A. E. Clegg (s), J. E. Cooper, S. Philip, R. D. Gloak, A. Griffith (s), A. Crittall F. Barnett, P. Smith, J. Cowden (s), T. W. Davey, G. Vallance, D. Drummond, J. Robley (s), R. Bradley, F. O. John, C. Myles, R. A. Cain (s), F. C. Dugmore, J. Moss, J. Atherton.

Callies: J. Cowden (s), G. Vallance, Major R. Gordon, C. Donaldson, A. Keay (s), W. McNair, W. Dunbar, D. Welsh, S. Philip (s), J. Houston, D. MacGillivray, G. Reid, P. Smith (s), R. Sinclair, J. Bowie, T. Forbes, J. Gibb (s), J. Wightman, W. Cunningham, C. Robb, and Mrs. Houston, Mrs. Vallance, Mrs. Hounsome and Mrs. Batwell.

Major W. Hurrell   H. R. Barbour
(Gwelo).   (Bulawayo).
Two Sporting Mayors.

Gwelo: Van Heerden, Franceys, Hartley, Macdonald (s), Gilbert, Chivers, Jackman, Morris (s), N. Mitchell, Daws, Shaw, Thorn (s), Windsor, Harrison, D. Mitchell, H. Harnell (s), Williams, Ferguson, Gordon, Hamilton (s), Mrs. Jackman, Mrs. Morris, Mrs. McIntosh, Mrs. Barnes (s).

PRETORIA RAILWAY BOWLING CLUB'S VISIT, 1926.

	Men.		Women.	
	Pret.	Byo.	Pret.	Byo.
v. Bulawayo Club	117	143	33	35
v. Raylton Club	59	66	52	28

Pretoria: Shevill, Rutherford, Noblett, Johnstone, Ellis, Hunt Howe, Goodwin, and Mrs. Shevill, Mrs. Rutherford, Mrs. Noblett, Mrs. Johnstone and Mrs. Ellis.

Bulawayo Club: R. A. Cain (s), F. C. Dugmore, T. W. Davey, J. Atherton, J. Cowden (s), D. Drummond, S. Philip, G. Vallance, Gibb (s), McNair, Perry, Cooper, Bradley (s), Pallister, Ginsberg, Granger, J. Moss, and Mrs. Griffith, Mrs. Childes, Mrs. Cowell, Mrs. Cottrell, Mrs. Downing, Mrs. Dickson.

Raylton Club: J. Robley (s), R. Bradley, A. E. Clegg, Griffith. Smith (s), F. O. John, W. Pickard, T. W. Osterloh, Mrs. Wright (s), Miss Charsley, Mrs. Dark, Mrs. Dodd.

BRITISH BOWLERS' VISIT, 1929.

```
Beat Raylton ...... ...... ...... ...... ...... ......   123 — 104
Lost to Bulawayo ...... ...... ...... ...... ......     107 — 111
Lost to Rhodesia ...... ...... ...... ...... ......      87 — 107
```

Britain: Mair (s), Reekie, Fleming, Frame, Binns (s), Eddy, Mathieson, Rowatt, Chapman (s), Malcolm, Hayward, Steel, McSally (s), Baines, Fenton, Arthur, Hawkins (s), Leeson, Jones, W. M. Grice, Watson (s), Day, Scott, Paul.

Raylton: Osterloh, Widdop, W. Pickard, A. E. Clegg (s), Roberts, S. Evans, F. D. Hockin, Griffiths (s), Nunn (s), Robson, Atherton, Denyer (s), Slater, R. Lumsden, R. Rayne, Bradley (s), T. W. Winter, McDougall, F. O. John, C. Myles (s), Harney, A. Edwards, C. H. Steel, G. Vallance (s).

Bulawayo Club: Johnson, Keay, H. Charles, R. A. Cain (s) Bowie, Payne, J. Cowden, F. C. Dugmore (s), Leather, Rouse, J. H. Ayling, Bradley, Rutherford, Sinclair, Davey, Drummond (s), Cooper, Huston, Gibb, Baker (s), Marris, Nicholson, McGarry, F. E. Briers (s).

Rhodesia: A. E. Marris, F. O. John, F. E. Briers, R. A. Cain (s), T. W. Osterloh, J. Atherton, G. Vallance, A. E. Clegg, C. Slater. R. H. Rayne, J. Denyer, R. Bradley (s), G. Baker, D. Drummond, M. McGarry, F. C. Dugmore (s), T. W. Winter, E. A. Payne, C. Myles, S. Bradley (s).

THE KIMBERLEY BOWLERS' VISIT, 1931.

	Kimberley.	Opponents.
v. Bulawayo Club	98	153
v. Bulawayo Raylton Club	151	136
v. Combined Bulawayo Clubs	119	123
v. Gwelo	Kimberley won by a few shots.	
v. Salisbury	151	122
v. Salisbury	154	138
v. Que Que	107	90

Kimberley: Oakley, Dengate, Silson, Delanely, Hutchinson, de Melker, Elliott, Scott, Irons, Alexander, Sneddon, James, Milner, Peat, Anderson, Wood, Mason, Ferraris, Watkins, de Smidt, Pearson, Sullivan, Bodley, Hermiston, J. Ogg, Kearns, Ferguson, Brand, Abrahams, and Mrs. Wooding, Mrs. Oakley, Mrs. Silson, and Mrs. Starling.

Opening of Raylton Bowling Green by Lt.-Col. C. F. Birney, D.S.O., December, 1923, under the distinguished patronage of H.E. the Governor, Sir John Chancellor, and Lady Chancellor.

Bulawayo Club: T. W. Davey, Johnston, Perry, R. E. Bayliss, D. Drummond, F. E. Briers, Munford, Dodd, G. Baker, Leather, Keay, Harrison, Bradley, Houston, Granger, Beaufort, R. A. Cain, M. McGarry, Taylor, More, J. Cowden, J. Wightman, Cooper, A. E. Marris, and Mrs. Beaufort, Mrs. Harrison, Mrs. Richardson and Mrs. Spearpoint.

Raylton Club: A. E. Clegg, G. Vallance, Van Rensburg, Osterloh, Robley, Winter, Robson, McPherson, Smith, C. Myles, Wolstenholme, Evans, Slater, Griffiths, Roberts, Holton, Denyer, Proctor, Miles, Marshall, Bradley, F. O. John, Roberts, A. W. Whittington, and Mrs. Wright, Mrs. Clegg, Mrs. Thompson, Mrs. Bell.

Combined Bulawayo Clubs: Clegg, Robley, Vallance, Whittington, Baker, Cowden, Harrison, Leather, R. Bradley, Griffiths, R. Rayne, C. Slater, S. Bradley, F. E. Briers, Houston, Johnston, Denyer, Proctor, John, Winter, F. C. Dugmore, M. McGarry, Davey, Bayliss.

Gwelo: Antoniadis, Bradley, Jacobson, Simpson, Butcher, Stanford, Gilbert, Doley, A. Swan, Cran, J. Swan, MacDonald, Hopkins, Anderson, Bourne, Hill, Harrison, Pearson, Brooks, Williams, Jenkins, Evans, Baxter, Seaward, Mitchell, Chandler, Windsor, Furnell, Stirling, Garland, Mrs. Butcher, Mrs. Cran, Mrs. Brooks, Miss Horrocks.

Salisbury: W. Templeton, Fairchild, P. McKie, Coleman, C. F. Walton, Farquharson, J. R. Mitchell, Busschan, A. W. Stodart, Furnell, B. Thomson, R. L. Thomas, Stewart, F. H. Allen, H. S. Taylor, W. J. Turner, Kinsey, D. R. Cook, Calder, A. D. Shalovsky, G. J. Jackman, W. E. Gooding, J. R. Whitlow, W. Mackie, J. Maxwell, G. Priest, J. M. Coull, H. Pollard, A. Ringrose, J. Sutherland, J. Irvine, Auld, J. Anderson, and Mrs. Hodkinson, Mrs. J. Sutherland, Mrs. R. L. Thomas and Mrs. P. McKie.

Que Que: Butcher, S. C. Davey, Baker, Dooley, Delport, Abrahams, Boby, Fowler, Shaw, Edney, Hutchinson, Young, Friend, Williams, Molam, Anderson, and Mrs. Roselt, Mrs. Watkins, Mrs. Field, and Mrs. Connolly.

C. Slater.   J. M. Coull.

THE RHODESIAN TEAM AT THE EMPIRE GAMES, 1934.

G. Baker,
G. Evans,
G. W. Baxter,
J. Houston,
C. E. Harrison,
H. S. Taylor,
A. W. Stodart.

They are wearing
the Rhodesian
International
Colours.

THE EMPIRE GAMES, 1934.

Singles.

Baker (Rhodesia) beat Keys (New Zealand) 21—8; beat Walker (Australia) 21—19; lost to Wales 15—21; beat Hong Kong 21—4; lost to Scotland 9—21; lost to England 17—21; lost to Ireland 17—21; lost to South Africa 14—21; lost to Canada 10—21.

Pairs.

Evans and Baxter (Rhodesia) tied with Australia 17—17; lost to Wales 15—32; lost to Hong Kong 16—35; lost to Scotland 13—29; lost to England 16—25; beat N. Ireland 16—15; beat South Africa 27—18; lost to Canada 13—22.

Rinks.

Rhodesia (Houston, Harrison, Taylor, Stodart) lost to New Zealand 16—20; beat Australia 19—18; beat Wales 27—11; beat Hong Kong 22—18; lost to Scotland 13—29; lost to England 8—29; lost to Ireland 14—22; lost to South Africa 8—37; beat Canada 22—16. Rhodesia's logs and positions in the final placings were:—

	P.	W.	L.	D.	F.	A.	Pts.	Pos.
Singles	9	3	6	0	145	157	6	8
Pairs	9	2	6	1	133	193	5	7
Rinks	9	3	5	1	149	194	7	7

RHODESIAN CHAMPIONSHIPS.

Men's Rink Championship—Imperial Cup.

1924—**Bulawayo Club:** J. H. Ayling, F. C. Dugmore, P. Rutherford, A. E. Marris.

1925—**Bulawayo Club:** J. H. Ayling, S. Philip, G. Vallance, G. Baker.

1926—**Bulawayo Club:** R. A. Cain, W. Batwell, J. Moss, J. Atherton.

1927—**Bulawayo Club:** R. A. Cain, F. C. Dugmore, H. Charles, O. C. Elton, J. Bowie.

1928—**Raylton Club:** R. Bradley, C. Myles, R. Rayne, C. Evans, Allan.

1929—**Salisbury:** W. Templeton, J. Hodgkinson, C. Walton, P. McKie.

1930—**Bulawayo Club:** S. Bradley, P. Rutherford, R. O. Rouse, C. N. Dodd, C. Harrison.

1931—**Salisbury Club:** W. Templeton, P. MacKie, C. F. Walton, R. Mitchell, J. M. Coull, E. W. Konschel.

1932—**Bulawayo Club:** D. Drummond, T. Shilling, C. Harrison, J. E. Johnstone, H. Cottrell.

1933—**Raylton (Bulawayo):** A. Clegg, C. Slater, E. B. Roberts, Osterloh, Holton.

1934—**Salisbury Club:** F. H. Allen, G. W. Jackman, E. A. Furnell, H. S. Ellis, J. M. Coull.

1935—**Salisbury Club:** A. W. Stodart, R. K. Cormack, H. Pollard, A. McPherson.

Men's Aggregate—Kimberley Pioneer Cup.

1932—**Salisbury Club:** A. W. Stodart, H. S. Taylor, F. H. Allen, R. L. Thomas, H. Pollard, A. Ringrose.

1933—**Raylton (Bulawayo):** A. Clegg, C. Slater, E. B. Roberts, Osterloh, Holton.

1934—**Salisbury Club:** A. W. Stodart, B. Thomson, C. F. Walton, H. Pollard, A. McPherson.

1935—**Salisbury Club:** A. W. Stodart, R. K. Cormack, H. Pollard, A. McPherson.

Perfection Cup.

Imperial Cup.

J. Wightman.

A. E. Clegg.

Ladies—Loyalist Cup.

1927—**Bulawayo Club:** Mrs. Cottrell, Mrs. Leather, Mrs. Dark, Mrs. Dodd.

1928—**Gwelo Club:** Mrs. McIntosh, Mrs. Calder, Mrs. Cran, Mrs. Butcher, Mrs. Hill.

1929—**Raylton Club:** Mrs. Wright, Mrs. Clegg, Mrs. Denyer, Mrs. Winter.

1930—**Bulawayo:** Mrs. Spearpoint, Mrs. Harrison, Mrs. Snelling, Mrs. McLean.

1931—**Gwelo Club:** Mrs. Cran, Mrs. Butcher, Mrs. Garland, Miss Simpson, Miss Horrocks.

1932—**Salisbury Club:** Mrs. J. Sutherland, Mrs. R. L. Thomas, Mrs. P. McKie, Mrs. F. Turner.

1933—**Salisbury Club:** Mrs. Thomas, Mrs. Jackman, Mrs. Studholme, Mrs. Johnston.

1934—**Salisbury Club:** Mrs. Thomas, Mrs. Jackman, Mrs. Studholme, Mrs. Turner.

1935—**Umtali:** Mrs. Rodie, Mrs. Davidson, Mrs. Harrold, Mrs. Booth.

Men's Singles Championship.

	Winner.	Runner-up.
1924	R. A. Cain	H. Charles
1925	A. Glasgow	W. Hamilton
1926	J. Robley	W. Hamilton
1927	J. Gibb.	S. Bradley
1928	D. Drummond	R. Rayne
1929	W. Templeton	R. Bradley
1930	S. Bradley	A. W. Stodart
1931	G. Baker	T. P. Morgan
1932	C. Slater	P. McKie.
1933	R. Rayne	A. Mitchell
1934	N. E. Denyer	A. Clegg
1935	A. E. Clegg	G. W. Jackman

Ladies' Singles Championship.

	Winner.	Runner-up.
1927	Mrs. McIntosh	Mrs. Houston
1928	Mrs. Houston	Mrs. Barnes
1929	Mrs. Crowther	Mrs. Pudney
1930	Mrs. Houston	Mrs. McIntosh
1931	Mrs. Cran	Mrs. Cottrell
1932	Mrs. Wright	Mrs. McKie
1933	Mrs. Brooks	Mrs. Clegg
1934	Mrs. Delamare	Mrs. Brooks
1935	Mrs. Studholme	Mrs. Delamare

CLUB CHAMPIONS.
Bulawayo Club.
Men.

1902 — C. R. Edmonds.	1919 — J. H. Williams.
1903 — W. Hadingham.	1920 — P. R. Smith.
1904 — R. B. Wood.	1921 — R. A. Cain.
1905 — R. B. Wood.	1922 — J. H. Ayling.
1906 — T. Gibson.	1923 — F. C. Dugmore.
1907 — J. Main.	1924 — S. Bradley.
1908 — J. Main.	1925 — J. Moss.
1909 — John Wightman.	1926 — D. Drummond.
1910 — S. B. Burns.	1927 — S. Bradley.
1911 — J. Main.	1928 — D. Drummond.
1912 — J. Main.	1929 — G. Baker.
1913 — J. Main.	1930 — G. Baker.
1914 — J. Main.	1931 — M. McGarry.
1915 — E. W. White.	1932 — S. Bradley.
1916 — J. L. McQuilton.	1933 — S. Bradley.
1917 — J. Cowden.	1934 — G. Vallance.
1918 — J. Cowden.	1935 — S. Bradley.

Bulawayo Club—

Sectional
Winners, S.A.
Bowling
Tournament,
1933.

A. Keay,
J. Houston,
J. Wightman,
G. Vallance,
D. Drummond,
G. Baker.

Women.

1921 — Miss Cowden.	1929 — Miss Spearpoint.
1922 — Mrs. Cottrell.	1930 — Mrs. Cottrell.
1923 — Mrs. Hodgkinson.	1931 — Mrs. Beaufort.
1924 — Mrs. Hodgkinson.	1932 — Mrs. Hounsome.
1925 — Mrs. Houston.	1933 — Mrs. Harrison.
1926 — Mrs. Houston.	1934 — Mrs. Houston.
1927 — Mrs. Houston.	1935 — Mrs. Crook.
1928 — Mrs. Cottrell.	

Raylton (Bulawayo).

Men.

1924 — A. E. Clegg.	1930 — A. E. Clegg.
1925 — C. Myles.	1931 — T. W. Winter.
1926 — A. Griffiths.	1932 — A. E. Marshall.
1927 — D. Bradley.	1933 — N. E. Denyer.
1928 — C. Myles.	1934 — R. H. A. Rayne.
1929 — D. Bradley.	1935 — R. McKenzie.

Women.

1925 — Mrs. Childes.	1931 — Mrs. G. T. Wright.
1926 — Mrs. G. T. Wright.	1932 — Mrs. N. E. Denyer.
1927 — Mrs. G. T. Wright.	1933 — Mrs. A. Edwards.
1928 — Mrs. G. T. Wright.	1934 — Mrs. G. T. Wright.
1929 — Mrs. A. E. Clegg.	1935 — Mrs. A. E. Clegg.
1930 — Mrs. F. W. Barnett.	

Salisbury Club.

1929 — A. W. Stodart.	1932 — J. R. Whitlow.
1930 — R. L. Thomas.	

Gwelo.

1925 — W. Hamilton.	1927 — D. Harrison.
1926 — G. W. Jackman.	1931 — E. J. Seaward.

Wankie.

1932 — T. Howie.	1933 — M. Wallace.

Umtali.

1933 — J. W. McCormack.	1934 — E. Harrold.

A Group of Bulawayo Bowlers.
G Baker, T. Leather, J. Pickles, S. Bradley.

BULAWAYO'S FIRST GOLF CLUB HOUSE.

Group includes: F. C. Dugmore, H. B. Heeley, H. B. Douslin and B. K. Ward.

GOLF

HE Pioneer Columns from Salisbury and Fort Victoria reached Bulawayo on November 4th, 1893, thus completing the conquest of Matabeleland and shortly afterwards they settled down to a peaceful occupation of the Colony.

The "Bulawayo Chronicle" of December 4th, 1894, published a letter from R. S. Egerton asking any golfers in town to communicate with him as he thought it feasible to start a club in Bulawayo. The result was the formation of a club on January 25th, 1895, with Mr. Egerton as Captain.

The Executive Committee was: P. V. Weir, J. A. Spreckley, J. E. Scott, C. Jefferson Clark, J. Macdougall, with C. R. Tompkins as Secretary and Treasurer. The annual subscription was set at £2 2s. od. and it was decided to telegraph at once for material and to draft rules and regulations.

Although the golf course was not formally opened until July, 1898, the first match under the auspices of the new club was played in July, 1895. The players (with handicaps) who participated in this historic game were: F. G. Shaw, H. A. Piper, Mitchell and W. B. Wright, each owing 12; R. S. Egerton, scratch; R. A. Siebert receiving 10 and P. V. Weir, H. Lamb, A. Thain and D. Sneddon each receiving 15. The course, which was more or less in the same position as it is to-day, was not easy, "owing to the number of wagon tracks and sluits."

In those early days play was possible for about six months only of each year, the grass being allowed to grow wild during the rainy season and being cut down as soon as the rains were drawing to a close. It is only within the last ten years that all-the-year round golf has been made possible by mowing the grass during the growing season.

The natural setting of the present course is picturesque with the Matjesumhlope stream winding in a fantastic manner through most of the fairways. Although for the greater part of the year this is nothing more than a dry river bed it nevertheless provides a natural hazard which presents some difficulty whenever it is encountered.

Of recent years, at the instance of expert advisers, attempts have been made to plant the indigenous couch or kweek grass, though it cannot be said that these efforts have met with any great success as yet, the poor results probably being due to

Bulawayo Golf Club is a fine building occupying a commanding position on the course. It cost approximately £3,500.

lack of continuous rain during the growing season and the ravages of insect pests. At various times experiments in soil improvement and grass cultivation have been made; quantities of loamy soil have been carted to the course, while lime, artificial fertilisers and natural manures have been distributed in the soil; but there is no denying the fundamental fact that grass will not grow to the required density without a sufficiency of rain, and that is where the shortcomings of the Matabeleland climate become strikingly apparent.

It may be found ultimately that a policy of taming and cultivating the rough veld grass and planting couch among such wild grass may make for better fairways in giving a mixture of grasses able to withstand the hard climatic conditions that exist here.

In former days greens made of finely sifted sand were the invariable rule and served their purpose fairly well. Grass greens were laid down as an experiment a few years ago on the Bulawayo course, most of them being the ordinary couch grass with one or two planted with Bradley. After an extensive trial, however, they were ultimately abandoned and the greens were reconverted to sand. During the 1934 season a quantity of fine slag from the Broken Hill lead and zinc mine was imported. This material appears to give a true putting surface when it is evenly distributed over the green, but its chief virtue over sand is that it is not easily blown away in a strong wind, and in this respect it may prove more economical in the long run.

Teeing-grounds are built of ant-heap or soil with a good proportion of sand added to the basic material.

In a long list of those who have given service for the Bulawayo Golf Club are J. Macdonald, H. Chapman (five times club captain), S. Marshall Symons, A. A. Colborne, A. H. Hill, who was honorary secretary for many years, and F. C. Dugmore. The latter was the first Rhodesian champion and he held the title three times. There have been few finer exponents of the game in the Colony. His son, H. B. Dugmore, by his performances here since leaving Oxford, where he played for the University with distinction, is acknowledged the best golfer Rhodesia has produced. The Dugmores have, indeed, a fine golfing record for both Mrs. Dugmore and Miss N. Dugmore have been Matabeleland champions, and the latter was runner-up in the Rhodesian championship in 1932.

HILLSIDE, UMTALI.

Of the professional golfers connected with the Club at different times one recalls the names of Day, Jack Fothering-ham, Howard, R. May and Walker. The last named is still with the Club and has as his assistant young Knight of Gwelo, who gives promise of becoming a good exponent of the game.

In Umtali there are two courses, over each of which the Rhodesian Championships have been played. Golf started there about 1906, when Hugh Tulloch, R. G. Snodgrass, J. T. Huxtable and Andrew Laing were among the founders of the Umtali Golf Club. B. E. Elkin, the well-known South African professional, did a great deal for the game in the early days, and others were Harry Dale, C. Wibberley, F. Webb, Teddy Davis, W. J. McIntosh and C. Eickhoff. In 1912 the Hillside (Umtali) Golf Club opened with a nine-hole course—extended to eighteen holes in 1916—and it is one of the best laid out courses in Southern Africa.

The crest of the Umtali Golf Club—a crow with a golf ball in its beak—has an interesting origin. Apparently these birds, especially in the early days, frequently flew off with players' balls, which were generally irrecoverable.

Golf has been played in Gwelo ever since the earliest days and the course has covered various parts of the commonage from time to time. It was not until the members erected a Club House near the Bulawayo road in 1928 that the Club began to go ahead.

Under the Presidency of Mr. H. W. Smart, and encour-aged by the example of an energetic Committee, the members turned out during week-ends armed with axes, picks and shovels and cleared the bush for a new course. As time went on it was decided to plant the fairways with grass suitable for a golf links and a policy was started whereby the fairways will be planted gradually, in sections, during the rainy seasons, so that ultimately the entire eighteen holes will provide one of the most pleasant golf courses in the Colony.

In 1928 the membership of the Club was from twenty to thirty players, which number has increased during the last seven years to a membership of over two hundred.

The work of constructing the golf course has cost a sum considerably more than the small membership could afford, but the Gwelo Town Council, wisely looking to the future amenities of their town, have made generous grants in assist-ing this Club in the same manner as other sporting bodies have been assisted in Gwelo.

A CENTRE OF SPORT IN THE CAPITAL.

An aerial photograph of the Royal Salisbury Golf Club's Club House and part of the course. Just behind can be seen the Salisbury Club's cricket and rugby fields and on the left a section of the Polo ground.

For ten years H. W. Smart was president of the Gwelo Club and he was responsible for a great deal of progress. Since 1933 F. Delano Thompson, M.P., who is interested in all branches of sport in the Midlands, has been president, with S. G. Rogers the popular captain of the club. The honorary secretary is J. W. Farquhar.

In Salisbury the first course was laid out by Major Hall and G. N. Fleming on the banks of the Makabusi River. This site, however, was declared by the Town Medical Officer to be unhealthy and was abandoned in 1900 for another situated where the present Prince Edward School, Victoria Memorial Library and Drill Hall now stand. The site of this nine-hole course was subsequently required for building purposes and the club moved to its present position at the northern end of the town, acquiring a lease of ground from the Town Council.

Salisbury's generous rainy season has been a valuable factor in assisting the building up of the present magnificent course. Smooth grass greens and fairways and interesting hazards set in delightful surroundings have made the course come to be recognised as one of the best in South Africa. There is also a very fine club house.

During the first five years of the club's existence E. Montagu (now Sir Ernest) was club captain and honorary secretary and he did great work. Among others who have furthered the club's interests are Mr. Justice Watermeyer, G. Duthie, T. O. McPherson who was three times Rhodesian champion, R. Swire Thompson and Colonel G. Parson, C.B.E., D.S.O., who has captained the club for ten seasons at various times. He was also principal in the formation of the Rhodesian Golf Union in 1925 and has been its president since that date. Colonel Parson, who is Officer Commanding the Southern Rhodesia Forces, has figured prominently in other sports, having rowed for Rhodesia and represented Mashonaland at rugby and cricket. For many years L. B. Waters has been the club's professional and his contribution towards the progress of golf in the Colony has been considerable.

In 1930, the Salisbury Club became the Royal Salisbury Club.

There is an increasing number of woman players in the Colony. One of the outstanding performers is Miss F. Waters (now Mrs. Parham), who won the Ladies' Championship on six occasions. There is a Rhodesian Ladies' Golf

Union functioning on much the same lines as the Rhodesian Golf Union. The present committee is: President, Mrs. Godfrey; Vice-Presidents, Mrs. P. H. Harvey and Miss S. Kennedy; Member of Executive, Mrs. Brereton; Hon. Secretary and Treasurer, Mrs. Humphrey Davy.

When the late Lord Gladstone was High Commissioner for Southern Rhodesia he generously presented a cup (known as the Gladstone Cup) as a trophy for the amateur championship of Rhodesia. This was open for competition by bona fide resident golfers in Southern Rhodesia, Northern Rhodesia and Beira, and the governing body, the Gladstone Cup Committee, was composed of delegates from the principal clubs.

In 1925 the Rhodesian Golf Union was formed with headquarters in Salisbury and it is now the controlling body in all matters pertaining to Rhodesian golf, including the running of amateur championships. Another competition which is held at the time of the championship meeting is the affiliated clubs' teams' match, for which a cup was presented by a late Governor of Northern Rhodesia, Sir Lawrence Wallace.

To-day there are over twenty clubs in Southern Rhodesia with a total membership of about 2,000.

A. R. Innes and G. A. Veale.

THE RHODESIAN AMATEUR CHAMPIONSHIP—GLADSTONE CUP.

1912 — F. C. Dugmore.	1927 — S. D. Timson.
1913 — F. Knott.	1928 — W. Compton.
1914 — F. C. Dugmore.	1929 — S. D. Timson.
1919 — F. G. Smith.	1930 — W. Compton.
1920-21 T. O. McPherson.	1931 — G. J. Humphrey.
1922-23 F. G. Smith.	1932 — S. D. Timson.
1924 — A. Smith.	1933 — W. B. Brown.
1925 — T. O. McPherson.	1934 — A. R. Innes.
1926 — P. R. McGregor.	1935 — T. V. Davidson.

THE RHODESIAN LADIES' CHAMPIONSHIP.

1926-27 Miss F. Waters.	1933 — Mrs. Chudleigh.
1928-31 Mrs. Parham.	1934-35 Mrs. Muir.
1932 — Mrs. Leete.	

AFFILIATED CLUBS' TEAMS' MATCH.

Men (Wallace Cup).

1920-21 Salisbury.	1928-29 Salisbury.
1922 — Bulawayo.	1930 — Royal Salisbury.
1923 — Livingstone.	1931 — Limbe.
1924 — Umtali.	1932-33 Royal Salisbury.
1925-26 Salisbury.	1934 — Umtali.
1927 — Livingstone.	1935 — Royal Salisbury.

Women (R.L.G.U. Challenge Shield).

1930 — Royal Salisbury.	1932-35 Royal Salisbury.
1931 — Bulawayo.	

PROVINCIAL CHAMPIONS.

Matabeleland (Haddon & Sly Cup).

1929 — G. A. Veale.	1932 — A. E. Farrell.
1930 — H. B. Dugmore.	1933 — S. R. Kirk.
1931 — E. A. Aitken.	1934-35 H. B. Dugmore.

Mashonaland.

1931-32 D. C. Cowan.	1934 — W. S. Grant.
1933 — S. D. Timson.	1935 — J. C. Robertson.

Midlands.

1926 — J. R. Anderson.	1932 — W. B. Brown.
1927 — W. B. Brown.	1933 — L. Myles.
1928 — J. R. Anderson.	1934 — W. B. Brown.
1929 — W. B. Brown.	1935 — G. J. Smith.
1930-31 H. B. Dugmore.	

Manicaland.

1915 — Bert Elkin.	1930 — Tom Cowley.
1921 — W. J. McIntosh.	1931 — I. Cuff.
1922 — R. Ainslie.	1932 — Len Waring.
1923 — Len Waring.	1933 — J. Day.
1924 — R. Ainslie.	1934 — Reg. Horne.
1925 — A. E. Farrell.	1935 — P. Mungle.
1926-29 Len Waring.	

CLUB CAPTAINS.
The Royal Salisbury Club.

1899-1903 E. Montagu.	1918 — E. S. Klette.
1904 — C. Townsend.	1919 — L. J. Orpen.
1905 — J. Robertson.	1920 — S. M. Symons.
1906 — H. B. Douslin.	1920 — T. O. McPherson.
1906-08 Mr. Justice Water- meyer.	1921-24 Maj. G. Parson, D.S.O.
	1925-27 R. Swire Thompson.
1909-10 G. Duthie.	1928-30 Col. G. Parson, D.S.O.
1911 — G. H. Eyre.	1931-32 R. Swire Thompson.
1911-14 G. Duthie.	1933-35 Col. G. Parson, C.B.E.,
1915 — G. R. Milne.	D.S.O
1916-17 T. O. McPherson.	

AT THE RHODESIAN CHAMPIONSHIP MEETING, 1932

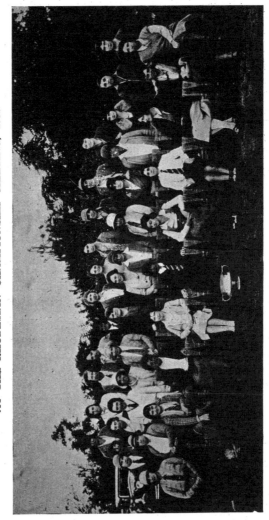

Back Row: Mrs. Dunbar, Mrs. Sanders, Mrs. P. H. Harvey, Mrs. Greenshields, Miss B. May, Mrs. Sinclair, Mrs. Parker, Mrs. Prew, Mrs. Pulbrook, Mrs. Hope Carson, Mrs. Parham.
Middle Row: Mrs. Vernall, Mrs. Ridgway, Mrs. Ross, Mrs. Britstone, Mrs. Garlake, Mrs. Crosbie, Miss Holland, Mrs. Golding, Mrs. Byrne, Mrs. Buxton, Mrs. Clarke, Mrs. Powell, Miss Pocock, Miss Wilson.
Front Row: Mrs. A. Smith, Mrs. Fraser, Mrs. Waters, Mrs. Cowan, Mrs. Humphrey Davy, Mrs. Leete (Holder), Miss N. Dugmore, Mrs. Godfrey, Mrs. Parson, Mrs. Cooper, Miss Gib.

AT THE CHAMPIONSHIP MEETING, 1935.

Back Row: L. R. S. Hill, E. S. Caudwell, W. A. Rezin, J. C. Smith, W. Barbour, W. Harris, G. L. Robertson, H. M. L. Brown, T. E. Jager, J. Hall, A. H. R. Dean, —?, G. Mansell.

Third Row: B. S. Waghorne, H. J. Binks, F. Sanders, O. Stenson, —?, J. Donnan, J. G. Simpson, A. E. Knight, C. C. W. Ingham, H. G. Surgey, J. D. Bold.

Second Row: A. Boshoff, C. G. F. Anderson, H. G. Brown, H. E. Elsworth, D. G. Elliott, E. Golding, H. A. M. Norton, W. H. Lowe, H. S. McVey, J. G. Robinson, R. Coombes - White, R. Johnstone, C. C. Michie.

Sitting: E. Humphrey Davy, S. D. Timson, R. L. Phillips, T. V. Davidson, K. A. Byrne, Sir Percy Fynn, Col. G. Parson, C.B.E., D.S.C., Sir Ernest Montague, J. M. McDonald, Alex Smith, W. B. Brown, D. H. Shepherd, A. McRobbie.

Umtali Club—Captains.

1903-10 J. Brown.	1921 — A. Holman.
1911 — W. J. McIntosh.	1922 — W. Potts.
1912-14 H. E. Dale.	1923-26 W. J. McIntosh.
1915 — B. H. Elkin.	1927-28 L. Waring.
1916-18 H. E. Dale.	1929-31 J. Easton.
1919-20 F. E. Webb.	1932-35 L. Waring.

Umtali Club—Presidents.

1903 05 C. Wibberley.	1920 — A. Laing.
1906 — R. H. Myburgh.	1921-31 D. M. Livingston.
1907-11 C. Wibberley.	1932-35 G. W. Chace.
1912-19 R. G. Snodgrass.	

Bulawayo Club—Captains.

1895 — R. S. Egerton.	1915 — J. Macdonald.
1896 — J. E. Scott.	1916 — B. K. Ward.
1897 — W. Forbes.	1917-18 H. Chapman.
1898 — F. C. Dugmore.	1919 — G. Young.
1899-1901 C. G. Ward.	1920 — J. Ellman Brown.
1902 — H. B. Douslin.	1921 — S. M. Symons.
1903 — B. K. Ward.	1922 — H. Chapman.
1904 — H. B. Heeley.	1923 — G. Johnson.
1905 — C. K. Garthwaite.	1924 — B. K. Ward.
1906 — C. W. Cosnett.	1925 — A. H. Ayres.
1907 — G. Johnson.	1926 — H. Chapman.
1908 — A. U. Ritchie.	1927-29 V. Swales.
1909 — L. P. Ashburnham.	1930 — J. H. Ayling.
1910 — D. McIntosh.	1931 — J. S. Dunbar.
1911 — J. Macdonald.	1932 — A. Gardiner.
1912 — J. Shiel.	1933 — A. A. Colborne.
1913 — J. Macdonald.	1934 — J. Ellman Brown.
1914 — H. Chapman.	

BULAWAYO CLUB CHAMPIONS (Rhodes Challenge Shield).

1901-03 F. C. Dugmore.	1924 — J. S. Wylie.
1904 — A. U. Ritchie.	1925 — C. H. Bennett.
1905 — F. C. Dugmore.	1926 — R. J. Thominet.
1906 — A. U. Ritchie.	1927 — J. S. Dunbar.
1907 — F. C. Dugmore.	1928 — H. B. Dawson.
1908 — A. U. Ritchie.	1929 — J. S. Dunbar.
1909-14 F. C. Dugmore.	1930 — R. Horne.
1919 — F. C. Dugmore.	1931 — A. Paterson.
1920 — R. D. Haves.	1932 — A. E. Farrell.
1921 — H. Chapman.	1933 — A. R. Innes.
1922 — S. M. Symons.	1934 — B. Myles.
1923 — H. Chapman.	1935 — H. B. Dugmore.

OFFICERS PAST AND PRESENT OF THE RHODESIAN GOLF UNION.

Presidents.—Col. G. Parson, C.B.E., D.S.O., 1925-35.

Vice-Presidents.—Mr. H. Chapman, C.B.E., 1925-32; F. G. Smith, Esq., 1925-31; Dr. T. R. F. Kerby, 1933-35; S. M. Symons, Esq., 1933; R. L. Ward, Esq., 1934-35.

Hon. Secretary and Treasurer.—P. R. McGregor, Esq., 1925-26; Alex Smith, Esq., 1927-33; Capt. A. V. Adams, 1934; Capt. K. A. Byrne, 1935.

Hon. Auditor.—E. P. Vernall, Esq., 1925-35.

The new Rhodesian golf champion, T. V. Davidson, of the Royal Salisbury Golf Club, photographed just after he had beaten Alex. Smith at the 36th hole in an exciting final.

H, Chapman, C.B.E.,
five times captain of the
Bulawayo Golf Club.

J. Ellman-Brown,
Captain of the Bulawayo Golf
Club for 1935.

M

SIR LEANDER STARR JAMESON.

HORSE-RACING

T the end of 1889 a detachment of the Royal Horse Guards (Blues), consisting of Major Trench-Gascoigne, Captain Ferguson, Surgeon-Captain Melladew, Corporal-Major White and a private, arrived at Gubulawayo. The party, which had travelled by mule-wagon from Kimberley, was from London and carried a letter from Queen Victoria announcing to Lobengula the incorporation of the B.S.A. Company by Royal Charter and advising him to give his confidence and support to the Company. A race meeting was held in honour of the Queen's envoys and a fairly good course was laid out with hurdles. All the Europeans entered those of their horses which had any pretensions to speed and with the addition of some of the king's and the indunas' horses there was a creditable muster for the Zambesi Handicap, the Gubuluwayo Plate and the two minor events that constituted the meeting. The racing was good and the king's horses won some of the stakes. Thousands of natives assembled to witness the white man's sport but beyond a few violent disputes tolerable order was kept. Thus the first race meeting in Rhodesia was held under royal patronage.

In July, 1891, Lord Randolph Churchill arrived in Salisbury after a long hunting trip. While awaiting the sale of his hunting outfit which, incidentally, realised more than the total cost of his expedition, he offered to race his stud against any of the local horses. The challenge was taken up by J. G. Cowan and his friend, T. Wignall, the latter a fine horseman who, with his grey, Inniskillen, beat Lord Churchill's stable. In October of the same year there was a match between Dr. Jameson's Moscow and a horse of Dr. Rutherford Harris, which was won by the former. Racing was very keen in Salisbury. H. J. Borrow imported a bay stallion Mintmark from the south and another notable from the same region was Pilot owned by Hugh Kerr. Major Forbes had a splendid jumper in Inniskilling and R. G. Snodgrass a fine grey named Hatfield.

Gymkhana meetings were held fairly frequently at this time. G. Graham's Makosi, D. Zeederberg's Fraud, F. Clayton's Black Diamond, Gould's Tomtit and Charlie Howe's Victor were some of the horses.

MAJOR ALLAN WILSON.

Such names as Sir Leander Starr Jameson, Bezuidenhout, R. Beal, Snodgrass, Jack Carruthers, Alf Smith and Henry Thompson will be remembered long in connection with the first racing in Salisbury. The Gymkhana Club later merged with the Mashonaland Turf Club.

Among the jockeys who came in with the column were F. Clayton and Willemite, light and welter respectively. The noted amateurs were Wignall, E. O'C. Farrell, cross-country men; H.Hay, medium weight, and later that splendid horse-man and sportsman, J. E. Nicholls.

Umtali had its first racing excitement in 1891. In May, 1892, a second meeting was held, consisting of one flat and one hurdle race, the latter won by Mr. Carden's Tommy, owner up, with Mr. Maritz's Cyclops, Mr. J. L. Crawford up, second. There was a dead heat in the flat race between these horses with the same riders.

In 1892 appeared Chess, a very fine galloway from Natal. This horse won everything, flat and hurdle, for several years. A memorable race was for the Umtali Plate in 1893, won by Mr. W. W. Taylor's Chess (H. van Reit) from Mr. C. Weissenbom's Inyama (owner), with Mr. H. Taylor's Rick-shaw (J. van Reit) third. At the same meeting there was a donkey race over a quarter of a mile. When the winner reached the post he evidently thought he had done enough for he stopped dead and the rider sailed through the air, to be picked up several yards away not much the worse for the mishap. The honorary secretary of all these early meet-ings was that fine all-round sportsman, J. L. Crawford, who in 1894 was chiefly responsible for the selecting of the present course in Umtali. Other early supporters of the turf were J. van Reit, Snodgrass, Wally Anderson, Harry Doll and D'Urban Barry.

The Victoria Turf and Sporting Club was formed in March, 1893, with Dr. Jameson president, Sir John Wil-loughby vice-president and J. Sampson secretary. The com-mittee consisted of C. R. Vigers chairman, Lord Henry Poulett, Napier, Capt. Chaplin, Allan Wilson, Bowen, Chinery, Finch, H. Smith and Tompkins treasurer. The annual subscription was fixed at five guineas.

At an early meeting in Bulawayo, on Boxing Day, 1893, a trooper who went mad through sunstroke turned the prison Maxim on to the bronzed, shirt-sleeved crowd, but fortunately no one was hit. Up to 1896 the race course was near where the Defence Force cricket ground is to-day.

BULAWAYO TURF CLUB.—Officials, 1933-1934.

Top Row.—A. G. Hay, H. Charles, W. A. Carnegie, G. C. Hooper Sharpe, P. W. Sherwell, V. Turnbull, B. A. Myhill, R. T. Little, J. B. McNeill, W. Gillespie, F. Barnett, P. O'Connor, Bottom Row.—F. E. Harris, Dr. H. J. Morris, P. J. Phillips, J. C. Coghlan, J. W. White, Dr. G. R. Ross, P. E. Landau.

The names of many well-known racing enthusiasts were connected with the foundation of the Bulawayo Turf Club. There was C. H. Zeederberg, Gordon Forbes, whose colours—chocolate and pink—were very popular, Teddy Hull, one of the best horsemen seen in this Colony, Alf Brown, Ted Slater, Harry Lloyd, Maurice Gifford, Douglas Pennant, Jonah White, W. R. Chennells, Fergus Peel, Halstead and Tommy Broughton.

E. A. HULL. W. A. CARNEGIE.

The Bulawayo Turf Club has been well served by a large number of sportsmen among whom are J. C. Coghlan, President, Dr. H. J. Morris, Dr. G. R. Ross, R. T. Little, Capt. B. A. Myhill, G. C. Hooper-Sharpe (Chief Veterinary Surgeon), F. Barnett, who was handicapper for many years, P. E. Landau, A. G. Hay, P. O'Connor, C. J. MacNamara, J. B. McNeill, W. A. Carnegie, secretary for some years, Major J. C. Jesser Coope, H. B. Ellenbogen, J. H. Bookless and F. E. J. Rosselli, the present secretary and handicapper.

The first meeting under the auspices of the Bulawayo Turf Club was on November 8, 1894. The chief event was the Bulawayo Spring Handicap for stakes of £150 and a cup presented by Mr. Rhodes, which was won by Mr. E. A. Slater's Master Cecil from Mr. C. H. Zeederberg's Chanticleer, with Mr. T. Broughton's Bonny Morn third. Mr. C. R. Vigers was judge, Mr. Hirschler starter, Sergeant Dykes clerk of the course, and Mr. C. H. Smith secretary. Other leading officials were Gordon Forbes, Zeederberg, D. Pennant and Ted Slater. The last meeting on the old course was in September, 1895, at which two-day meeting over £2,400 passed through the totalisator.

On February 3, 1896, the present course was granted to the Club. The pavilion, which is now used as the Members' Stand, originally belonged to the Bulawayo Athletic Club. It stood on what had been the site of the old Ingubu Kraal. From 1896 the Club grew steadily and, with money a more familiar commodity than it is now, meetings were frequent and some splendid racing was seen. There were at that time several hundred police in Bulawayo, among them Sergeant the Marquis de Busé, Corporal the Hon. Yard Buller and several other titles to be found in Debrett and they could ride anything with hair on it. A noted rough-rider was Corporal Sherwood Kelly—a Colonel, V.C., in the Great War. The police were greatly responsible for the stimulus given to racing at that time.

In November, 1897, the Gwelo Sporting Club held a meeting with a programme consisting of a Hack Race, a Pony Scurry and a Licensed Victuallers' Plate. In 1899 there was also a meeting at Selukwe.

In May, 1898, an expedition was sent by Mr. Rhodes to make a treaty by which the B.S.A. Company established its government in North-Western Rhodesia, which was then under the sway of Luanika. The expedition consisted of Capt. the Hon. Arthur Lawley, Administrator of Matabeleland (afterwards Lord Wenlock), his brother Colonel the Hon. Dick Lawley, 7th Hussars, his secretary (now Sir) R. A. Blanckenberg, Val Gielgud, Native Commissioner of the Sebungwe District of Matabeleland, Major R. Coryndon, Administrator of N.W. Rhodesia (afterwards Sir Robert and Governor of Kenya), Coryndon's secretary, and F. Worthington, who became the first Chief Secretary and Native Commisioner of N.W. Rhodesia. With them, to act as escort and to cut a road from Bulawayo to the Victoria Falls, went Captain (now Major) J. C. Jesser Coope and a small detachment of B.S.A. Police and armed Matabele. At the Falls Major Coryndon and Capt. Jesser Coope laid out a small race course and an excellent programme, consisting of a steeplechase, postillion, V.C. and bending races and several foot races was organised. The royal stand was a buck-wagon on which sat King Luanika, Letia, his eldest son, the Gambetta (Chief Councillor) and various other members of the Barotse court. The meeting was a great success and the king was hugely delighted with the fun. One of the results of the meeting was a challenge from Luanika to Lawley for a race on foot between their representatives. Capt. Jesser Coope and Val Gielgud represented Lawley's (or rather Rhodes's) young men against a formidable team of about twenty of the Barotse king's runners. They ran over a very sandy course and a desperate effort a few yards from the winning post gave Capt. Jesser Coope the race and, incidentally, the prize—a handsome ivory fly switch from Luanika and, from Lawley, a box of Cockle's Pills!

MAJOR J. C. JESSER COOPE.   TEDDY CAMPBELL.

In 1897 and 1898 Teddy Campbell won the Rhodes Cup on Cylinder. This Cup was presented by Mr. Rhodes in 1894. E. V. V. Campbell was truly a pioneer jockey. He came up in 1891 to prospect in Mashonaland, and fought through the 1893 war. He served under Major Allan Wilson and it was only because he fell sick and was sent back to the main body that he did not cross the Shangani with Wilson's ill-fated party. He served in the 1896 Rebellion and through the Boer War as a special scout. In between pro-specting he used to ride at various race meetings throughout

Rhodesia, where he enjoyed a tremendous popularity. When 53 years of age he won three races in the same day on one of Gordon Forbes's horses, Zamia. His farewell ride was in 1922, when he rode two winners. Teddy was then 60 years old and had been riding for 44 years.

A matter of interest is that the first dead-heat occurred on the Bulawayo racecourse in January, 1903. In the Polo Pony Sweepstake, Mrs. Russell's Delia, 12st. 9lbs. (Capt. Jesser Coope), finished level with Mr. Gormon's Billy, 11st. 9lbs. (Mr. Williams). In the run-off Delia won easily.

The Mashonaland Turf Club was formed in 1892, but it was not until 1897 that the first big Turf Club meeting was held. Several horses were walked up from the South, including African, an upstanding chestnut, and Recondite, a white horse which had been a Johannesburg Christmas Handicap winner. Doel Zeederberg entered horses which he brought up from Pietersburg.

This was known as the Carnival Meeting, and the big race, with stakes £1,250, was won by Recondite (Snodgrass-Fisher stable). This stable also owned Common, Master Grey and one other, and they won the Merchants and Licensed Victuallers' Race (value £850) with Common. Master Grey also won at this meeting. Other horses were Doel Zeederberg's Traveller, Gordon Forbes's Arquebus, an Australian horse, and Jack Brown's Cylinder. Jack Brown is now an outside bookmaker in Salisbury. Clayton's Black Diamond was another winner.

After the meeting Recondite was raffled and won by W. S. Taberer. He took the horse home and stabled him carefully, but in the morning the horse was found dead and it was believed that he had been poisoned.

From 1900 onwards there was little interest shown in racing until 1912, when an effort was made to put the sport on a sound footing. The Great War, however, put a stop to any further development and it was not until many years later that regular meetings were started again.

In 1922 the Mashonaland Turf Club was floated as a Limited Liability Company and, except for a period of two years during the past depression, the Company has always declared dividends.

In July, 1925, the Prince of Wales attended a meeting in Salisbury held in his honour. Sir Abe Bailey sent up a horse from Johannesburg named Manual II which led the field for six furlongs but could only finish third. The race was won by Dunhaven, owned by Jonah White, of Bulawayo.

Racing in Mashonaland has improved greatly during the past few years. Stakes cannot, of course, be compared with those of 1897 when the money was given by the Carnival Committee. Records have it that at the Carnival Meeting the total stakes for two days' racing amounted to £3,075.

Capt. C. E. Wells, O.B.E., may be regarded as the founder of the Mashonaland Turf Club, and it is mainly due to his unfailing energy that the Club possesses its present beautiful racecourse and is in such a flourishing condition.

J. W. WHITE.　　CAPT. THE HON. F. E. HARRIS,
D.S.O., M.P.
(Minister of Agriculture).

Capt. Wells, who, incidentally, was Secretary of the Carnival Committee in 1897, has been Chairman of the Mashonaland Turf Club for seventeen years and was Hon. Handicapper for fifteen years.

Handicapping is now in the hands of W. Rogers, who combines this work with the office of Secretary and ranks to-day as the best handicapper in Rhodesia.

The principal meeting of the year in Salisbury is held in August, during the Agricultural Show Week, and is known as the Show Meeting. The stakes usually amount to £800 for the two days.

Racing in Southern Rhodesia has passed through many vicissitudes. The 1896 Rebellion, the Boer War and the Great War have all provided serious checks, but except for these intervals racing has been carried on regularly and has made steady progress. At the present time Southern Rhodesia has a membership of 20 in the Jockey Club of South Africa and in all probability will shortly have its own Local Executive.

Amongst some of the prominent owners of recent times are Miss D. Addison, Capt. the Hon. F. E. Harris, D.S.O., M.P., Colonel H. F. Watson, Messrs. Jonah White, Digby Burnett, T. I. Furness, J. de Gray Birch and J. Willing.

CAPT. C. E. WELLS.

POLO

HE year 1895 saw polo played with great zest in Bulawayo. The Polo Club opened their ground on the new racecourse in Bulawayo in December, 1895, to stage the first game of polo ever played in Matabeleland. The teams were:

Army.—Major Villiers (Capt.), back; Capt. Kincaid Smith, No. 3; Capt. Mainwaring, No. 2; Capt. Llewellyn, No. 1.

Civilians: C. W. Halstead (Capt.), No. 3; H. R. Webb, back; R. Hamilton, No. 2; E. E. Reynolds, No. 1.

Civilians won rather easily by 5 goals to nil.

Other Army players were Col. Plumer, Capt. J. Carden, Capt. Brown, Capt. McFarlane, Capt. Nicholson, Capt. Laing, while among the civilians were H. Connop, M. G. Farquhar, Hon. M. R. Gifford, Reynolds, D. J. Dollar, M. Bainbridge, M. Gourlay, J. E. Jolliffe, A. H. Bramwell, C. E. Lenta, Bradley, W. H. Robinson, J. W. Colenbrander, D. Dollar, A. J. Forbes, M. Llewellyn and J. E. Scott.

The Jameson Raid and the Rebellion brought gaps when there was no play, but from 1897 to the Boer War polo fairly flourished. The Boer War caused another break, but thereafter there ensued many years of really first-class play. Polo matches were great social events. People went in large numbers and tea was provided by the ladies for players and spectators alike.

The officers of the B.S.A. Police formed the backbone of the sport, while others who contributed were the 7th Hussars, the K.O.S.B.'s, the Rhodesia Horse and, later, the S.R.V. mounted section. There were two grounds in the centre of the racecourse and very often both of these were in play. Regular matches two, and often three, times a week were played almost all the year round, under Hurlingham rules. The wet season made things difficult owing to the rapid growth of the grass and the softness of the ground. Matches or practices could be seen almost any day and twenty or more would turn out, for if ponies were not being used in matches they were always being trained.

The price of a pony ranged anywhere from £30 upwards and despite horse-sickness (though actually there was little of this in Bulawayo) the fitness of the ponies enabled them to survive this scourge and the game was kept going. In passing, it was very noticeable that on active service the hardiest mounts were those that had been used for polo.

There were five teams in Bulawayo. The B.S.A. Police Camp fielded two teams, A and B; there was the Bulawayo Club Team, the Town Team, generally captained by C. W. Halstead, and the Suburban Team. Play reached a very high standard and players who went South or overseas were well able to compete in any class of polo. The first captain of the Polo Club was Capt. MacFarlane, late 9th Lancers. The first Hon. Secretary was Mr. Reynolds, and the club suffered a great loss when he was killed in the action at von Secker's farm. Prominent among the military players were Capt. the Hon. Arthur Lawley, late 10th Hussars, afterwards Lord Wenlock; Col. the Hon. H. F. White of the Grenadier Guards; Col. J. S. Nicholson, 7th Hussars; Col. Chestermaster, 60th Rifles; Col. Holdsworth, commanding 7th Hussars; Major Mott, 60th Rifles; Capt. John Vaughan, 7th Hussars; Major Mockett, 4th Hussars and Adjutant, S.R.V.; Major Carew, 7th Hussars, and the Hon. John Beresford, 7th Hussars. From the B.S.A.P. there were Major R. Cashel, Capt. John Carden, Capt. J. C. Jesser Coope, Capt. Hoel Llewellyn, his brother, Mr. Llewellyn, Capt. MacQueen, Mr. Harold Chapman and the Hon. H. Beresford. Outstanding among the civilians were Val Gielgud, the Native Commissioner, C. L. Carbutt, J. C. Knapp, Gordon Forbes, Mowbray Farquhar, George Grey, Lionel Ludlow, Advocate W. Russell, H. E. M. Fynn, H. C. K. Fynn, Webb, Duncan Dollar and his brother, J. M. Sinclair, W. Wood, A. G. Hay, Bullock, Jackson and George Rich.

It was most difficult to get men and horses across the country, but several representative matches were played against Salisbury. The commencement of hostilities in 1914 marked the decline of the sport until finally it ceased to be played. Since the War it has not been possible to resuscitate the game and to-day there is no polo played in Bulawayo.

The Salisbury Polo Club was started on December 15, 1896. The Chairman and instigator was the late Colonel the Hon. F. de Moleyns, who was Adjutant of the 4th Hussars and first came to Rhodesia on the staff of Mr. Albert Gray, subsequently Lord Gray.

After the Rebellion was more or less in hand Colonel de Moleyns was sent as Colonel-in-Charge of the B.S.A. Police and he laid the foundation of that splendid discipline and efficiency which has always distinguished the police of this Colony.

There were also present at the first meeting of the Polo Club Major Gosling, Colonel Hopper, subsequently second in command of the Police, Capt. Gibbs, the first Adjutant of the old Rhodesia Horse who took such a prominent part in the Rebellion, George Graham, well known to Rhodesians as "Makosi" Graham because of a famous race horse he possessed, who came out to this Colony as a member of the Pioneer Police, Tyndale Biscoe, who was in the Navy and joined the Pioneer Column under Colonel Johnson and hoisted the Union Jack in Salisbury on September 12, 1890. Three years ago he visited Salisbury again on September 12 and hoisted the Union Jack on the Occupation Day anniversary.

Others present at the meeting were Dick Godley (now Colonel), a younger brother of the distinguished General Sir Alexander Godley who first gained his spurs in the 1896 Rebellion and gave such distinguished service in the Great War; Dick Godley joined up as a trooper in the Matabeleland Relief Force under the then Colonel, subsequently Lord Plumer); Moses Cornwall, who came up here in the very early days; Mr. Pidcock, Capt. MacQueen of the B.S.A.P., John Norton Griffiths, who, after leaving this country, became an English M.P. and well known to everybody as "Empire Jack"; P. E. Craven, who did yeoman service for the Club and subsequently for the Mashonaland Turf Club; the popular Jack Spreckley; Peter Potgieter, a well-known amateur jockey and a great polo enthusiast; Mr. Wilson Fox, who came up in 1894 from Johannesburg as the first Public Prosecutor in the Colony; and Harry Taberer, one of the most expert players. He held a wonderful record as an athlete and it is recorded of him that, standing in a barrel, he could throw a cricket ball 100 yards.

X. Feltham was another of the early polo players. In the Rebellion he dynamited the Mashona Caves and in doing so received a wound in his face which old hands say caused the finest flow of language it is possible to imagine. Others were Wilson Fox's brother, Frank; the well-known Colin Harding who served in the 1896 War with great distinction and received the C.M.G.; Marshall Hole, whose facile pen has written a history of the early days in Rhodesia; R. G. Snodgrass, and George Bowen, always a good man on a horse and a very keen player. He and Burnham were two of the fortunate ones who escaped from Wilson's Patrol on the Shangani, having been sent back, just before the river came down in flood, to bring reinforcements, if posible, to Allan Wilson's assistance. The horse Bowen rode when he escaped was a remarkably good roan, christened Blucher, which was given him by Mr. Rhodes.

With this splendid send-off the Polo Club was soon in a very flourishing condition and the first tournament was played during the peace celebrations in 1896, when the Rhodesia Challenge Cup was won by the 7th Hussars, who very generously left the Cup in Rhodesia.

The Club was fortunate enough shortly afterwards to secure the services of " Sonny " Taberer, a brother of H. M. Taberer. No matter what game " Sonny " took up, he excelled in it, and a more cheerful or sporting man to play with, or against, cannot be imagined.

One of the oldest members of the Club is Major J. E. Nicholls, O.B.E., who has been a member for over 40 years. He gave the author generous assistance with the compiling of this record.

Polo continued to be played and as the old original members gave up playing, new blood was added to the Club. Col. Chestermaster, who was killed in the Great War, became a member, and Gus. Bullock, one of the best riders ever seen in Salisbury. He it was who captured de Wet in the rising in South Africa and he devised the type of motor car with strong steel knives attached to the radiator for travelling through the veld and cutting through barbed wire fences.

There was, however, a period when the game lacked enthusiastic support, but the arrival of Capt. Shaw, who was seconded to the S.R. Volunteers from the 9th Lancers, saw a revival of interest, and Mr. St. Quintin was commissioned to go down to Johannesburg and buy new ponies. Incidentally, St. Quintin's brother, of the 10th Hussars, played in the first polo match ever held in England. A side consisted of six players then, instead of four.

Matches between Mashonaland and Matabeleland provided sufficient competition to keep the players keen, but Mashonaland did not succeed in beating the strong sides mustered by Matabeleland.

The Great War shut down polo entirely, and it was not until 18 months after the Armistice that Major J. E. Nicholls called a general meeting of players in Salisbury with the idea of reviving the game again. There was an enthusiastic response, and twenty new ponies were purchased in Natal by the well-known polo player Reggie Amos. Several officers returning from the Great War and resuming residence in Mashonaland helped to give a stimulus to polo and a cup was presented by Major Nicholls for competition in the Club. It is still played for to-day.

Polo in Salisbury is at present in a flourishing condition. There are several different teams, and players meet three times a week. The polo field is one of the best in South Africa, set in very pleasant surroundings and completely turfed. Thanks to the late Sir Charles Coghlan, the Club has free title to the ground as long as polo is played in Salisbury.

HOUNDS

The first pack of hounds in Matabeleland was imported in 1908 by George and Jim Harris from their home in County Limerick, Ireland. The opening meet was held at the kennels at Guinea Fowl Mine, and after forty minutes' hard going without a check "Gordon" pulled down the "Jack."

At sunrise the hounds moved off to draw the Lyndhurst kopjes but drew blank, and the next move was to draw the vlei at the source of the Gwelo river where Mr. Drinkwater viewed a jackal. Hounds were soon laid on and, with music from Favourite, Pilgrim and General (Wexford), and to the tune of the Master's horn, the hunt went in pursuit. The quarry was headed off from Lyndhurst kopjes, driven from refuge in a culvert and across the Gwelo and Selukwe road, and finally pulled down by Gordon (Limerick) in the open.

Among those present at the finish were G. W. V. Knight (Master), J. M. Harris and H. Williams (Whips), R. Holland, Normand, G. J. Harris, E. M. Rogers, Drinkwater, Talbot, Ringwood, Baynes and Reid.

INDEX

TO RHODESIAN REPRESENTATIVES

—◆—

U

T

V

W

ACKNOWLEDGMENTS.

The writer accords grateful thanks for donations from the Rhodesia Amateur Athletic and Cycling Union and the Mashonaland Rugby Football Board.